DEMOCRACY AND INTERNATIONAL TRADE

DEMOCRACY AND INTERNATIONAL TRADE

BRITAIN, FRANCE, AND
THE UNITED STATES, 1860–1990

Daniel Verdier

PRINCETON UNIVERSITY PRESS   PRINCETON, NEW JERSEY

Library of Congress Cataloging-in-Publication Data

Verdier, Daniel, 1954–
Democracy and international trade : Britain, France, and
the United States, 1860–1990 / Daniel Verdier.
p. cm
Includes bibliographical references and index.
ISBN 0-691-03224-6
1. Great Britain—Commercial policy—History. 2. France—
Commercial policy—History. 3. United States—Commercial
policy—History. 4. Democracy—Great Britain. 5. Democracy—
France. 6. Democracy—United States. I. Title.
HF1533.V47   1994
382′.3′0941—dc20   93-34315   CIP

This book has been composed in Adobe Goudy

Princeton University Press books are printed on acid-free paper
and meet the guidelines for permanence and durability of the
Committee on Production Guidelines for Book Longevity of the
Council on Library Resources Printed in the United States of America

10 9 8 7 6 5 4 3 2 1

A Mes Parents

Contents

List of Tables and Figures

Tables

Figures

Preface _____

THIS PROJECT began as a dispassionate, no-nonsense inquiry into the role of lobbying in the making of trade policy. It has ended as an apologia of the role of voting.

In traditional studies of trade policy, political economists have focused on interest groups. Institutionalists have focused on resourceful executives. Students of ideas on intellectual elites. And students of foreign policy on diplomats. Any focus on the role of voters is conspicuously absent from studies of trade policymaking, even though the policymakers—the legislators—are elected. To be sure, voters do not themselves legislate; therefore, they do not make policy directly; they do, however, decide who *does* make policy. In consequence, I argue here that voters play a far more significant role in the formulation of trade policy than has been previously recognized, despite the inevitable, disgraceful accompaniments to the process in a democracy—despite, that is, the corruption, rents, sleazy deals, clienteles, scapegoating of foreigners, and demagogic attempts to manipulate the electorate.

In this book, which is written for political scientists, political economists, and political historians alike, I propose an approach to trade-policy analysis that makes no prior assumption about who has the power to make trade policy decisions. Rather, the approach derives that information from the electoral arena, where every citizen has a vote. The argument for considering the role of the voters is made twice—first formally, then historically. Part one builds a theoretical framework based on standard assumptions about rational individualism. There, I show that self-maximizing individuals in a democratic context use electoral mechanisms to set the boundaries of trade policymaking. In part two, I present the argument in its rich historical context and retrace systematically the making of trade policy in Britain, France, and the United States, from 1860 to 1990.

I WISH to express my gratitude to those who have helped in the writing of the dissertation from which this book derives: to the late Gregory Luebbert for his inspiration, guidance, and support—his tragic death in a white-water boating accident was a personal loss to me, as well as a loss to the profession; to Vinod Aggarwal for his comprehensive comments, pertinent recommendations, and unfaltering support throughout the many years it took to steer this work to its final destination; to the late Aaron Wildavsky, Christine Paige, and Gary Bonham for valuable suggestions that helped immeasurably in clarifying my ideas; to John Zysman, Stephen Cohen, Beppe Di Palma, Ernst Haas, Ken

Jowitt, Robert Price, and many of my graduate-student friends at Berkeley for commenting on early parts of the manuscript; and to the Regents of the University of California and the Berkeley Department of Political Science for financial support.

I also wish to express my appreciation to those who have helped in the later stages of the manuscript: to my students at the University of Chicago for responding critically to my teaching; to my colleagues (and, nonetheless, friends) David Laitin, Bernard Silberman, and Mark Hansen for giving me invaluable comments on the never-final manuscript and for extensive demonstration of their collegiality; to Charles Lipson, Duncan Snidal, Atsushi Ishida, and the other participants of the Program on International Politics, Economics, and Security for a minute dissecting of the argument; to Gary Herrigel and the other participants of the Organization Theory and State Building Workshop, and to Gerald Rosenberg, Mark Hansen, and the other members of the American Politics Workshop for helpful discussions; to my other colleagues at the University of Chicago for an intellectually challenging environment. Also at the University of Chicago, I would like to thank Jim Fearon for constructive suggestions and the elegant game theoretic model reproduced in appendix one and Craig Koerner for making economics simpler, as well as Dale Copeland, Jason Cawley, Markus Fisher, Stuart Romm, and Ashley Tellis for a fruitful brainstorming session; and Denny Roy, Michael Dennis, Mark Schichtel, Erika George, Steve Karam, David MacIntyre, Melanie Stegman, and Henk Goemans for assisting this research by their time, zeal, and diligence.

My thanks go especially to Peter Cowhey, Peter Gourevitch, and Bradford Lee for a thorough, intelligent reading of the manuscript, extensive comments, penetrating criticisms, and a wealth of pointed suggestions, most of which I adopted without further acknowledgment. John Kroll, Jeff Frieden, David Lake, and Susanne Lohmann provided very helpful criticisms and assessments on parts of the manuscript. Serge Halimi literally shared his insightful thoughts on French socialism. The Social Science Research Council's Program in Foreign Policy Studies provided the means for time off at a critical stage of this project. The project would not have reached completion without their generosity.

I also wish to thank those who helped in the preparation of the final manuscript: to Malcolm De Bevoise for liking the manuscript from the outset and going out of his way to improve its readability; to Louisa Bertch Green for her tactful debunking of my franglais and her talented reworking of the manuscript into actual English; and to Roy Grisham for adding the final touch.

Errors and tenacious ambiguities that remain are all mine.

Finally—and, perhaps, most of all—I want to thank those who had less to do with this book than with its author: to my affectionate wife, Audrey, for her moral and material support; to our baby girl, Natalie, for bringing joy in our life; and to my parents, André and Paulette, for making it all possible. This book is dedicated to them as but a token of my deep appreciation.

Daniel Verdier
Chicago, October 1993

Introduction _____

Why is it that I and my American colleagues are being
constantly taken to court—made to stand trial—for
activities that our counterparts in Britain and other
parts of Europe are knighted, given peerages or comparable honors?
  (*Crawford Green, chairman of Du Pont*)

Anticlericalism is not for export.
  (*Gambetta, founder of the French Republican party*)

THE AIM OF this work is to explain how foreign trade policy is made in democratic regimes. It offers a general theory predicting the relative role played by
interests, parties, and state officials, and uses that theory to account for the
trade policies of France, Britain, and the United States during much of the
nineteenth and twentieth centuries. Its main conclusion is that foreign trade
policy is the outcome of a process influenced by voters.

Emphasis on voter influence is seldom encountered in the study of foreign
policy, and it challenges two analytical traditions in the field of international
relations. Analysts of international politics, who operate at what is called the
systemic level, hold that the preferences of a country's citizens, including
those of voters, have little or no influence on the country's relations with
other states. Analysts of domestic politics, who operate at what is called the
unit level, do consider the preferences of domestic actors but rarely the preferences of voters, on the ground that voters are unorganized, uninformed, or
powerless. The extent of voter influence, this work suggests, is far greater than
is ordinarily assumed.

The Systemic Level of Analysis

The first tradition underrates the importance of domestic factors because it
assumes that the anarchic character of the international system discourages
individual states from pursuing aims not directly related to national security.[1]
National security, however, is an elusive concept. In cases of national emergency—for instance, when a country is attacked—the concept is clear
enough; in the absence of emergency, especially when no enemy has been
identified, national survival, in and of itself, may become the justification for

almost any policy: alliance or neutrality, free trade or protection, or protection for steel or for wristwatches.[2] Because indeterminacy lends itself to controversy, a country's trade preferences—and ultimately its foreign policy—are subject to vigorous political debate.

Indeterminacy at the international level implies that foreign policy is not analytically distinct from domestic policy. In both cases, nations can pursue one of two courses: the maximization of a short-term, *particular* interest (for example, through protection, devaluation, annexation, arms, or environmental laissez-faire); or the pursuit of the *general* good (in the form of free trade, currency stability, territorial self-restraint, disarmament, or self-sustaining development). Policies of the first type yield immediate and visible benefits: a tariff salvages an industry's revenues; a devaluation delivers a competitive jolt to industry; territorial annexation, by increasing access to coveted resources, boosts national prestige; an arms build-up increases security (or at least the perception of it). Unregulated pollution keeps production costs low. Yet the hidden costs of these policies are not fully borne by the main beneficiary. Instead, the costs are unloaded onto weaker states, onto future generations of fellow citizens, and, if other countries retaliate, onto the present generation as well. Under such circumstances, how do countries determine their interests, and over what period of time? The answer depends largely, though not exclusively, on the domestic policy process. If the process allows the government to take a comprehensive, long-term view, costs will be minimal. In contrast, if the domestic policy process rewards only short-term expediency, then the policies pursued by governments will yield collectively suboptimal outcomes, which may take the form of high prices, currency instability, war, waste, or pollution.[3]

Foreign policy is fully determined by international factors only in the event of a national security crisis. In all other situations, the making of foreign policy, like that of domestic policy, requires that choices be made between particular and general goals. In both foreign and domestic policymaking, domestic politics is a determinant of the outcome.[4]

The Unit Level of Analysis

An emphasis on voter influence also contradicts unit-level interpretations of trade policy. Since Schattschneider's seminal work on the Smoot-Hawley Tariff, voters have been consistently theorized out of the trade-policy process.[5] None of the three dominant paradigms of political economy—which emphasize, in turn, markets, institutions, and ideas—pays attention to voters. Market-oriented political economists treat trade policy as reflecting the preferences of small, concentrated economic interests; voters who (by definition) have broad, diffuse interests, are left out of the analysis.[6] For institutionalists, trade policy reflects the institutional interest of autonomous state officials; voters, because they lack institutional affiliation, are ignored.[7] For students of social ideas, trade policy changes in response to modifications in economic doctrine and as a result of shifts in shared beliefs transmitted among policymakers through extra-electoral channels; voters who are assumed to have no ideas of their own, and who merely borrow the ideas of others, are redundant participants.[8] In either case, little importance is attributed to voters, despite the fact that electoral democracy typically is the system of government in the countries studied, in which every official appointment proceeds directly or indirectly from the ballot box.

Yet, leaving voters out of the study of democracy is like leaving soldiers out of the study of war. In any analysis of democracy, voters are the greatest source of uncertainty, no matter how informed they are. If, for instance, voters are completely informed about what is at stake in a given situation, politicians find themselves faced with the awkward situation known as "cycling majorities." [9] This situation arises when there is no possibility of putting together an electoral majority large enough to defeat all other possible coalitions. A winning majority of this sort is possible only when a single issue is at stake—which is never the case when voters are completely informed. Because of this indeterminacy among the electorate, the legislative outcome depends on the order in which issues are taken up. Yet, although cycling majorities work to the advantage of the institution that sets the legislative agenda (since the agenda-setter determines the majority),[10] uncertainty persists. Only now, it is at a remove from the legislative process, since, in a democracy, voters determine who sets an agenda.[11]

Even if, as I assume in this book, voters are only partially informed about issues and candidates, uncertainty does not disappear, although it changes form. In this situation, politicians are confronted with *rational ignorant voters*, Anthony Downs's term which captures an intuitively correct idea: The impact of an individual vote on the electoral outcome is so negligible that the ordinary voter is uninterested in casting an informed ballot (unless provided with a financial incentive), and will instead choose candidates on the basis of rules of thumb related to party ideology.[12] Rational ignorant voters operate at a superficial level of analysis, reducing both important and trivial issues to a simple ideological opposition between the Right and the Left. Although such simplification eliminates the risk of cycling (because only one issue is left to be decided), it does not remove the uncertainty about which substantive issues politicians will choose in constructing competing ideologies. Therefore, precisely where the Right-Left cleavage occurs in the electorate remains similarly uncertain.

In consequence, the principle of electoral uncertainty undermines theories of trade policy that fail to take voters into account. Chapter one shows the dissolving effect of including voters in the modeling of four key variables:

policy process, preference formation, the unit of interest organization, and policy instrument. From parameters defining the boundaries of the political competition, they turn into a stake of the political competition.

Findings and Case Studies

Three case studies are explored: France, Britain, and the United States during much of the nineteenth and twentieth centuries. The conventional wisdom in comparative politics holds that pressure groups play a greater role in the United States than in Britain or France, that state officials play a greater role in France than in Britain or the United States, and that parties (and thus voters) play a greater role in Britain than in France or the United States.

The picture that emerges from the present analysis is rather different. A first step is to distinguish between two questions. The first question—Who decides on the policy?—asks which interests have a say in the actual formulation of policy at the policymaking stage.

A second, and more fundamental, question is, *Who decides who should make the decisions, and how are these decisions made?* This question asks who has a say in the building of the trade policy process, which is defined in a preliminary way as the set of rules that identifies who decides and which rule is followed. I argue that it is voters who determine the policy process; and thus, it is the voters who indirectly control policymaking. This entirely new way of looking at policymaking—i.e., by treating the policy process as a variable whose value is determined by electoral competition—is systematically applied to the experiences of Britain, France, and the United States throughout the period 1860–1990.

The fact that the voter decides who makes the decisions does not imply that voters will always choose to assign themselves (through their elected representatives) the responsibility for deciding. Rather than adjudicate trade matters themselves, voters may instead authorize their representatives to delegate that task to others (to special trade interests, for example, or to diplomats), depending on the degree of voter concern for trade issues relative to nontrade issues. So the answer to the first question —Who decides on policy?—is not necessarily the voters; rather, the answer is subject to cross-national and longitudinal variation.

An important consequence of the electoral-delegation argument is that special interests play a contingent, residual role in process-building. The "special-interest lobbies"—small groups, large firms, concentrated sectors—are mainly process-subscribers. Far from influencing the design of the policy process, they merely accept and adjust to it. Some producers are successful in adjusting their preferences to the process. If the process favors lobbying and rent seeking, producers organize into trade associations and lobby for their particular preferences. However, if the process favors the articulation of general interests, they tailor their policy preferences accordingly. This adjustment, it must be added, is neither smooth, complete, nor cost-neutral. Some producers are unable to adjust their preferences; even for those who can, acting with voters as allies is often risky and costly. Where it exists, private political power exists at the tolerance of the voters, typically as a result of voter indifference. The political power of "big business," therefore, is to be understood as an electoral construct.

With respect to the question—Who decides on the policy?—the analysis in this book differs with prevailing views of the trade policy process in the United States and France. The American trade policy process is convention-ally seen as contaminated—and dominated—by special industrial interests.[13] This is an exaggeration. For the past century, U.S. industry has maintained adversarial relations with Washington; between the large corporations and Washington, relations have reached enmity (see the epigraph in which former Du Pont chairman Crawford Greenwalt rails against U.S. antitrust legisla-tion). Whereas special interests may be said to have predominated in earlier periods, most lastingly in the postbellum era from 1865 until 1887, U.S. trade policy in modern times has been governed by popular considerations. Unable to exercise control over the state, American industry generally has preferred self-help to rent seeking.

The standard view of business-government relations in France is that of an autonomous state bossing industry around.[14] The view I offer is exactly the opposite: French voters have consistently delegated the formulation of trade policy to business. The reality is that for almost a century (1892 until the late 1970s), French industrialists have enjoyed a stable, privileged, collusive rela-tionship with state officials. Politicians have rarely let ideology interfere with the promotion of business interests. When asked to take a stand on the protec-torate over missions which the Roman Catholic Church had conferred in the Near East and China, and on which French influence in these regions de-pended, Gambetta, the founder of the Republican party, responded that anti-clericalism, the rallying cry of Republicans, should not get in the way of export promotion.

This pragmatic relationship was reflected in the combined ability of indus-trialists and farmers—the electorally dominant producer group of the Third Republic—to reach agreement over trade policy. Their agreement was inter-rupted twice, logically enough, in 1936, during the Great Depression, and in 1945 during the *Libération*, when the demands of a newly mass-based producer group—the workers—which until then had been ignored, suddenly won ac-cess to government. In 1947, with the expulsion of the Left from governing coalitions because of its Communist affiliations, the workers were effectively disfranchised. Once again, France was a safe haven for industrialists and one of the most creative laboratories for state intervention in industry—that is, until the 1970s, when a reorganized Left was able to win back from the Right the right to govern. Industry-government relations in France since the election of 1978 have not differed significantly from those in the United States.

Only the case of Britain corresponds at all closely to the prevailing view in the literature (though not with Crawford Greenwalt's opinion).[15] Here, industry and government have historically maintained an arm's-length relationship. From 1881 on, when Britain pulled out of the 1860 tariff treaty system, the orientation of trade policy reflected the preferences of the median voter—preferences identical to those of the working class until the 1970s, and with those of the middle class since the 1970s.[16] Variations in the orientation of British policy are largely attributable to variations in these median preferences: free trade until the 1920s; indifference between free trade and protection in the 1930s; and intervention after the war, until the neoliberal revolt of the middle class in the 1980s, which was provoked by the proven unreliability of the state in distributing rents to industry. In the case of Britain, government aid to industry, where it has existed at all, has been limited, indirect, and inconsistent.

Organization of the Book

A book that deals with both theoretical and historical materials, such as this one, can be organized in one of two ways. Either the theoretical argument can be laid out first, as a preface to the historical cases, and run the risk of seeming merely to have been deduced from general principles. Or the theoretical argument can follow the historical material, as historians prefer, so that it will seem to have been derived exclusively from experience, with no reference to general principles. As a social scientist, I have chosen the first option, although I do not wish to unfairly tax the patience of historians. This work owes as much to inductive inference as it does to a priori reasoning, and it is aimed at historians and social scientists alike.[17]

Part One

A POLITICAL THEORY
OF INTERNATIONAL TRADE

One

Trade and the Voter

A SURVEY OF THE EXISTING LITERATURE

L'enjeu, c'est la règle du jeu
(The rules of the game are the stakes of the game)

Tout est politique!
(Everything is political!)

THE FACT that the voter has been left out of the study of trade policy is attributable to a tendency in the field to define the stakes of political competition too narrowly. Four variables are commonly assumed to be parametric (or non-varying) or exogenous (varying, but in accordance with events that stand outside the political arena): (1) the identity of the decisionmakers and the rules for deciding (policy process), (2) the preferences of the interests thus represented, (3) the unit of interest organization (sector, factor, etc.), and (4) the type of trade policy instruments to be investigated. The result is not just a simplification but a misrepresentation that occults important aspects of the democratic process. In contrast, I argue that these four variables must reflect political competition.

The Trade Policy Process

Producers and politicians formulate trade policy according to a set of rules and procedures called the trade policy process (hereafter *policy process* unless otherwise noted). The policy process identifies both the decisionmakers and the rules for decisionmaking. Chapters two and three elaborate on the definition of policy process and offer a typology. A question of immediate concern is the analytical status of the concept: Is the policy process exogenous; i.e., does it obey rules of transformation that stand outside the realm of political competition? Or is it part and parcel of that realm? The standard view, one shared by nearly all writers on the subject, is that the policy process is exogenous. I argue to the contrary—that electoral politics requires that the policy process be endogenized.[1]

The existing literature contains several competing models that exclude the policy process from political competition. Political economists of the Chicago school postulate a process that they assume to be universally valid—rent seeking.[2] This is a formal model for what is generally referred to as "interest-group politics," or "pressure politics." The model features tenure-maximizing politicians who sell policies (called "rents") to wealth-maximizing individuals in exchange for campaign funds. Political economists attribute the existence of this exchange to the inefficiencies of the electoral market, in which rational ignorant voters are inclined to cast uninformed ballots. Only voters whose interests are sufficiently concentrated for them to overcome the dilemma of collective action and to lobby politicians directly can extract significant rents. The rest of the voters, who may only cast their individual votes, subsidize rents.

Appropriately, institutionalists have questioned the universality of the rent-seeking model of policymaking. They have proposed, instead, a richer scale of state institutions, one that ranges between two extreme types, the weak state and the strong state.[3] The weak-state model corresponds roughly to the political economist's rent-seeking model, whereas the strong-state model is characterized by state officials who are free to act independently of predominant societal preferences. Although not all recent institutionalist theory relies on the weak state/strong state dichotomy, it nevertheless still characterizes the impact of state institutions on coalitions as exogenous.[4]

Another model, the median-voting model, has occasionally been applied in the field of trade policy.[5] Borrowed from studies of American political parties, this model is an economist's version of the political scientist's notions of party government and party politics.[6] The median-voting model features two parties that vie for the support of the median voter. Although the voters are conceptualized as rational ignorant, their ignorance is not a source of inefficiency, as in the rent-seeking model, because they use party ideology as a proxy for a party's true position on specific issues. Knowledge of party ideologies makes voters sufficiently well-informed to vote. In two-party systems, party ideologies also enable the median voter to choose the trade policy (assuming the two parties take opposite stands), as the winner manages to attract the median voter's support. In multiparty systems, however, the policy outcome is indeterminate.

Despite the differences, these three approaches are united in considering the rules of the political game not as a stake of the game but as fixed independently of it and deserving of separate study. The point is especially clear with respect to political economists, for whom the exogeneity of the policy process is a matter of assumption.[7] It is also clear with respect to students of parties and institutions, who consider exogeneity the logical consequence of a historical process. This point deserves elaboration.

Central to both the institutional and the party approach are two theoretical propositions: path dependency and historical precedence. Students of parties and institutions subscribe to a theory of change according to which institutions figure less often than do policies on the political agenda—owing to the fact that institutional change is incremental and path-dependent, except at "critical junctures" (those rare moments in history when institutions are overhauled).[8] Students of parties and institutions also rank institutions according to historical precedence; prior institutions are viewed as shaping more recent ones. The checks and balances of the U.S. Constitution, for instance, are said to obstruct the creation of a centralized trade-policy process, because the former is historically prior to the latter. The combination of these two postulates—path dependency and historical precedence—yields a trade policy process that is fully and exogenously determined by the network of institutions in which it is embedded.

In this book, I show, instead, that the policy process is variable and that its variation is not necessarily determined by historically prior institutions. I will also show that democratic institutions are not tightly organized, but, rather, are the variable and complex products of strategic interaction. Consequently, institutions exhibit a degree of slack which, it should be noted, has a stabilizing effect; the Constitution and its principles are cushioned against the daily legislative grind. If institutions were as tightly and hierarchically organized as institutionalists suppose them to be, policy conflicts at each level would be relayed to the level immediately above, until the whole institution is embroiled. Slack acts as a firebreak.[9]

Treating a formal institution as an organization of loosely linked layers makes it possible to view process-building as a function of electoral politics. The policy process is not securely fastened to venerable texts and customs, but is flexible enough to be shaped by minor policy disputes. The driving force behind the politicization of the rules of the game is electoral politics. Politicians compete for reelection in part by taking advantage of this flexibility. Since their primary goal is to be (re)elected, they are motivated to make the most of whatever they have. If they fail to get their way on an issue, they contest the rules. They are the natural and indefatigable agents of institutional change. In a democracy where voters are sovereign, politics knows no fixed boundaries; the domain of politics can, in principle, be expanded indefinitely, until "*tout est politique.*"[10]

The policy process thus does not have fixed parameters, nor is it a variable that is determined fully and exogenously. Rather, it is the product of political competition, in a redistributive game governed by electoral considerations.

Trade Preference Formation

Any individual not indifferent to trade policy will favor either freer trade or greater protection. The field is divided unequally on the question of how trade preferences arise. The majority take individuals' trade preferences as a given, whereas a minority treats preferences as social constructs. By and large, students of tariff-making treat individuals' revealed trade preferences as given. Trade preferences are assumed to be a reflection of the producer's position in the economy. Producers in import-sensitive sectors endorse higher tariffs; those in export-oriented sectors endorse lower tariffs. This view has been rightly criticized for its unreflective reliance on the primitive concept of material interest. However, although students of social groups, cultures, and ideas have advanced a more nuanced notion of material interest, placing it in the context of socially shared beliefs or ideas, few have succeeded in supplying an alternative formalization, and none have sought to reduce material interest to political competition.[11] This book adopts a quite different position, treating trade preferences as political strategies.

The assumption of exogeneity is questionable even for perfectly informed, self-maximizing producers. (Note that if exogeneity does not hold for this class of individuals, then, a fortiori, it does not hold for anyone.) Such producers seek profits. They choose the trade preference which simultaneously provides them with the highest return and has the greatest chance to succeed. Although "return" is an economic variable, "chance" (the chance of winning the return through lobbying) is a political variable. Producers try to maximize the product of the two variables (return discounted by political risk). High risk might make an expected high return look less attractive, whereas low risk might make an expected low return appear more attractive.

The contribution of political risk to the formation of trade preferences becomes clear if one keeps in mind that many (but not all) producers can choose among more than one policy to maximize trade gains. In principle, producers have fundamentally mixed preferences; they seek competition on what they consume but a rent on what they produce. Import-sensitive producers, for instance, can benefit either from lower tariffs on their inputs or higher tariffs on their outputs. Correspondingly, export-oriented producers can benefit either from lower tariffs on their inputs or from bounties on their outputs. It is not unimaginable that even an import-dependent distributor could be indifferent to free trade and import licenses if these provide him, and a few others, with monopoly rents by effectively excluding potential newcomers from the distribution business. To a great extent, producers choose sides on the basis of political feasibility.

In sum, for many producers—especially those who belong to growth sectors—the claim can be made that the policy is likely to weigh more heavily than the economy on the choice of trade preferences. In these cases, whether a firm supports a tariff cut or an export subsidy depends not on the firm's position in the economy but on the relative political cost of each option. Since political costs are set by politicians, the industrialist's calculus internalizes the politician's calculus, and thus voter preferences.

The Unit of Interest Organization

There is a third question that trade analysts tend to answer a priori: Should the unit of analysis be the *sector*, as in the specific factors model, or the *factor of production* (land, labor, and capital), as in the Heckscher-Ohlin model?[12] For some time, economists by-passed the question by way of assumption, whereas political scientists became embroiled in a professional dispute over the relative merits of the concepts of "group" and "class." Owing partly to Olson's demonstration of the steep organizational costs faced by members of large reference groups, the dispute seems to have been resolved in favor of sector and "group." Yet, a sector's capacity to organize a trade lobby does not, as political economists invariably assume, simply reflect that sector's size and degree of concentration. The capacity to organize also depends on the type of organization that will be required for political expediency. If the policy process is responsive to particular interests, forming a special interest group is the right strategy; if the policy process is more responsive to general interests, then the public interest group (or, better, the political party) is the best form of organization for lobbying. The special-interest-group formula favors small, concentrated producer groups, such as sectors; whereas the general-interest-formula favors large, diffuse producer groups, such as factors. In sum, interest organization cannot be treated solely as an exogenous parameter any more than trade preference formation can. Both take into account the question of political feasibility.

Trade Policy Toolbox

Export subsidies, imperial preferences, tariffs, and quotas are all instruments of trade policy. Does this category also include antitrust, planning, industrial policy, income policy, health and environmental policy, regional development policy, defense procurements, aid to small business, and so on? Although it is standard practice to treat each of them as a separate topic, the rationale for doing so is unclear, since trade flows reflect differentials in prices that are generated by many different variables, including wages, subsidies, and all sorts of regulations. The repertoire of trade policy instruments cannot be defined a priori; instead, it must be determined endogenously.

The question of what tools the toolbox contains has been addressed by both institutionalists and political economists. Institutionalists have proposed making the choice of policy instruments a function of state institutions. Strong states, the argument goes, are able to pursue micro, targeted policies more effectively than are weak states. Just as institutions are considered an exogenous variable by institutionalists, so are policy instruments. The present study takes the opposite tack by arguing that the trade policy pursued by "strong states" does not reflect institutional givens but is shaped by electoral competition.

Magee, Brock, and Young offer an endogenous interpretation of trade policy tools.[13] They have tackled a question that has puzzled many economists: Results show that when protective mechanisms are ranked in terms of the damage they cause to the economy, governments invariably choose the most damaging; quotas are preferred to tariffs, and tariffs are preferred to subsidies.[14] The reason for choosing suboptimal policies—Magee, Brock, and Young argue—is that the negative effects of quotas are less detectable by rational ignorant voters than are those of tariffs, and the negative effects of tariffs are less detectable than are those of subsidies. Therefore, the less ignorant the voter, the greater the need for a government (for electoral purposes) to resort to suboptimal policies. Later in this study, I point to a similar correlation. The point to be emphasized here is that the determination of appropriate policy tools requires a close analysis of electoral politics. The choice of certain tools does in fact reflect historical and technological constraints; other choices are determined largely by the demands of political competition.

Even so rapid a survey of the field as the present one suggests that numerous restrictive assumptions have worked to obscure the importance of electoral politics as a factor in the formation of trade policy. A wider net must be cast in order to include the role that voters play. This is true because voters stand outside the assumptions of most studies about process, preferences, and tools, as well as the unit of interest organization. To place these variables beyond the influence of political competition not only impoverishes the analysis, but also occults important aspects of the democratic process. My goal is not to offer a rival line of argument, but to construct a general framework in which existing theories (rent seeking, median voting, state autonomy) function as local explanations, with specified boundary conditions, and explicit rules of transition.

Two

The Electoral Regulation of Access

THE ARGUMENT of this book—that voters indirectly control the making of policy, and that they do so by setting the rules according to which lawmakers make policy—can be represented by means of the following chart:

FIGURE 2.1
Variable Chart of the Theory of Electoral Delegation

Electorate ———▶ Policy process ———▶ Policy outcome

The idea of voter control defined herein differs from two versions commonly encountered in the literature. One characterizes the relationship between voters and representatives as a mandate; the other characterizes the representative as a delegate or a free agent.[1] The mandate theory asserts that voters select representatives on the basis of ex ante commitments to substantive policies. Once elected, representatives are obligated to support the policies. The mandate, however, is an overly stringent and not very practical theory of electoral control. Rational ignorant voters are more likely in the first place to choose a personality and an ideology rather than a program. Even in an ideal world of perfectly informed voters, the theory of the mandate runs into the objection that majority voting cannot yield a stable, social choice in the presence of more than two programs.[2]

The free-agent theory is flawed for different reasons. The theory asserts that the role of voters is not to elect representatives with strict mandates to support definite policies, but is to hire representatives who will then act as the representatives judge best for the community. Where the mandate theory assumes too much control, the free-agent theory assumes too little. The voters' task of predicting which candidates will prove the most competent and exhibit the soundest judgment is complicated by the fact that delegating to an agent is insufficient to ensure representation; according to recent developments in agency theory, the slack allowed a free agent induces shirking.[3]

In this book I suggest a third theory of electoral control, one which asserts that elections allow voters to do more than simply choose agents, but less than actually choose policies. What elections do, above all, is allow voters to choose the rules by which their agents make policies. In this sense, an election is comparable to a legislature's delegation of authority to an independent agency: The legislature authorizes an agency to act on its behalf. At the same time, it guards itself against possible abuse, deception, and shirking by setting up strict rules for information transfer, publicity, consultation, and representation—all of which the agency must respect in formulating policy.[4] In a similar fashion, by means of elections, voters set the rules of representation, information transfer, and publicity, all of which lawmakers must respect when deliberating about policy. Then, within the limits set by voters, lawmakers charge the administrative branch with the responsibility for carrying out policy. This argument is referred to as the theory of electoral delegation.

Politicians at election time decide what position to take on a trade issue, and how much visibility to confer on it, based on their assessment of voters' expectations. These campaign decisions effectively determine the policy process, which is defined as the rules of access to policymaking after the election. If the trade issue is salient among the electorate, voters' interests will be more fully represented in policymaking than if it is not salient. Similarly, if the trade issue is divisive among the electorate, voters' interests will also be more fully represented in policymaking than if it is not divisive. However, if the trade issue is neither salient nor divisive, rent seekers tend to crowd out voters' interests.

What role do producer groups play in this process? It is argued that producers choose a position to take on the trade issue, as well as the tactical alliances to form, based on their assessment of what is politically feasible.

I first sketch a generic industrialist's calculus (first step), the policy options that person faces, and the lobbying tactics available. Then I explain how these options are constrained by the politician's calculus. Next, I present the politician's calculus, then model the setting of the electoral agenda, derive the consequences for the layout of the policy process, and use this information to complete the analysis of the industrialist's calculus (second step). The penultimate section discusses the potential objection that campaign funds overdetermine voters' preferences. Throughout, the argument is deliberately cast at a high level of generality; the references made to trade policy are essentially illustrative. This chapter can be read along with its mathematical appendix (appendix one).

The Industrialist's Calculus: First Step

It is possible to categorize the various interests seeking influence over postelection policymaking. The main contenders are free traders, on the one hand, and the seekers of rents (tariffs, quotas, export subsidies), on the other.[5] The dichotomy between free trade and rent seeking is a subset of a class of problems concerned with the choice individuals often face between maximizing their interests by means of a particular policy (a rent) and a general policy. A particular policy allows an individual to self-maximize by generating negative externalities which are borne by others; for instance, a tariff increases an industry's profits at the expense of consumers.[6] In contrast, a general policy allows an individual to self-maximize while minimizing negative externalities; for instance, free trade reduces overall prices without shifting the cost onto consumers.

Who will seek rents and who will support general-interest policies is not entirely determined by the structure of the economy. Economic indeterminacy is especially present in the domain of trade policy, for reasons mentioned in chapter one, which need only to be briefly recalled here.[7] Industrialists can benefit either from freer trade on their inputs or from rents (tariffs or subsidies) on their outputs. For most of them, their position in the economy as producers reveals nothing about their trade-policy preference. This fact suggested, therefore, that the concept of trade preference be replaced by the more encompassing notion of *trade strategy*, whereby free trade, protection, and export promotion are not preferences but rather a set of strategies from which producers choose in order to maximize profits. The principle of economic indeterminacy also suggests that the relative access of rent seekers and supporters of general-interest policies to policymaking cannot logically be inferred from the economic structure but must be sought instead in politics. Whether a firm supports a tariff cut (general strategy) or an export subsidy (rent) depends not on the firm's position in the economy but on the relative political cost of each strategy. Since political costs are set by politicians, the calculus of the politicians is examined next.

The Politician's Calculus

Lawmakers determine access to the policy process by deciding whose interests they wish to represent when initiating, debating, and passing a piece of legislation. Although the criteria on which they base their decision may be diverse, the argument developed in this chapter is that, because lawmakers are chiefly concerned about (re)election, the decisions they make regarding access are intended to maximize their chances of (re)election. The logical starting point is the setting of the campaign agenda.

Setting the Campaign Agenda

The first point to establish is how much visibility parties decide to confer on the trade issue at election time, based on their assessment of voters' expectations. Assume that voters are rational ignorant, that is, that they are pocketbook maximizers with imperfect information about the differential financial impact of various policies and policy positions.[8] Rational ignorance imposes two constraints on the electioneering strategies of parties. First, elections hinge on a mere handful of issues selected by parties from among dozens, even hundreds, of possible issues. In setting their campaign agendas, parties have to decide which issues should figure prominently and which are to be buried in the dense script of party manifestos. Second, voter rational ignorance obliges parties to go to great expenses and efforts to sell their issues to the voters. Given that a party must assign priorities to issues and publicize the result, under what circumstances will that party decide to commit a substantial portion of its resources to promote its position on the trade issue?

A party decides where to rank an issue with an eye to the number of votes that are likely to be won as a result of giving the issue special attention. The party's decision depends on two calculations—the first regarding salience, and the second, divisiveness. Parties are more likely to stress the trade issue on election day if the issue has the potential to force voters to take a position instead of allowing them to express indifference, and if it promises to divide voters rather than unite them. Neutral, consensual issues are less likely to be emphasized.

Salience and divisiveness are two electoral parameters whose respective values may be assumed, at least for now, to be exogenously set. (This fiction will be lifted in chapter 4, when elements of strategic choice are introduced.) Together, salience and divisiveness define a two-dimensional space on which each point represents a trade issue's possible location. This space can, for the sake of simplicity, be reduced to four typical values. In table 2.1, each cell records the spending level simultaneously chosen by each of two competing parties. Each party's choice is constrained, first, by the values assumed by each electoral parameter; and, second, by the other party's anticipated decision. (Appendix one develops a spending model to predict the ranking of the trade issue on two competing parties' respective agenda, together with a numerical simulation of different levels of salience and divisiveness.)

If an issue is popular with the voters (upper row), both parties have an interest in addressing the issue. If the issue is also divisive (case I)—that is, if there is a normal voting distribution of, say, free traders and protectionists— then the parties each have an approximately equal opportunity to increase significantly their respective chances in the election if they take strong opposing positions on the issue.[9] Each party, therefore, will spend considerable effort to promote its trade stand among voters. The trade issue, that is, will figure at the top of both campaign agendas. In contrast to this, if the issue is both popular and consensual (case II), then those on one side of the issue—say, free traders—will dominate, and their party will spend disproportionately more on the issue than the protectionist party, though not as much as it spends in case I. The free-trade party spends relatively more in case II in order to capitalize

TABLE 2.1
Typology of Two Parties' Decisions to Promote the Trade Issue

| | Degree of Divisiveness of the Trade Issue | |
	High	Low
Degree of Salience of the Trade Issue		
High	CASE I Both parties devote substantial resources to promoting the trade issue, having about an equal chance of sharply increasing electoral support	CASE II One party devotes substantial resources to promoting the trade issue, having a disproportionately greater chance of sharply increasing electoral support
Low	CASE III Both parties devote few resources to promoting the trade issue, having about an equal chance of only slightly increasing electoral support	CASE IV Both parties devote few resources to promoting the trade issue, one party having a disproportionately greater chance of only slightly increasing electoral support

Table 2.1 is derived from table A.1 in Appendix 1.

on its comparative advantage; the party does not spend as much in case II as it would have in case I, because it faces less competition from the other party, whereas the protectionist party spends some money, though not much, to limit the gains of the free-trade party.

If, however, the voters show little interest in the trade issue (lower row), the only constituents for trade issues left are special interests. In this case, parties would have to make great efforts to marshal public support. They prefer instead to concentrate their resources on other issues, spending only a token amount to publicize their respective trade stands, but an amount sufficient to attract the financial support of well-informed trade interests. On balance, spending in this case is less than in the former two cases. Spending is further reduced if the interest groups converge in their positions (case IV) than if they diverge (case III), for reasons analogous to those noted in comparing cases II and I. These four ideal cases can be ranked transitively according to the total effort spent on the trade issue by the parties: More is spent in case I than in case II, in case II than in case III, and in case III than in case IV (consult appendix one for a numerical illustration). In summary,

parties are more likely to make an effort to promote the trade issue on election day if the trade issue is perceived to be salient than if it leaves voters indifferent, and parties are more likely to devote equivalent resources to promoting the trade issue if it is divisive rather than consensual.

It is clear, then, that the electorate determines the campaign agenda. It remains to be demonstrated that the campaign agenda, in its turn, determines who will have access to policymaking.

Deciding Access: The Electoral Delegation

The amount of effort parties devote to the trade issue on election day both reveals and finalizes voters' expectations about how trade policy will be made after election day. The effect of massive spending on the trade issue (cases I and II) is to make the issue one of the yardsticks by which to judge the winning party's performance in government. Massive spending has the effect of turning voters' trade preferences into a public mandate. Conversely, low spending (cases III and IV) leaves the issue safely in the shadow of voters' ignorance—voters may have an opinion about trade, but they have no access to information about where parties stand on the issue and no means of expressing their opinions. The relative spending behavior of the parties also determines whether the trade debate will be conflictual or consensual. Where the two parties spend with roughly equal success (cases I and III), the opposition party may be expected to put up a fight at the policymaking stage, if only to honor campaign promises, by accepting debates and contesting votes. If, instead, one party has spent (and won) much less than the other (cases II and IV), it is likely to adopt a low profile in the policy process, since promoting a minority line yields little benefit.

The amount and relative distribution of effort spent on election day on articulating public preferences on the trade issue determines how the policy process is structured. To see this, it is necessary first to define how policy processes operate. A policy process is a set of informal rules that determines the relative weight of three classes of deciders: those for, those against, and those not in a position to participate. The last category, "Absent," refers to nonparticipants; these are not to be confused with abstainers, who have the power to participate in the decisionmaking process but who decide to abstain from doing so. "Abstain" is a distinct analytical category that does not add enough explanatory value to warrant discussion here.

A policy process is fully specified by two rules. The first rule determines the relative weight of those absent to those present (those for and those against, combined). This is the quorum. *Quorum* is ordinarily defined as "the number . . . of officers or members of a body that when duly assembled is legally competent to transact business."[10] If this definition is modified to reflect the principle of popular representation, by which voters transfer to their representative the power to decide for them, a quorum is the number of voters who, duly represented, allow their representatives to transact business. The second rule determines the relative weight, among those present, between those for and those against. This is the decision rule.

Given this definition of the policy process, the link between the agenda for spending and the policy process becomes clearer. The *total* amount of effort expended on the trade issue by the parties to influence the election day result determines the size of the quorum. Large spending on the trade issue translates into a high quorum in the trade-policy process, because lawmakers have committed themselves, at great length and untold expense, to make the legislative case for their voters' trade preferences. Low spending on the trade issue, however, in effect excludes voters from the trade policy process, because the parties articulated no policy promise during the election. Simultaneously, the *relative* spending of the parties determines the type of decision rule; symmetrical spending gives rise to an adversarial process in which decisions are made by a simple majority of representatives, whereas asymmetrical spending leads to a consensual process in which it does not pay the minority side to take an opposing position. In this case, decisions are made as if they did not obey the actual majority rule but required the consent of all.

This analysis is unavoidably abstract. The abstraction arises from the fact that such concepts as "quorum" and "decision rule," which I use informally here, also have formal definitions in legal theory, which are analogous to the one used here, but which are void of explanatory content. All deliberative bodies, for instance, have by-laws that explicitly specify the quorum and the decision rule once and for all, irrespective of the nature of the issue, the importance of that issue for the deciders, or how much effort they spent on publicizing their position on the issue. Yet the fact remains that these formal rules do not tell us anything about whose interests actually get represented in the process. What we need to know, and what these formal rules are presumed to tell us (although, in fact, they do not), is not how many representatives have to be physically present in the lower house for the trade debate to proceed, nor how many must vote "in favor" for the bill to pass. Instead, we need to know how many principals' interests must be truly represented by their elected political agents for debate to take place, and how many of these truly represented principals must reach agreement with one another through their agents for the bill to be passed. Procedural appearance is not necessarily a good indicator of political reality. The full legislature might be present to debate a bill, for example, where the interests spoken for are those of only two private lobbies. Conversely, a half-empty legislature could pass a bill that has the explicit support of the electorate at large. *Quorum* and *decision rule*, as used here, are unobservable categories meant to capture the informal reality behind the forms of legislative debate.

The realism of the unanimity rule may also be questioned. After all, nowhere on earth are laws passed unanimously. There are cases, however, when disagreement does not pay. Policymaking in time of war is one such case; nations at war are averse to seeing their politicians fight rearguard battles. Policymaking in low quorums is another; if, for instance, industrialists are averse to "playing partisan ball" to such an extent that they would rather see their agents settle their differences in private than in public. Conversely, there are instances in which agreement does not pay. Consider, for instance, the disrepute into which logrolling has fallen. Logrolling, a coalition-building technique by which politicians exchange promises of mutual support for one another's pet legislation until unanimity is reached, was the standard mechanism of tariff-making in the United States after the Civil War. From 1888 onward, however, as the tariff became a partisan issue, this time-honored vehicle of consensus came to be seen as a threat to partisan discipline and was relegated to intraparty use, as a means of securing unity among factions within a single party. Logrolling remained an intrapartisan device until the passage of the Smoot-Hawley tariff in 1930, when it suddenly became an interpartisan device again, making shambles of party discipline and delegitimating congressional tariff-making.[11] Interpartisan logrolling had become anathema to an electorate by then used to being mobilized along party lines.

The argument so far asserts that the degrees of salience and divisiveness of a given issue on election day determine the level of priority assigned to that issue by each party on its respective campaign agenda. Different levels of priority on campaign agendas lead to different policy processes. High-level priority on an agenda leads to a public mandate; that is, voter preferences are given corresponding weight in the policymaking process. Low-level priority on the agenda means that voters are effectively excluded from policymaking. In the following discussion, I will refer to the former case as *high quorum* and to the latter as *low quorum*. Furthermore, symmetry between competing agendas leads to an adversarial process, which I call *majority rule*, whereas agenda asymmetry leads to a consensual process, which I call *unanimity rule*. This institutionalization of the electoral parameters into the policy process I call *electoral delegation*, because it can be studied as a delegation of power from the electorate to the lawmakers. As with more formal cases of delegation, the power to decide for a principal is transferred to an agent, and the agent is subject to various institutional checks.[12] Within the microcosm of a legislature, electoral delegation reproduces the degree of salience and divisiveness of issues as they are perceived by voters at the time of the campaign.

Cui Bono? It remains to determine the implications of different mixes of quorums and decision rules on our generic industrialist's calculus.

The Industrialist's Calculus: Second Step

We have already seen that industrialists can maximize net returns either by pursuing a particular policy (rent) or a general policy (free trade), and that the choice between these two strategies, in large part, depends on the political feasibility of each policy. In light of the typology of political processes just laid out, we now assess the political feasibility of each strategy by successively considering the impact on the cost of lobbying of the quorum and the decision rule.

Quorum and Trade Strategy

A high quorum (inclusion of voters in the policy process) makes general policies politically profitable, whereas a low quorum (exclusion of voters) opens the way to rent-seeking behavior. A high quorum implies: (1) the organizing advantage enjoyed by rent seekers over voters, under other circumstances, is reversed by a high quorum in favor of the voters; (2) rent seekers face greater lobbying costs. These are developed successively.

ORGANIZING ADVANTAGE

The advantage that concentrated interests enjoy over diffuse interests is the ability to overcome free-riding. This advantage is canceled if diffuse interests are organized into voters by political parties. Hence, whenever a trade issue is seized on by parties—that is, whenever the quorum of the trade policy process is high—concentrated interests lose their exclusive access to lawmaking.

Further, not only does a high quorum cancel the organizing advantage normally enjoyed by concentrated interests, it actually gives the advantage to diffuse interests. A high quorum implies a large-scale coalition, which concentrated interests are less able to stabilize than are general interests. Lord Derby expressed the point well in the debate over free trade and protection in Great Britain in 1887:

> The strength of [the free traders'] position is this, that every free trader is the ally of every other free trader, whereas every protectionist looks with jealousy on those who wish to protect articles in regard to which he is a consumer, and not a producer.[13]

Lord Derby's quip about the tariff anticipated an important and more general analytical finding: Large-scale rent-seeking coalitions are fundamentally unstable. This instability arises from the fact that a rent seeker's gains come at the expense of the rest of society, which includes other rent seekers. Rent seeking is feasible when it benefits only a small minority, because then the burden of the rents obtained can be spread over an exploited majority. If the ratio between payers and rent seekers becomes less asymmetrical, however, rents begin to cannibalize each other, because the full burden can no longer be borne by the exploited majority without risking a payers' backlash, as well as a full-fledged debate on redistribution.[14] Organizing a coalition around a general interest is much easier.

COSTS OF RENT SEEKING

The cost of rent seeking increases in direct proportion to the level of quorum, for three main reasons: (1) the need to organize diffuse interests involves "field" expenses that rise with the size of the quorum; (2) the larger the quorum, the smaller the set of feasible policy alternatives; and (3) the risk of shirking on the part of political agents becomes greater.

Field Expenses

Field expenses are the costs incurred by special interests in rallying public support. If the quorum is low, there is no need to marshal public support. To the extent that the public is demobilized, the policy process operates according to the rules of compromise or logrolling; the smaller the number of participants, the less expensive the rent. In contrast, if the quorum is high, agents for rent seekers cannot rely on compromise or logrolling to ensure passage of the legislation granting the desired rent. The participation of a large number of outsiders makes pork-barrel politics too costly, logrolling unstable, and compromise sometimes damning. Agents must, instead, assemble these outsiders in the form of a massive electoral constituency in favor of the rent. This coalition cannot be "general" (rents cannot be easily generalized), but has to be "tangential" (most of its members support the rent for related but distinct reasons). A vivid instance of tangential coalition can be found in the "Bootlegger-Baptist coalition" of the Prohibition era in the United States. Bootleggers and Baptists alike had a common interest in closing corner liquor stores on Sunday, though for obviously different reasons.[15]

The costs incurred in building tangential coalitions are likely to be both high and uncontrollable. Assuming that the party is favorable to the lobby's demand for a rent, the party will publicize the demand, provided the lobby contributes field expenses. The amount of these field expenses is hard to determine in advance, however. The electoral and legislative chances of the rent are dependent on the chances of other issues endorsed by the party. Indeed, a party is like a locomotive pulling a long train of controversial issues: If one car jumps the tracks, the entire train may be derailed. This kind of issue interdependence implies that by investing in one issue, a special-interest group is effectively obliged to underwrite the entire platform, and so becomes financially liable for bailing out any part of the platform. Moreover, given that it is impossible in a multiissue environment for the agent to allocate costs by issue, sponsors find themselves caught up in a game of collective action. The result is that those with the greatest interest in obtaining the rents end up paying for the rents of others.

A lobby faces an additional hurdle if, in addition to the field expenses just described, it must convince a party to champion its cause. In that case, it must seek an alliance with a public-interest group with sufficiently large popular appeal to influence the party leadership. Such a marriage of convenience is not only burdensome from the point of view of the special interest, which assumes the role of provider, it can also be a source of uncertainty if the public-interest group has an independent agenda. In the Bootlegger-Baptist case, the bootleggers' search for tangential support made the fate of the desired rent (the creation of a captive Sunday market for booze) closely dependent on the Baptists' success in mobilizing an anti-booze "moral majority."[16]

The Choice Set

A high quorum reduces the choice set of available policy options. By forcing special interests to turn the trade issue into a general issue, or to attach it to a general issue, a high quorum has the effect of simplifying the choice set, because a quantitative issue (the rent) is converted into a qualitative one (the ethical principle that the policy is alleged to exemplify); thus, for example, free trade ideologues want free trade for everyone. This "clotting" of the choice set removes room for maneuver and compromise, and this effect is compounded by the "contagion" effect.[17] Since a general issue is more easily merged with other popular debates than is a specialized issue, the risk that further restrictions will be imposed on the choice set is much higher in a high quorum (in which the range of popular debates is constantly being enlarged) than in a small quorum setup (in which policymaking is sheltered from the contamination of general ideas). The restrictions placed on the choice set by clotting and contagion, together with high field expenses, make a high quorum an expensive environment for rent seekers.

Agent's Shirking[18]

Irrespective of the size of the quorum, representative agents have an interest in increasing campaign contributions, which they can then apply against the costs of securing election or reelection. A lobbying group can guard against shirking by monitoring the behavior of agents. The cost of this varies. In a low quorum, monitoring costs are low; concentrated interests know exactly what they want, and they state their demands in minute detail. Legislative slippages are easily detectable and, where they cannot be reversed, usually lead to renegotiation of the initial understanding. Moreover, campaign support, which the lobby offers in exchange, is divisible and amenable to fine-tuning. Detail and divisibility make for a principal-agent relationship that is easy to monitor. In contrast, a high quorum provides agents with greater leeway in their dealings with lobbies. The public opinion leader is the depository of a noncodified expertise akin to that of the lion tamer. Moreover, lobbies have good reasons for thinking that agents will shirk precise, enforceable commitments, since rents for special interests are unpopular among large groups. In order to repackage a rent as a credible application of a general principle to a particular case, an agent needs flexibility.

A low quorum provides ideal conditions, then, for the pursuit of a particular, rent-seeking strategy. It encourages free-riding among diffuse interests. It keeps lobbying costs for concentrated interests low, because it involves no field expenses. It keeps participants' options open. And it offers little opportunity for agents to shirk. A high quorum, in contrast, reverses the asymmetry in organizing advantage in favor of diffuse interests. A high quorum also raises the costs of lobbying on behalf of concentrated interests by triggering sizable, and uncontrollable field expenses, by restricting the choice set through clotting and contagion, and by tempting agents to defect from prior engagements.

Decision Rule and Trade Strategy

The decision rule influences the quality of information made available by participants—a valuable good in conditions of voter rational ignorance. Where the decision rule takes the form of majority rule, the rule generates an adversarial process which is highly productive of information and which leads each side to submit the other's claims to systematic scrutiny. Candidates have a vested interest in uncovering and publicizing negative information about their opponents; this extra information, in turn, promotes voter participation. The unanimity rule, in contrast, generates a consensual process that is not productive of information. Unanimity fails to generate the extra information characteristic of the majority rule and thus offers fewer opportunities for the public monitoring of lawmaking.

Generating a higher level of public monitoring, the majority rule restricts rent seeking regardless of the value of the quorum. If the quorum is low and the debate is limited to two lobbies, then, under a majority rule, competition between the lobbies will end in compromise or with the defeat of one lobby or the other. The lobbies will pocket less rent in either case than if they had achieved unanimity at the sole expense of the voters, as this would be the case under a unanimity rule.

If the quorum is high, a majority rule will, similarly, restrict rent seeking more effectively than a unanimity rule. Even though high quorum ensures that the voters are represented in policymaking, public monitoring always suffers in the absence of opposition. Indeed, electoral promises are usually cast at a very high level of generality, such as "free trade for industry." A party that comes into power with a broad popular mandate for its policies enjoys a certain degree of latitude in specifying the details, since, during the campaign, these lay in the shadow of the voters' rational ignorance and were unspecified. The possibility exists, then, for the party, once in government, to resell this residual to private lobbies. In theory, therefore, rent seeking can occur on a small scale even in a high quorum. There are some limits to the growth of rent seeking, however; there exists a danger, for example, that a collusive transac-

TABLE 2.2
Impact of Electorate on Policy Process and Policy Outcome

	ELECTORATE		→	POLICY PROCESS		→	POLICY OUTCOME
			Rules				
Case*	Salience	Divisiveness	Quorum	Voting	Costs of private lobbying	Information	Type of policy
I	high	high	high	majority (adversarial)	high	rich	general interest
II	high	low	high	unanimity (consensual)	high	poor	general interest with a minor rent dimension
III	low	high	low	majority (adversarial)	low	rich	particular rent with compromise
IV	low	low	low	unanimity (consensual)	low	poor	particular rent with logrolling

* Numerals refer to table 2.1 and table A1.1 (Appendix 1).

tion between the winning party and a private lobby might be publicized by alienated insiders to discredit the government, thereby forcing the government to move swiftly to close the covert "secondary market" for rents. In an adversarial setup, where a defeated party pledged on election day to oppose government policy, the risk of scandal is real and is usually sufficient to deter the winning party from engaging in covert rent seeking. The risk to the winning party is less serious in a consensual setup, where no institutional vehicle exists for articulating dissent.

The implications of the decision rule for the cost of lobbying can be summarized as follows: a majority rule produces a policy process that is information-rich and therefore favors the implementation of policies in the general interest, whereas a unanimity rule generates a policy process that is information-poor and therefore favors the implementation of policies in the interests of particular groups.

When the argument of this section is combined with that of the previous sections, the result is as follows:

> The higher the quorum, and the more adversarial the decision rule, the easier it is for individuals (including concentrated interests) to pursue policies in the general interest, rather than policies tailored to their particular interests. In contrast, the lower the quorum, and the more consensual the decision rule, the easier it is for concentrated interests to extract rents.

Policy processes characterized by high quorum and majority voting promote public participation, whereas policy processes characterized by low quorum and consensus restrict public participation. Therefore, producers—such as industrialists, who have flexible trade preferences—will decide whether to pursue free trade or protectionist rents, depending on the structure of the policy process.

Table 2.2 recapitulates the entire argument up to this point. The possible combination of the two electoral parameters, salience and divisiveness, define four possible policy processes, which are distinct from each other in quorum level and type of decision rule. Each process is "stacked" in favor of different principals and a policy of different scope.[19]

A Potential Objection: The Cash Connection

We are now ready to tackle the issue regarding the relative importance of money and votes. Political economists argue that under the assumption of voter rational ignorance, parties need financial contributions in order to market their respective policy stands. Since funds are contributed mainly by organized industries (to a greater extent in the United States than in Europe), these industries thereby gain preferential access to policymaking, bypassing the cumbersome electoral channel. Parties write their platforms, political economists argue, with an eye as much (if not more) to money than to votes.[20]

However, the present argument suggests that the importance of the cash connection is not given, but closely tracks the state of the electoral market. Indeed, what do parties need cash for? Not to create voters' preferences de novo, as the successful parties are those that work with existing preferences.[21] Parties need money to advertise their positions and to inform voters. As a result, the demand for money varies in proportion to the degree of voter ignorance. Money matters most when voter ignorance is high, and least when voters are well-informed. Whenever an issue is salient or divisive or both, it is because voters already enjoy a modicum of information about the issue, or, at least, they have the capacity to learn about it quickly. In the final analysis, the marginal efficiency of cash depends on the nature of the policy process, which in turn depends on the intuition of politicians about which issues are most salient and most divisive.

This argument may seem open to two objections. The first is that industrialists can take advantage of their relatively large financial resources to prevent parties from responding to high salience and divisiveness with high quorum and majority voting, two rules averse to rent seeking. If money is needed to place a salient and/or potentially divisive trade issue at the top of the policy agenda, those who are in a position to provide it dominate the agenda. It might be argued that private interests faced with the prospect of an unfavorable policy process would not necessarily have to adjust (as I argue here). They could threaten either to take control of the party or suddenly to leave it, thus choking off the party's access to funds. The takeover threat is implicit in the "investment theory of parties" advanced by Ferguson, in which political parties are seen as controlled by small "blocs of major investors," with the consequence that party leaders address only issues that are approved by business and confine public debate to safer, noneconomic questions.[22]

Neither the threat of takeover nor of exit seems, in practice, to be a realistic option. The takeover of a party by investors might help cut shirking costs, but it would not reduce field costs.[23] Nor would it improve the choice set, since money can buy media specialists and prime television time but not always a winning electoral issue. Because a popular issue is, by definition, almost a winning issue, investors tend to rally round the most popular candidates. The strategy of confining the public debate to unimportant "noneconomic" issues would be feasible if the political debate were tightly compartmentalized into issues; in reality, issues are linked. (The recurring debate in France over religious education, for example, is not a diversion from economic issues but part and parcel of the redistributive conflict.) Party takeover is not sufficient to control the real source of uncertainty—voters.[24]

Nor is it plausible that a particular group could prevent a party from pursuing policies contrary to the group's interests by threatening to leave and thus deprive the party of the group's financial contribution. The threat of exit carries weight in a one-issue election, where the choice set is predetermined, the stakes are known in advance, and the political risk predictable.[25] But the leverage of major financial contributors is much reduced in a multiissue campaign that is vulnerable to issue contagion. Partisan rivalry raises the cost of exit for lobbies, since the trade issue becomes linked to larger issues, which serve to draw voters' attention back to the trade issue. In this case, defeat implies more for special interests than the mere failure to collect on the rent. It may also imply losing on related issues, such as tax, subsidies, or regulatory legislation. Raising the stakes automatically leads to an increase in contributions, since, in polarized closely contested elections, it is the marginal contribution that decides the electoral outcome. Ironically, this control over the outcome does not increase the contributors' control over the policy process, but instead makes them captive creditors.[26] The likely effect of a parametric increase in salience is not to scare off lobbies, but instead to turn them into loyal contributors.

In fact, in high-quorum situations, parties are more likely to fear free-riding than they are the attempt by strong-minded interests to impose their will. When a party is electorally committed to implementing a given policy, the effect is to induce firms that stand to benefit from the policy to reduce their campaign contributions, not out of a desire to curtail partisan debate but from a conviction that partisan debate is self-perpetuating.

There is a second, more fundamental objection to the argument presented above. It proceeds from the belief that salience and divisiveness are not parametric but are instead manipulated by parties and organized interests. I will defer consideration of this issue until chapter four, where elements of strategic choice are introduced in the determination of respective degrees of salience and divisiveness. The position provisionally adopted here is that only interest groups that can credibly speak on behalf of broad classes of voters (e.g., farm associations or trade unions) are capable, under particular circumstances, of determining the salience and divisiveness of a given issue. It is interesting, and important, that "big business" is not capable of doing this.

Summary and Implications

In this chapter I have proposed a novel way to think about electoral control. Voters may be seen to control policymaking, because elections provide law-makers with incentives for reproducing within their deliberative microcosm the parametric characters of the electorate. The delegation operates in two stages. In the first, elections force parties to rank issues in order of importance according to their perceived salience and divisiveness. Parties are more likely to emphasize an issue if it is salient than if the issue leaves voters indifferent and if it is divisive rather than noncontroversial. In the second stage, the amount and distribution of effort expended on an issue on election day struc-tures policymaking after the election. Large spending institutionalizes a high quorum (by opening the policy process to individuals pursuing more general interests), whereas low spending reserves the process for rent seekers. Sym-metrical spending institutionalizes majority voting, which yields an informa-tion-rich process favorable to general interests. Asymmetrical spending, in contrast, institutionalizes the unanimity characteristic of an information-poor process that favors rent seeking.

The notion of election-as-delegation is to be opposed to the notion of elec-tion as legislative mandate. First, the delegation hypothesis is more encom-passing than the mandate hypothesis. The latter is, in fact, a subset of the delegation hypothesis, corresponding to case I in tables 2.1 and 2.2, where the mandate proceeds from high salience and high divisiveness, a combination that translates into high quorum and majority rule, the process best suited to diffuse interests. Second, the theory of delegation also escapes the quandary that besets the mandate. Under delegation, the policy process is not subject to the instability (known as "cycling") typical of majority voting in the presence of more than one issue. Salience and divisiveness are not subject to cycling; neither is the choice of the policy process.[27] Underlying this unusual result is the idea that agenda-setting is not an institutional response to an electoral problem, but the natural outcome of electoral campaigns.

Finally, delegation theory is pregnant with implications for business-gov-ernment relations in a capitalist democracy. Business lobbies function most effectively in the fragmented world of rent seeking. The opening of policymaking to general interests makes investment in party bonds less attractive to business. In a process that is unfavorable to rent seeking, business finds reasons to champion market liberalism—the ideology of limited government. While liberal discipline is no insurance against nationalization, it does leave business in a much stronger position than if it were subject to frequent state intervention and vulnerable to charges of collusion and profiteering. Conversely, business tends to strengthen its contacts with government when the policy process disfavors general interests. In this context, championing liberalism would be absurd, for it would imply that rent seekers contribute to a fund whose proceeds are used for the purpose of making the state unavailable for rent seeking.

The rest of part one applies the framework of the present chapter to trade policy. Chapter three offers a fourfold typology of the trade policy process: "party politics" (defined as party government), "executive politics" (a variation on state autonomy), and "pressure politics" (an intermediate concept subdividing into "pluralist competition" and "logrolling"). Chapter four elaborates the first causal arrow (see figure 1.1), linking the electorate with the policy process, and explores the question of the origins and rules of transformation of policy processes (i.e., what makes the trade issue salient or divisive). It also offers testable hypotheses for what causes a switch from pressure to party politics, from party to pressure politics, from either pressure or party politics to executive politics, as well as the reverse in each case. Chapter five investigates the second causal arrow—the impact of the policy process on the outcome—and shows how the policy process influences the orientation and the tools of trade policy.

Three _____

The Trade Policy Process

A TYPOLOGY

THE THEORETICAL FRAMEWORK presented in chapter two is deliberately cast at a high level of generality, and the references to trade policy are essentially illustrative. Specifics, however, are needed to turn the general framework of chapter two into a predictive theory of trade policymaking. This chapter, therefore, specifies concepts for both particular and general interests and fills in the details of four types of policy process.

Chapter two argues that the relevant actors in the making of trade policy are self-maximizing individuals who are mobilized either as voters in support of a general interest policy or as special-interest groups pursuing rents. By drawing from trade theory, it is possible to be a little more precise in the definition of particular and general interests. International trade theorists have offered several ways of aggregating trade interests. The specific factors model (two fixed factors and one mobile) makes the sector, or industry, the effective unit of analysis, whereas the Heckscher-Ohlin model (with two mobile factors) makes the factor of production (land, labor, or capital) the basic unit of analysis.[1] To this pair, I add the *nation*, in recognition of the security dimension of international trade, which affects all citizens of a country equally.[2] Rarely, however, have economists or political scientists raised the question of boundary conditions. For instance under what circumstances is one grouping more important than another? In this book I look for the answer in the policy process, arguing that the policy process determines the identity of the producer group to whom the political agent is directly accountable.

Drawing on chapter two, we can identify four types of policy process: party politics, executive politics, and pressure politics, the last with its two variants, competition and logrolling (see table 3.1). The party politics process (case I in tables 2.1 and 2.2) is the parties' response when the trade issue has a high degree of both salience and divisiveness. Typically, two disciplined parties (or coalitions thereof) use the trade issue to compete for votes, and the eventual policy outcome reflects the electoral promises of the winning party. In this process, the factor is the principal level of interest aggregation.

The executive politics process (case II) is the parties' response to high salience and consensus. Basically, one party assumes a position of dominance on

TABLE 3.1
Typology of Trade Policy Processes

Case*	Rules		Principal	Name
	quorum	voting		
I	high	majority	factor (class**)	party politics
II	high	unanimity	nation	executive politics
III	low	majority	sector	pressure politics, competitive variant
IV	low	unanimity	sector	pressure politics, logrolling variant

* Numerals refer to tables 2.1 and 2.2, and table A1.1 (Appendix 1).
** The class (i.e., farmers, workers, capitalists) is the social outgrowth of the factor.

the trade issue, a position which the other party eventually emulates. This process is often analyzed in the literature as a manifestation of "state autonomy." The nation (not the state) is the principal actor of executive politics.

The pressure politics process has two variants, depending on whether the relevant interests—the sectors in both variants—compete or logroll. The competitive variant (case III) is the parties' response to low salience and high divisiveness. Parties adjudicate the issue on the basis of competition among the private lobbies.

The logrolling variant (case IV) is the parties' response to low salience and low divisiveness. The parties treat the trade issue as one to be adjudicated through logrolling among private lobbies.

Each process is reviewed in turn below. I then address the potential objection that these four categories may not be mutually exclusive.

Party Politics

The principal in the party-politics process is the factor of production (or the producer class). Historically, the factor became a political category with the advent of mass politics. Modern mass parties, which developed when electoral machines and local worthies were no longer capable of securing electoral majorities, shifted the focus of political debate from the locale to the factor. Because the factor is a general and parsimonious level of interest aggregation (there are only three factors: land, labor, and capital), modern parties helped stabilize the uncertainty introduced by a burgeoning electorate.[3] Because parties were interested primarily in large-scale constituencies, they endorsed the partition of the economy by factor and they formed around two distinctive lines of cleavage—farm-factory and employer-employee—in the process defining three distinctive socioeconomic groups: farmers, workers, and capitalists.[4]

Party politics, or party government, is a policy process that relies on partisan discipline. The party leadership systematically requires party representatives to follow party directives in voting, for example, on the trade issue. Debate over trade policy provides substance for partisan cleavage, around which elections are fought and, from which, in the case of multiparty systems, compromises toward the formation of coalition governments are excluded.[5]

The fact that parties are the inevitable brokers of electoral politics, however, does not imply that all issues, at all times are processed through party politics. Party leaders invoke partisan discipline only with regard to issues that are important in defining their electoral profile. When trade policy is not part of this profile, parties qua parties play no role in trade policymaking. The existence of modern mass parties, therefore, is a necessary but not sufficient condition for the advent of the party politics process.

A partisan cleavage exists when relevant parties take opposite stands on an issue or a bundle of issues and elevate those stands to the status of party doctrine. When a party makes a given issue a component of its profile in order to win elections, it does so by linking those issues that are salient and divisive with its own side of an existing partisan cleavage. Cleavages also serve to sustain party cohesion. Once a party has successfully captured a constituency with respect to a given cleavage, reiteration of its commitment in future elections suffices to collect the votes of the same constituency.

Because a high degree of generality is essential to its working, party politics invites the participation of diffuse and tangential interests in policymaking; the quorum is high. The factor of production provides a politically convenient framework within which to aggregate a variety of issues in addition to the trade issue. Consequently, party politics finds itself accommodating issues likely to interfere with the trade issue. When partisan rivalry thereby makes the trade debate a component of the class debate, it coexists with more or less distant ideological kins, which, too, happen to be part of the party's profile. As the party is hard-pressed to show a coherent line, it is not unlikely that the cleavages that constitute the profile of the party end up overlapping one another. All issues become relevant to all debates. The less salient ones are rewritten by the more salient ones; or they are all synthesized into an all-embracing conflict. In this ideological environment, it is easier for firms and farms to promote their class rather than their sectoral interests.

However, when a party loses its ability to promote class as a universal, it reverts to sectoral, parochial, or provincial appeals. Elections no longer restore political autonomy. To win elections, party leaders must abandon the old, class-based slogans and endorse a multitude of specific, but ideologically undigested demands. The "issue-voting" and "catch-all" parties thus produced, in turn, result in governments that are bound by an excessive number of particular electoral promises, and party politics degenerates into a noisy specimen of pressure politics.

Some recent developments in party systems may call for amendments to the present analysis. Although the party is not an obsolete institution (since electoral democracies cannot function without it), the rise of the white-collar workforce has weakened traditional class politics, and the electoral marginalization of farmers and the decline of the class cleavage have thrown parties into a crisis.[6] The study of the French and British cases in the 1980s will show, however, that predictions of the end of class politics may be exaggerated.

Executive Politics

The principal of executive politics is the citizenry constituted as a nation. Executive politics (case II of tables 2.1 and 2.2) is the case in which one party manages to establish a dominant position in the area of trade policy, a position other parties must emulate if they wish to govern. The party leader casts his or her message above partisan politics and invites the voters as citizens to rally under that banner. This process features a high quorum and unanimity.

In theory, there are a number of situations that might meet these two conditions. All citizens might, for instance, believe free trade to be a Pareto-optimal policy, an argument often advanced to account for British free-trade policy before 1914.[7] In practice, however, very few issues have the capacity to arouse popular interest and simultaneously transcend partisan cleavages. Trade, because it is a redistributive issue, is no exception. Alone, it cannot elicit consensus but must be linked, if only tangentially, to an issue that is both consensual and paramount. The only issue that has served this purpose with even a modicum of consistency is national security. Indeed, historically, it has taken a trade-security linkage to elevate the trade issue to the realm of consensual politics. The free-trade consensus in late-Victorian Britain was exceptional and has never been replicated elsewhere; it was also a residual phenomenon, since it reflected British mercantile fortune. More important, it was short-lived; although the policy endured, the ideological consensus had ended by the late 1860s. Note that the linkage of trade with security is a necessary but not sufficient condition for consensus; equally important, security itself must be a salient and consensual issue, not a partisan one.

The "executive politics process" is so called because the executive's position is the most effective position from which a party leader can take a national stand. Such is the case for several reasons. One, national unity is more effectively embodied by a single position than a collective one. Two, in most countries, authority over foreign affairs traditionally is invested in the executive. And, three, chief executives tend to be elected by national rather than local constituencies (as in the case of presidents) or by nationwide institutions (as in the case of parliaments that choose prime ministers).

Like party politics, executive politics promotes tangential issues, such as national security, that have no more than an indirect relation to trade. Trade policy provides the basis for international commitments engaging the country's international prestige, an effective focus for voters qua nation. Consequently, the security issue can affect trade alignments in ways that are at odds with the trade debate. Diplomacy involves the selection of international friends and foes for the purpose of maximizing one's own national security. Trade protection is lowered to reward friends and raised to penalize enemies. Security concerns, therefore, transform the goal of trade policy from an instrument for maximizing wealth into one for maximizing national prestige. Attempting to fit the trade debate into the procrustean bed of national security is likely to entail unexpected consequences for trade interests. In France, for instance, the need to reduce the German threat was used by successive governments first in 1947, to subsidize the French steel industry, then to sacrifice that same industry to German competition three years later.

Pressure Politics: Competitive and Logrolling Variants

In pressure politics, the principal of interest aggregation is the sector. Pressure politics corresponds to the political economists' rent-seeking model discussed in chapter one. It is a process dominated by concentrated interests which pursue particular strategies. We can quibble about how particular a strategy already common to all or most of the producers of a single sector can be. A truly particular strategy would be one endorsed by a firm or, in agriculture, a farm. Still, there are good reasons to skip that basic level and focus on the sector instead. The most rudimentary level of effective political aggregation in matters of trade is not the individual firm. Until the middle of the nineteenth century, the standard political unit was the town or locality, which quite often was organized around a single trade. By the 1860s, when this study starts, the political unit had become the sector, or industry (in this book I use the two words interchangeably).

Pressure politics is characterized by the exclusion of diffuse interests—the quorum is low. The main actors of pressure politics are special interests. In the trade area, these special interests are the trade associations (for example, the American Iron and Steel Institute, the National Association of Wool Growers, and the British Sugar Refiners' Association) and, by implication, the trade unions. As usual, party leaders are the brokers; but the distinctive features of party politics—partisan discipline and ideological commitment—are absent. In pressure politics, a party may lean more in the direction of free trade than protection, but the leadership makes no attempt to enforce partisan discipline. Typically, different factions in different parties take up different sides of the trade debate. If the party cannot govern alone and seeks a coalition with other parties, the trade issue is never an obstacle to coalition, but instead becomes an object of compromise. In pressure politics national elections are never contested on the basis of the trade issue; instead, politicians use their articulation of the trade issue to attract cash from firms and farms, cash which can then be used to promote other issues.

Individual voters are excluded from pressure politics because the sector offers very little edge to general (class or national) interests. To be sure, the sector does serve as vehicle for issues tangential to trade, such as marketing agreements, production control, and licensing. Tackling these issues does not raise the quorum, however, because it seldom attracts groups other than industrialists who already belong to the sector. That is, the debate is self-contained. Furthermore, the intrusion of general or tangential interests is insignificant.

Although not prone to ideological manipulation, the sector is not free of conflict. Typically, trade associations handle two kinds of trade conflict. In the first, a trade association serves as an arena in which member firms with divergent interests compete with each other for direction of the association. Sectoral consensus is reached usually after a power struggle, at the end of which the losing minority is confronted with two equally implausible alternatives: stay in and subvert or exit and outflank.

In the second kind of conflict, one trade association must reach an agreement with the other trade associations situated along the same production stream (direct suppliers and direct consumers) short of the final consumer. The need for agreement among these trade associations arises because producers of raw materials and their direct consumers—the manufacturers of finished or semifinished goods—have, by definition, immediate and antagonistic economic interests. Consequently, a trade policy position with regard to one stage in the production process will have a direct impact on the other stages. When a trade association fails to settle its difference with other associations, by creating a compact, it runs the risk that its own claims will be contested and perhaps defeated by the others.

Depending on how successful trade associations are in containing intrasectoral and intersectoral conflicts, the policy process will resemble the competitive model (case III) or the logrolling model (case IV). Most accounts of tariff policies too hastily assume that logrolling is a "default" process; rather, it is a complex, exacting process requiring trade association officials to secure two kinds of agreements—the first within their own association, the second with the associations located along their production stream—before presenting their demands to politicians. Trade association officials can be reasonably sure their demands will not be dismissed or distorted by the political system only when both types of agreement have been negotiated successfully.

In all cases, member firms that do not expect to gain from a consensually agreed-upon trade policy may seek arbitration by politicians on behalf of their position. If those firms find themselves in a minority, both within their own association and among the other relevant associations, their only alternative is to seek the support of firms or associations located in other sectors, along other production streams—a precarious move at best. In fact, trade demands are processed sector by sector, so that conflicts are confined to single sectors. Associations on opposite sides of an issue—provided they operate in unrelated sectors—never confront one another.

A Potential Objection: Compatible Simultaneity

The present typology assumes that the four policy processes are mutually exclusive. Are they? There are two answers to this question. The first is empirical and will be considered in part two. The second, considered here, is a logical one: Does the reverse assumption about the four policy processes—i.e., that they are simultaneously compatible—lead to contradictory statements? In the following, each policy process is paired in turn with the others, in order to assess relative degrees of compatibility.

Party Politics and Logrolling

The case for coexistence of party politics and logrolling could be made because each operates toward principals—factors and sectors—with different access to information. Promises made to voters are cast at a high level of aggregation: the factor. The agent is bound by a broad mandate, such as "free food for the workers." The agent did not promise to modify specific duties, but instead enjoys the latitude to define the quantity and the distribution of such duties, as voters strongly support the social philosophy of their party and leave the task of day-to-day interpretation to party leaders.[8] But if the party leader is accountable only for maintaining the party line, anything that is "below the line," so to speak, falls under the shadow of voters' rational ignorance. Hence, as I argue in chapter two, the likely result is the emergence of a covert, secondary market in which the party in power "resells" the specific duties to industry lobbies. Therefore, the conditions for the simultaneity of logrolling with party politics seem to have been met.

The conditions for this simultaneity, however, are fragile. Survival of the pocket of rent seeking depends on an informational asymmetry between voters and sectors that may not be sustainable over a long period. Party politics is an adversarial—and, thus, an information-rich—process. Voter ignorance about political scheming is likely to be disturbed when the opposition seizes on a particularly shady transaction and publicizes it as an example of government duplicity. Lobbies will anticipate correctly that at the first electoral threat the agent will close the secondary market. Party politics, therefore, acts as a check on logrolling by eliminating it from interpartisan relations, though not necessarily from interfactional relations within a single party.

Executive Politics and Logrolling

The case for the coexistence of logrolling and executive politics is a strong one. Unlike party politics, in executive politics, there is no readily available vehicle for the articulation of dissent; executive politics is thus an information-poor process. As a result, a politician can take advantage of the wider band of voters' rational ignorance to engage in the profitable practice of rent making. While it would be imprudent to exclude the possibility of a "virtuous" government, in general a government has no electoral incentive to resist the temptation to engage in rent making, because issues of broad agreement (e.g., the national interest) rarely arouse the same passion as contested ones. Morris Fiorina has suggested that the electorate is "ungrateful," because voters do not reward politicians for delivering values they all share as much as they do for delivering values that divide them.[9]

In summary, in both party politics and executive politics (albeit less so in the former than in the latter), a pocket of logrolling may develop, subject to one constraint: The growth of such a pocket is bound by, and subordinate to, the functional requirements of the high-quorum process. This functional requirement is much more strongly felt in party politics than in executive politics because of the information differential that exists between an adversarial and a consensual process.

Competitive Pressure and Party Politics

The third pairing is definitely unstable if we consider the possibility of a discrepancy in the outcome of the two processes. What would happen, for instance, if the protectionists expect to win on the sectoral front, and the free traders expect to win on the partisan front? The answer was supplied by Schattschneider: The losing sector in pressure politics has an interest, after the fact, in appealing to party politics in order to counter its losses.[10] The winning sector, anticipating the loser's move, has an interest in escalating to party politics from the outset by investing all its political resources in the protectionist party. The dynamic of escalation turns each sector into a client of its party, a client that raises funds for the party and shares in the party's spoils and vicissitudes. Pressure politics, for all practical purposes, is absorbed by party politics and disappears.

Competitive Pressure and Executive Politics

The fourth pairing is also unstable. Executive politics cannot accommodate a pocket of pressure politics in which sectors openly compete for spoils. The government cannot allow competition, for it would generate too much information and oblige the government to curtail its own activity. The government—torn between raising money through rent making and preventing rents from reaching a level that would scandalize the voters—must monitor the market closely. The government is safer channeling rent-seeking activity into administrative and quasi-judicial procedures, which helps to control the growth of the covert secondary market, as well as legitimizing exceptions to the accepted policies. Executive politics is not compatible with any form of competitive politics, but can accommodate only logrolling.

Party Politics and Executive Politics

This fifth pairing would imply that the parties agree on the main orientation of the trade policy, but disagree on minor aspects, hardly a stimulating combination. When there is consensus among the electorate on the main orientation of the policy, there is little room left for "party politics." Parties may still differ over implementation, but this is not an issue that easily arouses voters. If, however, implementation becomes a salient and divisive issue, then the consensus on orientation is likely to be submerged in the conflict, as the partisan dynamic places the emphasis on what divides parties most rather than on what unites them. The political dynamic, therefore, will follow either executive politics or party politics, but not both simultaneously.

Competitive Pressure and Logrolling

The two variants of pressure politics seem a priori compatible. The making of a tariff, for instance, covers a large number of products. The absence of conflict over some products facilitates logrolling by legislators; conflict over other products forces legislators to work through compromise. The question is, how stable can a combination of logrolls and compromises be? The answer depends on how easy and stable the compromises are and, if the compromises are unstable, the significance of the losing interests. The stability of the combination therefore depends on politicians' capacity to marginalize loss. This is an empirical question, which is considered in part two. A priori, though, the two processes are compatible.

The objection on the grounds of compatible simultaneity turns out to be sustainable in only two of the six possible pairings. In the first pairing, some logrolling is likely to nest within the executive politics process, because this process generates insufficient information to prevent the formation of a non-competitive secondary market for rents. In the second pairing, logrolling can coexist with the deadlocks and compromises typical of the competitive pressure process.

Summary

This chapter has elaborated four types of policy process. Each process is a manifestation of electoral politics as managed by parties. Parties, the universal actors in democratic politics, can articulate the trade issue in one of four different ways:

1. As a salient, divisive issue (party politics). Two disciplined parties (or a coalition thereof) use the trade issue to compete for the votes of factor owners.

2. As a salient, but consensual, issue (executive politics). One party has the dominant position on the trade issue as a result of linking it with a security issue that enjoys a national constituency.

3. As a private, divisive issue (pressure politics, competitive variant). The issue is allocated between or among competing sectors.

4. As a private, consensual issue (pressure politics, logrolling variant). The issue is allocated between or among logrolling sectors.

The next chapter examines the circumstances under which one process or another prevails.

Four

Origins of the Trade Policy Process

CHAPTER TWO DERIVES the policy process from two parameters of electoral politics, salience and divisiveness. In the present chapter we consider the origins of these parameters and examine the conditions under which the trade issue is salient rather than inconspicuous, divisive rather than consensual.

There are two possible origins of the parameters. One, salience and divisiveness are set exogenously; that is, they reflect a choice made collectively by some individual voters in response to events external to policymaking, such as wars or great depressions. Two, salience and divisiveness are set endogenously; that is, they reflect a choice made collectively by some individual voters in reaction to or anticipation of the choices of other players, who may be parties, private lobbies, or other voters.

Endogenous determination implies that voters can coordinate their vote, as parties are not responsive to isolated individuals. This raises the issue of collective action. The capacity of a group for collective action generally is a reflection of group size.[1] Recall from chapter three the typology of policy processes according to producer groups of different sizes. There, it is established that high salience is associated with the factor or the nation, whereas low salience is associated with the sector; and that divisiveness is associated with the sector or the factor, whereas consensus is associated with the sector or the nation (see table 3.1). The requisites for party politics, therefore, are the same as the requisites for factor mobilization, those for executive politics the same as those for national mobilization, and those for pressure politics the same as those for sectoral mobilization. (One drawback of this formulation is that it collapses into one category both variants of pressure politics, competitive and logrolling, because both operate at the sectoral level. The argument will bear this in mind.)

The nation as a group is not capable of collective action, because it has no collective identity outside politics. As a result, little strategic calculation (in the game-theoretic sense) is entailed in the advent of executive politics; exogenous events play the central part. The sector readily lends itself to collective action, since it needs no political help to come into existence. It is too small a group, however, to attract the attention of the parties; thus it is unlikely to be in a position to arbitrate between pressure politics and party politics. The factor occupies the intermediate position. A large and disparate group, it is rarely amenable to comprehensive organization on its own. Nevertheless, factors always embody an organized subset that claims to speak on behalf of its whole—for example a trade-union confederation or a farm lobby. If such an organized subgroup is able to earn the credibility of politicians, then the conditions that favor strategic choice are present for determining electoral salience and divisiveness. When external circumstances are ripe, such a lobby is able to play indifferently on the two boards of pressure politics and party politics, thereby introducing an element of strategic choice in the process of determining policy.

Preferences over Processes

In its most simplified form, the game of process-building involves both politicians organized in parties and sectors organized in lobbies. Lobbies choose between lobbying on behalf of the sectors they represent and lobbying on behalf of a factor that has a mass membership—land or labor. Parties choose to articulate the demands of sectors, the demands of one or more factors, or the demands of the nation. Ideally, a party prefers a higher level of aggregation to a lower one. Executive politics is preferred to party politics, and party politics to pressure politics. Indeed, pressure politics provides a party with cash, and party politics generates both cash and votes; executive politics, on the other hand, translates into the dominant position. Parties are also engaged in a zero-sum game with one another, so that a politician winning his or her first choice often means that another politician ends up with his or her last choice.

The lobby's ideal preference-ordering is the reverse of the party's. Pressure is preferred to party and executive because concentrated interests have better control over the policy outcome in a low-quorum environment than in a high one. Lobbies, however, often have incompatible policy preferences; the side likely to lose may be willing to support a costlier process in order to get its first policy choice.

The next step is to identify the circumstances responsible for orienting the choices of parties and lobbies in a particular direction. The following analysis proceeds on a case-by-case basis, investigating first what causes a switch from pressure to party politics and from party politics back to pressure politics, then the causes of a switch from pressure or party to executive politics and finally from executive politics back to pressure or party politics.

From Pressure Politics to Party Politics

The switch from pressure politics to party politics implies a switch from a debate among sectors to one between factors. This section argues that such a switch is predictable when a factor of production with a mass constituency is mobilized against the status quo. More precisely, there are two requisites for partisan articulation to obtain. First, there must be a sectoral difference that cannot be resolved through pressure politics. Second the aggravated sector(s) must be able to enlist the electoral support of a mass-based factor of production.

The first requisite—dissatisfaction with pressure politics—was identified by Schattschneider. When trade interests agree to compromise over their differences or when logrolling is stable, there are no grounds for partisan escalation. As Schattschneider noted:

> It is the losers in intrabusiness conflict who seek redress from public authority. The dominant business interests resist appeals to the government. . . . It is the weak who want to socialize conflict, i.e., to involve more and more people in the conflict until the balance of forces is changed.[2]

Dissatisfaction with pressure politics is a necessary but not a sufficient condition. Indeed, although dissatisfaction is a permanent feature of policymaking, partisan articulation is not. Thus, the first requisite must be supplemented by a second one. The alienated interest must be able to speak on behalf of a mass-based factor, whether land or labor. It must be ready to flex its electoral muscle in favor of a party willing to champion its cause. The rationale behind this requirement is easy to intuit: A party does not commit itself to a cause without assurance that the electoral benefits will exceed the costs. As Mark Hansen puts it, the politician is concerned about "competitive advantage" and "recurrence."[3] Competitive advantage is assured by the broad electoral base of the two factors of production referred to above—land and labor. Land and labor have the numbers that can make the trade issue salient and thereby draw the attention of the parties. In contrast, industrialists in general can never deliver large numbers of votes directly; they can only contribute to campaigns that target workers or farmers. The notion of recurrence stipulates that the demand for partisan articulation will be sustained in the future, since a partisan commitment always has a long-term opportunity cost. Once committed, a party is loathe to change its orientation, lest it damage its reputation for dependable, principled action.[4] The need for recurrence rules out marriages of convenience. Even if, for example, industrialists were successful in rallying the support of farmers or workers, the future of such a coalition—like that of the bootleggers and Baptists—would be very uncertain.[5] To keep farm or labor in the coalition, capitalists might have to agree to redistributive policies, such as welfare payments or support prices, which could cost industrialists more than the coalition is worth. Furthermore, promises from capitalists to support redistributive policies are not credible. Credibility requires that the lobby soliciting partisan endorsement share an identity of goals with the broader class it claims to represent; belonging to this class is a necessary condition for credibility.

The partisan alternative therefore exists for both unions and farm lobbies. These lobbies hold the wild cards; they have the organization that allows them to play the pressure card. And they can rely on sufficiently large numbers of voters to play the partisan card as well. Unions and farm lobbies thus serve both as special interest groups and as spokesmen for large constituencies.

Two caveats must be addressed. The first concerns the ideological location of the voters of mass-based factors. Large numbers of voters per se are unavailing unless they are located near the median of the political spectrum. For instance, until the 1930s the French organized working class was much too far to the left of the ideological spectrum to attract plausible bids from the parties of the center and right. Similarly, the British agrarians were too far to the right to entice even the Conservative party, for example, to support food duties in order to secure a farm vote that would certainly be conservative.

The second caveat concerns the identity of mass-based factors. Farmers and workers are not always the only mass-based factors capable of appealing to parties. Workers did not become a mass constituency until the end of the nineteenth century, whereas farmers ceased to be a mass constituency about the time of World War II. Moreover, small businesses might conceivably constitute a voting group large enough to be able to play the swing role attributed to land and labor. At the same time, they would provide big business with the troops they so badly need to play the game of process-building strategically. As we will see, the fairly comprehensive historical survey presented in part two fails to uncover such occurrences—with one interesting exception: the political turn to the right in the 1980s, felt equally in France, Britain, and the United States. Only recently, and because farmers and workers are no longer the effective players they used to be, have the middle classes—self-employed, small employers, crafts, small merchants—gained or regained some importance in mass (party) politics. It is unlikely, however, that these new *petits bourgeois* have become the moving force of party politics. Their power is residual; they are decisive only when others are powerless. Thus, their power warrants no special theoretical consideration.

In sum, there is only one case in which a party leader should find the trade cleavage a good investment: When a labor movement or farm movement takes an independent stand on the trade issue and provides a reliable core of constituents to the party willing to advocate that movement's demands.

From Party Politics to Pressure Politics

The change from party to pressure politics implies a realignment of the trade debate from one divided according to factors, to a debate divided according to sectors. Either the conflict between factors (as articulated by the party system) must be neutralized, or, more likely, the trade issue must be separated from that conflict. Such realignment occurs through a corporatist bargain, defined as a negotiation between peak associations (the Trade Union Congress and the Confederation of British Industry, for example), each of whom represents a factor of production. Two conditions are necessary for a corporatist bargain to take place. First, the peak associations must be willing to remove the trade debate from partisan competition; second, the parties must be willing to relinquish the trade issue to the associations. The first condition is easily realized, the second is not. Let us review each one.

Sectors dislike partisan articulation because it makes rent seeking costly and risky. Even farm and labor lobbies, which hold their electoral power in reserve, have difficulty controlling their party, because a threat to scuttle an election is not credible.[6] Moreover, the risk of electoral setback, always present in party politics, gives lobbies an incentive to "institutionalize" their temporary gains in the form of a settlement, with the opposite side. Unless the opposite side can be sure of winning decisively, it too is responsive to compromise. Finally, appealing to party politics may make sense for some pressure groups whose potential electoral power is underrated by the narrow lobbying market. Once the partisan correction has occurred, however, all lobbies, including those that benefited from the correction, will eagerly dispose of this expensive formula and return to the world of safe and affordable lobbying—pressure politics.

A privileged instrument for puncturing the partisan bubble is the corporatist agreement.[7] The peak associations of the factors active in party politics—farm, labor, and industry—agree to defuse the class conflict and restore the conditions necessary to allow the policy debate to return to the pressure mode. The goal of each association is to centralize discussions on the trade issue and demobilize their respective memberships. Indeed, demobilization of the rank and file is critical to the survival of the corporatist agreement, since the agreement cannot occur without some sacrifice from both sides, sacrifice that is usually borne by the weakest members of each side. If successful, the corporatist agreement ensures that the trade issue loses its two initial electoral characters—salience and divisiveness. The only successful instance encountered in this study, however, is the "alliance of cotton, iron and wheat" in France in 1892.[8] Failed attempts, on the other hand, are numerous, including two in the United States between big labor and big business and a countless number in Britain.[9]

The literature on corporatism, although it was not applied to trade policy, is relevant nonetheless to our discussion. That literature identified several institutional requisites for corporatism. It has been argued, for example, that a corporatist bargain cannot be reached in the absence of corporatist institutions, which are defined as "centralized," "comprehensive," and "authoritative" peak organizations, capable of entering into a bargain and delivering on their promises.[10] Although this formulation may be useful for short-term predictions, it underestimates the strategic origins of institutions; namely, where a viable collective strategy exists, it usually is institutionalized.

The conditions for corporatism must be looked for in the very policy process that corporatism is designed to bypass—party politics. The parties' primary concern is attracting voters, a costly undertaking. For parties, capturing mass-based groups and wealthy contributors in their ideological nets makes good business sense, but parties do not like the idea of peak associations depoliticizing the issue and terminating ideological speculation. Worse, in the competitive logic of party politics, corporatism, politically speaking, is a losing proposition.

This point deserves elaboration. Let us consider a two-party system, where one party represents workers and another represents industry. A corporatist bargain requires leaders of the party in power to go out on a limb and make an offer that is attractive to the opposition's peak association. Even if such a pact were made, and even if it held good until the next election, it would then collapse. Indeed, regardless of which party wins or loses, the extreme wing of the losing party will blame the defeat on the corporatist bargain—which the moderate wing presumably ratified. Extremists easily find support for their positions among some members of the rank and file of the peak organization, whose interests were sacrificed in the bargain. In two-party systems, the possibility—indeed, the certainty—that an election will alter the balance of power within the defeated party by bringing extremists to the fore is enough to encourage early defection from bargaining, if indeed it did not deter bargaining in the first place. Peak organizations cannot depend on each other because they cannot depend on their own rank and file, and they cannot depend on their own rank and file because they cannot depend on their own party.

It should come as no surprise that countries with two-party systems do not exhibit the institutional attributes of corporatist institutions. In such countries, corporatism as an institutional strategy never made political sense for the reasons noted above.[11] Corporatism is more likely to exist in countries with dominant party systems—that is, systems in which the same party dominates all governments. Examples of stable corporatist bargaining on price and wage policies appeared in Scandinavian countries, where the working-class movement has achieved political hegemony. In this case, industrialists were freed from the negative influence of rightist backbenchers; they were also deterred from defecting. To defect was to risk trouble for themselves in the form of unrestrained wage demands and statutory controls they had no hope of overhauling at the next election.

A party will look favorably upon a corporatist bargain only if the bargain allows the party to stabilize its own coalition. Sometimes such a bargain has the effect of securing a shift to pressure politics, while sometimes it consolidates party politics. The Méline tariff (1892) falls in the first category. In France, Méline's Republicans had a vested interest in the formation of an urban-rural producers' coalition to shore up their electoral base, which the tariff issue threatened to splinter. The bargain prevented politicization of the trade debate. In contrast, the New Deal is an instance of a corporatist bargain that consolidated party politics. Franklin D. Roosevelt's electoral success rested on his ability to bring farmers, organized labor, and (later on) export sectors to support the Democratic platform and accept positions in his administration. The bargain gave a boost to the partisan debate. Union ratification of price supports for agriculture reconciled the agrarians to free trade, thus allowing the Democrats to challenge the protectionist Republicans head-on.[12]

In sum, the conditions for a corporatist bargain are highly restrictive. Party politics does not allow for bargains that cross the partisan cleavage; it allows only for intrapartisan bargains. The only conceivable case in which corporatism can be used to keep the trade issue out of party politics is that in which the power of a dominant party is threatened when the trade issue becomes partisan. In such a situation the dominant party cannot afford a clash between the two factors, but, instead, tries to engineer a compromise between them. Hence, we have the hypothesis: The trade issue is likely to revert to pressure politics when a party becomes dominant, for reasons unrelated to trade, and when it is in the party's electoral interest to have rival factors of production reach a corporatist agreement on the trade issue. The qualification "for reasons unrelated to trade" is important: If the party becomes dominant, thanks to the trade issue (or because of an issue linked to trade), the switch is not toward pressure politics but toward executive politics.

From Pressure (or Party) Politics to Executive Politics

One effective way of expropriating sectoral interests, or of retreating from the partisan battlefield, is to pair the trade issue with an issue that is both salient and consensual. The security dimension of trade—that is, the fact that trade can be used to reward allied countries and penalize rivals—has made national security the issue most consistently and effectively paired with the trade issue. When security becomes a salient, consensual issue, trade is likely to follow in its wake. Voters are thus rallied as a nation on one side or the other of the trade debate; and either protectionists or free traders are offered a unique opportunity to rout the other side.

The origins of the trade-security-linkage are exogenous. The linkage materializes when a country faces an external challenge that is both military and inescapable. The external challenge must be military or, if it is economic, it must have direct military implications. Economic challenges usually have a military implication, except when the distribution of military capabilities between the challenger and the challenged is notably uneven. For small European countries, war was never the continuation of politics by other means (as Clausewitz professed) but the end of politics. War had to be avoided either by seeking the protection of a powerful patron or by petitioning the international community for neutral status. The military aspect is also absent if the economic challenge comes from a militarily weak power; for example, Japan is not at present a security threat to the United States.

Besides being military, the challenge must be inescapable. That is, meeting the challenge must require the mobilization of domestic resources. This condition means that the security market does not clear through a shift in alliance patterns; thus, by way of inference, the path of least resistance (balancing through alliance with other powers) must be closed or uncertain. This condition is met in a bipolar system, where two superpowers cannot switch alliances to cope with each other and competition takes the form of an arms race.[13] In a multipolar system, by contrast, the incentive to check an external threat through mobilization of domestic resources is mitigated by the option of forming a coalition.

Regardless of the nature of the system, other powers, those not self-reliant, may opt for disarmed neutrality, thereby averting the domestic impact of the external threat. Or they may seek military protection by declaring allegiance to a patron. If, in the latter case, the patron requests the signing of favorable commercial treaties in exchange for protection, then the trade-security linkage is inescapable. The postwar General Agreement on Tariffs and Trade (GATT) and Comecon were two examples.

I propose the following general hypothesis: Whenever a country is confronted with an external threat that is both military and inescapable, trade policy will be processed through executive politics. Furthermore, the transformation to the executive politics process should take place regardless of whether the initial policy process is pressure or party politics.[14]

This hypothesis has an important corollary. In the absence of an inescapable military threat, the foreign policy establishment does not enjoy the popular support necessary to take trade policy out of its domestic format—whether pressure or party. Rather than elevating the trade issue, they risk lowering the security issue. In the late 1870s and early 1880s, the British Foreign Office was pressed by export-oriented industries to alleviate the negative effects of the worldwide protectionist backlash to British trade by negotiating reciprocity treaties with major trade partners and threatening retaliatory measures against unfair trade practices. The Foreign Office demurred, in part because of Lord Salisbury's fear that meddling with the trade issue, an issue of high salience in the electorate at the time, would constrain his margin for maneuver. More generally, Salisbury's concern about growing parliamentary control played a role in his fixing on a policy of "splendid isolation," a noninterventionist policy that offered no edge to domestic debate.[15] Fifty years later, Cordell Hull, the U.S. Secretary of State under Franklin Roosevelt, was bolder. In 1934 Hull's office took over the determination of tariff rates with no other justification than the statement that Congress could no longer handle the making of the tariff. Rather than freeing the setting of individual tariff rates from the chimera of pressure politics, however, as was initially intended, the transfer of tariff authority to the State Department reduced the executive's diplomatic autonomy and freedom of action. This move had debilitating consequences for Anglo-American relations at a time when fascism was on the rise.[16] In sum, if the nation is not mobilized by an external emergency, diplomats seeking to convert trade into an instrument of diplomacy risk turning diplomacy into an instrument of domestic politics.

The Retreat from Executive Politics

The hypothesis runs as follows: Executive politics lasts as long as public sanctioning does. Public sanctioning, in turn, lasts as long as the executive is able to convince the nation of the persistence of an external challenge. This transformation is far from being clear-cut, because executive politics initiates two dynamics that point toward an earlier and a later demise, respectively.

The first dynamic involves the creation of a pocket of pressure politics—the "secondary market effect" already discussed. Recall the argument: The high quorum characteristic of executive politics provides the policymaker with the capacity to pursue a relatively independent course. The policymaker is able to reject demands from organized interests on the grounds that rents might antagonize public opinion. The public, however, is uninformed; it must be mobilized, and mobilization of public opinion is a cumbersome tool. Mobilization of public opinion is effective in breaking up wide fronts of rent seekers, but not in disciplining petty profiteering—for example, by defense contractors who charge $600 apiece for toilet seats or $7,600 for coffeemakers, or the U.S. zinc, lead, and oil industries using their potential wartime value as an excuse for imposing quotas.[17] In addition, public opinion as a weapon is difficult to turn against industries that demand compensation for damages suffered in competition with foreign producers. Because free traders tend to free-ride policymakers cannot check these rent seekers by allying with free traders. Thus made vulnerable, the policymaker constantly engages in the practice of providing "indulgences" to industry. Hence, a pocket of pressure politics develops in the shadow of the national interest. This dynamic leads to the early emergence of rent seeking—before the dissolution of public sanctioning—and thus, to a reduction in the scope of the application of executive politics.

This secondary market effect is supplemented by a second dynamic, the "reputation effect." Paradoxically this effect supports the persistence of executive politics even after public sanctioning has dissolved and the process has been left to run its course. Typically in executive politics, the legislature authorizes the foreign secretary to transform the country's trade policy from an exclusively domestic matter into one that is subject to binding international agreements which can be repudiated only at the expense of the violator's international reputation. Therefore, as long as the agreement remains in force, and even if the security threat that gave rise to the agreement recedes, the risk to a country's reputation from unlawful violation of international obligations is sufficient to ensure continued domestic support of the agreement. Public sanctioning in these instances does not disappear. More precisely, its focus shifts from a specific threat to national security toward a diffuse notion of protecting national reputation or prestige. By weaving international networks of obligations, executive politics creates high opportunity costs.

Moreover, international bargaining tends to dissolve the sectoral nature of trade policy and instead to centralize policymaking in one encompassing decision. The give-and-take that eases negotiations involves more than one sector at a time, making a high tariff on one sector dependent on a concession from another sector. In the end, a country's trade policy and that of its trade partner are interdependent. One industry's tariff and another industry's tariff are also interdependent. The intersectoral character of trade policy makes it extremely difficult for industries to lobby for a change on their own. Nor can these interdependent industries bring about a change by organizing a sufficiently broad coalition through logrolling, since logrolling cannot stabilize oversized coalitions. Only a political party can play that role, either by championing the cause of the sectoral interests in a context of party politics or, if the party is dominant, by engineering a corporatist bargain between antagonistic factor interests. Without the mediation of a party, sectors are more likely to press their claims from inside than they are to confront the process from outside. Hence, we have an amendment to the initial hypothesis: Even after the initial international emergency dissipates, the executive-politics process, by contracting international obligations that engage the reputation of a country and by centralizing policymaking, makes it difficult for sectors to displace executive politics. More briefly, even after public sanctioning has dissolved, sectoral interests cannot displace executive politics without the help of a party.

The Detour of Administrative Delegation

It is useful to open parentheses and address the question of administrative delegation. Does the delegation of authority from legislature to executive, in and of itself, modify the nature of the policy process? Some scholars and analysts equate administrative delegation with pressure politics, others with state autonomy. The point is not merely a theoretical one; it is of empirical import as well, because the making of trade policy was transferred from the legislature to the executive in France, Britain, and the United States between the two world wars. I argue in this section that administrative delegation per se makes no difference to the policy process, and that the typology presented in chapter three applies across the legislative-executive divide.

Two arguments have been made with respect to the consequences of delegating policymaking to an administrative agency. The first is derived from the "capture theory" of regulation, a subset of the rent-seeking approach, which asserts that regulatory agencies pursue the welfare of the very sectors they were created to regulate.[18] From this argument, it follows that administrative delegation is, with corporatist bargaining, another instrument of ideological deescalation. The lesser visibility of bureaucratic politics and the existence of stiff procedural constraints make it easier for concentrated interests to reassert control over the outcome.

The argument that administrative delegation yields pressure politics contains two weaknesses.[19] One, the legislator has full control over the nature of the interests to which it intends the new agency to be responsive. That is, the legislator can "stack the deck" in favor of sectoral or general interests by setting informational requirements, providing independent resources, and representing the public.[20] Two, elected representatives cannot rationally delegate trade policymaking to an agency unless they are confident that the agency will reproduce the electoral parameters of relative salience and divisiveness to which the representatives themselves are liable. Delegations are more likely to reinforce the policymaking status quo than to alter it.

A second argument equates administrative delegation with a switch to bureaucratic autonomy (executive politics, in my typology). This argument builds on the Weberian notion of the specificity of the administrative process; it posits that the effect of the delegation is to empower an autonomous actor, endowed with its own institutional interest, broadly or narrowly defined.[21] The argument is either trivial or at variance with the tenet of rational choice. It is trivial if all it amounts to is the idea that the legislator-administrator relation, like all principal-agent relations, allows for some shirking on the part of the agent. It is nonrational if it implies that the administrative process irremediably distends the electoral connection. If it does, it places elected representatives at risk of frustrating the voters, a risk few will take. It is a risk that can be avoided simply by not consenting to the delegation in the first place. Administrative delegation does not yield executive politics. Nor is executive politics defined by the location of the policy process in the administrative branch (although this is an incidental consequence) but by the nature of the electoral delegation.

Summary

In this chapter I have sought to identify working propositions on the etiology of the three policy processes described in chapter three—pressure politics, party politics, and executive politics. Specific to trade policy, the propositions are listed in the order of discussion:

Hypothesis 4.1 (mass-based factor): The shift from pressure politics to party politics is to be expected when a labor movement or a farm movement takes an independent stand on the trade issue and provides the party advocating its demands with a reliable core of constituents.

Hypothesis 4.2 (corporatism): The trade issue is likely to revert to pressure politics when a party becomes dominant for reasons unrelated to trade and when it is in the party's electoral interests to have rival factors of production reach a corporatist agreement on the trade issue.

Hypothesis 4.3 (security emergency): Executive politics will obtain whenever a country is confronted with an external threat that is both military and inescapable.

Hypothesis 4.4 (end of security emergency): Executive politics will be displaced when the external challenge subsides and a party endeavors to displace executive politics in accordance with the hypotheses on mass-based factors or on corporatism.

Five

The Making of Trade Policy

CHAPTERS THREE AND FOUR have operationalized the concept of policy process and proposed hypotheses to account for its variations. This chapter first defines and maps the variations of the dependent variable, then delineates the implications of the different types of processes for the orientation and tools of trade policy.

Trade Policy: Definition and Variation

Trade policy is not a stable category across time and borders. It can be defined but only in the most general terms, as the policy that purports to affect trade flows between domestic and world markets. Any finer definition must concern itself with historically contingent events, which I present here, and with endogenously determined outcomes, which are the subject of subsequent sections.

The nineteenth century settled on a highly parsimonious definition of trade policy. Tariffs became the universal (and almost unique) instrument of state intervention in foreign trade. Export prohibitions from the mercantilist past were obsolete; import prohibitions were eliminated and converted into tariffs. Bounties, still used in France and several other countries, were fast receding. Indirect regulatory tools, such as navigation laws and preferential trade with colonies (imperial preferences), were headed toward extinction. Such parsimony reflected the spread of liberal ideas, which called for carving out an economic sphere free of state intervention, both at home and in international relations. In this liberal context, the tariff was justified as a provider of revenues.

The picture becomes considerably complicated in the twentieth century. The tariff, subverted from its revenue function, began to be used in conjunction with private cartels to build up artificially competitive industries that charged monopoly prices in their home markets and sold at dumping prices on the world market. In retaliation, governments of countries being dumped in adopted antidumping regulations. Navigation laws and imperial preferences returned in the wake of colonization. The collapse of the gold standard in 1914, and the use of currency manipulation to boost exports and protect domestic producers after 1918, led to further regulatory measures aimed at canceling predatory devaluations. The economic throes of the 1930s ushered in the generalization of the import quota. Although most of these measures were introduced with the intention of controlling for spurious practices—cartels, monetary instability, abnormal surplus capacity, which undermined the efficiency and transparency of the tariff—in the end, the measures produced the opposite result: subverting tariffs and rendering cross-national comparisons meaningless.

The post-World War II era brought still more exceptions to the tariff. Effective international regulation of tariffs and quotas under GATT led countries that could not cope with the successive tariff reductions to seek new means of subversion. Bounties, now called subsidies, returned in strength in a variety of arrays: subsidies for exports, production, sectoral concentration and modernization of the tools of production, R&D, retraining, and so on. Over time, the name on the overall package changed from planning to industrial policy and then to supply side. To achieve what tariffs had previously done more simply, governments annexed almost every regulatory tool within reach: public procurements, health and safety regulations, exchange controls, and patents, including restrictions pertaining to national defense. This panoply of offensive tools begat one of defensive tools, including countervailing duties and smarter procedures aimed at curbing unfair trade practices of wider scope. Because GATT banned unilateralism, quotas became voluntary; they were negotiated bilaterally and imposed by exporters. Trade policy has long since lost its classical simplicity and transparency—today, no one knows how to measure protection.

How are these historical variations to be coded? The definition of trade policy can be mapped along two dimensions: the orientation of trade policy and the mix of policy tools. The first dimension, orientation of trade policy, is usually said to vary between free trade and protection. Although I use this conceptual short-cut whenever convenient, it is important to note that the distinction, in itself, offers no edge to conceptualization. Rather, the dichotomy that lends itself to rational prediction is one between *general* policies and *particular* ones.

A particular measure is defined as a measure destined to be enjoyed by a sector. In contrast, a general measure is one that applies to a diffuse group—a factor or a nation. Political economists usually posit an identity as being between free trade and general policy and between protection (or subsidies) and particular policies. The logic is that a rise in the tariff—say, on metals—is a particular measure, generating benefits for the metal producers only; whereas a decrease in the tariff on metals generates benefits for all consumers of metals, which is a diffuse group. Subsidies provide another illustration. The benefits of a subsidy go to the firm or sector that receives the monies, whereas a cut in the subsidy accrues to taxpayers.

This basic identity—between free trade and general interest on the one hand, and protection (or subsidies) and particular interest, on the other— makes sense within the assumptions of economic theory; but, in a political framework, it is theoretically inadequate. It is the voters who—by sharing, dividing, or ignoring an idea—decide whether an idea is general or particular. Moreover, if one assumes, as political economists do and as I do here, that voters are rational ignorant, then it can be said that voters are never sure whether or not free trade is socially optimal or whether consumption brings them closer to each other. Only classical economists know such things.[1] For voters, free trade is one ideology among many, which claims to know the formula for collective happiness. That is, there is no reason to equate protection (and subsidies) with rent. Protection (and subsidies) can be general when substantively linked to a general idea, such as national security, imperial expansion, or even redistribution in favor of a majority of the population. Conversely, free trade is a general-interest policy unless it is perceived as endangering national security, imperial expansion, and so forth. The orientation of trade policy, therefore, varies between general and particular goals, a dichotomy often, but not always, reducible to free trade and protection, respectively.

The second dimension of trade policy is the complexity of the trade policy toolbox: *parsimonious* or *complex*. Until World War I, the trade policy toolboxes of Britain and the United States were limited to the tariff, whereas that of France included not only tariffs but bounties, drawbacks, imperial preferences, and tied loans, as well. Since World War II, France more than Britain, and Britain more than the United States, have resorted to subsidies, whether to exports, modernization, concentration, bail-outs, retraining, or R&D. These two measures, orientation and tools, are our two dependent variables and are developed successively.

Orientation of the Trade Policy

The Screening Effect

The policy process does not directly determine the trade policy orientation.[2] What the process does, however, is point to the exogenous events most likely to affect policy orientation, such as business cycle, factor endowment, or trade dependence. Indeed, policy orientation is always a reflection of the preferences held by the principals. Therefore, to the extent that the policy process determines the identity of the principals, it indirectly affects the policy outcome. The process can be visualized as a grid laid over a cloud of exogenous, causal events that blocks some events and allows others. (See figure 5.1, which is a refinement of the flowchart in figure 2.1, with "orientation" as the dependent variable.) A change in the policy process is the equivalent of changing the grid, thus blocking some events previously allowed while allowing some new events.

FIGURE 5.1
Variable Chart with Orientation as Dependent Variable

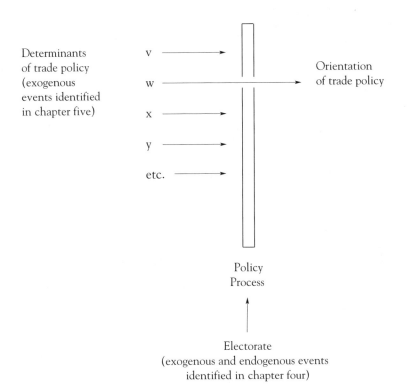

Determinants
of trade policy
(exogenous
events identified
in chapter five)

Orientation
of trade policy

Policy
Process

Electorate
(exogenous and endogenous events
identified in chapter four)

What are the screening rules? There is a fundamental connection between the size of a group and the scope and timing of the exogenous problem the group takes on. A group with a membership of a certain size cannot optimally tackle a problem that affects a population larger than the group membership; this is so because of the collective-good dilemma.[3] Nor can this group effectively tackle a problem that only affects a subset of its membership, because of the risk of disintegration.[4] A similar reason applies to timing; small groups can refocus their attention more quickly on new problems than large groups, but they are at a disadvantage with respect to problems that do not avail themselves of a quick fix, requiring sustained action instead. The screening effect therefore operates in two stages. First, the electorate defines the policy process and thus the identity of the principal—sector, factor, or nation. Then the principal targets a class of exogenous events. Once this class of exogenous events is known, it is possible logically to derive hypotheses about the orientation of the trade policy simply by varying the value of the exogenous event. I begin with the case of pressure politics.

Predicting Trade Orientation in Pressure Politics

In pressure politics, the level of efficient political organization is the sector. Industrialists belonging to one sector usually organize a trade association for dealing with what directly affects the price of their products. Trade associations typically are output-oriented organizations, differentiated by product. These associations rarely deal with inputs, because the same inputs are common to multiple sectors. Trade associations tackle events that affect the profit expectations of firms—that is, events which occasion changes in the demand for, or changes in the price of, their products. Typical of such an event is the business cycle.[5] In periods of boom, demand is large enough to accommodate all producers, even import-sensitive ones. In periods of lull, demand shrinks; in consequence, as price-competition intensifies, import-sensitive interests organize and press their governments to raise trade barriers. Trade associations are well equipped to deal with a business downswing, because a downswing can be allayed by closing or enlarging the domestic market, product by product.

Not all trade associations were created to lobby on the tariff; some were also directed at price-fixing. The two types of association are easily distinguishable, however, because protective-tariff lobbies respond to the ups and downs of business cycles differently than do price-fixing cartels. Periods of prosperity strip protective lobbies of their raison d'être, but, because rising demand makes price-fixing profitable and easy to achieve, such periods foster the cartels. Conversely, periods of recession reanimate protective lobbies but undermine price agreements by tempting members to undersell one another. Protective lobbies are "countercyclical," whereas cartels are cyclical.

Other kinds of events occasion changes in demand and prices. In contrast to sudden swings in the business cycle, for example, there are secular or incremental changes affecting terms of trade, factor endowments, trade dependence, and so forth. These events, however, are unlikely to be detected by firms and acted upon at the sectoral level. This does not mean, of course, that divergences in factor endowment among sectors will not translate, ceteris paribus, into cross-sectoral variations in pressure and thus, if pressure politics is the existing policy process, into cross-sectoral variations in rent levels. What this means is that tipping points in long-term changes will emerge in coincidence with a downswing in the business cycle and be processed as a change in the business cycle. In pressure politics the business cycle is the universal vehicle for longitudinal changes in trade orientation.

In sum, the business cycle is a good predictor of trade orientation. Thus we have the following hypothesis: In pressure politics, trade orientation moves toward protecting losers during periods of economic lull and promoting winners during periods of boom.

A basic rule of pressure politics is that it works best for those who are most organized. Hence, the second hypothesis: The policy outcome reflects the preferences of the most organized interests. The difficulty, however, is to assess differential organization. Cross-sectoral economic proxies, such as the degree of industrial concentration, the size of firms, and good performance, are double-edged. On the one hand, they give us an idea of which firms are most capable of taking advantage of pressure politics. On the other hand, the same indicators also measure a firm's capacity to play by the rules of the market—large, concentrated, and performing sectors are the least in need of a rent. To my knowledge, there is not a single cross-sectoral economic proxy capable of capturing the political phenomena at work in pressure politics. Justification for this assessment is supported by the inconclusive state of the evidence presented so far by political economists intent on showing that recent U.S. trade policy conforms to the rules of rent seeking (see chapter twelve). Because of the ambivalence of the economic variables, the only fact one can actually assess is whether industries are organized to reap political rents—the underlying assumption being that industries do not incur lobbying costs unless they see an opportunity. The existence of strong, widespread networks of trade associations engaged in lobbying for trade rents usually is a good indicator of pressure politics, while the relative balance among rival networks is a good predictor of the policy outcome.

Predicting Trade Orientation in Party Politics

The level of efficient political organization in party politics is the factor of production. Producers belonging to one factor are mobilized by political parties. Whereas trade associations are output-side organizations, parties are input-side; they articulate the demands of producers arrayed in factors—land, labor, and capital.

Parties are sensitive to variations in the relative prices of inputs. These variations are not linked to the business cycle but are the product of secular trends. For example, both land prices since the 1870s and wages for unskilled labor since the Great Depression have lost ground to profits on capital. This trend has been fueled by the competition experienced by Europe and North America since the nineteenth century from developing countries in Latin America, Asia, and Africa—all richly endowed with land and unskilled manpower. Party systems responded to the changes by taking up the urban-rural cleavage in the late nineteenth century and the class cleavage later on.[6] Despite this correspondence between relative input prices and partisan competition, it is difficult to arrive at any firm conclusion about what determines the electoral success of one factor rather than another. Rogowski's analysis comes closest to this determination.[7] He showed that the alignment of land, labor, and capital is a reflection of long-term trends in world trade: Expansion leads the well-endowed factors to gain economically more than do others and to claim more political power. Conversely, a contraction leads well-endowed factors to lose economic and political ground to poorly endowed factors. Rogowski acknowledges, however, that knowledge of the coalitional structure is insufficient to determine the election winner, thus to determine the outcome of trade policy. This electoral indeterminacy is itself the result of interference from a host of other issues that party systems articulate.

Here, the goal is less ambitious. Since the party that will be in power cannot be predicted scientifically, the fact will be accepted as historically given. Hence, we have the rather trivial hypothesis: The determining event for trade policy in party politics is the profile of the victorious party.

It is less trivial, however, that the external events that are decisive in pressure politics should be of less relevance in party politics. In party politics, the effect of the business cycle should not be as systematic as it is in pressure politics. There is only one scenario in which the partisan cycle would work in harmony with the business cycle: if the free-trade party won in periods of boom but lost to the protectionist party in periods of lull. The probability of this happening is low, since rationally ignorant voters have no interest in elucidating the impact of the business cycle on trade, and of trade on their pocketbook. What is more likely to happen in the presence of rational ignorants is that the incumbent party loses power every time the economy slows down. Under this assumption, the business cycle and the party cycle are bound to fall out of phase.[8] A third possible scenario, and probably the most realistic of the three, is that election results are not sensitive to the business cycle; instead, they are determined by voter perceptions that run the gamut of issues over which parties compete. There is little reason to believe that parties swing in tune with the business cycle. Hence, we have the next hypothesis: The role of the business cycle in party politics is mediated by the party cycle in a way that, a priori, makes indeterminate the impact of the business cycle on policy outcome.

Predicting Trade Orientation in Executive Politics

The environmental events that are key in determining the orientation of the trade policy in executive politics have their origin in security concerns. Typically, executives have viewed increases in commercial intercourse between two countries as a prime requisite for strong alliances. Conversely, they have generally viewed the damming of commercial flows as a sanction calling for retaliation. In that respect, diplomats (backed by the nation) may be expected to favor trade relations with their allies while urging blockades against their enemies. Diplomats should be expected, as well, to resist domestic demands that would harm their allies' commerce and submit every potential policy change to negotiation with the country's trade partners. We thus have the following hypothesis: Changes in trade policy reflect patterns of reciprocity between trade partners.

The diplomat's capacity to barter trade preferences for strategic advantages is likely to be subject to a budget constraint. Hence the corollary to the preceding hypothesis: As soon as the economy of one country shows signs of fatigue relative to the economy of its allies, that country's voters will resist further trade concessions and request the executive to reassess its grand strategy.

The external events that play a determinant role in the other two institutional processes are of little relevance here. The profile of the party in power, for example, is of little consequence. In fact, the trade policy conducted by the executive typically receives transpartisan, if not multipartisan, support. Also, the business cycle, which should play a decisive role in pressure politics, does not play a role in executive politics, especially if its impact is in phase with those of its trade partners. Indeed, if a crisis affects all economies at once, the crisis may strengthen the hand of the protectionist opposition; but the crisis also sharpens the acuteness of the threat—the trade partners are then more vulnerable to the external threat—and thus strengthens the hand of the executive.[9]

The Tools of Trade Policy

Trade policy varies in the nature of the tools employed. The toolbox can be either parsimonious or complex. The relative definitions of parsimony and complexity have varied overtime. Until World War I, the standard toolbox was limited to tariffs; by 1930, it included quotas. By World War II, it included export subsidies. This evolution is a reflection of the wide erosion of the tenets of classical liberalism and the consequent growth of state intervention in the economy; this longitudinal variation is accepted here as a given.[10] The cross-national variation observed at any given time, however, merits explanation. The trade policy of certain countries exhibits a variety and complexity well beyond the cross-national median of the time. In the nineteenth century, in addition to tariffs, certain governments resorted to imperial preferences, tariff assimilation of the colonies, tied loans, and "buy national" policies. By the 1920s, currency devaluation was added to the toolbox by some, but not all, countries. Since World War II, the complete toolbox typically has included subsidies to modernization, concentration, investment, research, and many other measures which fall under the category of "planning" or "industrial policy." In order to account for the cross-national variation, I address these two questions: Why should lawmakers complicate the trade toolbox? Under what conditions will industry tolerate state intervention greater than the cross-national median?

Governments' Rationale for Supplying Additional Tools

Consider the government's rationale. When do policymakers need a complex toolbox, and when can they manage with a simplified one? A standard rule of thumb in economics is that a government needs as many policy tools as there are economic problems to solve.[11] In political science, we do not know what an economic problem is, but we do know what a political problem is. A government is confronted with a political problem whenever it needs to reconcile the demands of conflicting constituency groups, each of whom is equally necessary to sustain the government's electoral support.

Conflicted interests can be reconciled by means of either general or particular policies, the general policy by targeting the policy denominator common to all interests, the particular policies by tailoring state aid to the particular need of each interest. A general policy is appropriate when trade conflicts can be subsumed under one broad category—for example, land versus capital, France versus Germany—because the policymaker needs to solve only one conflict. This is the case in a high-quorum process, whether party politics or executive politics. In contrast, particular policies are more useful when trade conflicts are decentralized—for example, wool growers versus woolens manufacturers—because the policymaker is confronted with a multiplicity of conflicts. This is the case in a low-quorum process such as pressure politics.

Ideally, policymakers would like to be able to use both types of policies simultaneously, a general policy to reach a large class of voters and a battery of side-payments to accommodate the requests of sectors harmed by the general policy. But policymakers may be bound by their electoral promises. If they win by mobilizing voters against special interests (monopolies, plutocrats), they can accommodate these special interests only at the risk of perjury. Strongly felt in party politics, this constraint is somewhat relaxed in executive politics because of imperfect information (see chapter three).

A general policy is more parsimonious than a set of particular policies. Whereas the former applies evenly—for example, free trade for all, protection for all—the latter tries to accommodate interests of both types—both import-sensitive and export-oriented—thereby justifying a more sophisticated toolbox.

Hence, from the politician's point of view, a high-quorum process is less likely to require a complex toolbox than a low-quorum process. Ceteris paribus, party politics favors parsimony, pressure politics favors complexity; executive politics may, in certain circumstances (when a secondary market for rents emerges, for example) accommodate a relative degree of complexity. Populists, nationalists, and class ideologues have little need for instrumental imagination. Only agents with limited substantive autonomy need deploy their stores of procedural ingenuity.

This proposition must now be checked against the industrialist's point of view. Is the propensity of trade interests to demand side-payments also inversely correlated with the size of the quorum?

The Industrialist's Rationale For Demanding Tools

The demand for particular (as opposed to general) policies is higher in pressure politics than in party or executive politics—for two reasons. First, the demand for side-payments is analogous to the demand for rents. Industrialists want side-payments they can appropriate; that is, they desire measures that apply to the sector and that trade associations can lobby and claim credit for. Side-payments that apply to the factor are less easily captured by sectoral interests.

The second reason is that sectoral lobbies enjoy greater control over policymaking. Side-payments are generated in pressure politics by incremental *spillover* of the trade issue into neighboring issues. For example, a publicly owned railroad is pressed to "buy national" to compensate for low tariffs on imported engines. In party or executive politics the trade debate spills over into other debates as well, but with the important difference that it is trade that is annexed by other issues with which it has an ideological connection. Let us say that a tariff has been reduced to break a trust or several trusts. This situation is more similar to *contagion* than to spillover, since the trade debate loses its independence and is rewritten by the class (or security) debate.[12] Private-interest groups enjoy very little control over the dynamic of contagion—which, indeed, may turn against them. Therefore, the demand for it is limited.

Combining the politician's and industrialist's rationales yields the following: At a given time, high quorum is correlated with a simple toolbox, whereas low quorum is correlated with a diverse toolbox.

Public and Private Refinements

A specific manifestation of the preceding hypothesis is the occurrence of subsidies since World War II, especially of subsidies to production (also known as "industrial policy"). Unlike tariffs and quotas—whose impact on a single firm ultimately is mediated by the market—subsidies are allocated directly by the state. Subsidies call for a greater level of collaboration between industry and government. Industrialists must share with the government information of a sensitive nature regarding investment decisions. The closeness of the collaboration varies with the degree to which the subsidy is automatic; tax deductions and regional development grants involve no special negotiations, whereas subsidies targeted to individual firms require negotiation of a special quid pro quo. Industry's attitude toward this type of microintervention is mixed. On the one hand, subsidies seem to be an attractive option because they allow firms to rely on the extraordinary powers of the state and because they allow firms access to the public purse. On the other hand, subsidies are risky; the government may use them to pursue goals that do not completely overlap with corporate goals or, worse, that are incompatible. It thus seems reasonable to argue that business, especially the upper levels of business, would not, over the long run, consent to state interference in sectoral and microeconomic decisions if they suspected state officials of serving interests hostile or indifferent to the welfare of business. State officials will only be invited to expand the scope and sharpen the focus of their policy tools if they establish a workable partnership with big business; such a partnership is possible only in the context of pressure politics. In comparison, in a policy process dominated by partisan rivalry or strategic goals, the policymaker enjoys too much autonomy vis-à-vis industrialists for industry to entrust its fate to that policymaker. Therefore, we have the hypothesis: Since World War II, whenever trade policy is the outcome of pressure politics, trade officials will resort to subsidies. By contrast, wherever trade policy is the outcome of party politics or executive politics, state officials will have no more than regulatory means at their disposal.[13]

The final hypothesis in this chapter concerns the private-policy toolbox: Ceteris paribus, an industrialist whose government has few policy tools at its disposal is at a comparative disadvantage vis-à-vis a foreign competitor whose government has more policy tools at its disposal. To make up for this deficiency, the first industrialist must adopt private countervailing measures. To some extent, a deficient public toolbox must be compensated for by means of a more sophisticated private panoply, whereas a rich public toolbox allows the firm to dispense with the adoption of a sophisticated private panoply. Among the private tools sectors have used to compensate for a deficient governmental policy are vertical integration, cartels, systematic dumping, multinational relocation, and banker-sponsored restructurings. Hence, we have the hypothesis: There is an inverse relation between the degree of refinement of the public policy toolbox and that of the private policy toolbox.

Summary

This chapter has defined trade policy and derived hypotheses about its orientation and tools. The orientation is indirectly derived from the policy process: the process screens out environmental events unlikely to be aggregated by the sector in pressure politics, by the factor in party politics, or by the nation-at-war in executive politics. The tools are derived directly from the nature of the policy process. Hypotheses are listed below, numbered and labeled for later reference:

Hypothesis 5.1 (business cycle): In pressure politics, trade orientation reflects the business cycle, being more protectionist in periods of lull and less protectionist in periods of boom.

Hypothesis 5.2 (collective action): In pressure politics, trade orientation reflects the preferences of the most organized interests.

Hypothesis 5.3 (party cycle): In party politics, trade orientation reflects the profile of the party in power.

Hypothesis 5.4 (indeterminacy of the business cycle): In party politics, the impact of the business cycle on the policy outcome will be indeterminate.

Hypothesis 5.5 (international reciprocity): In executive politics, changes in trade policy reflect patterns of reciprocity between trade partners.

Hypothesis 5.6 (economic constraint): In executive politics, the ability of the executive to barter commercial favors for strategic advantages, and/or make or maintain trade policy as the outcome of a process of reciprocal negotiations with allies, depends on the relative strength of the domestic economy.

Hypothesis 5.7 (public policy toolbox): At any given time, high quorum is correlated with a simple toolbox, whereas low quorum is correlated with a diverse toolbox.

Hypothesis 5.8 (industrial policy): Trade officials show a greater readiness to use subsidies in pressure politics than they do in party politics or executive politics (this hypothesis applies for the period after World War II).

Hypothesis 5.9 (private policy toolbox): There is an inverse relation between the degree of refinement of the public policy toolbox and that of the private policy toolbox.

Recapitulation of the Overall Argument

The theory of electoral delegation proceeds in two steps: (1) elections allow voters to define the trade policy process; and (2) the trade-policy process indirectly determines the policy orientation but directly determines the policy tools. I consider each step successively. First, the electorate determines the identity of the principal to whom it wants the government to be accountable in the matter of trade policy: sectors (pressure politics), factors (party politics), or the nation (executive politics). It is, in fact, the politicians who make this determination based on the degree of salience and divisiveness of the trade issue in the electorate. In turn, salience and divisiveness may be determined exogenously. For instance, an inescapable, military threat leads the electorate to delegate trade policy to a government entrusted with a consensual, public mandate. Or, salience and divisiveness may be determined endogenously. A lobby able to speak on behalf of a dissatisfied mass-based factor may arbitrate between pressure and party politics. Also, a dominant party able to command a corporatist bargain may arbitrate between pressure and party politics.

Second, once the policy principals are known, it is possible to determine the events to which these principals are responsive when lobbying on the issues of policy orientation and the composition of the toolbox. In pressure politics, where the principals are the sectors, the policy orientation reflects the business cycle over time, as well as the relative levels of sectoral organization across sectors. Sectors also have an interest in adopting a sophisticated policy panoply, because they directly control its use. In party politics, where the principals are factors of production organized politically by disciplined parties, the trade orientation is that of the winning party. The toolbox is simple and unsophisticated, in part because parties are not responsive to the demands of sectors, but also because too few sectors are willing to trust politicians to pursue sectors' interests. In executive politics, where the principal is the nation, the trade orientation reflects security imperatives, and the toolbox is simple and unsophisticated.

Part Two

THE MAKING OF TRADE POLICY IN BRITAIN, FRANCE, AND THE UNITED STATES, 1860–1990

Six

The Case Studies

THE SECOND PART of this book provides the empirical support for the theoretical propositions of the first part. My aim is not to submit the propositions to a systematic test, nor to deliver the definitive versions of British, French, and American modern trade history, but rather to show how easily the facts of these three national experiences line up with the categories and causal statements of part one and to contribute a new interpretation of these three cases.

Selection of the Case Studies

The choice of case studies was determined by the simultaneous use of three criteria. Each case had, first, to fall within the boundary conditions of the theory, second, to offer an extended timeframe for analysis, and, third, to provide fertile ground for alternative interpretations. The constraints suggested Britain from the Second Reform Act of 1867; France from the early days of the Third Republic, in 1870, and the United States from the close of the Civil War, in 1865.

The first criterion (boundary conditions), is that each country have institutionalized legal, unrestricted, and recurring elections. The theory thus applies to all advanced industrial democracies. Authoritarian regimes are excluded because they either do not hold elections or, if they do, they exclude the possibility of party competition. To be sure, most authoritarian regimes are partisan—Vichy, for instance, was furiously antilabor.[1] Hypotheses relative to party politics, however, are of no use in such cases, precisely because it is the purpose of a partisan regime to eliminate the uncertainty inherent in party politics. In large part, French business confidently invested in the Vichy regime—not in spite of the regime's partisanship, but because of it.

The second criterion was the length of time democratic institutions had been in operation in each country. An extended time frame was deemed essential for observing changes in the policy process.

The third, and final, criterion was to choose cases already well researched, which provide plenty of developed information, and whose interpretations have been hotly disputed. Among the interpretations encountered along the historical and comparative paths simultaneously traveled in this book, two recur with consistency: political economy and institutionalism. Political economy, recently erected on reclaimed pluralist and revisionist foundations, offers an interpretation of trade policy that is rooted in the economic preferences supposedly held by concentrated economic sectors—heavy industry, cartels, banks, multinational corporations. This interpretation links policy variations to historical trends and differences in national industrial structures.[2] In contrast, institutionalists have emphasized the role of institutions and institutional changes. Among those encountered in this study are the functional centralization of industry in the 1870s;[3] the advent of the mass party in the 1880s;[4] the transfer of lawmaking responsibilities to the executive branch during World War I and in its aftermath;[5] and the centralization of producer groups and promotion by the state of procedures for corporatist intermediation.[6] Institutionalists also point up cross-national differences: the existence of a centralized and enterprising state in France, of a centralized but inaccessible public service in Britain, and of fragmented and penetrated institutions in the U.S.[7]

Preview of the Chapters

The theoretical framework of part one casts a new light on the history of trade policy and policymaking in France, Britain, and the United States. The 120-year time span covered by the three case studies is divided into five periods by four turning points: the lowest point of the Great Depression of the 1880s, World War I, World War II, and the turn of the 1960s. In the following, I sketch the leading themes, by chapter.

CHAPTER SEVEN

Chapter seven starts with the wake of the Cobden-Chevalier Treaty (1860), a treaty that represents the apex of international free trade in the nineteenth century. This period ends in the mid-1880s, after the first jolts of the depression of the 1880s had shaken the complacency over free trade that characterized the previous decade. The trade policies of the three countries during this period show great disparity. The United States emerged from its civil war resolutely protectionist, and it remained so throughout this twenty-year period. Britain and France, in contrast, began and ended the period with record low tariffs. Protectionism in the United States reflected the advent of pressure politics. The weakening of the Democratic party led to a suspension of party politics; industrialists who until then had favored free trade began to invest resources in the organization of trade associations, as well as scrambling for rents. The organizational trend in the United States had no equivalent in France and Britain, however. France was suffering from executive hangover. The Second Empire, an authoritarian regime that institutionalized executive dominance in the trade policy area, had signed trade treaties which seriously restricted the republic's margin for maneuver. Meanwhile, protectionists longed for a return to the pre-1860 system of pressure politics. Repealing the international agreement under which the French parliament labored would have required no less than the creation of a universal coalition of concentrated trade interests—an organizational feat that particular interests could not accomplish on their own. Moreover, no political party saw any electoral advantage in supporting such a coalition. At the end of the period, the protectionists had failed at logrolling and the free traders had won a victory by default. The victory of free trade in Britain was not a victory by default; nor was it the reflection of an ideological consensus (as has often been argued). Rather, free trade in Britain was the result of active engagement on the part of the Liberals (the free-trade party), who undertook to transform the tariff into a partisan issue. In response to rising protectionist agitation, and in the midst of a difficult renegotiation of the treaty with France, the Liberal government decided, in 1881, to ax the trade agreement, exit from the conventional trading regime, and commit the party to a defense of free trade. This move allowed the Liberals to make a bid for the support of the newly organized trade unions, all of which supported free trade, and to force the Conservatives into championing an unpopular cause. Conservative leaders barely evaded the trap by dodging the issue and censuring its backbench.

CHAPTER EIGHT

In this chapter, the depression of the 1880s is covered, from its lowest point to its aftermath. The period has provoked a wealth of interpretations which focus variously on producer coalitions, the advent of modern mass parties, and, at the systemic level, the decline of British trade hegemony. No interpretation, however, can account for all three cases. The key to trade policy during this period lies in the way each political system responded to discontent on the farm. By the mid-eighties, the depression had reached Britain's rural areas, and trade had become a salient issue for the farm vote. French and British farmers were asking for protection, while U.S. farmers sought free trade. The sudden availability of the farm vote destabilized the existing policy process in all three countries. In the United States, the network of trade associations that had been carefully constructed earlier was swept away when the Democrats endorsed free trade. Democrats saw in the farmers' dissatisfaction an opportunity to rebuild their antebellum free-trade coalition. Thus, trade policy in the United States became a partisan issue in 1888 and remained so until 1914. In France, the farm revolt did not trigger the same partisan escalation that had been triggered in the United States. The Republican leadership in France, whose political dominance depended on their ability to straddle the widening urban-rural cleavage, took it upon themselves to persuade farm and industrial organizations to negotiate a corporatist agreement designed to keep the matter out of party politics. The outcome was the Méline tariff of 1892, which drew France from the treaty system of 1860 and made the tariff an issue for pressure politics. In Britain, the electoral consequences of the agrarian crisis had less impact, because of the marginal nature of the farm vote. But by 1907, the Conservative leadership could no longer resist the combined demands of agrarians and industrialists and were forced to endorse protection. Thus, by 1914, trade policy was part and parcel of the farm-factory conflict in the United States and the class struggle in Britain, whereas, in France, it was a matter of sectoral pressure.

CHAPTER NINE

This chapter focuses on World War I and its immediate aftermath. The military emergency allowed executives of all three countries to break free of existing constraints and pursue policies heretofore regarded as forbidden. In France, where sectoral interest had ruled unopposed for several decades, the war allowed the state to regain the initiative from the sectors and launch an institutional offensive intended to perpetuate the primacy of the executive long after the war's end. In Britain and the United States, where the state had enjoyed autonomy within the ideological bounds of party politics, politicians broke free to pursue policies of national scope. Hence, in Britain the war neutralized partisan bickering, thus allowing the Tariff Reformers to win a place in the Liberal government and force protectionism on the Liberal party for the duration of the war and its aftermath. In the United States, the outbreak of war tempted a Democratic president to release his party's trade position from its populist hold and use it to expand American corporate capitalism abroad.

This surge in executive autonomy everywhere, however, was predicated on the war emergency. Peace froze the surge in its tracks; in all three cases the end was swift because executives had not taken advantage of the war to establish a trade treaty network that would remain in effect after peace had been restored.

CHAPTER TEN

Chapter ten spans the two world wars, a period that saw the generalized relocation of tariff-making from the popular assemblies to the administrative branch. The period saw official government consultation as well. Policy processes, however, remained largely unaffected by the relocation. Where pressure politics dominated—as it did in France—the administrative arena replicated familiar aspects of penetration, decentralization, and universality. In contrast, where party politics obtained, as in Britain and the United States, the administrative process bore the marks of autonomy, centralization, and partisanship. Further, in France, consultation degenerated into clientelism, whereas in Britain and the United States, it served for the transmission of government policy.

CHAPTER ELEVEN

Chapter eleven takes up the post-World War II years. The Cold War combination of military bipolarity and America's economic hegemony enabled the U.S. executive to link trade to security and to exact the same link from its allies. The period thus witnessed the institutionalization of the longest, most universal trade-security linkage in modern history. This linkage was institutionalized primarily in the GATT and secondarily in the EEC (whose continued functioning was declared to be a condition for the unity and security of the West). Because the GATT regulated the use of traditional tools of trade policy, countries such as France and Britain, whose governments could ill afford to expose their industries to world competition, developed a new set of protective and promotional tools—mostly subsidies—that fell outside the purview of international regulation. The trade-policy toolbox, until then parsimonious, was expanded to include a host of loosely related policies such as planning, industrial policy, countervailing duties, and VERs. Because these new instruments fell outside the scope of the GATT, they were not subject to executive politics but to domestic debates in which the working class was a full-fledged actor. Trade policy thus remained a partisan issue in Britain, where the adoption of planning and industrial policies was delayed and implementation was hampered by the instability inherent in the partisan policy process. Trade policy would have been a partisan issue in France as well had not the Cold War disqualified the Communist party and made it impossible for the French Left to govern. The Cold War made the French state safe once again for private lobbying, turning France into privileged ground for business-government collusion.

CHAPTER TWELVE

Chapter 12 undertakes an analysis of the most recent decades—the 1960s, 70s, and 80s—a period marked by world economic crisis. The crisis had no real effect on the trade policy administered by the GATT, because it was protected by the trade-security linkage. The crisis did, however, disqualify state intervention in the form of industrial policy, a form that had developed in France and, to a lesser extent, in Britain as an adjuvant to the liberal prescriptions of the GATT. This disqualification of industrial policy, which occurred at the close of an electoral realignment favorable to the Right, was carried out by the traditional middle classes—small business and the self-employed. The advent of party politics coincided with the displacement of pressure politics in France and with the end of corporatist experiments in Britain. U.S. politics, in comparison, registered a similar electoral undertow; but the making of trade policy was not affected, since trade policy was still administered according to the letter, if not always the spirit, of GATT. Executive politics remained the dominant process in the United States even though the relative decline of the U.S. economy led to extensive rent seeking.

In the epilogue to chapter twelve, I address the challenges of the new decade. The 1990s have opened on a new era in world trade. The crash of the Soviet bloc severed a trade-security linkage which, since 1947, had been built into the bipolar power structure. Currently, the question of the future of the GATT, and of the corresponding policy processes in the three countries, is high on the agenda of both theory and policy. In the epilogue, the theoretical tools of this study are applied to this formidable subject.

CONCLUSION

In the conclusion, the general theory of electoral control is recalled, and its related propositions are expanded.

Except for the concluding chapter and the relatively brief chapter nine, each chapter follows a standard outline—division into three sections, one per country. Each section, in turn, first, develops the origins of the policy process, and, second, the respective roles played by lobbies, parties, and the executive (usually in that order). Finally, I take a look at the consequences for trade-policy tools and trade orientation.

Seven

Descent into Depression, 1860–86

BRITAIN AND FRANCE signed the Cobden-Chevalier Treaty in 1860. This treaty, which served as the cornerstone for the international trading regime of the period, was popular on both sides of the English channel. The two governments had signed it to calm public fears over the tension that resulted from France's annexation of Nice and Savoy. By offering to open the French market to British goods, Napoleon III helped Palmerston appease British voices calling for countervailing action. In both countries, the effect of the Anglo-French agreement was to place tariff-making in the realm of the executive (executive politics in Britain, dictatorship in France), with the terms to be determined by international reciprocity and frozen for the duration of the agreement.

The two countries soon followed divergent paths, however. British Liberals countered early signs of disaffection with free trade among the electorate with a successful bid for popular support for free trade. Britain traded executive politics for party politics. Following the collapse of the Second Empire and the advent of the republic, France traded dictatorship for pressure politics, albeit an imperfect kind. For two decades international engagements that had been contracted by the empire continued to make tariff-making a highly centralized process, a process that robbed protectionists of the advantage they usually enjoyed in such a process.

Embroiled in a civil war that interrupted two decades of liberalization, the United States did not join the European tariff treaty system. That war effectively removed tariff-making from the parties and placed it in the hands of the lobbies. Postbellum America thus provides us with a textbook case of the logrolling variant of pressure politics. By the end of the period, tariff policymaking was being carried on at the sectoral level in the United States, at the national level in France, and at the class level in Britain.

These divergences in the policy process shaped lobbying and industrial organization differently in the three countries. Decentralized pressure politics in the United States implied that the basic level of interest aggregation was the trade association, with party factions serving as the political conduit. Conversely, centralized-pressure politics in France (and, to a greater extent, executive politics in Britain before 1881 and party politics after 1881) disqualified trade associations.

The state played an important role in France, a receding role in Britain, and a nonexistent one in the United States.

Free trade survived in the policy process most capable of articulating general principles, the nascent party politics of Britain in the 1880s. Free trade in the context of centralized pressure politics also proved resilient in France. Free trade suffered its worst setback in the United States, amid decentralized pressure politics. There, the tariff debate bore exclusively on the sector, offering no edge to macroeconomic generalizations.

For each case, I identify the origins of the policy process, then examine the lobbies, parties, and executive, and finally arrive at the policy outcome.

The United States

The Policy Process

From 1846 to 1860, the United States moved in the direction of free trade at about the same pace as Britain; but the American Civil War reversed this trend. Two arguments have been advanced to explain the protectionism of the postbellum period in the United States. Revisionists argue that U.S. industry was protectionist before the Civil War and that the war was fought for protection.[1] Taussig, on the other hand, argued that the war expanded industry's surplus capacity to such an extent that protection became a necessity.[2] The two arguments are essentially economic because they argue that the protectionists triumphed in the absence of free-trade supporters. There are limits to these arguments, however. I will show that, although the American Civil War had a definite impact on the industrial structure of the United States, its decisive impact with respect to the tariff was on the policy process. The war led to the replacement of party politics by pressure politics, thereby creating the conditions for the triumph of rent seeking. I first address the existing arguments, then focus on the institutional dynamic.

ECONOMIC VERSUS POLITICAL EXPLANATIONS

The revisionist argument that the Civil War was between a protectionist north and a free trading south has not stood up under close historical analysis. Historians have shown that the tariff was not a sectional issue, and that the North as a whole was not protectionist.[3] The reduction of the tariff in 1857, which John Sherman dubbed the "manufacturers' bill," was accomplished by Southern and New England votes together. In 1861, most manufacturers in New England took no part in the debate over the Morrill Act (an upward revision passed after Southern senators walked out of Congress), probably because they were content with the status quo.[4] The only known exception was the Boston woolens manufacturers, who descended on Washington to fight an increase in the duty on wool and, if they were not successful in checking the increase, to obtain adequate compensatory duties on woolens.[5] Written for the Pennsylvania ironmasters and the Ohio and Michigan sheep raisers, the bill was not representative of Northern opinion in general.[6]

Taussig's argument—that the war so expanded industry's surplus capacity that it made protection a necessity—has merely added to the confusion. The Civil War, Taussig argued, disturbed the normal flow of trade and itself acted as a prohibitory tariff, thus encouraging otherwise inefficient domestic producers to begin production. These newcomers, because of their inefficiency, would not have survived a return to the status quo ante. Instead, they swelled the ranks of the protectionists and blocked the phase-out of war duties.[7]

Taussig's argument is not compelling. In those sectors that supported free trade before the war, the war created a two-tier productive system. The first tier consisted of established producers who had reached world competitiveness before the war, while the second tier was composed of new producers who were less efficient but still made profits, thanks to the abnormal level of protection afforded by the war. The decision whether to return to prewar openness or maintain the war tariff was more likely to rest with the first tier (concentrated in New England) than with the second tier (loosely scattered throughout the Midwest). The core of New Englanders could hope to hold on to their market either by closing the American market to foreign competition, but sharing it with the new domestic entrants, or by reducing the duties low enough to allow foreign competition to suppress fledgling western competition. On strictly economic grounds, their choice could go either way.

The nature of the choice between domestic and foreign competition was not lost on contemporaries. Edward Atkinson, president of the cotton spinners of New England and a director of the Boston Board of Trade, wrote in 1866:

> The strongest men in the trade are more afraid of the unskillful competition built up at home by high duties than they are of foreign competition.[8]

Militating in favor of openness to foreign competition was the growing dependence of New England manufacturers on foreign imports for raw materials. As local sources of raw materials were rapidly exhausted, New England manufacturers found themselves farther from available domestic sources than their competitors in the American West. Their natural suppliers, in fact, were foreign. Inland transportation costs made iron ore from Britain and Sweden cheaper than iron ore from Minnesota. The same was true of iron and scrap iron from Europe. Coal from Nova Scotia was cheaper than coal from Pennsylvania or West Virginia. Chilean copper delivered in New York was cheaper than Michigan copper. Wool from Canada, Spain, and even Australia was cheaper than a clip from Ohio. Linseed from India and hemp from Russia and the Philippines were imported into Boston at lower prices than from the

West.[9] As a result of the high tariffs on raw materials, New England products were vulnerable not only to foreign imports but to competition from the American West as well.

Note that the problem continued even as the frontier of industrialization moved farther and farther from New England. In the textile industry, New Englanders' foremost competitors were Pennsylvanians in the 1850s and 60s, and Southerners thereafter.[10] In the iron and steel industry, the rolling mills of New England and New York first faced competition from New Jersey and Pennsylvania and then from Ohio, Michigan, and West Virginia.[11] In the leather shoe industry, a similar trend took place at the turn of the century, as St. Louis became the third largest manufacturer in the country.[12] In all these cases, the migration of the center of industry toward domestic sources of raw materials was caused by high protective duties on imported raw materials and was facilitated by equally high duties on finished products. In every case, those New England and Atlantic manufacturers who could not follow the migration were increasingly receptive to the idea of free trade.

Why did New England manufacturers choose protection rather than free trade? The answer does not lie in the economic reality of the 1860s, but in the political reality. The Civil War did not affect the manufacturers' competitiveness—at least not for those manufacturers who were organized and politically active—as much as it affected the parameters of political competition. The manufacturers, in fact, took their cue from the policy process, and the policy process that governed tariff-making after the Civil War was a textbook example of the logrolling variant of pressure politics (case 4 in table 3.1). Moreover, the process reflected a trade issue that was neither divisive nor salient, as well as orienting trade interests toward the pursuit of short-term, particular interests. Given the protectionists' natural organizational advantage in a process articulated around the sector, free traders were bound to be underrepresented. New England manufacturers in a nonpartisan process were no longer confident of securing a free-trade policy for their raw materials; therefore, protection for their products was the logical choice. In sum, those New England manufacturers who were long established and well networked were not protectionist. They might have been able to prevail over foreign competition in the economic market, but they could not prevail over protectionist competition in the political market. For this reason, they chose to play the protectionist card.

EVIDENCE FOR THE END OF PARTY POLITICS

A simple way to identify the operative presence of party politics in postbellum tariff-making is to determine the level of partisan discipline observed over time in congressional roll-calls on the trade issue. The method used to summarize these observations is presented in appendix three. Comprehensive results for the U.S. House of Representatives are presented in figure A3.1 and for the U.S. Senate in figure A3.2 (also in appendix 3).

As the data suggest, until 1887 the trade debate was not partisan. Whereas Republican leaders were committed to protection, and leaders of the Democratic party favored reductions in the tariff, each party accommodated a minority. Within Republican ranks, the antiprotectionist clamor was heard from New England export-oriented towns, which found factional expression in the "Johnson Clubs" (1886) and the "Mugwumps" (1884), as well as the grain-growing areas of the West (the "liberal Republicans" [1872] and the "reductionist Republicans" of Minnesota and Nebraska [1887]). On the Democratic side of the aisle, dissonant views came from a strong protectionist faction led by Samuel J. Randall of Pennsylvania, Speaker of the House from 1875 to 1881. Randall's followers included the eastern groups of the Democratic party, who represented predominately manufacturing districts in Ohio, Pennsylvania, and New York. Randall also found ready allies among the Louisiana sugarcane growers and two industrial enclaves in Alabama and West Virginia.[13] Until 1887, he and his fifty-two followers held the balance of power in the House. In the 1884 presidential election, the Democratic platform straddled the two factions, comparing favorably with the Republican platform.[14]

ORIGINS OF PRESSURE POLITICS

The cause for the collapse of party politics and the advent of pressure politics rested with the defection of the agrarians. Having been the bedrock of antebellum free trade, agrarians suddenly were no longer responsive to free trade. Even though American farmers were suffering from falling prices, they did not blame this condition on the industrial tariff. The farmers exported to Europe, which remained open to U.S. wheat until the late 1870s and early 1880s. Their initial response to the price decline was to pressure the railroads to reduce freight rates.[15] In the 1880s, American farmers pinned their hopes on a policy of inflation through the remonetization of silver, which they hoped would sustain and perhaps raise prices. Certainly trade was not an unimportant issue; in fact, it was gaining prominence as the depression deepened. But the issue was overshadowed by trust and currency issues. After the Civil War the tariff simply did not have the salience it had earlier.

The theory cannot predict the agrarian defection. Hypothesis 4.2 is not applicable (the hypothesis states that party politics is displaced when one party becomes dominant and has an electoral interest in bringing conflicting factors to a corporatist agreement). It was not the corporatist agreement between farm and factory but a civil war that put an end to party politics. The Republican party, dominant for some years after the war, had no need to engage in conflict management, because agrarians were indifferent.

Agrarian defection is the reason why the tariff lost its antebellum salience.

The agrarians were the only mass-based producer group engaged in politics at the time. But the defection is not the reason why the process lost its divisiveness. For this, we need to look more closely at the lobbies.[16]

Lobbies

Pressure politics encompasses two types of conflict, intrasectoral (between the firms of a same sector) and intersectoral (between different sectors). In the pluralist variant of pressure politics (case 3, table 3.1), conflicts are settled by politicians in a process that is competitive. In the logrolling variant of pressure politics (case 4, table 3.1), these conflicts, or at least a significant number of them, are settled outside the policy process. Politicians simply endorse the agreements reached among trade interests. The postbellum tariff was of the logrolling type. A comparison of this tariff-making process with a prior instance of the pluralist variant, the tariff of the pre-Jacksonian era, is useful in highlighting the properties of logrolling.

In the pre-Jacksonian era, interest organization was not by sector but by local community. As Pincus notes in his study of the 1824 tariff, industry memorials to Congress represented local industrial communities, not industries. Other participants were agricultural societies, state legislatures, and chambers of commerce—all local organizations. Pincus explains the existence of this parochial mode of representation in terms of excessively high transaction costs: "The costs of obtaining information about the actions of others and of coordinating and monitoring efforts can be expected to rise with distance, especially in periods such as the 1820s in which communications were slow and costly."[17] Transactions took place in a highly ineffectual system in which "most interstate and inter-product bargaining took place among the members of Congress, rather than outside Congress."[18] Congressmen had to arbitrate intraindustrial conflicts between producers belonging to the same sector but living in different districts, and interindustrial conflicts between industrialists living in the same town but belonging to different sectors. With Congressmen in charge, the danger of contamination by issues other than trade were real.[19] In addition, the system generated as much conflict as it helped resolve. The "cohesiveness of industry lobby," Pincus writes, "made for more pressure, but narrowness, for more Congressional resistance."[20] In other words, the geographic concentration of lobbying minimized intraindustrial conflicts but maximized interindustrial ones, whereas geographical diffusion minimized interindustrial conflicts but maximized intraindustrial ones.

By the 1860s, communication had improved and constraints on coordination were eased. When industrialists were given another crack at pressure politics after the Civil War, they were able to devise a more rational system of interest representation, one in which neither intra- nor interindustrial conflicts would any longer be entrusted to politicians but would instead be handled among producers themselves. The postbellum era saw the end of two previous bottlenecks through the organization of sectors into nationwide associations and through the signing of minicorporatist agreements (known as primary producer-manufacturer "compacts") between upstream and downstream sectors. The compact was particularly effective. Since primary producers and manufacturers were often located in different parts of the country (as was the case with agricultural crudes such as cotton, wool, flax, hops, and oleaginous seeds), the compact could guarantee wide political support. The new setup considerably aided the working of pressure politics by decreasing friction between politicians and improving the ability of producers to monitor the performance of the politicians. In the best hypothesis, the demands of the industry would be communicated to the politicians who would incorporate the demands without further discussion into the general tariff bill and then logroll. Trade associations and compacts helped stabilize tariff-making because they were vulnerable from two sides only—the side of the final consumer and that of the free trade dogma—neither of whom enjoyed a ready-made institutional entry into pressure politics.

This transformation took place after the Civil War. The earliest instance was the wool compact of 1865. In 1864, New England woolens manufacturers faced two alternatives: seek a reduction in the duties on wool, and thus antagonize farmers from Ohio, Michigan, Pennsylvania, New York, and Vermont; or come to terms with those farmers and use their support to promote further protection for woolens. The path to be preferred seemed obvious. The Democratic party was not interested in carrying out a crusade against protection, and in 1864 the South was absent from Congress anyway. Therefore, in November 1864, a group of woolens manufacturers from Massachusetts, Rhode Island, and Pennsylvania founded the National Association of Wool Manufacturers (NAWM).[21] Soon afterward, they induced wool growers to organize an association similar to their own and arranged for the two trade associations to meet in Syracuse on 12 December 1865, to discuss the tariff. A month later, a bargain was struck, according to which the manufacturers accepted the growers' demand for increased wool duties, provided the growers accept the principle of compensation without qualification.[22] The manufacturers wrote a tariff schedule that increased duties on imported wool, gave compensatory duties to manufacturers to offset the extra cost, and conceded to the manufacturers an extra duty equal to the protection to which they thought they were entitled. The chairman of the Ways and Means Committee, Justin Morrill of Vermont, included the proposal verbatim in his general tariff bill of 1866. Although the bill died in the Senate, its wool and woolens schedule survived as a separate bill, which was passed by both chambers and signed into law, thus becoming the first protectionist legislation to reach the statute book after the Civil War.

A similar scene unfolded in the iron and steel industry, albeit after a long decade of fumbling. The American Iron and Steel Association (AISA) was founded in November 1864, but its ability to speak for the industry as a whole was immediately challenged by the secession of various groups and by the founding of rival organizations.[23] Pig-iron producers formed their own association in 1871; they were imitated by the nail manufacturers, crucible manufacturers, eastern ironmasters, and other iron manufacturers.[24] The fragmentation of the iron industry made it an ineffectual lobby in Congress, easily challenged by New England consumers of British iron, such as the shipbuilders and axe manufacturers. Until 1873, the fight for protection in the industry was waged chiefly by a local organization, the Industrial League of Pennsylvania.[25] Things began to change in 1874. At a joint meeting held on February 5 of that year, two parallel iron manufacturers' associations and the old AISA combined under the name AISA. Moreover, at Cresson, Pennsylvania in September 1882, the AISA hosted a national convention of manufacturers of iron and steel, and the producers of iron-ore organized as the Western Iron Ore Association. The compact agreed to a comprehensive system of duties that was recommended to the Tariff Commission and finally adopted by Congress.[26]

National trade associations flourished in all industries.[27] In addition, compacts were agreed to between malsters and brewers in Baltimore in June 1878, and beween flax and hemp growers and manufacturers in Saratoga in July 1882. In charge of numerous products, the Manufacturing Chemists' Association, in 1882, mailed about a hundred questionnaires to its members, prepared a comprehensive schedule of tariffs, had the full association ratify it, and then gave it to the U.S. Tariff Commission, which, in turn, endorsed most of the schedule and had Congress adopt it.[28] By 1882, of the fourteen schedules on the tariff bill, six in effect were covered by either a single trade association or a compact (metals, chemicals, paper, wool, silk, flax and hemp); a seventh was partially covered by a trade association (earthenware, in the "earthenware and glassware" schedule).

Parties

The lobbies went a long way toward suppressing the conflict inherent in the policy process. They were not completely successful, however, because not all minority interests could be articulated. Lobbies needed the help of politicians to contain incipient dissension which might have broken the ranks of the lobbies. Politicians aided the associations by granting them exclusive access to policymaking. This access conferred on trade associations a kind of official recognition that reduced the associations' costs of policing free riders and helped them overcome conflicts within their respective bailiwicks. Access and

organization thus became mutually reinforcing. Further, this circularity generated stability, since the policy process operated in a closed circuit.

None of the associations mentioned above were representative of the minority interests in their industry—and, sometimes, not even of the majority
interests. Although the National Association of Wool Manufacturers
(NAWM) claimed to represent the whole industry, it was actually controlled
by the carpet and worsted wool segments. Carpet and worsted manufacturers
imported a type of wool (carpet and combed) not grown in the United States.
They feared that an open conflict with the third segment of the industry—the
woolens manufacturers and their domestic supplier—would result in high duties being imposed indiscriminately on all imported wools—carpet and
combed, as well as carded. Therefore, the carpet and worsted manufacturers
calculated correctly that, if the domestic growers were allowed to write their
own ticket in regard to carded wool, those same growers would certainly allow
carpet and combing wools to enter the country at a nominal rate. This was the
essence of the Syracuse bargain of 1865, institutionalized as the Wool and
Woolens Act of 1867. The act, however, discriminated against woolens manufacturers who chaffed under an effective level of protection lower than that
enjoyed by the worsted manufacturers, with whom they actually competed.[29]
Not happy with the deal, the woolens manufacturers were divided among
themselves, between those who needed protection and found the deal better
than nothing, and those who did not need protection and from the outset had
advocated free trade.[30] Many woolens manufacturers bolted the association.
Of those enrolled as of November 1864, about 80 percent were no longer
members at the end of 1875. In 1869 and thereafter, the woolens faction
regularly petitioned Congress to reduce duties on clothing wool, but in vain.
Attempts to organize were unsuccessful. In 1878, a hundred of them created
the American Woolens and Wool Association to lobby for a moderate wool
bill; but there is no evidence that the lobby survived its infancy.[31] Counteror-
ganization was futile, for the NAWM alone could deliver.

The National Association of Wool Growers (NAWG) was hardly more
representative of the wool-raising branch than the NAWM was of the manufacturing branch. The NAWG represented the interests of wool growers "east
of the Mississippi and north of the Mason and Dixon line."[32] For example, the
association did not reflect the preferences of Iowa, one of whose senators opposed protection for wool-raising, nor of the South, the Southwest, Texas, or
California, where the cost of maintaining a sheep was one-eighth or less the
cost in New England or New York.

The American Iron and Steel Association (AISA) was no different. At its
second founding, in 1874, several rail manufacturers organized a parallel association of rolling-mill owners located east of Pittsburgh, Pennsylvania. In
1882 and again in 1884, a large group of New England members demanded
that the AISA move to have coal, iron ore, and semifinished materials placed

on the free list. Although this was not surprising, it was to no avail. In general, the association privileged the smelters located near the rich beds of Bessemer ore on the shore of Lake Superior, at the expense of the seaboard establishments that had to import their ore from Cuba, Elba, and Spain and pay a duty on it.[33] Finally, AISA was not representative of the opinion of its most successful members, such as Andrew Carnegie and Abraham Hewitt, who openly asserted their disbelief in the necessity of high tariffs.[34]

Why did the politicians condone such undemocratic practices? The politicians had an interest in helping the associations stabilize tariff-making. The tariff, a burning issue before the Civil War, might be reignited at any time. More important, the tariff was the main source of federal revenue; as such, it was a recurring item on the Congressional agenda, since every change in the business cycle affected the revenue and called for revision.[35] The party in power could not afford political malpractice.

The party most sympathetic to the plight of the trade associations was the Republican party. The major associations in the United States established a privileged relationship with Republican leaders. The woolens manufacturers were almost all Republican, and most of them were politically active and powerful in their communities. In the case of the iron and steel association, the connection was decidedly overt. In 1886, the AISA campaigned against and defeated the previous Democratic chairman of the Ways and Means Committee, William R. Morrison of Illinois. B. F. Jones of Pittsburgh, a prominent figure in the AISA, was chairman of the 1884 Republican National Convention. In 1888, the position passed to Matthew Quay, the political boss of Pennsylvania, who had raised $3 million for the Republicans' war chest.[36]

Protectionists chose the Republican party for instrumental, not ideological, reason. The GOP harbored a larger protectionist faction than the Democrats. In addition, the GOP dominated postwar politics; of the twenty-six years between 1861 and 1887, the GOP controlled the House for sixteen, and the Senate and Presidency for twenty-four. The protectionists thus enjoyed a de facto monopoly on representation. But the protectionists were quite willing to support the Democratic protectionist faction led by Randall—indeed, a Republican district had sent Randall to Congress. As Ida Tarbell put it, "[the protectionists'] great desire was that both parties should agree to protection as the American system, [and that] the question should practically be taken out of politics."[37] Until 1887, protectionist forces were not compelled to settle in favor of one party or the other.

THE UNEXPLAINED RESIDUAL

The tariff was a transpartisan issue; yet it was not a consensual one. In Congress, the majority faction of the Democrats and the minority faction of the Republicans consistently voted against the tariff, which introduced a dissonant note into a process otherwise dominated by logrolling. In fact, despite the efforts of trade associations to suppress intrasectoral conflict, the efforts of the compacts to overcome intersectoral conflict, and the monopolization of the channels of access to policymaking by the trade associations in complicity with the members of the Ways and Means Committee, there was an irreducible residue of discontent. The reverse would surprise us, since trade is fundamentally a redistributive issue, incapable of drawing universal support on its own.

It is remarkable, however, to see the extent to which the postbellum policy process was successful in suppressing or neutralizing dissent. The tariff may have attracted its regular contingent of opposition on the floor of Congress; but this opposition was merely symbolic, since the process was entirely controlled by rent seekers. Whenever the Ways and Means Committee was in Republican hands, to get a protectionist tariff adopted, the Republican leadership relied on its own majority alone or, when necessary, extended the advantages of protection to the Randall faction. As long as the Democratic leadership would not make protection an issue of partisan discipline, the Randall faction incurred no penalty for cooperating with the Republicans.[38] Whenever the Democrats controlled Ways and Means, no tariff legislation was ever passed. Typically, the committee reported a bill to reduce the tariff, which would then be defeated on the House floor by the Democrat-protectionist minority in alliance with the Republicans. Thus, the bill never reached the Senate. This happened three times between 1875 and 1881, and three more times between 1883 and 1887.

The Executive

The executive branch played no specific role in formulating trade policy in the United States in this period. The Reciprocity Treaty, signed with Canada in 1854, was denounced in 1866. The administration tried to sign subsequent treaties, with no success. A winning majority in Congress could not be mustered for a reciprocity policy because this policy was openly designed to favor export-oriented manufacturers at the expense of agriculture. Of all the treaties successfully negotiated before 1890, only the Mexican treaty was approved by Congress; even then no positive action was ever taken to provide enabling legislation. Domestic opposition to the treaty was strong and could have been predicted, since, according to the treaty, almost all Mexican products that would have been authorized to enter the United States duty-free were agricultural: beef, barley, coffee, fresh fruits, raw hides, hemp, sugar, and nonmanufactured leaf tobacco. By contrast, almost all U.S. products that would have been allowed to enter Mexico duty-free were manufactured: locomotive engines and rolling stock, machinery, sewing machines, steel bars for mines, crude petroleum, and some farm products. Enabling legislation was thus opposed by the tobacco-growing or sugar-producing states, Virginia, South Carolina, North Carolina, Maryland, Kentucky, and Louisiana, on the grounds that these states would directly suffer from Mexican competition. The legislation was opposed by the NAWM and the AISA on the grounds that reciprocity opened a breach in the protective system.[39]

The Policy Outcome

According to hypothesis 5.7, spillover is the usual correlate of pressure politics, because the logic of interest accommodation calls for complicating the toolbox. This hypothesis is not confirmed by tariff-making in the postbellum United States. The reason lies in the gigantic size of the American market, which allowed incremental generalization of protection to become a unique solution to problems encountered by a majority of the domestic industries.

Pressure politics makes policy orientation highly sensitive to events of sectoral scope. In chapter five, I formulated two hypotheses about the orientation of the trade policy, both of them observable in the present case. Hypothesis 5.1 predicts a correlation between trade-policy orientation and business cycle. Hypothesis 5.2, which predicts that policy outcome reflects the preferences of the best organized interests, will be discussed first.

Did organization pay off? I tried to devise a test that could help us answer this question systematically. The oral testimony of all the witnesses who appeared before the Tariff Commission in 1882 was coded according to type and degree of interest organization represented by each witness. Witnesses for each product considered before the Tariff Commission were grouped in one of four categories, those representing (1) themselves, an individual firm, or several firms; (2) a local, regional, or sectional industry organized as a trade association or a local organization; (3) a nationwide, nonorganized industry, usually authorized by a petition; (4) a national trade association. Testimony was also differentiated according to whether a witness favored more protection or less (thus making eight subcategories). Finally, the policy outcome for each witness's request was coded according to whether the request was granted. An ordinary least-squares regression of the policy outcome was then run on these variables. The results, shown in table 7.1, provide strong evidence that industries that were organized as trade associations were more likely to obtain what they wanted than were more loosely organized industries, local organizations, or individual firms. Most interestingly, the results are indifferent to the orientation of the trade interest. Fewer trade associations asked for reductions than for increases (seven against fourteen), but with comparable effectiveness. Finally, the results seem to be indifferent to the fact that the 1883 tariff resulted in an overall reduction of customs revenue—most duties were lowered.

TABLE 7.1
Duties Regressed against Requests Made at Tariff Hearings by Oral Witnesses
Differentiated by Trade Orientation and Degree of Organization, 1883

Variable	Expected sign	Coefficient	t-value
Protectionists:			
nationwide trade association	+	0.2826	(3.54)*
industrywide ad hoc delegation	+	−0.1388	(−1.06)
local organization	+	0.1058	(2.35)
individual firm	+	−0.0505	(−1.92)
Nonprotectionists:			
nationwide trade association	−	−0.2666	(−2.74)*
industrywide ad hoc delegation	−	0.3411	(2.01)
local organization	−	−0.0600	(−0.85)
individual firm	−	0.0053	(0.18)
Constant		0.5137	(8.65)*
Number of observations		146	
R-squared		0.190	

* significant at the 0.01 level.

Coding rules:
    The basic unit of observation is the testimony, not the product. Approximately 100 witnesses referred to thousands of products. The coding rule, therefore, had to reflect the condition that a single witness could address more than one product and different witnesses could address overlapping baskets of products. For example, assume that five witnesses testified on behalf of the same trade association in favor of a higher tariff on 100 products. Assume, further, that three additional witnesses—two protectionists and a free trader—each representing his own firm, followed suit, the two protectionists singling out product "a" and the free trader singling out product "b." The coding in such a case would be the following:

observation$_{01}$ (100-basket): TA-Pro. = 1; 0 for other variables

observation$_{02}$ (product a): TA-Pro. = 1; Indiv.-FT = 2; 0 for other variables

observation$_{03}$ (product b): TA-Pro. = 1; Indiv.-Pro = 1; 0 for other variables.

    The dependent variable is the policy outcome. An outcome reflecting the protectionists' demand was coded "1"; an outcome reflecting the nonprotectionists' demand was coded "0"; an outcome compromising between the two sides was coded "0.5."

    Sources: For hearings, U.S. House of Representatives, *Report of the Tariff Commission*, 1882. For actual rates, both preceding and following the tariff revision, Young (1874); *Comparison of the Customs Law of 1883* (1890).

Hypothesis 5.1 (the correlation between trade policy orientation and the business cycle) was tested by Gallarotti.[40] During the period under study, the tariff was revised four times and the correlation is indeed observed in all four cases: tariff reductions in 1870, 1872, and 1883 were preceded by a boom in business, whereas the increase in 1875 succeeded a slump. Although these results accord with our predictions, there are two caveats. One, fiscal constraint makes the results somewhat spurious; and two, the use of customs revenues as a proxy for actual levels of protection makes the results unreliable.

The first caveat concerns fiscal constraint. Tariff revisions were not called for as a response to producers' demands, but for fiscal reasons. The effect of prosperity was to increase imports and thus government revenues. The effect of a slump was the opposite. Since revenue accruing from customs duties represented more than 50 percent of total government receipts, customs revenues had to be adjusted to the business cycle—upward in periods of lull, downward in periods of boom.

The second caveat, that the aggregate measure used to estimate the level of protection actually measures customs revenues and not actual levels of protection, compounds the predictive difficulty. Two kinds of duties were imposed, protective duties and "duties for revenue." The latter were imposed on products grown in the United States in small quantity or not at all—sugar, coffee, tea and spices. In consequence, the Committee on Ways and Means had some room in which to maneuver. By adjusting the various rates, the committee could simultaneously reduce the total revenue generated by the tariff while maintaining (or sometimes increasing) the effective level of protection. Taussig argues that such was the case with the "reductions" of 1870 and 1883. The only documented reduction in protection, which occurred in 1872, took the form of a 10 percent reduction across the board. Note that the second caveat is not specific to the United States, but plagues all longitudinal and cross-national comparisons. In light of these two caveats, the evidence in favor of the business-cycle hypothesis must still be considered tentative.

There is a third aspect of the policy outcome that fits the hypothesis of pressure politics. In their study of the U.S. tariff in 1870, the only cross-sector analysis of the tariff available for the period, Baack and Ray found a significant association between (final) consumer goods and higher tariffs.[41] Baack and Ray interpreted this result as evidence of pressure politics, a process that makes consumers more vulnerable than producers to exploitation. Unfortunately, the fact that Baack and Ray used nominal (as opposed to effective) rates as their dependent variable renders the test inconclusive. Their findings may simply be a manifestation of the widespread practice of granting manufacturers both protective duties and compensatory duties (the latter reflect the negative impact of duties on raw materials or semifinished goods).[42] Still, the fact that manufacturers felt free to pass on to the final consumer the compounded cost of upstream tariffs is, in itself, evidence of the apathy of that consumer. The case is compatible with, but not reducible to, pressure politics.

The post-Civil War tariff was a case of logrolling. Because U.S. farmers were indifferent to the tariff, policymaking was captured by sectors. The policy reflected both cross-sectoral variations in organization and changes in the business cycle. In Britain, to which we now turn, we find the opposite case.

Britain

The Policy Process

Between 1860 and 1914, the British tariff was stripped of its protective content and turned exclusively into a source of revenue. Most of the explanations proposed for Britain's unflinching adherence to free trade focus either on the competitiveness of British industry or on the ideological commitment of British public opinion to laissez-faire.[43] Neither the economic nor the cultural propositions, however, are fully convincing; by 1880, many industries were clamoring for protection against foreign competition and disturbing the free-trade consensus. Continued free trade was bought at the price of a dramatic change in the nature of the policy process. In 1881, the tariff-making process in Britain was switched over from executive politics to party politics. By severing the link between trade policy and the international treaty system, then turning trade policy into a purely domestic issue, Gladstone, as the leader of the Liberals, ensured that successive British governments remained loyal to free trade. I first discuss the existing explanations, then I present my own interpretation.

ECONOMIC AND CULTURAL EXPLANATIONS

Economic and cultural explanations point to evidence that is highly similar. In 1860, Britain was the hegemon of world trade. British industry enjoyed higher levels of labor productivity than did industry on the Continent or in North America.[44] Britain's share of world trade was about twice that of any other country.[45] Protection had lost all domestic support. Even the ineffectual silk industry was willing to settle for an indirect subsidy, a derogation of the application of the Factory Acts, an industrywide statute that limited the labor of women and children.[46] Free trade commanded widespread support, in part because it was associated with the twenty years of unparalleled economic expansion that followed repeal of the Corn Laws in 1846. Free trade appeared to be a well-tested policy; the burden of proving otherwise naturally fell to its critics.

Though faithful to the reality of 1860, this exquisite picture rapidly became outmoded. As early as 1865–66, the ribbon, silk, glove, and watch industries were protesting against free trade. By 1869–71, they had been joined by manufacturers of straw hats and bonnets, boots and shoes, woolens and worsted, and iron. In 1881, the wisdom of unilateral free trade was questioned by manufacturers of refined sugar, jewelry, steel, hardware and cutlery, tinplates, guns, bicycles, earthenware, farming, and shipping.[47] The Royal Commission of 1886 heard testimony to the same effect from manufacturers of iron and steel, refined sugar, carriages, paper, watches, agricultural implements, wood spirit, and growers of rye and timber.[48] The first organized expression of this backlash came from the "Revivers of British Industry," founded in 1869, which disbanded after two years. A Reciprocity Free Trade Association took up the task, but it too soon disbanded. The National Fair Trade League, created in 1881, managed to exist until 1891.[49] Had the policy process been responsive to sectoral pressure, as it was in the United States after the Civil War, free trade would no doubt have suffered exceptions. Yet, it did not; the reason rests with the policy process and its nature.

FROM EXECUTIVE POLITICS TO PARTY POLITICS

Between 1860 and 1881, the British tariff was bound by two tariff treaties—the comprehensive Anglo-French Agreement (1860) and a minor agreement with Austria. Thus, duties on products traded with these countries were set and frozen for the duration of the treaties. The British tariff was also bound by an array of most-favored-nation (MFN) treatment agreements which extended to Britain's other trade partners the duties set by the tariff treaties. The technical distinction between a tariff treaty and an MFN agreement is an important one in terms of policymaking. A tariff treaty requires the parties involved to negotiate specifically designated duties and forego the right to alter the duties; whereas an MFN agreement entails no real bargaining, only the promise not to discriminate against each other's goods. The agreement places no limit on the discretion of the governments to change their respective tariffs. The core of the British tariff system thus was the Anglo-French Agreement, signed in 1860 for a ten-year period and renewed for another decade in 1871. William Gladstone, then chancellor of the exchequer, and Cobden, his main negotiator, were ill disposed toward tariff treaties. They believed that free trade was best defended by avoiding the "haggling and higgling" of diplomacy.[50] However, for security reasons, they agreed to the Anglo-French Agreement; they wanted to reduce the tension between Britain and France after the annexation of Nice and Savoy by the French. Had the tariff negotiations fallen through, Gladstone would still have included in his domestic budget proposal the reduced duties that Britain conceded to France in the treaty. The treaty thus made no difference with respect to the orientation of British trade policy, although it made a big difference to the policy process (which thus became executive politics) and not party politics. Almost immediately, the security threat lost its salience; but, for reasons unrelated to security, the international engagement remained for ten years and in 1871 was reconducted for another ten years.

This situation was not optimal for the free traders, since executive politics is a process that is somewhat vulnerable to particular interests. The reciprocal nature of the policy process, according to which reductions are exchanged for reductions or withdrawn in retaliation for unilateral defection, invites state intervention in the setting of the tariff, thereby creating opportunities for rent seeking. Under executive politics, export-oriented interests—which, under other circumstances, would support laissez-faire and abstain from pursuing their sectoral interests—have a vested interest in requesting the executive to pursue an activist economic diplomacy to open or preserve foreign markets. Hence, as Britain's trade partners turned protectionist with the onset of the depression of the 1880s, export-oriented industries became sensitive to protectionist demand for "fair trade." Many export-oriented sectors suffered from foreign tariffs, losing market share not only in protected markets, but in neutral markets as well. For instance, many witnesses before the Royal Commission of 1886 complained that high tariff walls allowed European and American competitors to charge monopolistic prices at home and dispose of their surplus abroad, at cost price, thus cutting into the profit margins of their British rivals and sometimes underselling them outright. Potential support for countervailing and retaliatory duties in Britain in the 1880s was broad, extending far beyond the small group of ineffective producers. Executive politics tended to blur the sharp distinction between free trade and protection, merging import-sensitive and export-oriented producers into a heterogeneous coalition for "fair trade." Hence, there was the possibility that executive politics would accommodate a pocket of rent. Joseph Chamberlain, as president of the Board of Trade under the Gladstone government and still a free trader, foresaw this undesirable outcome with an acumen worthy of leading, modern rational-choice theorists:

> [A]s [protectionists'] individual interests will be direct, important and capable of easy organization they are not unlikely to outweigh as a political force, the more widespread, indirect, and less readily appreciated national interests which would be prejudiced by any reversal of our Free Trade policy.[51]

Dogmatic free traders like Gladstone thus had good reasons for disliking tariff treaties.

Further, executive politics entailed tampering with fiscal resources as British exporters tried to talk the executive into exchanging the existing tariff for revenue on wine to secure access to wine-producing countries. During negotiations with France in 1871, the Bradford (England) Chamber of Commerce suggested the British government deter higher duties on English textiles by threatening retaliation in the form of higher duties on French wine and silk. The late 1870s witnessed mounting support for a proposal to use wine duties to overcome hostile tariffs in wine-exporting countries.[52]

As long as the tariff was in force, however, all British governments were bound by its terms, and tariff-making was subject to the logic of international bargaining. In the late 1870s, at a time when support for reciprocity was rising among export-oriented industries, the Conservative government appointed a select committee to inquire into the operation of the wine duties and their possible use as a bargaining chip in negotiations with wine-producing countries. The committee recommended the reduction, but Gladstone and the Liberals returned to power before any action had been taken on the committee's report. Still, even Gladstone and the Liberals could not escape the bargaining dynamic. Gladstone endorsed the committee's report. He requested from Parliament a one-year authority to bargain wine duties down in his negotiations with France, which was granted; but the year ended before an agreement could be concluded. Again, in May 1881, the Gladstone government collectively agreed to threaten the French with retaliation. Regardless of their dogmatic beliefs, and like any other government, the Liberals were forced to extract a "good deal" from the French.

Being a doctrinaire liberal, Gladstone was unhappy with this state of affairs. He saw that executive politics could not keep free trade unadulterated, and that an end to the parliamentary consensus was the price to pay for maintaining doctrinal purity. He saw a unique electoral opportunity as well. By freeing the trade issue from its international entanglements and promoting it as a partisan issue, Gladstone would score electoral points. Free trade was still popular in spite of the growing stream of discontent; it had the support of industrial pillars such as cotton, coal, traditional machine tools, shipbuilding, and the alkali section of the chemical industry. Merchants, bankers, and insurers also were staunch advocates of free trade. Most important, free trade was popular with the majority of the voters. The mass base of support for free trade was the British workers, for whom the memory of the "bigger loaf campaign" of the 1840s against the agrarians was still vivid and could be revived at any time. As heirs to the doctrine of Cobden, the Liberals found in free trade an issue that would isolate the Conservatives at the polls if the latter gave in to the siren call of protectionism. An incidental advantage of recasting the trade debate in terms of mutually exclusive principles would be a return of the export-oriented sectors to the free-trade camp, which had temporarily been seduced by talk of "fair trade" and "reciprocity."

Hypothesis 4.1 states that if a mass-based group is unhappy with the orientation of trade policy, it thus provides a political party with a unique electoral opportunity. Gladstone seized this opportunity. In Leeds, on October 7, 1881, in the middle of negotiations, Gladstone delivered a speech in which he stated his "thorough-going opposition to retaliation and protection generally," undoing in two hours the bargaining position it had taken the Foreign Office two years to consolidate.[53] Negotiations with the French did not recover. Since, for all practical purposes, the Cobden-Chevalier Treaty was the only link Britain had with the tariff treaty system, Britain ceased to engage actively in setting tariff rates and was content thereafter to sign and honor MFN agreements. Executive politics was terminated; parties had regained full control over tariff-making.

The Conservatives understood very well the scope and nature of this electoral challenge by the Liberals. Under the rules of executive politics, more and more Conservatives had become receptive to pleas for protectionism. As early as 1869, two conservative MPs had been active in the Revivers of British Industry. The leaders of the party refused to commit themselves, thus enabling individual MPs to advocate the interests of their constituents. Lord Salisbury adopted the position that "each case could only be dealt with its own merits." He affected sympathy with the demand for retaliation but would not commit himself to pursue that course in Parliament unless the partisans of fair trade presented him with an overwhelming public demand—a most unlikely event.[54] In short, the Conservative leadership was happy with the slack afforded by the existing executive process, for it allowed them to dodge a potentially divisive issue.

After 1881, the pragmatic attitude of the Conservative leadership became untenable. The party needed a statement of policy in response to the Liberals' rhetorical onslaught. At first, party leaders sought a syncretic solution, aptly summarized by B. H. Brown:

> What was needed was a statement of policy, which, while freeing the party from the charge of protection, would yet permit a measure of experimentation in constituencies where "Fair Trade winds" were stirring.[55]

The ambiguity of this position became harder to maintain after the Conservatives reassumed power in 1885. The Conservative Salisbury government tried to delay the problem by appointing a commission of inquiry.[56] Nevertheless, in 1885, for the first time fair trade became an electoral issue. The Liberals had little difficulty adopting an unequivocal position on the issue; but the Conservatives remained hopelessly muddled. Sixty to eighty Conservative deputies were committed to fair trade, while the rest of the party straddled the issue.[57] Fortunately for the Conservatives, trade was not the central issue of the 1885 election, which was fought mainly over the issues of Ireland and Joseph Chamberlain's "unauthorized program." The roots of the party's defeat were firmly planted, however; it was only a matter of time before the trade issue brought down the Conservative leadership, forced by its rank and file to champion a cause fundamentally unpopular with the voters. Gladstone had initiated a partisan dynamic which, although it would not come fully to fruition until 1907, already in 1881 ensured that tariff-making would not soon become a refuge for particular interests.

Lobbies

Evidence for the absence of rent seeking in Britain during this period can be found in the relative weakness of special-interest lobbying. British trade interests were not as efficiently organized to formulate and push for their trade interests as were their American counterparts. A systematic survey of British industrial organizations shows that relatively few national trade associations and compacts existed. The lobbying scene was dominated instead by public-interest organizations.

In the British case, the only expression of trade lobbying available is the Royal Commission's Inquiry into *The Depression of Trade and Industry* (1886).[58] The commission sent to the chambers of commerce and "other Associations representing the interests of the trading and industrial classes" a series of questions on, among other things, how British and foreign trade policies had contributed to the depression and how the depression might be remedied. The commission received responses from 57 chambers and 32 associations. Among the 32 associations, 21 were local and 11 were national. Four among the 11 national associations expressed no particular opinion concerning trade policy, either because they had received no authority from their members (the Alkali Manufacturers' Association and the Mining Association of Great Britain) or because they were strictly domestic industries. There were thus only seven nationwide trade associations with an expressed trade interest: the British Sugar Refiners' Association, the Papermakers' Association, the Starch Trade Association, the Tinplate Manufacturers' Association, the Wire Trade Association, the General Shipowners' Society, and the Agricultural Engineers' Association. The absence from this list of the three pillars of British industry—textiles, coal, and iron—is significant. Overall, the dominant mode of business organization in Britain in 1886 was not the national trade association but the local organization.

Local organizations fell into one of two categories. Either they represented several trades equally, as did most chambers of commerce, or they were dominated by one trade, as were local trade associations and certain chambers of commerce (Manchester, Sheffield, or Batley). By the end of the century, most of the chambers of commerce belonged to the former category—with a heterogeneous membership. They were incapable of playing a role in the trade debate because they were divided and unable to take a stance (5 were in that position),[59] because they had delegated that authority to their product-by-product sections (6),[60] or because they had committed themselves to some remedy more general than either free trade or protection. Such remedies included the removal of hostile tariffs through diplomacy, improved consular assistance, better regulation of railway rates, improved technical education, lower wages, creation of a Ministry of Commerce and Industry, and so forth (34). Only 12 chambers out of 57 took a stand on the trade issue, 4 for free trade, 8 for protection.[61] This low figure suggests that the aggregate effect in a system of representation based on chambers of commerce is biased toward preserving the status quo, since absence of agreement leads to inaction. Action, if any, is feasible only on issues of general interest to commerce and industry.

The second category of local organization with homogeneous membership was ill equipped to cope with intraindustrial conflicts of interest. Both the coal industry and the iron and steel industries were organized into regional groups, which were unable to coordinate their views.[62] The truth is that most existing trade associations were created to deal with matters other than trade, mostly price-fixing. Combinations were more effective when concentrated locally. The Alkali Manufacturers' Association, formed in 1866 to regulate the price of soda, was concentrated in Liverpool; the Tinplate Manufacturers' Association was exclusively Welch. Because coal mining and iron manufacturing were widely distributed geographically, the national organs of these two industries, the Mining Association of Great Britain and the British Iron Trade Association, were not responsible for price-fixing; rather, their regional units were. Even these local associations, however, were unable to articulate a position regarding the tariff. Among the three local associations of ironmasters, two declared themselves unable to state an opinion with respect to trade policy. The third suggested, instead, the development of a customs union with the other members of the empire, carefully dodging the issue of how a tariff-less Britain could be part of such a union. The Birmingham Chamber of Commerce, in contrast, took a definite—protectionist—stand on the issue.

This analysis of the 1886 inquiry establishes that British lobbies were weak and inefficient. But what explains this weakness? Certainly there was no lack of demand for protection. As we have seen, the early years of the depression of the 1880s witnessed significant agitation in favor of protection. Another argument, inspired by the institutionalist school, would point out that British industry was constrained by organizational choices made earlier, which now precluded effective reorganization. A comparison of British and U.S. industrial development is quite telling in this respect. British industry, like U.S. industry, originally developed in a pattern of local specialization. In Britain, since specialization yielded high returns, early penetration of rapidly expanding foreign markets strongly reinforced district specialization. In the United States, industrialization followed the westward drift of the frontier, leaving in its wake a more dispersed industrial implantation.[63] In addition, differences in trade policy and transportation costs reinforced the U.S.–British divergence. Given two such different modes of industrial development, the argument could be made that the local mode of business-interest mediation in 1880s Britain was a natural reflection of its concentrated implantation, whereas the functional mode of industrial mediation in the United States was a reflection of the need to overcome geographic dispersion.

Certainly, such is the case. What the argument fails to answer, is, why did British localism not bend in the face of adversarial change? Inertia furnishes a compelling explanation, provided British industrialists had remained altogether unorganized at the national level. They did organize, however, though following a pattern incongruent with a pressure model of politics. Rather, the pattern reflected the implicit, albeit unmistakable, partisan nature of the policy process.

A test case for the partisan politics hypothesis is the fate of the antibounty campaign launched by the British Sugar Refiners' Association. The BSRA had the rare distinction in 1880 of having organized a planter-refiner compact à l'américaine. Both West Indian planters of cane sugar and British refiners were severely battered by the competition from beet sugar, which most continental governments subsidized on a grand scale. Organized in separate committees, planters and refiners, in 1882, combined to found the National Anti-Bounty League. The workers involved in the refining of sugar organized themselves as the Workmen's National Association for the Abolition of Foreign Sugar Bounties. All of these organizations pressed the same demand: imposition of a countervailing duty, to be followed by an invitation to foreign producers to remove the duty on sugar, in exchange for an abolition of the bounties. Organized to the last man and advancing a reasonable request, the industry, judged by American standards, should have stood a good chance of seeing its plans ratified; but such was not the outcome. The Gladstone government branded the request "protectionist" and turned it into a partisan issue. Responding in kind, the industry sought the support of public opinion and the Conservative party, and solicited help from the National Fair Trade League. The workers, for their part, appealed to the Trades Union Congress and, after being turned down there, appealed to the London Trades' Council and other working-class societies.[64] In 1887, the industry succeeded in forming a "parliamentary committee." Though unwilling to join the fray, leaders of the Conservative party announced that they would consider the industry's request and called for an international conference. After three inconclusive sessions, the Conservative government announced that it would present an antibounty bill to the House of Commons. The government, however, ended up postponing a vote and withdrawing the bill after the Liberal opposition launched an all-out free-trade campaign. The upshot was that Britons continued to sweeten their tea with freely admitted, bounty-fed sugar. As B. H. Brown aptly put it, "the question of bounties was not one that could be dealt with 'above party' as the [Conservative] Government hoped."[65]

The sugar episode illustrates the impossibility of reaching a pragmatic compromise on issues related to trade when the policy spectrum is successfully split between the antagonistic principles of free trade and protection. By forcing the split, the Liberals banished from serious consideration a whole panoply of fair-trade and reciprocity measures that might otherwise have attracted support from a broad range of manufacturers. The split also obviated the need for industrywide associations. What was needed, rather, was an organization similar to the old Anti-Corn Law League, with its simple, general message able to reach beyond the industries' usual audience and capable of linking the interests of protectionists to those of the Conservative party. To that study, we now turn.

Parties

Even in its embryonic state of 1886, party politics in Britain had visible consequences for business organization. The protectionists, shifting their lobbying from the sector to the factor, created in 1881 the National Fair Trade League, whose mission was to popularize retaliatory duties and preferential trade with colonies.[66] The National Fair Trade League endeavored, with little success, to show that a large number of workers were sympathetic to fair trade (as hypothesis 4.1 calls for). Protectionists' attempts to organize included electioneering committees at the district level, since, in the end, policy outcome would depend on which party was in power. The National Fair Trade League's role was to help Conservative local unions select Conservative protectionist candidates and get those candidates elected. It is worth noting that the partisan process did not alter the local base of business organization, but actually reinforced it.

The protectionists could not persuade party leaders that fair trade had a mass following, and thus were not noticeably successful in getting the Conservatives to articulate their demands. The attempt in 1881 to create an organization of workmen and "gentlemen" and use it to infiltrate the Trades Union Congress was a resounding failure. With the possible exception of the sugar industry, the working class remained wedded to the "big loaf" cry of the earlier Anti-Corn League. As a result, the Conservative party was not persuaded to articulate fully the protectionists' demands. To be sure, the party system witnessed a rise in voting discipline in 1881 (see appendix three, figure A3.3). These two votes strongly suggest the trade issue's capacity to polarize the House of Commons along party lines. Still, the trade issue was not, however, at the top of everyone's agenda, a state of affairs attested to by the low level of participation (fewer than half the MPs took sides). Yet, trade definitely was a partisan issue; the Liberal side of the spectrum was disciplined and ready to strike down any proposal hinting at protection.

The Fair Trade League's difficulties in converting the Conservative leadership to protection hindered its fund-raising effectiveness, since it had so little to show in return for the costs incurred by its contributors. Similarly, the Liberals had difficulty convincing import- and export-oriented sectors to mobilize against an enemy viewed as weak.

The Executive

Initially during this period, Great Britain became deeply involved in trade diplomacy. After signing the Cobden-Chevalier Treaty, many state officials showed a keen interest in maintaining the tariff-treaty system. Sir Louis Mallet, until 1872 a high-ranking official on the Board of Trade and with the India Office thereafter, regarded the promotion of tariff treaties as the key to establishing multilateral free trade. In 1875, Chancellor of the Exchequer Northcote suggested organizing a European congress for the purpose of negotiating an international tariff union. That same year, Charles Kennedy, another high-ranking official with the Foreign Office, proposed circumventing the threat of foreign protectionism by renewing trade treaties with France, Austria-Hungary, Italy, Spain, and Portugal and by offering concessions on wine duties. And in 1876, the Foreign Office considered a German offer to sign a tariff treaty if the British government would reduce its duties on imported spirits.[67]

As party politics assumed pride of place, the Foreign Office disengaged itself from international commitments. We have already noted that, by the early 1870s, Britain had signed tariff treaties with France and Austria and most-favored-nation agreements with all its other major trade partners. In the 1880s, however, Britain renounced the use of tariff treaties, content to protest upward revisions and request MFN treatment. By the end of the 1880s, Britain had only MFN agreements with her major trade partners. The government had tariff treaties only with minor partners, peripheral countries such as Rumania (1880), Serbia (1880), Montenegro (1882), and Spain (1886).[68] Clearly, the British government was moving away from trade intervention.

The argument can be made that, in the long run, the state's withdrawal from active diplomacy ultimately hurt the prospects of free trade. Fair trade and reciprocity are not inherently protectionist practices; free trade might have been better served had the British executive used its diplomacy tools to foil protectionism on the Continent. The pragmatism and fine-tuning required for the diplomatic promotion of free trade, however, could be accomplished only through a policy process dominated by an autonomous executive. The intricacies of such negotiations are incompatible with party politics.

The Policy Outcome

In 1860, Britain eliminated all protectionist duties while maintaining a tariff intended exclusively to raise fiscal revenue. Most duties were levied on items not produced in Britain. All the duties levied on products produced in Britain were instituted to offset an existing domestic excise tax.[69] This situation remained unchanged until 1914. In sum, British trade policy was parsimonious with respect to the policy tools it adopted (as hypothesis 5.7 would predict). With respect to policy orientation, British trade policy was neither responsive to the business cycle nor to cross-sectoral variations in organization. This result is compatible with both executive politics (hypothesis 5.5) and party politics (hypothesis 5.4), but not with pressure politics (hypotheses 5.1 and 5.2). However, hypothesis 5.3, which states that the policy outcome should reflect the profile of the party in power, is not observable, since the profile of the Conservative party was not clearly articulated but rather was deliberately evasive. Upon winning the 1885 election, for instance, the Conservatives appointed a commission of inquiry into "The Depression of Trade and Industry." This result confirmed the aforementioned embryonic nature of party politics in the 1880s. It is not until the next period that the partisan process reached full maturity.

France

The Policy Process

The trade-policy process of France's Second Empire lasted well beyond the end of that government in 1870. The network of bilateral trade agreements that linked France to the free-trade system of the nineteenth century was not dismantled until 1892. (The Cobden-Chevalier Treaty formally expired in 1882, but the French Parliament unilaterally renewed it until 1892, the date all the other treaties were due to expire.) The period under review in this chapter therefore begins about 1870 and ends with the failure of the protectionists to consolidate the oversized logrolling coalition necessary for overthrowing the "conventional tariff." Meanwhile, trade policy was dominated by free traders. How could the imperial legacy last so long?

The Second Empire was authoritarian. Technically, the government was not responsible to the parliament until the last year of the regime. In the area of trade policy, the emperor and his ministers held sole authority to conclude trade agreements with foreign governments and thereby to modify tariff rates. Until 1860, the emperor refused to use this prerogative, preferring instead to involve the senate and the elected *Corps législatif* in the process of reducing the tariff. Both chambers, however, were dominated by a coalition of protectionist interests that counted among their ranks textile manufacturers, cattlemen, colliers, ironmasters, and, most important, the charcoal-iron industry and its fuel suppliers—the owners of large wooded estates.[70] After three frustrated attempts (1853, 1855, and 1859) to sway the *Corps législatif* toward free trade, the emperor finally altered the rules of the game in favor of the free traders. Availing himself of his extraordinary powers, he opened secret

negotiations with the British government and, on January 23, 1860, announced the signing of a ten-year agreement to remove all prohibitions on
imports and lower import duties on all manufactured goods. This move was
soon followed by negotiation of similar treaties with most of France's other
trade partners and by a series of decrees abolishing import duties on most
primary products.[71]

It is clear that the policy process governing this unprecedented liberalization was one of executive dominance. Negotiations were kept secret from the
Corps législatif until the very end. Although a legislative debate and vote were
allowed three months after the January announcement, the scope of both was
restricted to a narrow aspect of the new policy.[72] The protectionists resorted to
civil disobedience, stirring up discontent among their workers—the only alternative left to them.[73] But the protest provided a unique opportunity for a
regime whose founding principle was the maintenance of public order. Representatives of the movement were summoned and served notice of the emperor's intention to jail all industrialists who tried to shut down their works or
entice their workers to commit acts of violence by other means. The protectionists immediately withdrew all petitions.

Tariff-making under the Second Empire, however, was not a case of executive politics, but one that falls outside the scope of the present theory. The
regime was authoritarian, and the theory applies only to democratic regimes.
The origins of executive dominance in 1860 cannot be found in the electorate, since there were no competitive elections. In the absence of competitive
elections, it is impossible to tell whether the emperor's decision found any
support among the electorate. Presumably, even authoritarian rulers have at
least some interest in anticipating popular sentiment; but the discretion such
rulers enjoy with respect to the agenda provides them with the capacity to
disregard popular dissatisfaction in the short term.

At its peak in 1860, dictatorship was progressively phased out as a result of
the emperor's decision to liberalize the regime. In 1867, deputies were granted
the right to challenge the government on a given policy and, at the close of
debate, to call for a vote. Then, in September 1869, the *Corps législatif* was
given full authority to make tariff decisions. Although the elected chamber regained its pre-1860 authority, thereby giving sectors the opportunity
to shape the content of the policy, this policy deviated little from its free-trade
orientation. By the end of the 1860s, the protectionists were effectively
isolated, incapable of organizing a solid coalition to reverse the liberal policy
of the empire. The Brame interpellation, intended to force the Ollivier government to renounce the Anglo-French Treaty in 1869–70, received only
thirty-two votes.[74] The collapse of the Second Empire and the coming to
power of a team of politicians devoted entirely to protection—Thiers as Chief
of the executive and Pouyer-Quertier as minister of commerce—did not affect
the outcome. The Third Republic thus presents a paradox: How could the

return to a policy process which, for all practical purposes, falls in the broad category of pressure politics, yield a free-trade outcome in the face of rising protectionism?

There are two reasons for this apparent paradox. One has to do with the economic consequences of the repeal of a rent. The reform of 1860 broke the back of the protectionist coalition by accelerating the conversion of the French iron industry from inefficient charcoal furnaces to more cost-effective coke furnaces.[75] With the disappearance of this rural metallurgy, whose interests were mingled with those of the owners of large estates, the protectionists lost their only secure outpost in the agrarian countryside. Moreover, in easing along this process of attrition, the empire adopted measures attractive to particular protectionists: a general reduction of freight costs; a program of drainage, reforestation, and clearing for cultivation; and loans to industry (forty million francs were lent at a low rate of interest to help specific factories update their equipment).[76] The empire thus had engineered a coalition of industrialists, importers, bankers, and the urban mob, among others, in support of a policy of cheap primary products.

The second reason for the paradox has to do with the conventional nature of the French tariff. Because the tariff was part of a web of commercial agreements, it could legally be renounced only on fixed dates, which meant that the tariff appeared on the political agenda only intermittently. Conveniently for the protectionists, the two most important conventions with Britain and Belgium could be renounced as early as December 1871. The protectionists, however, passed up this opportunity, and the tariff remained frozen for the next period.[77] Again in 1878–81, they failed to revoke the tariff. Only on the third attempt, in 1888–91, did the protectionists succeed in withdrawing France from all international commitments and reducing tariff-making to a strictly domestic affair. Meanwhile, the tariff could not be an issue between revisions, since reneging on international commitments was not an option.

The conventional tariff presented protectionists with another drawback. Lobbying was divided into two successive phases: first, adoption of the tariff by the legislature; and, second, negotiation of bilateral conventions with France's trading partners. The second phase was informed by a logic of give-and-take which, given the relative position of France at the high end of the tariff, invariably was biased toward tariff reductions. The protectionists, therefore, were placed at a perpetual disadvantage in the negotiation of trade treaties.

It is at this point that an apparent contradiction in the overall argument of this chapter needs to be addressed. In the study of Britain, I argue that Gladstone swept away the conventional tariff because that tariff gave too great an edge to particular interests. In the present section, I argue that particular French interests continued to be excluded from tariff-making because the conventional tariff denied them an edge. The contradiction is only apparent, however. The conventional tariff offered a third option besides free trade and protection, one entailing advocacy of "reciprocity" or "fair trade" as an issue, around which a constituency of mixed interests could be gathered. Whether fair trade is synonymous with free trade, or whether it is a code word for protectionism, depends on the observer. In Britain, where free trade had a popular base of support, fair trade smacked of protectionism. In France, where free trade enjoyed no such base, reciprocity was tantamount to free trade.

What was required to repeal the conventional tariff in France? The universal scope of the treaties meant that the skirmishing tactics at which small groups of protectionists usually excel were of little use. An industry could not hope to extract an advantageous tariff on its own. Nothing less than a universal (or transsectoral) coalition was necessary to defeat institutionally entrenched free traders. There were no means available to protectionists for mustering such a coalition. The partisan route was closed; no party wanted to endorse the protectionist project because there was no mass support for protection. The only workforce industrialists could expect to manipulate was a highly localized one subject to the same collective-action problem as the industrialists themselves. Workers were less important to the early governments of the Third Republic than the urban crowds from Paris and other large cities who were generally ill-disposed toward protection. As for agriculture, the farmers were not yet interested in protection. The Société des agriculteurs de France (SAF), the dominant agrarian association at the time, endorsed protection, but in 1880 it was still a fairly elite club, unrepresentative of the farm population.[78] Moreover, the conventional nature of the tariff deterred parties from investing in the tariff as an issue, since, if the partisan takeover were to fail, the party attempting it would be left with a nonissue for eight of the ten subsequent years. In any case, there was no guarantee that the existing government, if attacked on the tariff, would call an election during, or just prior to, the period for renegotiating the trade agreements.

Logrolling, the second possible means for reforming the policy process, was impractical. Two attempts at stabilizing the oversized logrolling coalition required to dismantle the conventional tariff failed. The first attempt was initiated by Thiers, in 1871, when protectionists were a small, disorganized group. As chief of the executive, well connected to the iron industry, Thiers sought to engineer a universal coalition of producers by subordinating renunciation of the treaties and an upward revision of the tariff to an extension of the principle of protection to primary products—wood, raw wool, silk cocoons, flax, hemp, oleaginous seeds, olive oil, beet sugar, and hides, among others. The attempt divided industrialists, many of whom refused to pay import duties on raw materials in order to benefit from protection on their finished goods, and they allied themselves with the free-trade camp to defeat Thiers' proposal.[79]

In 1880, leaders of the protectionist movement, seeking to resuscitate Thiers' universal coalition, made another attempt.[80] In February 1880, the agrarian bloc and the protectionist industrialist bloc of the legislative chamber made a deal: If the pro-industrialist deputies supported high duties on silk-worms and livestock, the farm bloc would support higher duties for manufactures. The bargain fell through, because the industrial deputies were unable to maintain discipline in their ranks.[81] The two main associations—the SAF, for the primary producers, and the *Association de l'industrie française* (AIF) for the manufacturers—could not reach a corporatist entente.[82] The two sides tried again when the Senate took up the bill. Less concerned about the popular vote than about their fellow deputies, the senators representing protectionist industrialists voted for the agricultural duties; this time, however, the agrarian side failed to maintain unity.[83] Indeed, the agrarians' stand was fraught with ambiguity. Golob recounts that a section of the SAF demanded reductions of the duties on agricultural machinery and on "the raw materials used by French mechanics and builders in order to maintain fair competition with foreign producers in the interest of French agriculture."[84]

The failure of the primary producers and the industrialists to institute a corporatist bargain capable of stabilizing a logrolling coalition was a direct reflection of the indifference of the parties. As I argue in chapter four, corporatism cannot survive in a competitive political environment; rather, it operates as part of the electoral strategy of either a dominant party or a dominant coalition. In 1871 and again in 1881, no party had developed an interest in stabilizing a trade dispute that was limited to two particular groups, manufacturers and a handful of affluent agrarians represented in the SAF. (The SAF was not then the public lobby it eventually became.) Logrolling in a nonstabilized political environment proved as futile for the lobbies as stone-rolling was for Sisyphus.

In sum, France suffered from executive hangover. The Second Empire, an unpopular dictatorship, had devised to the republic a policy process with properties and consequences similar to those encountered in executive politics: the orientation of a tariff that reflected the moderating influence of international negotiations, a tariff that could be modified only once every ten years (even then, the scope of interest organization necessary to modify the tariff substantially necessitated the services of a party). As of 1886, the protectionists had not found such a party. Deprived of a mass support base, they were unable to persuade an opposition party to champion protection and launch an ideological attack on the treaty system. Nor would they have been able to interest a dominant party (had one existed) in arranging a corporatist bargain conducive to pressure politics.

Lobbies

French industrial organization during this period resembled British organization more than it did American. Sectors were not organized effectively to push their trade preference through politics. This fact is all the more significant because, at an earlier time at least some of the sectors were quite well organized.

Business under the *Monarchie de juillet* was well organized. For example, in 1840, forgemasters from all parts of the country organized into a national *Comité des maîtres de forges* to check the government's free-trade vagaries. Because the franchise was so restricted, the Comité exercised influence mainly through election of individual ironmasters to the chamber. The Comité also used the press to turn public opinion against government projects. These organizational feats were probably unique to the forgemasters, who still used charcoal as their main fuel and could thus count on the widespread support of the landowners whose wood was used to make the charcoal. Another powerful tariff lobby was the *Comité des houillères*, created in 1851 to check imports of British coal. The machine builders were yet another group organized as a comité. Most other trades were concentrated in a single geographic area—winemaking in Bordeaux, cotton spinning in Alsace, linen in Lille, silk weaving in Lyon. Their interests were represented by local chambers of commerce and elected deputies.[85]

The *empire autoritaire* was able to loosen the grip of business organizations on trade policy by weakening the legislature and censoring the press; the emperor's decision, in 1860, to make the tariff conventional eliminated that grip altogether. With the tariff no longer on the parliamentary agenda, the nationwide organizations lost their raison d'être. Ironmasters then concentrated their efforts on price-fixing, a tactic regional associations were better equipped to deal with than was the *Comité des maîtres de forges*. Suddenly confronted by international competition, ironmasters developed divergent interests. Within the coke-iron industry, Le Creusot and Terrenoire took advantage of the new markets opened by the treaties in Central Europe. In contrast, Blanzy, Commentry-Fourchambault, and producers in the Nord and Pas-de-Calais continued to oppose the treaties while depending on local markets. The ironmasters comité was so divided that its leadership finally had to be reorganized in 1868, to avoid open conflict between its president, Schneider of Le Creusot, and a powerful rival member, de Wendel of Hayange (Nord).

A similar divergence occurred in the cotton textile industry, in the *Syndicat des industries cotonnières de l'Est*. The spinners and weavers of the Nord, Normandy, and the Vosges opposed the treaties, whereas the textile printers of Mulhouse and Rouen supported them. An attempt in 1869 to reconcile differences within the syndicat lasted only seven months, until the printers seceded and created the *Comité d'impression de l'Est*. Only the colliers seem to have maintained their comité.[86]

Organizational disarray is to be expected in a policy process dominated by an authoritarian executive.[87] When decisions are made by a small imperial coterie, it makes little business sense for industrialists to invest resources in maintaining nationwide trade associations. Personal contacts were probably

TABLE 7.2

Number of Witnesses, Differentiated by Organization, Who Appeared before the *Commission du tariff général des douanes*, 1878–79

Chamber of commerce	17
Local or sectional trade association (except Parisian)	13
Parisian trade association (member of *Union Nationale*)	17
Self-proclaimed delegate(s) of a local industry	7
Trade association	9
Self-proclaimed delegate(s) of a national industry	19
Transsectoral association	2

Sources: *Commission du tariff général des douanes* (1878–79). The transcripts were also published in various issues of the *Journal Officiel* from May 23, 1878 through June 14, 1879.

more useful to them, but the secret nature of the contacts makes investigation impossible.

Restoration of the powers of Parliament provided a check on the arbitrary actions of the state and should have provided renewed incentive for business to organize. A glance at the list of witnesses who appeared before the *Commission du tariff général des douanes* throughout 1878 and 1879 reveals the dominance of local organizations over national and recalls the British situation (see table 7.2).

If all self-proclaimed delegates are discounted and only organized interests considered, the ratio of national trade organizations to local organizations in France at the time was nine to forty-seven.[88] Another factor also recalls the British situation: the presence of national coalitions of interests organized along ideological lines—the protectionist *Association de l'industrie française* (AIF), founded in 1878; and the free-trade *Association pour la défense de la liberté commerciale*. Each was a tentative public-interest group; each sought to reach outside its member industries and use the press to turn public opinion against the other. In addition, the AIF orchestrated a national campaign of petitions to rally the working class to its cause. As in Britain, moreover, there was only one compact, which spanned the coal, iron and steel, and machinery industries. Although the French compact was more important economically and politically than the British sugar compact, the French compact was almost as ineffective at representing its preferences as was the British sugar compact. Only coal duties were maintained; other duties were cut by half or more.[89] Generally speaking, the 1881 tariff was a free-trade victory almost across the board, and business organization in France in 1878 was as tentative and ineffective as business organization in Britain.

The explanation for this state of affairs is to be found in the conventional nature of the French tariff. An industry could not hope to extract an advantageous tariff on its own. The scope of the conventional principle made modification of the duties an all-or-nothing affair; only a parliamentary majority mobilized in debate over the overall concept of protection could accomplish that. Until they could overwhelm the free traders on a broad front of general trade principles, protectionists would not get a single tariff increase passed.

Note the contrast with the U.S. case. In the United States, sectoral tariffs such as the Wool and Woolens Act of 1867 were passed in their own right. True, most of the time, individual schedules were considered altogether in general revisions. This practice reflected the need to balance expenditures with revenues, of which more than half came from customs duties. But the practice should not obscure the fundamental difference between the French and American cases. In the United States, unlike France, firms in one sector may fail to agree on a level of protection for the products of that sector without negatively affecting the ability of other sectors to promote their own interests. In fact, if one sector abstained from asking for a higher duty, it had the effect of improving the chances of another sector to secure such a duty, given that the House Ways and Means Committee always kept revenues in line with expenditures. In France, by contrast, an unsolved dispute in any sector endangered the entire coalition. As long as protectionists could not reach an agreement on the overall structure of the tariff, they would not be able to free tariff-making from its international bonds. The policy process in the United States rewarded sectoral organization, whereas the French process deterred sectoral organization, rendering it both unreliable and ineffective. Instead, the French process called for a universal (transsectoral) coalition of protectionist interests. The coalition had to comprise a parliamentary majority and engage in a wide-ranging debate likely to attract participation by all organized producers. Whereas the American process rewarded compacts arranged between primary producers and manufacturers at the sectoral level, the French process called for a corporatist bargain between the agrarians organized in the SAF and the protectionist manufacturers organized in the AIF.

The cause of the relative failure of the French protectionists in comparison to their American equivalents reduces to a difference in organizational requisites, which, in France, were steeper than in the United States. Primary producers and manufacturers in France had to form a single, central compact, whereas in the United States, sectoral compacts were sufficient. The French therefore had to fight a single, general battle, while the Americans were free to engage in sporadic, sectoral skirmishes. In consequence, protectionism in France would come about only all at once, if at all, and only if the conventional tariff were repealed. In the United States, protectionism crept in sector by sector.

Caught in an inhospitable policy process, French protectionist lobbies, like their British equivalents, withered. They enjoyed no real access to policymaking, especially not to the executive; and they were saddled with an issue that figured only intermittently on the parliamentary agenda. Therefore, they failed to attract members. The free traders, on the other hand, won the battle of 1881 and disbanded, entrusting their preference for free trade to the logic of the conventional system—a system which, after 1881, made it very difficult for either side to use "access" as a justification to its troops for continued investment in organization.

Parties

In France, the party was not the unit of mediation, even though the multipartisan nature of the party system might obscure this fact. Consider the partisan breakdowns presented in appendix three, table A3.1. A priori, there are elements of a left-right polarization in the votes regarding trade policy: the Right was protectionist, the Center divided, and the Left free trader. The Right, however, was divided between traditional protectionists and Bonapartists who remained loyal to the legacy of Louis Napoléon. Only on the extreme Left did trade-policy voting exhibit the partisanship characteristics of discipline and consistency. The question, therefore, is whether the uniform ideological voting on the Left was sufficient grounds for declaring the entire process partisan.

The dynamics of the system suggests that the answer is no. In the French multiparty system of the time—a political system in which all governments depended on the center—the peripheral location of the free-trade principle rendered its supporters unlikely participants in the government. Advocacy of free trade was apt to be more ideological than pragmatic. In the long run, all parties moved to the Right. Groups once constituting the extreme Left found themselves, several decades later, to be part of the Left or the Center. This rightward drift was partly the result of the appearance of new political families on the extreme Left and partly the result of a desire by extremists to share in the honors and responsibilities associated with governing. In all cases, a prerequisite for moving away from the extremist ghetto was successful electoral appeal, the Left party becoming so large that centrist leaders could no longer ignore it.

Given this trend, the obvious test for the partisan hypothesis lies in the resilience of the free-trade message. Did the rightward drift of extreme-left parties represent an extension of their free-trade constituency, or did the drift represent a reduction in the parties' initial commitment to free trade? In the latter case, one might conclude that the free-trade principle was a political contingency and thereby rule out the party-politics hypothesis.[90] This is precisely what is observed. The first group to appear on the extreme left was Léon Gambetta's *Union Républicaine*. Ten years later, Gambetta was invited to form a government; a former splinter group had become a relevant party. The evolution of the party's antiprotectionist vote anticipated such an outcome: 95 percent in January 1872, 57 percent in 1878, and 62 percent in 1881. By 1891, the group had lost even its nominal identity and was part of a Left and Center-Left whose free- trade vote was 13 percent. The next group to appear on the extreme Left was the *radicaux*, a party that had by the turn of the century assumed a pivotal role. The evolution of the party's anti-protectionist vote was: 54 percent in 1878 (a vote that may be considered an exception, since the bill stirred anti-Italian sentiment among the wine pro-ducers of the southeast of France, a Radical stronghold); 96 percent in 1881; 48 percent in 1891; 24 percent in 1903 (total of the three Radical tendencies); 41 percent in 1909 (total of the two radical tendencies); and 4 percent in 1910 (total of the two radical tendencies).[91] The partisan hypothesis, therefore, is rejected.

The unit of mediation in France was not the party, as in Britain, but the parliamentary bloc. A bloc is a specialized voting group that does not call for the exclusive allegiance of its members, as parties do. The results of bloc poli-tics are similar to those of factional politics, although the two differ, in that blocs are transpartisan, single-issue organizations, whereas factions tend to be parties within parties, articulating several issues simultaneously. In the end, however, both types of politics deliver a transpartisan coalition. Two blocs of deputies—a free trade bloc and the protectionist *groupe Feray*—formed in the Chamber of Deputies in 1871, to resist Thiers' protectionist program. Three blocs—protectionist, free trade, and farm—formed to legislate the 1881 tar-iff.[92] The debates and the outcome were determined by interaction among the blocs; parties qua parties were irrelevant.

The Executive

The role of the state in France has already been addressed. From 1860 until the *Senatus Consulte* of September 11, 1869 (which returned to the *Corps législatif* the power to regulate the tariff), the role of the state was central and the policy process was dominated by an autonomous executive. During these years, the executive signed tariff treaties with Britain, Belgium, Prussia (acting on behalf of the Zollverein), Italy, Switzerland, Sweden-Norway, the Hanseatic cities, Spain, the Netherlands, Austria, Portugal, and the Vatican. Each new treaty required modifying some aspect of France's conventional tariff. After 1869, under the republic, the state assumed a secondary role, negotiating foreign treaties subject to parliamentary invitation and ratification. The treaties with Britain and Belgium were terminated and renegotiated in 1872–73; in 1882, all extant treaties, with the exception of the Anglo-French Agreement, were renegotiated for another ten-year period. By 1886, the French tariff was set by six treaties—with Belgium, Spain, Italy, Portugal, Sweden-Norway, and Swit-zerland—that froze the rates for ten years, until 1892. France remained the linchpin of the European tariff treaty system throughout the period. In theory, the discretion of state officials was limited in several ways. Reductions could not exceed a certain percentage (24 percent in the tariff of 1881). More important, each treaty had to be approved by Parliament. In practice, the discretion left to state officials was substantial. They could choose the countries with which to negotiate, as well as the mix of concessions to make and extract. They could, in effect, shape the scope, intensity, and (if they were politically shrewd) the outcome of the final debate in Parliament. This degree of administrative discretion reflected the enduring centralized nature of the postimperial pressure politics process, a structure that persisted because of its enemies' quandaries about organization.

The Policy Outcome

The fact that the Republican tariff was but intermittently on the agenda makes predictions regarding its policy outcome somewhat intricate. To simplify things, I will assume that the tariff obeyed the rules of pressure politics (competitive variant) when it was on the agenda but not when it was off. Whenever the tariff was on the agenda, French tariff policy reflected the business cycle. The reason why slumps did not trigger protectionist legislation is that they occurred at times when the conventional tariff was not up for renewal. When the tariff was on the agenda (1871–72, 1878–81), the economy was growing, and the outcome was not favorable to the protectionists. The French tariff remained low in the 1870s and relatively low during the 1880s. Although the tariff allowed for a slight increase in protection, nevertheless it was billed as a triumph for free trade in light of the protectionism that engulfed the rest of Europe. Moreover, when Parliament passed an increase, it was negotiated away by the executive.

Little information can be gleaned from the nature of policy tools. The tariff remained the essential instrument. To my knowledge, protectionists made no attempt to bypass this cumbersome instrument during periods when the tariff could not be modified. The free traders probably would have thwarted any attempt in that direction.

Summary

In the United States after the Civil War, the tariff lost its prewar salience, because the agrarians lost interest in the tariff, preferring instead to take up the antitrust and silver issues. Moreover, improvements in transportation and communication made possible organization of nationwide trade associations, and these trade associations endeavored to overcome the prewar divisiveness on the issue. They succeeded in part by internalizing intrasectoral conflicts, controlling intersectoral conflicts through the creation of compacts up and down a common stream of production, and gaining exclusive access to the policy process. The trade issue—without salience and, for all practical purposes, without divisiveness—was processed according to the rules of low quorum and unanimity. The U.S. policy process in this period, therefore, was a textbook instance of the logrolling variant of pressure politics (case 4, table 3.1). Accordingly, U.S. trade policy reflected cross-sectoral variations in organization and longitudinal variations in the business cycle.

In Britain, the Franco-Austrian crisis produced public support for a tariff agreement with France, leading Gladstone to recast tariff-making as a case of executive politics governed by high quorum and unanimity. The executive process generated consensus on fair trade and created a pocket for rent seeking in the shadow of public ignorance. Anticipating this development, Gladstone moved to sacrifice the consensus on fair trade by tapping widespread electoral support for free trade. The British policy process thus evolved from executive politics (case 2) into party politics (case 1), characterized by high quorum and majority voting. Party politics was still embryonic at the end of the period, because the Conservatives were dodging the issue. The policy outcome, however, reflected the incipient quality of party politics.

In France, Napoleon III accepted the treaty with Britain in part as a quid pro quo for French annexation of Nice and Savoy and partly because he preferred free trade and had the power to force his preferences on resentful industrialists. The Second Empire set the agenda for the republic, however. Even though, after 1870, pressure politics became the trade policy process, the conventional nature kept tariff-making so centralized that many French manufacturers did not regard the sectoral pursuit of protection as their most attractive option. The intermittent, comprehensive, and reciprocal nature of tariff-making raised the cost of lobbying and disqualified sectoral organization, calling instead for an organizational effort along transsectoral lines, which only a party could be expected to stabilize. Unable to hire the services of a party, the protectionists were unsuccessful; the policy thus perpetuated the status quo of 1860.

The lesson to be learned from the study of the period 1860–86 is that free trade exhibits an affinity for debates of general scope. In both Britain and France where free trade found institutional vehicles of a national scope (Liberal ideology in Britain, international obligations in France), protectionism failed as a political strategy. In the United States, where producers were mobilized on a sectoral basis, free trade enjoyed no edge in the debate with protectionists. The different case in the United States did not reflect a different economic reality, but rather a difference in policy process. Tariffs are rents, which sectors are adept at capturing. In the United States, where the policy process brought forth sectoral organization, producers lobbied for protection irrespective of the economic category (import-sensitive or export-oriented) to which they belonged. In France and Britain the unit of interest aggregation was not the sector, as it was in the United States, but a broader reference group: industry at large in France after 1870; the nation in Britain until 1881; thereafter, the factor. In these two countries, protectionism was a less viable political strategy. Rent seeking did not pay, because the high quorum allowed manufacturers to pursue a general preference (a low tariff on inputs), while confronting particular interests with high entry barriers. In France, for example, manufacturers had to create a universal, transsectoral coalition which, as a rule, could not be stabilized by vote trading but which required a modicum of party leadership. In Britain, protectionists had to rely on the Conservative party. Consequently, there was little sectoral organizing either in France or Britain; and protection did not fare well. Free traders, in contrast, fared much better.

Eight

Crisis and Response, 1887–1913

Le protectionnisme, c'est le socialisme des riches.
(Protectionism is socialism for the rich.)
  (*Léon Say*)

Le libre-échange, c'est l'anarchisme des millionnaires.
(Free trade is anarchism for the millionaire.)
  (*Jules Méline [parliamentary exchange reported*
  by Jean Jaurès])

THE GREAT DEPRESSION reached its lowest point in the mid-1880s. In each of the three countries, farmers were the hardest hit, and in each case they sought relief through political channels. Also in each country, politicians responded differently to the farmers' plight. In Britain, the outcome was free trade; in France and the United States, it was protection. This divergence in outcomes has attracted wide scholarly interest to the period, making it a fitting testing ground for the present theory. At some risk of oversimplification, the contending interpretations of the period can be divided into three camps, according to whether the main emphasis is on producer coalitions,[1] partisan cleavages,[2] or the nation's place in the international trade system.[3] Each interpretation emphasizes the facts sympathetic to its analysis; none, however, is able to explain both process and outcome for all three countries.[4]

The first explanation—producer coalitions—suggests that trade policy in this period reflected the interplay of economically concentrated producers. Yet, the explanation could not predict which coalitions won. Why, for example, did the French version of the iron-and-wheat coalition win protection, while its British equivalent failed? Why did U.S. protectionists lose in 1894, win in 1897, and lose again in 1913? Part of the reason the producer-coalition theory does not help predict the winner is that the theory offers no precise measure of power. Is the winning coalition the one that maximizes cash or votes? Part of the reason for this lack of predictive capacity is the indeterminate boundary of the issue at stake. Was the relevant issue simply the tariff, or were other concerns included? If the boundaries of the issue are undetermined, the relative sizes of the prospective coalitions are also indeterminate. As the U.S. case shows, establishing the limits of the debate can be a decisive factor in the outcome. Free traders would have had a better chance of prevailing had they managed to separate the tariff debate from the silver and antitrust issues.

The second explanation—partisan cleavage, which places the emphasis solely on parties, party systems, and the advent of mass parties in response to popularization of the franchise—misses the French case altogether. In all three countries, the economic crisis of the 1880s resulted in an urban-rural cleavage over the tariff issue.[5] That cleavage was reflected in two of the three party systems. In Britain, this cleavage reinforced existing party cleavages, while in the United States, it resulted in a partisan realignment. In France, however, the urban-rural cleavage existed, but it was neither absorbed by existing party cleavages; nor did a realignment occur. Instead, the trade issue was resolved outside the French party system by means of a corporatist agreement between the peak organizations of the agrarians and the protectionist industrialists.

The third explanation—the international trade system—cannot account for Britain. This argument suggests that the existence of a trade hegemon facilitated free trade, that the decline of the hegemon later brought about protectionism. This evolution is observable in the case of France and, to some extent, the United States, but not in the case of Britain, which kept its flag solidly nailed to the mast of free trade.

All three explanations fail for want of investigation into the policy process. The end of the century witnessed the escalation to party politics in the United States, the delayed maturation of party politics in Britain, and the consolidation of pressure politics in France. The starting point for any explanation of trade policies is the agrarian crisis that led farmers in Britain, France, and the United States to solicit political intervention. The demands of farmers were granted in France and the United States, where the farm vote counted; but not in Britain, where the agrarians were a captive constituency of the Conservative party. Political attention to the trade issue, where granted, manifested itself in one of two ways, depending on the nature of the relevant party system. In the United States, where the party system was competitive, trade policy became a partisan issue. In France, the party system was managed by a dominant center party which suppressed debate while engineering a corporatist bargain between primary producers and manufacturers, and thereby turning tariff-making into an example of pressure politics.

In Britain, where farmers were no longer a decisive force at the polls, protectionist manufacturers were left in the lurch. On one side, Liberals denied to farmers the hearing that organized interests are normally entitled to. Appreciative of the vote-getting power of free trade, Liberals rendered pressure politics impossible by reinforcing their already uncompromising stand on free trade. On the other side, Conservatives resisted the appeal of the protectionists, on the grounds that protection failed to draw enough support from the electorate to justify making trade a partisan issue. Unable to condemn free trade, but not willing to endorse it either, the Conservative Tory leadership struck Tariff Reform off the party agenda; for the next two decades, Tariff Reform was relegated to the backbench. Tariff Reform finally returned to the agenda in 1907, when Tariff Reformers set out to rally working-class support.

It was a pyrrhic victory for British reformers, however. They gained control of the Tory party but divided its electoral base. Their bid for the popular vote failed because it did not take into account the broader class issue that defined the party. The class cleavage overwhelmed the tariff issue, and workers were mobilized with the Liberals behind free trade, condemning the protectionist Tories to indefinite opposition. Paradoxically, in the United States where the tariff became a partisan issue, it was the free traders who ultimately lost. Although free trade was the choice of most voters, partisan articulation exposed the trade issue to contamination by the silver and antitrust issues, which were more controversial. In the end, the antitrust and silver issues dominated the debate, and free trade lost at the polls. As noted, in France the iron and wheat coalition overwhelmed the free traders by keeping the issue out of the partisan debate, and thus sheltered it from the unpredictability of French party politics.

The United States

Escalation to Party Politics

In his annual message, in December 1887, U.S. President Grover Cleveland irrevocably committed the Democrats to a general decrease in the tariff. His plan was to have the Democratic House of Representatives write a reductionist tariff bill—the Mills bill of 1888. Then, instead of trying to force the bill through the Republican-controlled Senate, Cleveland would use it as the principal plank in the Democratic platform for the 1888 presidential campaign. What motivated the Democratic initiative to champion free trade and make the protective tariff a campaign issue?

The two conditions of party politics, salience and divisiveness, are met simultaneously when a mass-based group is alienated by the status quo (hypothesis 4.1). U.S. farmers were one such group. Their absolute number, as well as their geographical dispersion, made them a strong electoral force. Hurt by protection, they were demanding free trade as the only solution to the problem of excess production. American labor was in no position to play such a role. Workers were a distinct minority in the population, usually disorganized. When they did organize, along trade lines, they took no independent position on the tariff, but assumed the position held by their respective industries. It was not until the 1940s that the two national confederations, the AFL and the CIO, took a position on the tariff.

The primary problem for American farmers was falling prices for produce. Chronically in debt, farmers used their land as collateral for mortgage and thus risked foreclosure if the nominal value of their land depreciated. Moreover, unlike industrialists, farmers could not take advantage of labor-saving technology to offset a decline in prices. They could check their falling profits only by tilling larger fields. As new lands became available for farming, however, and large-scale production became the norm in the United States, as well as in such countries as India, Australia, and Russia, supply outstripped demand and prices sagged further.[6] Finally, because domestic production exceeded domestic consumption, tariff protection was superfluous to sustaining domestic prices.

In 1869, when prices first began to decline, the farmers' first response was to pressure the railroads to reduce freight rates for produce.[7] In the 1870s and 80s, the attempt by farmers to have the railroads regulated not only did not abate, but rather, took on a new life when a trend toward cartels allowed the railroads to charge monopoly rates, a development that further antagonized the farmers. Farmers also favored the remonetization of silver, which they hoped would sustain prices and perhaps even raise them.

These two issues, silver and monopoly, split Democrats and Republicans alike along sectional lines, and new movements (the Farmers' Alliance and the Anti-Monopoly party, for example) surfaced in the West. Republican leaders tried to stop the splintering in their party by taking up protectionism, a stand with anti-British, nationalist overtones which they expected to appeal to voters beyond immediate import-sensitive interests. The Democrats, for reasons we saw in chapter seven, were for a long time divided between free trade and protectionism. The leadership refused to commit the party to free trade, fearing a consequent realignment.

As the Democrats regained electoral ground lost during the Civil War, and as their leaders regained confidence by confronting the Republican platform head-on, the chances of keeping the tariff issue out of partisan competition grew slimmer. The protectionists dominated only the industrial sectors; free traders dominated agriculture. Moreover, farmers constituted a large population of consumers who could be mobilized by a Democratic platform committed to free trade. Free trade promised to become the basis for a national coalition capable of extricating the Democratic party from its sectional ghetto. This coalition would include the cotton planters of the South, the grain growers of the West, and the export industries of the East and North.

In December 1887, President Cleveland moved in the direction of free trade for circumstantial reasons.[8] In May 1887, the economy had fallen into a mild recession that affected especially Western and Southern farmers. As farmers hoped for monetary inflation, the Democratic party, then in power, fell prey to a sectional conflict: the party's Western and Southern wings were advocating the coinage of silver, with the Eastern wing upholding the gold standard. To preempt the split, Cleveland downplayed the currency debate, emphasizing instead issues that might bridge the incipient urban-rural divide. Free trade was the obvious common denominator of both the supporters of the gold standard and the surplus-ridden farmers in need of foreign outlets. Although a campaign based on free trade would wreck the Randall faction, the sacrifice was small compared with abandoning the leadership of the party to the silverites.[9]

If the Democratic leadership refined its act, even the import-sensitive manufacturers could be added to the coalition. The effective socioeconomic pillars of protection were the compacts between primary producers and manufacturers formed after the Civil War. If these compacts were ended, protection would end, too. An obvious strategy for driving a wedge between primary producers and manufacturers, and scuttling the protective system, was to adopt a tariff bill that would offer manufacturers duty-free raw materials while maintaining protection for their finished products. Free raw materials, indeed, would mean that New England manufacturers would no longer be at a disadvantage vis-à-vis their Western and Southern competitors, who were located nearer to sources of raw materials. Mandated free raw materials, furthermore, would mean that manufacturers could withdraw their support from the domestic primary producers without risking immediate retaliation on duties protecting finished products. As for the free trade ideologues of the Democratic party, free raw materials could easily be presented as a first step in the generalization of free trade. The second step—reduction of the duties on manufactured products—would not happen in the immediate future and could easily be forgotten if political necessity required. The Mills bill sought exactly these terms.[10]

Although the bid failed to deliver immediate victory to the Democrats, it did corner the Republican-controlled Senate and force it to pass a protectionist bill—the Allison bill—and to use it as a campaign platform. The Democrats thus succeeded in transforming the tariff into a partisan issue. Henceforth, the fate of protection was closely tied to the electoral success of the Republican party, and the fate of free trade was tied to the success of the Democratic party. Systematic evidence for this development is to be found in figures A3.1 and A3.2 (appendix three). These figures track the historical evolution of partisan bias on votes on tariff bills in the House of Representatives and the Senate. The index surged in 1888 and remained at a high level until World War I.

Displacement of the Lobbies

Once political parties began to articulate trade interests, the trade association network lost its raison d'être. Among the first victims claimed by the new policy process were the weakest compacts. Transcripts of congressional hearings in 1890 reveal the collapse of three compacts: the brewers-hop growers compact of 1889; an importer-manufacturer compact applying to kid-glove leather dating from 1890; and the growers-manufacturers flax-hemp-jute compact established in 1882.[11] In all three cases, one side to the agreement defected at the last minute and still managed to get what it asked for. In the first two cases, victory went to the more protectionist side—hop growers and manufacturers of kid gloves. In the jute case, both sides were protectionist; for unknown reasons, victory went to the manufacturers of jute goods. These compacts collapsed because one side lost interest in keeping its part of the bargain, since it knew that Congress was on its side. Partisanship preempted the outcome by making unnecessary cooperation among competing interests.

Party politics claimed a second wave of victims among the compacts that the Democrats deliberately targeted. We have already seen that the Democrats' strategy in 1888 was to drive a wedge between primary producers and manufacturers. In the Mills bill, the Democrats singled out the wool compact. If they could unravel that compact, other compacts would follow suit. The Mills bill provided for free wool and an ad valorem duty of 40 percent on most wool products, more than the National Association of Wool Manufacturers had ever demanded. As one would expect, manufacturers of woolens, supported the measure, but so did some worsted manufacturers.[12] In 1888, the compact withstood this first shock, probably because the Mills bill had no legislative future in a Republican-controlled Senate. In 1893, the Wilson bill renewed the assault on the nineteen-year-old compact, this time successfully. The National Association of Wool Manufacturers had sacrificed the woolgrowers to the partisan game.

When the Republicans returned to power, the NAWM renewed its support for the growers' demands. The 1897 Dingley tariff reenacted the McKinley rates for raw wool; yet the compact never really recovered from the Democratic interlude. The wool schedule that was finally incorporated in the Dingley Act was not the result of an agreement between growers and manufacturers. Moreover, the NAWM, never representative of the industry as a whole, was now a ghost of its former self. As we have seen, the association lost the woolens segment of the industry in the 1870s.[13] In 1890, the NAWM lost more of its most prominent—and efficient—members, including the Bigelow Carpet Company, the association founder's very own affair. Then, during the 1909 tariff revision, it lost the entire carpet segment. Nevertheless, the NAWM, which by then represented only the worsted segment, managed to prevail; the duties were left unchanged.[14] Clearly, it succeeded, not because it was representative of the industry (it was distinctly not that), but because the Republicans were in power. Protection was part of Republican ideology, and the wool schedule was the symbol of protection. In the partisan battle, the wool schedule had come to resemble a military stronghold, on which entire wars might turn. In 1909, the Republican leader, Nelson Aldrich, referred to it as "the very citadel of protection."[15]

The iron and steel compact fared no better. The disintegration originated within the American Iron and Steel Association. Abraham Hewitt and Andrew Carnegie had argued since 1874 that American foundries were strong enough to hold their own without protection from foreign competition. At the time, however, these men were unique in their views and had little influence. Carnegie's case was typical. A formidable competitor, making war on the others, and owner of the most efficient steelworks in the world, Carnegie was also a Catholic to whom the Episcopalian and Presbyterian elite circles of Pittsburgh were closed. His standing in the AISA was hardly more favorable. When Carnegie suggested a resolution to reduce protection at the Cresson Convention of 1882, he was declared out of order and excluded from working committees.

The marginal position of Carnegie and Hewitt improved when Cleveland took up the torch of free trade. In 1892, Carnegie and Henry Frick, another AISA member, reduced their donation to the Republican campaign and instead contributed heavily to the Cleveland campaign. In 1893, Hewitt and Carnegie appeared at the hearings on the Wilson bill, urging cuts in the duties; Senator Gorman, who cosponsored the bill, actually asked Carnegie to write the metal schedule for the new bill. The compact between the AISA and the Western iron-ore producers collapsed when the president of the AISA asked for a cut on the duty on iron ore. The partisan battle thus provided an avenue of expression for minority views in the steel industry.[16]

After the compacts, the trade associations were on death row. The best-documented case is that of the steel industry. Steelmasters faced the antitrust movement, which had grown out of a widespread belief that protection as a trade policy fostered the development of industry trusts. As the concentration in steel grew and the industry came under the scrutiny of the trustbusters, the largest and most advanced steel producers sought to deflect criticism by substituting informal price-fixing schemes for the far more visible duties on foreign imports. This reorientation led to the demise of the AISA. In April 1908, such prominent firms as U.S. Steel, Bethlehem, Cambria, and Jones & Laughlin left AISA and founded their own organization, the American Iron and Steel Institute. The new generation of executives wanted an association that would foster collective action, regulate production, and fix prices; they did not want protection. Executives withdrew their support from the American Protective Tariff League. At their request, the 1909 tariff lowered duties on coal, iron ore, scrap iron, and several steel products. In 1912, the old AISA was terminated, and its facilities were absorbed by the AISI.[17]

More generally, in the 1890s and afterward, many firms within various sectors and many sectors within particular industries began to voice their support for lower rates of protection, if not for free trade altogether. The 1909 tariff revision saw the leather industry split between two roughly equal coalitions, with the shoemakers and tanners stumping for free trade and the ranchers and meatpackers for protection. After 1890, the lumber industry splintered along sectional lines, with the loggers of Michigan and Wisconsin on the free-trade side and the lumberjacks of the West Coast and South on the side of protection. In 1909, the oil industry divided between Standard Oil, which advocated free admission of all petroleum products, and the rest of the industry, which lobbied for maintaining the tariff. Cotton manufacturers split along a Northeast-South line. The former, producing finer grades, was protectionist; the latter, which fabricated coarser grades, was indifferent to protection.[18]

The resurgence of antiprotectionism has generally been ascribed to the maturation of U.S. industry.[19] Indeed, every sector that took part in the trend toward concentration and managerial efficiency around the turn of the century felt a much reduced need for protection against foreign competition. Although this trend was, no doubt, an important factor, it does not completely explain why firms in these sectors found it profitable to abandon the sectoral discipline heretofore enforced by the trade association. Why did dissident firms suddenly prefer, in Albert Hirschman's terminology, "exit" to "voice"? The answer lies in the redundancy of trade associations in a party process. Once the parties began to articulate trade interests, firms felt that they could effectively represent their views to politicians without having to maintain sectoral consensus.

More importantly, sectoral organization no longer paid off. Trade associations could no longer deliver. Table 8.1 recapitulates the regression analysis of the 1883 tariff (table 7.1) and extends it to the 1890 McKinley tariff and the 1894 Wilson-Gorman tariff. Each of the special interests appearing at the hearings or inquiries on the three tariffs was coded according to whether it was articulated by an individual firm, a local organization, an ad hoc delegation representing a nationwide industry, or a formal, nationwide trade association. Also, each case was coded according to whether the interests thus represented got what they asked for. For 1890 and 1893, the hearings before the House Ways and Means Committee were selected for analysis; for 1883, the only hearings available were those held by an specially appointed tariff commission.

The results of this analysis suggest that sector organization became ineffective under the Democrats and somewhat redundant under the Republicans. Organization paid off for both protectionists and free traders in 1883, for protectionists only in 1890, and for no one in 1894. These results are compatible with the present contention that tariff-making after 1888 fell under the aegis of party politics, with the corollary that trade organizations per se were no longer decisive in promoting their members' interests. Trade organization still paid off for protectionists in 1890, when the Republicans controlled Congress, because rate increases were set according to demand, not according to some prescribed system. But the payoff was less than it had been in 1883, because tariff increases in 1890 were increasingly offered on principle to any producer who asked for one, regardless of the intensity of lobbying. Neither did lobbying pay off for free traders in 1893, when the Democrats controlled Congress; Ways and Means chairman Wilson made reductions according to his overall plan for undermining the compacts—free raw materials and a less than pro-

TABLE 8.1

Duties Regressed against Requests Made at Tariff Hearings by Oral Witnesses, Differentiated by Trade Orientation and Degree of Organization, 1883, 1890, 1893

Variable	Expected sign	1883	1890	1893
Protectionists:				
nationwide trade association	+	0.2826 (3.54)*	0.2111 (2.78)*	−0.0538 (−0.69)
industrywide ad hoc delegation	+	−0.1388 (−1.06)	0.0336 (0.38)	0.1288 (0.92)
local organization	+	0.1058 (2.35)	−0.0256 (−0.43)	−0.1058 (−1.56)
individual firm	+	−0.0505 (−1.92)	0.0610 (1.45)	0.0206 (0.44)
Nonprotectionists:				
nationwide trade association	−	−0.2666 (−2.74)*	0.0229 (0.18)	0.0681 (0.26)
industrywide ad hoc delegation	−	0.3411 (2.01)	0.0339 (0.20)	
local organization	−	−0.0600 (−0.85)	−0.0158 (−0.18)	0.0219 (0.22)
individual firm	−	0.0053 (0.18)	0.0104 (0.16)	0.1445 (2.17)
Constant		0.5137 (8.65)*	0.5508 (11.07)*	0.1894 (2.44)
Number of observations		146	131	92
R-squared		0.190	0.098	0.092

* Significant at the 0.01 level.

Note: The coding rules are the same as for table 7.1. The dependent variable is the policy outcome. A outcome reflecting the protectionists' demand was coded "1"; outcome reflecting the non protectionists' deman was coded "0"; outcome compromising between the two sides was coded "0.5".

Sources: For the Tariff, of 1883, see table 7.1. For the hearings in 1890 and 1893, see U.S. Congress, Hous Committee on Ways and Means 1890, 1893. For actual rates respectively preceding and following each tari revision, see *The Tariff and Administrative Customs Acts of 1890, and the Bill H.R. 4864.* Washington, D.C. : U.S Government Printing Office, 1894; U.S. Treasury Department, *The Tariffs of 1894 and 1897 on Imports into th United States.* Washington, D.C. : U.S. Government Printing Office, 1897.

portional reduction of compensatory duties on manufactures (thus amounting to a decrease in nominal protection but an increase in real terms). In 1893, "the hearings were perfunctory," a commentator wrote, "and were conducted principally as a defense measure against criticism . . . they had little bearing on the making of the Wilson Bill."[20] Although the Senate eventually amended the bill beyond recognition, Wilson's blueprint initially had a debilitating effect on the lobbies, especially those in favor of free trade. Only two requests for a reduction emanated from trade association officers in 1893.

In sum, party politics displaced the postbellum lobbying network. In party politics, firms need not form coalitions at the sectoral level, as in pressure politics; instead, they can deal directly at the next higher level. Trade associations and compacts operated most effectively before 1887—that is, during a time of internal division within the political parties. Once the parties had purged their ranks of minority views, the sectoral organizations fell apart.

Issue Contagion

Party politics during this period did more than weaken private lobbies; it turned the tariff debate into a proxy for the public debate—indeed, the class war—between farm and factory. Party politics brought issue contamination in its wake in two ways. First, the escalation to the level of values and principles took the trade issue to a level of speculation and polemics that facilitated cross-issue linkages. For example, in 1887, President Cleveland sought to discredit protection by linking it to trustification. Although, by the turn of the century, there was concrete evidence of this alleged causal relationship, Cleveland's claim seemed exaggerated at the time. The connection between the two issues was provided by the farmers, who were suffering from both monopoly shipping rates and tariff-induced inflation on farm supplies and thus were receptive to the idea that there was a large industrial conspiracy against them.

The trade issue was contaminated through the play of a second mechanism besides negative propaganda, a mechanism initially intended to muster support for the trade issue, but one which irresistibly, though unintendedly, led to its demise. Partisan discipline required leaders to abstain from seeking support outside the membership of the party; it required members to vote only for measures sponsored by their leaders. The Republicans, therefore, could no longer get protectionist legislation passed by seeking the support of the protectionist minority of the Democratic party. The Democrats crushed this minority by threats of penalties, and by 1888, Randall's following in the House fell from fifty-two to four.[21] Henceforth, the Republican party had to rely on the votes of its own minority. To gain these votes, it had to promise side-payments to them on other issues. The necessity of providing these payments is precisely what propelled the trade debate into the broader farm-factory conflict.

The McKinley tariff of 1890 well illustrates the second process of issue contamination. The bulk of the Republican minority was in the West, among corn and wheat growers. To persuade these Republicans to support the McKinley tariff bill, the Republican leadership first offered Western farmers a stake in protection by proposing to raise tariffs on agricultural goods. Useless for grains, protection was effective against Canadian barley, beans, hay, eggs, and animals imported into markets along the border—all Republican territory. Protection was equally effective against Scottish potatoes, which competed with Maine potatoes.[22] Republican leaders next offered to foster the growth of beet sugar, an import-sensitive industry, in order to dilute the cereal growers' political strength in the West; and a bounty was paid for domestic sugar production. Then, because farmers wanted an export-promoting measure that would dispose of unwanted surplus abroad and prevent price demoralization at home, the Republicans revived the policy of reciprocity. Reciprocity was thus a means of reconciling Western flour, grain, and meat producers to a policy of protection. The tariff of 1890 enabled the president to negotiate reciprocity treaties with Latin America.[23]

None of these measures addressed the two foremost demands of the cereal growers: silver and breaking up the trusts. Both issues fed the class conflict between agriculture and industry, a conflict that sprang from the growing imbalance in terms of trade that obtained in almost every industrialized country in the late nineteenth century: Agricultural goods simply bought fewer and fewer industrial goods. To ease the imbalance, the representatives of U.S. farmers advocated inflation by means of the remonetization of silver—that is, subversion of the gold standard. The conflict was also fueled by a disequilibrium in the degree of organization of agriculture and industry. Scattered farmers faced concentrated industrial sectors, at first as railroad monopolies, then as trusts in farming equipment, fertilizers, paint, nails, and so forth. To overcome the disadvantages of their lack of organization, farmers clamored for antimonopoly laws at the state and federal levels.

Whereas the extension of protection to the farmers, subsidies to sugar beets, and reciprocity were side-payments that had the effect of associating the farmers with the trade debate as a trade group, currency and antimonopoly measures subordinated the passage of a protectionist tariff to the realization of a compromise on two extraneous, redistributive, and highly controversial issues. The Republican leadership persuaded Congress to pass the Sherman Antitrust Act (1890) in order to answer Western complaints that Republican tariffs bred trust.[24] Also in 1890, they got the Sherman Silver Purchase Act passed, which required the U.S. Treasury to increase its annual purchase of silver and inflate the monetary mass accordingly.[25] This linking of issues antagonized bankers, capitalists, and industrialists—groups which, however, were not greatly victimized. Nevertheless, the measures were too charged ideologically for conservative financiers and narrowminded self-made businessmen, who now looked to the Democratic candidate, Grover Cleveland.

Partisan sanction of the tariff-trust-currency synthesis soon followed. Until 1892, both parties had harbored both silverites and "goldbugs," both agrarian and probusiness elements. In the Democratic party, Cleveland was the leader of the Eastern, or gold, faction. In 1893, back in the White House, Cleveland read the silverites out of the party for good, thus making the Democratic party a vehicle for an all-out free-trade policy that favored both the gold standard and lower tariffs. This position enjoyed the warm support of financiers and export industries alike. Cleveland called a special session of Congress to repeal the 1890 Sherman Silver Purchase Act. He then asked Congress to adopt the Wilson tariff bill—a replay of the ill-fated Mills bill of 1888, which granted manufacturers free raw materials.

This second ideological realignment was more than the party could stand. The repeal legislation passed Congress, but with greater support from sound-money Republicans than from Democrats.[26] The vote, strictly sectional, split the parties between the industrial East and Great Lakes and the agrarian West and South. The tariff bill fared little better. Here, Cleveland was able to maintain partisan discipline in the House but not in the Senate. The latter amended the bill upward, beyond recognition, and managed to prevail in the conference committee. The breach of discipline among Democrats did not sit well with Cleveland, who publicly criticized the Democrats in the Senate and allowed the bill to become law without his signature. Historians have berated Cleveland for his tactical ineptitude. The Democratic leaders of the Senate Finance Committee, however, were even more inept. By allowing logrolling to breach partisan discipline, they betrayed Cleveland's campaign pledge, which cost him credibility among the farmers. Functional in the context of pressure politics, logrolling wreaks havoc in party politics. The split in the Democratic party was completed during the presidential campaign of 1896, when the Bryan silverites took over the Democratic convention and the Cleveland Democrats walked out. Cleveland's attempt to make the Democratic party the party of gold and free trade succeeded only in making it the party of silver and free trade. In the context of two-party politics, the GOP became the party of gold and protection.[27]

The Democrats were momentarily shattered by the populist fight. Ten years later, it was the Republicans' turn. As Cleveland had tried to placate the populists by advocating free trade, House Speaker Joseph Cannon and Senate Finance Committee chairman Nelson Aldrich tried to maintain Republican unity by advocating protection. However, the Western wing of the Republican party, led by Senator Robert La Follette, cared only about antitrust. Though nominally protectionists, they objected to tariffs, which, they said, would bolster the trusts.[28] One of these Western Republicans, Cummins of Iowa, popularized the "Iowa Idea," which called for reductions in rates that sheltered monopoly. As early as 1901, Congressman Babcock introduced a bill that proposed to add to the free list "all manufactures of iron and steel, imported from abroad, the like of which are made in the United States by a 'trust.' " Regarding raw materials, Western Republicans advocated raising the tariff in some cases to encourage development of new resources, and lowering it in others to conserve domestic natural resources. Although their goal was to make the tariff advantageous to the West, their tactic was destructive of the protective system as a whole. They not only asked for reductions on manufactures' rates, more important, they reinforced the potential cleavage in the debate along class lines: Western farmers against Eastern trusts, a cleavage along which, three years later, the party would fold.

In the Great Plains, antitrust took precedence over the tariff. Acting on their belief that protection bred trusts, farmers supported free trade to break them. On the other side, large companies such as Standard Oil and International Harvester, both of whom were under investigation by the Justice Department for alleged violations of the antitrust laws, sought to deflect criticism by requesting Ways and Means chairman Sereno Payne to lower the duties on their products. Despite a common interest in free trade, wheat growers and International Harvester waged a class war. Cattle ranchers and the meat industry were similarly divided. The duty on hides was eliminated mainly because the tanners were able to persuade the public that the main beneficiaries of protection were not the scattered cattle ranchers but the Meat Trust, which had nearly complete control over the supply of hides and was threatening to take over the tanners.[29]

Once again, free trade served as proxy for antitrust, when the Democrats returned to power. The opening sentences of their campaign platform lashed out at the "high Republican tariff" responsible for the "unequal distribution of wealth," the "high cost of living," and the "trusts."[30] In 1913, the Underwood tariff was passed by Democrats, to reduce duties and afford farmers relief from the trusts. In prior years, mainstream Democrats had given up on free trade per se as an issue and had acknowledged that "legitimate" industries ought not be endangered by lower duties. In 1909, Ways and Means chairman Underwood had declared that

> the differences that exist between the two great parties are not the issue of protection against free trade, but the true issue is that one desires to write a protective tariff that leans toward prohibition of imports and the other a revenue tariff that favors fair competition. Although we occasionally find a free trader within the ranks of the Democratic Party, the great rank and file of the party do not favor the doctrine of free trade.[31]

Even the principle of a "tariff for revenue only," for so long the Democrats' alternative to protection, could no longer be fitted into what had become a class debate. A tariff for revenue only meant high duties on sugar, that is, a fiscal policy that placed the heaviest tax burden on the lower classes. To conform to their declared populism, Democrats, for the first time, legislated a cut in sugar duties and then a graduated income tax, to make up for the loss in revenues.[32]

The collapse of the protective system in 1913 was directly attributable to the disrepute into which its allies of 1896 had fallen. The protective coalition was not defeated by opponents of protectionism—the export industries—but by the opponents of monopoly—the farmers. The farmers, of course, were also to be counted among the export-oriented trade groups, but the issue around which they mobilized was not protection per se. For the farmers, allying themselves with export industries was out of the question.

Export Industries Disfranchised

Because the tariff debate was forced to merge with issues with which it entertained but a remote, ideological connection, the debate lost its flexibility. As expected in a high-quorum setup, the range of available policy options shrank (hypothesis 5.7), with the result that export-oriented interests were disfranchised.

The export-oriented industries of the United States were the offspring of the managerial revolution of the late nineteenth century, a revolution felt most in industrial machinery, petroleum and related products, and durable and nondurable consumer goods for mass urban markets (sewing machines, packaged meat, and eventually automobiles and photographic materials). These sectors were those able to take advantage of labor-saving technology and in which vertical concentration worked best, both upstream and downstream. A few large firms controlled a large share of the output of the sector. These were the industries that became increasingly critical to the continuing strength and growth of the U.S. national economy as the century progressed. By contrast, no significant level of concentration was to be found among import-sensitive industries.[33]

After 1896, however, these economic giants were political orphans. Their first policy choice, gold and free trade—until 1896, advocated by Cleveland—found no ready-made political vehicle afterward. The Republican party supported gold and protection, while the Democratic opposition advocated silver and free trade. With no means of getting their first choice, export-oriented industries had to settle for second-best: gold and protection.

Export-oriented sectors did not give up completely on political action, but instead sought to "take the tariff out of politics." They demanded that an independent tariff commission be appointed to investigate and make recommendations for tariff rates.[34] In 1909, in a move worthy of European corporatist ententes, representatives of the National Association of Manufacturers (NAM) and various farm associations founded a joint organization, the National Tariff Commission Association, to lobby for an independent commission designed to oversee revision of the tariff. Two "insurgents"—Senators LaFollette and Beveridge—were among the leaders of the movement. The protectionists and the Republican leadership (Cannon, Payne, and Aldrich) opposed the plan, while the Democrats refused to support a measure they deemed too timid a move toward lower tariffs, and a Republican idea anyway.[35] The legislative outcome was the Tariff Board, a fact-finding panel created by the Payne-Aldrich Act of 1909. The board, however, had no power other than to publish findings; congressional prerogatives were left untouched. The idea of a tariff board was not dead, though. By 1910, William Howard Taft and all Republicans endorsed it, hoping thereby to bridge the gulf within the party between the Progressives and the Regulars. But they lost the House to the Democrats, who blocked the bill. The Underwood tariff of 1913 made no provisions for a commission and the NAM–farm lobby soon fell apart.

In a party process that pitted free trade against protection, there was no room for a tariff commission. Protectionists (the NAWM, AISA, American Protective Tariff League, Boston Home Market Club, etc.) opposed the measure on the grounds that it could be used to reduce the tariff, whereas Democrats dismissed the measure on the grounds that it would demobilize electoral support for free trade. Farmers and industrialists disagreed about the extent of the powers of the Tariff Board. Mindful of the abuses perpetrated under the postbellum system of pressure politics, the Midwest asked for a strong commission, equipped with subpoena powers as well as the power to examine industrialists under oath and study the financial records of business firms. Needless to say, the industrialists were unwilling to grant extraordinary powers to a state agency whose control they might have to share with the Republican insurgents.[36] It might have been possible to resolve this disagreement under the auspices of a dominant party or an executive committed to promoting exports, but, in the context of party politics, the problem was insuperable.

The Executive and Reciprocity

Export sectors looked to the White House and the State Department for help. These sectors were particularly impressed by Secretary of State James G. Blaine, a Republican. Blaine endeavored in 1890 to use the resources of his office to bridge the farm-factory gap with an export-promotion platform that was compatible with the Republican stance on protection. The revival of the reciprocity policy, already touched on in the discussion of the McKinley Tariff, is worth detailing here.

The new feature this time around was that the agreements, once concluded, required neither ratification by the Senate nor the approval of Congress to go into effect. This extraordinary delegation of power to the executive, however, would be nominal unless Blaine found the appropriate goods with which to bargain. Politically, wool was out of reach. Hides were available but insufficient. Sugar would be sufficient but was now unavailable, because Ways and Means chairman William McKinley intended to put it on the free list to reduce the treasury surplus and to appeal to farmers as consumers. Blaine and

McKinley then agreed on a tortured compromise. Congress would first put sugar on the free list, then it would require the executive to threaten sugar-exporting nations with reimposition of the duty on import-shares if reciprocal advantages to U.S. products were not granted. Sugar would be free until then and would most likely remain so, since most of these nations were likely to agree to grant these advantages. The president alone would have the discretion to decide whether or not the reciprocal advantages were satisfactory. Congress passed the new provisions in 1890, and agreements were concluded with eleven countries—all the Latin American nations except Colombia, Haiti, and Venezuela, and three European beet sugar-exporting countries, Germany, Austria-Hungary, and France.[37]

Republicans touted reciprocity to all exporters as the miracle cure for the drawbacks of protection. Their implicit goal was to reconcile the export-oriented sectors (including the grain growers) to the protective policy. The Democrats understood very well the threat and in 1894 disabled reciprocity. The Democratic House pulled out the teeth—the President's retaliatory powers—and the Senate removed the bait—free sugar.[38] All previous treaties but two were canceled and no new ones were signed.[39]

Export industries responded in 1895 with the creation of the NAM whose lobbying agenda was devoted entirely to export-promotion by means of a revival of reciprocity with Latin America and a series of government measures to cut transportation fees—federal subsidies to merchant marine, improvement of internal waterways, and a Nicaraguan canal.[40] The Republicans warmly endorsed the plan and, in the tariff of 1897, revived reciprocity.

Yet, this second experiment ended in failure, too.[41] Protection and reciprocity did not go hand in hand, but instead were incompatible. Indeed, reciprocity was, by definition, a give-and-take procedure in which concessions had to come from both sides. It worked as long as Republican leaders could exclude from the protective system the products they needed to use as bargaining chips. Tea, coffee, spices, tobacco, sugar, and hides were such products in 1890, the first three because they were not produced in the United States, the next two because they were produced on Democratic soil, the last because cattle raisers were disorganized. With the extension of protection to sugar, tobacco leaves, hides, and other new products in 1897, the secretary of state was bereft of viable concessions. He could promise only reductions on coffee, tea, tonka, and vanilla beans. The tariff of 1909 formally discarded reciprocity, substituting a French-like maximum-minimum tariff that reduced executive discretion to nil. The tariff of 1913 restored the previous schedule.

Reciprocity policies failed because tariff-making was a domestic affair. Protectionists would not grant the executive or any tariff board more than fact-finding authority. To that effect, the State Department, in 1897, expanded its Bureau of Statistics and renamed it the Bureau of Foreign Commerce. Beginning in 1906, appointments and promotions in the Consular Service were made according to merit, a change long sought by exporters. In addition to refurbishing the State Department, a new department was created in 1903, the Department of Commerce and Labor, to centralize all information facilities related to foreign trade. In 1905, Congress staffed the new department with a corps of special commercial agents to investigate trade opportunities abroad.[42] These institutional innovations were aimed at updating information on foreign markets and dispatching it promptly to nationals with products to export. This public service was especially important to small and medium-sized firms that could not afford to investigate prospects abroad. Larger firms, with their own facilities, were either indifferent to or affected sheer ignorance of the service. Indeed, American protectionism got such bad press in Europe that some American firms engaged in production there preferred to hide the fact of American ownership rather than avail themselves of local U.S. consular services.[43]

The Private Toolbox

Unable to rely on the government, and even hurt by its policies, export industries played the card of laissez-faire: they developed their own countervailing policy toolbox (hypothesis 5.9). Under the aegis of private banking houses on Wall Street, modern business endeavored to neutralize the negative impact of the tariff, if not to transform it into an export-promoting device. Investment houses provided large manufacturers with the resources needed to integrate vertically and thereby to negate the costly impact of protection on raw material prices. Good investment banking connections provided leading firms with the contacts needed to coordinate secret price-fixing ententes. Sectors such as steel, farm implements, and heavy electrical engineering, for instance, were products of J. P. Morgan's gigantic consolidations and all accounts were managed by the House of Morgan.[44] The House made no attempt to direct the activities of business; rather, it provided an environment in which companies, by means of secret ententes, could escape cutthroat competition and reduce market volatility.

Like price-fixing, export promotion became a private, informal affair. The amount of production in excess of domestic consumption could be disposed of abroad at prices lower than at home. Through systematic dumping, big business could undersell foreign competitors abroad and thus secure new outlets for their mass-production factories. Dumping was carried on at a loss, or at least at a reduction in profits (insignificant when measured against the super-profits amassed in the huge American market). As early as 1888, the *Chicago Tribune* reported that American-made farm implements were being sold cheaper abroad than at home.[45] A report in 1909 by the president of the Tariff Reform Committee established evidence of dumping practices by such sectors as petroleum, illuminating oil, lubricating oil, lead, tubes, wire rope, files, plows and harvesting machinery, boilers, sugar and coffee machinery, arms and ammunitions, safety fuses, sewing machines, typewriters, safes, condensed milk, and cornstarch. Besides U.S. Steel, the most commonly named offenders were other steel producers, International Harvester, Standard Oil, Vacuum Oil, Winchester, Hall Safe, American Screw, Underwood Typewriter, and National Sewing Machine.[46] Additional evidence of dumping comes from foreign responses to American dumping. The first-ever general antidumping law, passed by Canada in 1904, was directed primarily against American dumping. Canada was soon imitated by New Zealand and Australia. Joseph Chamberlain, a leader in British industry, frequently used evidence of American dumping in his campaign for imperial trade protection. In fact, the Republican Campaign Text-Book of 1906 not only acknowledged the U.S. practice of dumping but gloried in it. Finally, U.S. Steel's resort to dumping was so systematic that the firm had other American producers benefit from it; domestic manufacturers who bought material from U.S. Steel, from which to make products for export, were granted rebates on the usual domestic price.

Concentrated businesses found another way to use protection to their advantage: the extensive establishment of branch factories abroad. Opening production units abroad was a defensive response to the worldwide tariff hikes at the end of the century. Since the United States took a more than active part in that protectionist trend, many a company's decision to go multinational may be seen as a necessary adjustment to offset the adverse effects of Republican tariff policy. International Harvester, for instance, decided to locate a plant at Croix, after it became clear that the reciprocity agreement of 1898 with France would not go into effect.[47] In addition, manufacturers who might otherwise develop an extensive export business from the United States were induced to establish branch factories in Europe and the British dominions, where they could avail themselves of U.S. dumping prices on their supplies. To the extent that dumping was met with retaliatory import taxes by foreign governments, relocating abroad became a necessity for many American business.[48]

Not all exporters could afford to relocate abroad. Most of the companies that transplanted part of their production overseas were those that occupied a monopolistic or oligopolistic position at home. Moreover, once the branch was established abroad, it developed a vested interest in the maintenance of high foreign tariffs. High tariffs acted on exporters like natural selection: Few adapted, but those who could were the mightier and the wiser.

In sum, American big business had to adjust to a hostile domestic political environment, and it did so very effectively. Even though initially protection was not the first choice of big business, export-oriented firms turned protection into such an export-promoting device that they themselves developed a vested interest in protection.[49] The question, however, is not whether large firms took advantage of their close association with Republican politicians. Large managerial concerns normally find ways to adjust, simply because they are the most powerful economic force in society. What is interesting is *how* they adjust. Expecting nothing good from the political system—not even from the Republican party, which eventually fell apart under the antitrust on-slaught—American big business played its laissez-faire card. Instead of relying on the government to promote sales abroad, industrialists kept the govern-ment at bay while transforming themselves into self-reliant multinationals. As they became self-reliant, the companies grew mightier economically and less vulnerable politically. This strength, however, did not reflect political power as much as the adaptability of the fittest in a hostile environment.

The Policy Orientation

Hypothesis 5.3 states that in party politics, tariffs reflect the profile of the party in power. A study by Baack and Ray, however, concludes that parties were irrelevant. This study, a cross-industry analysis of the tariff rates of 1910 and 1914, finds the share of industrial value-added in Republican states to be re-lated significantly to protection in 1910; but the relation was signed nega-tively, as if free traders had been elected by industrial constituencies, and protectionists by rural ones—a rather odd finding. Their methodology was questioned in 1991 by Conybeare, who overturned the negative findings in a study of the McKinley rates. Conybeare found that Republicans delivered on their promises. He also found that roll-call votes in favor of protection were cast by representatives whose districts already had, or were about to receive, high levels of protection.[50] Since voting was strictly partisan, the partisan mediation seems unmistakable.[51]

The importance of the impact of party politics on trade policy in the United States is further supported by the irrelevance of the business cycle to the policy outcome (hypothesis 5.4). Indeed, the party cycle displaced the business cycle. In 1890 and 1897, the tariff was raised following an economic upturn, whereas in 1894 it was reduced in the midst of an economic crisis. Only in 1909 and 1913 was the tariff reduced after a recovery—that is, in accordance with the business cycle. In contrast, the party-cycle hypothesis predicts all the changes correctly, fumbling only on the tariff of 1909, which reflected the factional conflict that soon afterward split the Republican party. The important point here is not that the business cycle suddenly became irrelevant after 1890, but that its impact on the policy outcome was mediated differently than it would have been by pressure politics. The electorate blamed each policy crisis on the incumbent party and voted subsequently to turn that party out of office. In 1890 and 1892, voters penalized the Republicans for their ineffective tariff and currency policies and blamed the Democrats in 1896 for Cleveland's equally ineffective policies of free trade and deflation.

Table 8.2
United States: Determinants of Tariff Changes, 1887–1913
(ordinary least squares estimates)

	Coefficient	t-statistic
Business cycle	−0.0108	−1.09
(Percent change in GNP)		
Party cycle	0.026	2.06*
Insurgents	0.019	1.77
(dummy coded 0		
until 1901, 1 afterward)		
Constant	−0.027	−2.03*
Number of observations	27	
R-squared	0.19	

*Significant at the 0.05 level.
Note: The dependent variable is the yearly change in the tariff.
Coding rules and data sources:
Changes in the nominal tariff: Logarithm of the yearly percentage change in the average ratio of customs revenues collected to dutiable imports. U.S. Bureau of the Census 1976, Series U-207 and Y-353.
Party cycle: This is the trade orientation of the governing party, with Republicans coded "1" and Democrats coded "0".
Business cycle: Logarithm of the yearly percentage change in the GNP. I used the Maddison Index. Maddison 1982, 173.

Table 8.2 seeks to capture these historical facts in a systematic way. The dependent variable is the percentage change in the average rate of duty for dutiable imports.[52] The independent variables are the business cycle (variations in GNP/Maddison Index), the party cycle, and a dummy standing for the intra-Republican split after 1901. The results show all three variables correctly signed and a high significance test for the party cycle variable.

In sum, U.S. tariff-making at the turn of the century exhibited all the signs of party politics: high salience and divisiveness, high quorum and majority voting, weak lobbies, issue contamination and disfranchisement of export-oriented sectors, the substitution of private policy tools for inefficient public policies, and a trade orientation mostly responsive to the party cycle. Interestingly, in France, the case differed in every respect.

France

The Corporatist Bargain of 1892

What the protectionists had dreamed of realizing since 1871 finally grew to fruition in 1892: The peak associations of the industrialists and the agrarians reached agreement to overthrow the conventional tariff of the Second Empire. The process by which the agreement was reached is an empirical illustration of hypothesis 4.2 about corporatism. After the political defeat of the monarchists in France, the Republican party became the dominant party of the period. The party discovered an electoral interest in halting the developing farm-factory cleavage and to this end applied itself to engineering the "iron and wheat coalition."

The remarkable fact about the making of the tariff of 1892 is that party politics did not sweep out pressure politics, although one prerequisite for the displacement was satisfied: Agrarians were experiencing the worst depression of the century. As a result, farm organizations were requesting protection for primary products. Many industrialists, however, whether export-oriented or import-sensitive, considered this request unacceptable. As chapter seven shows, the industrialists had twice defeated the farmers' move for protectionism, in 1872 and 1882. Had they defeated protection in 1892, the trade debate would surely have divided the French party system down the middle, with the Left favoring free trade and the Right favoring protection. This cleavage did not occur. The agrarians were able to find powerful allies among the industrialists and strike a deal. This long-awaited corporatist bargain between primary producers and manufacturers held firm in the end, and the French tariff was freed from its international commitments. Tariff-making thus shifted from the centralized form of pressure politics that it had inherited from the empire into the more common, decentralized form of pressure politics; and interest organization began to withdraw from industrywide lobbying and concentrate instead on the sector.

The changeover originated in the countryside. The agrarians responded to the second slump of the depression by organizing. In less than ten years, those whom Marx had earlier derided as a "sack of potatoes" grew into a versatile political force equipped with a lobby adept at pressure politics and an electoral base no serious party could afford to ignore. This surge of organization in the years when the tariff was not on the agenda requires explanation. Among the multiple trade-offs that made the tariff of 1881 possible was a stipulation granted by the free traders to the agrarians. No agricultural duties could be altered or frozen by international agreements. At the time, this concession was thought by the free traders to be insignificant since most agrarian duties were merely nominal. Eventually, however, this concession played a substantial part in routing free trade. Unlike industry and commerce, the countryside remained available for mobilization throughout the 1880s, since the duties on agricultural products could be upgraded whenever economic conditions got so bad that protection was unavoidable. Sure enough, the surtax on beet sugar was raised in 1884; duties on cereals and livestock were raised in 1885 and 1887; and duties on spirits and certain wines were raised in 1887 and 1890, respectively.[53]

The agrarians organized. Still a society of aristocratic landowners in 1881, by 1890 the *Société des agriculteurs de France* (SAF) had become a peak organization with a nationwide and interclass constituency. Between 1886 and 1890, SAF benefited chiefly from the unprecedented organization of agrarian *syndicats*. The number of syndicates rose from 93 to 648, with a total individual membership of something over three hundred thousand. The *Union centrale des syndicats des agriculteurs de France*, a creation of the SAF, comprised 340 syndicates in 1890. In addition, two other syndicates were active in advancing the cause of protection for agriculture: the *Syndicat des viticulteurs*, founded in 1887 by the Midi winegrowers, and the *Syndicat général des sériculteurs*, formed the same year to raise the prices of cocoons and raw silk.[54]

The first consequence of this surge in organization was that the agrarians were prepared to confront the industrialists, who were organized in the *Association de l'industrie française* (AIF), on an equal basis. Now organized as a peak association, agrarians boasted a leadership with a specific mandate from its membership. In 1888, the SAF and AIF exchanged guests at their annual banquets and appointed a common electoral committee to finance the campaigns of protectionist candidates in the 1889 election.[55]

The second consequence of the organizational surge was that, by the election of 1889, the SAF was no longer a private-interest group but a formidable electoral force, competent and willing to flex its muscles. For the election, the SAF leadership recommended that its affiliated syndicates ask candidates to endorse a manifesto recently approved by a well-attended national Congress. Agrarian leaders claimed that some 500 candidates had pledged their support for the manifesto and that 220 were elected. Eventually, the agricultural bloc that formed in the Chamber of Deputies just after the elections numbered 301 members, with Jules Méline the president.[56]

The specific mandate of the agricultural bloc was to extract from the industrialists a tariff favorable to primary producers. Méline, architect of this corporatist collaboration, was a parliamentarian who represented a cotton textile district in the Vosges. As Minister of Agriculture in 1884, he had officially endorsed protection for farm products by introducing the first legislation to raise the duties on grains and livestock. Méline played a decisive role in working out those points, which were still in contention when debate opened in Parliament in 1890. Industrialists had agreed to the taxation of imported foodstuffs, a principle eventually ratified by Parliament. However, they had reservations about the taxation of raw materials. In 1885, the AIF had accepted the principle of duties on raw materials, provided the duties were accompanied by a system of drawback and compensatory duties.[57] But Méline and many others rejected the drawback system as impractical.[58] The industrialists then asked for the free admission of hemp, flax, cocoons, raw silk and raw wool, hides, and oleaginous seeds.

The outcome of the debate was favorable to the industrialists. All of the raw materials listed above were admitted duty free.[59] Still, Méline made sure that, for several products, victory for the industrialists did not imply defeat for the agrarians. The cultivation of hemp, flax, and cocoons received subsidies from the state, while woolgrowers were indirectly protected by higher duties on imported sheep. The agrarians suffered outright defeat only on hides and, more important, on oleaginous seeds. Although Méline had granted protection to the seeds in the proposal of the Chamber commission, he faced stiff opposition from the government, which was won over to the cause of the Marseille soap interests.[60]

Republican Mediation

Méline's solicitude for the agrarians clearly was prompted by electoral considerations. Méline was a leader of the Republican party, a party which, from the rout of the monarchists in 1879, had governed the republic from the center. The Republicans, then called Opportunists, were a dominant party with a vested interest in straddling the cleavage between farm and factory, rural and urban areas. Léon Gambetta initiated this expansion of the Republican party into the countryside in a speech at Bordeaux on June 26, 1871, at a time when other Republican leaders were still indignant that the rural vote had rallied to the Royalists in the election of 1871. Gambetta made another speech in April 1875, in which he took up the defense of the Senate, a body most Republicans wanted to destroy on the ground that it overrepresented the rural-aristocratic Right. In 1880, in order to organize the countryside behind the republic, Gambetta promoted the *Société nationale d'encouragement à l'agriculture* (SNEA), the Republican response to the SAF.[61] When, in December 1881, Gambetta formed his first (and last) government, he created the Ministry of Agriculture.[62] The obvious payoff for the Republicans was penetration of the countryside at the expense of the Right. The drawback was growing tension within their movement between protectionists and liberals. Only by keeping the tariff out of partisan politics could the new Republican leaders—Méline and Jules Ferry—prevent the extremists from capitalizing on Republican division.

A Republican fumble would benefit the conservative Right, since affinities between the agrarian syndicate movement and the conservative Right were numerous indeed. As members of the nobility, the conservative leaders of the SAF were looking for alternative occupations after their forced retirement from politics. The ideology of the movement—corporatism—was a doctrine of Catholic inspiration with definite antistatist implications, in perfect harmony with the conservative Right's stand in favor of clerics and against state intervention and higher taxes.[63] The conservative Right's stronghold was in the countryside, and the voting record of its representatives in favor of protection was exemplary: 64 percent (January 1872), 93 percent (1878); 94 percent (1881); 96 percent (1892).[64] Had Méline deviated from his role of impartial facilitator and shown greater receptivity to his fellow industrialists than he did to the agrarians, the Right was prepared to launch an ideological offensive on the issue of the tariff.

Hence, amid the polemics of a constitutional crisis ignited by the Boulanger affair, Monarchists and Republicans found a way to collaborate on the tariff. The Republican cottonmasters avoided taking a position on the regime issue and joined the conservative forgemasters within the AIF. The Republican SNEA rallied the Monarchist SAF to the farm bloc in the Chamber; free traders of diverse political stripes organized the *Union pour la franchise des matières premières et pour la défense de l'exportation.*[65] The debate over the tariff thus unfolded along nonpartisan lines.

That party politics was bypassed is confirmed by analysis of parliamentary roll-calls on tariff bills in 1891, 1903, 1909, and 1910 (table A3.1 in Appendix 3). The only parliamentary group united against the tariff were the Socialists. Their antiprotectionist vote evolved as follows: 83 percent in 1903 (adding the two existing groupings together), 92 percent in 1909 (idem), and 56 percent in 1910 (17 percent for the independent Socialists, 76 percent for the SFIO). As with the Radicals at an earlier time, however, the Socialists were not a party of government; thus their free-trade vote was of marginal importance in the making of the tariff.

From Corporatist Compact to Sectoral Lobbying

Trends in French business organization moved in the opposite direction from those in the United States. With the passage of the Méline tariff, sectoral organization assumed a new prominence. Yet, until that tariff effectively freed the French tariff from its web of international agreements, tariff lobbying had to be transsectoral.

The Méline tariff was passed by a coalition of farm and industry. This corporatist compact was the offspring of the two peak associations, the *Association de l'industrie française* (AIF) and the *Société des agriculteurs de France* (SAF). The peak associations and the corporatist compact provided protectionists with winning organizational weapons. In contrast, sectoral compacts were unimportant until 1892. The recurring conflict within the sectors, which pitted primary producers against manufacturers, was noted by Villey.[66] The leather industry was split between tanners, on one side, and shoe, glove, and saddle manufacturers on the other; woolgrowers disagreed with woolens manufacturers. Even the coal-metal-engineering compact of 1881 collapsed. The consistently influential *Comité des forges* was paralyzed by internal strife on the issue of temporary admissions.[67] The protectionist ironmasters used the AIF as their main lobbying vehicle, even though they probably comprised a majority within the Comité. Similarly, their free-trade opponents—to be found among the makers of high-quality steel in the Loire, the foundries working for St. Nazaire shipyards, and the electrical engineering industry—joined the free-trade lobby, the *Union pour la franchise des matières premières*.[68] Industrialists gave up on bargaining at the industry level, preferring instead to concentrate their resources on their respective transsectoral associations. Intrasectoral bargaining was not only insufficient, it offered no policy advantage; in a corporatist setup, a compromise at the sectoral level might easily be overwhelmed by a sweeping last-minute bargain engineered at the top.

The principle that governed the making of the tariff of 1892 was accommodation of interests. Even though the protectionists dominated the process, they made sure to include in the tariff compromise the most powerful free traders. Several staunch free traders lost the doctrinal, but not the practical, battle. Lyons silk spinners, Marseille soap makers, Reims and Fourmies worsted manufacturers, Paris leather manufacturers—all won free raw materials over the opposition of the cocoon, oil seeds, sheep, and cattle growers.[69] Accommodation of these interests served to neutralize powerful opponents of protection and help set the compromise on the tariff of 1892 on a broad, secure, economic base.

Sectoral organizing became relevant after 1892, largely owing to transformation of the French tariff into a strictly domestic issue. Parliament recovered mastery of tariff-making; henceforth, duties could be altered one by one and at any time. The result was proliferation of laws modifying the duties on one or more items at a time. Arnauné lists about thirty such modifications for the period 1892–1910.[70] Not only did the allowance of piecemeal adjustment eliminate the need for a general revision every five to ten years, it now became possible for specific organized interests to rewrite the schedule of their concerns according to the more immediate needs of their trade.

In no sector other than agriculture was the capacity for responsiveness to cyclical variations so carefully institutionalized. With the *loi du cadenas* passed on December 13, 1897, the government was entrusted with raising duties by decree on grains, flours, breadstuffs, wines, and livestock and meats—whenever international conditions threatened to depress the price of these products. Each decree was subject to subsequent ratification by Parliament. If domestic supplies then proved insufficient to meet demand, discontented consumers would have to rely on urban deputies to reduce protective duties or momentarily suspend them. Urban deputies were successful in doing so with respect to wheat in 1891 and 1898, but regularly failed afterward.[71]

The protectionist transsectoral organization did not disappear altogether. In 1893, the AIF was expanded to include agrarian interests, becoming the *Association de l'industrie et de l'agriculture française* (AIAF). However, as S. M. Smith writes, "its very size and the diversity of its composition made it less and less an agency of combat and more and more a ceremonial body dedicated to defending the status quo. Therefore, never again did it play the aggressive role in economic policymaking that, as the AIF, it had played between 1878 and 1892."[72] The AIAF remained the vigilant guardian of the balance of interests reached in 1892. The purely ceremonial character of the organization was evidence of the solidity of a bargain that persisted largely unaltered until the 1950s.

This process of interest accommodation reached its climax during the general revision of 1910. Trade associations were asked to present their wishes to the Chamber Tariff Commission which, in turn, was to communicate its wishes to the full Chamber in the form of industry reports. A typical report contained a schedule of duties, listing or quoting for each product the requests made by the interested associations. This format favored sectors capable of presenting a common front, leaving to the politicians the onus of arbitrating in conflicted cases. According to Villey, in sectors such as hides and leather, lime and cement, cotton yarn, garments, iron and steel, automobiles, and chemicals, the commission's recommendations confirmed the wishes of the respective associations.[73]

The definition of the role assumed by a well-organized trade association in the context of pressure politics could not have been better described than by the reporter for the Chamber Tariff Commission himself, Jean Plichon. In his remarks regarding the *Comité des forges*, Plichon noted:

> The complexity of the revision would have been difficult for the Tariff Commission had it not had the good fortune to receive a remarkable study made by the *Comité des forges*, a gathering not only of metallurgists, but also of important and numerous machine builders. And this *Comité des forges* played in this circumstance the difficult role of conciliator of opposing interests, who eventually agreed, through mutual transactions, upon a common set of demands, signed remarkably by both producers and consumers; this did not prevent the Commission in turn from arbitrating.[74]

Problem-Solving through Instrumental Spillover

We saw in the U.S. case that issue contamination occurred when the trade issue was merged with conflicts over more general issues. Export-oriented interests, disfranchised along the way, were left to devise their own commercial policies. In the French case, the opposite process—spillover—occurred, in which trade remained an issue at the sectoral level, although, in its search for new policy instruments, it captured other issues.

Spillover is the usual correlate of pressure politics (hypothesis 5.7). The logic of interest accommodation calls for the extension of trade policy beyond the narrow boundaries of tariff legislation, whenever those boundaries prove too restrictive to sustain accommodation. Since the French government during this period was concerned more with maintaining a particular balance

among trade interests (the balance reached in 1892) than with using a particular policy tool (the tariff), it had to adjust its use of the tool each time
changed economic circumstances threatened the balance of interests. In the
face of an ever-changing economic environment, maintaining the political
status quo called for more or less continuous policy adaptation.

We did not encounter any noteworthy instance of spillover in our review of
tariff-making in the United States after the Civil War, even under a process
of pressure politics; this was because of the exceptional size of the U.S. market.
In contrast, the extension of protection in France in 1892 was bound to raise
problems of a different order, since the smaller French economy obliged most
industries to look for supplies and markets abroad.

One problem duties alone could not solve was a deficiency in the domestic supply. The tariff of 1892 maintained and expanded the earlier system
of temporary admissions whenever the system facilitated a compromise between primary producers and manufacturers. (Temporary admission admitted,
free of duty, raw materials or semifinished goods to be finished in France,
provided the goods were then exported.) The tariff also experimented with
bounties for production. Silk yarn, flax, and hemp, for example, were imported
free, whereas flax, hemp, and silk cocoon growers were compensated with
bounties.[75]

Another problem that duties could not solve was deficiency in domestic
demand. Private firms needed some form of government-sponsored sales promotion. Two policies stood out as possibilities: imperial preferences and tied
loans. Regulation of colonial trade created new prospects for interest accommodation. Several French industries requested "tariff assimilation"—that is,
the extension of the metropolitan tariff into the colonies. Whereas French
goods could enter French colonies duty free, foreign goods had to pay metropolitan duties. The first colony to be assimilated into the tariff system was
Algeria, in 1884. The driving force behind this move was the French rail
industry, which was losing its domestic market to foreign suppliers. Thanks to
tariff assimilation, by 1886, French suppliers had regained the upper hand.[76] In
1887, it was Indochina's turn. This time, the French petitioners were the wool
and cotton textiles industries. The latter's request was not new; as early as
1872, producers of coarse cotton fabric from Rouen requested that the Second
Empire end its experiment in tariff autonomy for the colonies. In 1887, the
request was heeded by a Republican majority in dire need of shoring up its
Tonkin policy after the military disaster of 1885. Even the Right, which from
1885 to 1887, systematically opposed colonization of the Tonkin, in 1887
unanimously voted to assimiliate its tariff.[77]

The Méline tariff of 1892 not only increased protection for industry, it
systematized French colonial tariff policy. From then on, colonies were divided into three categories according to their trade status. The first, and by far
most important, group included those colonies whose tariff was "assimilated."

French goods could flow freely into their markets, whereas, until 1913, most colonial goods would continue to pay half-duties upon entry into the metropole, allegedly to raise revenues. The second group—referred to as "nonassimilated"—included those colonies whose tariff was not assimilated, either for reasons of diplomacy or of geographical impossibility, but which nonetheless were required to grant tariff preferences to French products. The third category included colonies for whom an international convention guaranteed an open-door policy. Here, the only trade advantage enjoyed by French merchants was the advantage conferred by French predominance in financial, maritime, and administrative domains. After 1906, the most important colony in this category was Morocco.

The policy of tariff assimilation increased the relative share of French exports to the colonies, thus coming to the aid of declining industries such as cotton fabrics, soap, candles, shoes, rope, and rails by helping them find new outlets and thus remain a force in the economy. The policy also provided a substantial market for such food industries as refined sugar, cooking oil, and beer and liquor.[78] The policy, of course, entailed costs, mostly in the form of military and railroad expenses; but these were borne by colonial consumers and French taxpayers. French taxpayer money was invested or spent on populations which provided a captive export-market for declining and consumer-good industries.[79] Although the restrictions on colonial trade frustrated those businesses with an interest in the volume of exchanges (railroad companies, the French merchant marine, the port shipping constituencies of Bordeaux, Le Havre, and Marseille) those interests benefited from a monopoly on colonial shipping.[80] The silk weavers of Lyons probably were the most vociferous opponent of tariff assimilation. Yet, even they had a stake in colonial expansion, for they hoped to secure a dependable supply of raw silk, as well as reliable markets, for their finished products.[81]

The colonial market was a plausible solution for a traditional, consumer-oriented industry such as textiles; but it was too backward for an equipment industry such as metal engineering. More than textiles, French engineering suffered from a restricted domestic market. Prior to 1892, engineering firms had sided with their free-trade consumers—railroad companies, steamship lines, municipalities, and technical ministries. The advent of pressure politics, in 1892, had the effect of squeezing the engineers between the powerful *Comité des forges*, on one hand, and insufficient domestic demand, on the other. Engineering companies split into two groups—the builders of locomotives, railroad equipment, armaments, ships, and heavy electrical machinery, allied with their protectionist suppliers; and the builders of machine tools, who continued to press for reduction of duties on pig iron. Internal division spelled ineffectiveness, both in 1892 and in 1910.[82] Nevertheless, neither steelmasters nor politicians could remain indifferent to the fate of the industry. Any blatant disequilibrium between the sectors threatened the principle of interest accommodation that had been institutionalized in 1892. Together, they sought to resolve the conflicts in the metal industry by finding outlets for French heavy machinery. Producing the goods in this industry required large financial outlays, while their promotion required the participation of the financial community in the form of export loans.

The first branch of the metal industry to avail itself of government help was that of the armament industry.[83] Only one major builder continued to make field artillery into the 1890s: Schneider, from Le Creusot. The weakness of the French field-artillery industry was not technical; and was commercial only to the extent that Schneider's German competitor, Krupp, could undersell it. Rather, the determining factor was financing. Although many nation-states wanted to equip their armies with modern artillery, few could afford to do so without large loans from such modern financial markets as London and Paris. As long as the French financial market remained neutral, Krupp would continue to undersell Schneider and would be paid with funds that, in a large part, were raised in Paris. If, however, French bankers could be persuaded to tie their participation in the loan market to French sales, Schneider would gain the upper hand.[84] At first, the banks opposed tied loans, claiming this practice would complicate the negotiation of foreign loans and jeopardize collaboration with German financiers.[85] More generally, bankers had little vested interest in the well-being of industry, preferring instead to lend to public treasuries, both foreign and domestic.[86] Yet the bankers had to compromise, because the French government, prodded by Parliament, possessed the regulatory power to bar placement of foreign values on the stock exchange. Although no government policy was ever systematized, the decisionmaking process governing the quotation of foreign values thus became complicated by considerations of an industrial nature. The policy of tied loans was requested not only by Schneider but also by the mechanical construction industry, for the same principle could, and would, be applied to any expensive equipment.[87]

Trade interests were not always successful in annexing new trade-policy tools. Certain policy arenas were partisan; if encroached upon, they might have engulfed the trade debate. A good example is the "Buy French" policy, which the locomotive builders vainly hoped the railroad companies would adopt. In 1899, the builders closed ranks by forming the *Chambre syndicale des fabricants et constructeurs de matériel de chemins de fer* and taking their case to the deputies in Parliament. The *Comité des forges* gave its support to the locomotive builders. In 1909, their interests were supported by the Chamber, once again by a commission of investigation but no binding legislation was passed, and the railroads refused to comply.[88] The fact is, the politicians could not be persuaded to require the railroads to reserve their contracts for French nationals, because the conventions of the banker-railroad nexus (1883) made the state responsible for absorbing the railroads' operating deficits. A "Buy French" policy would strain the state budget and supply ammunition to the Socialist

Left, which kept urging nationalization of the railroads.[89] The principle of accommodating particular interests thus faltered over an issue that had been explosive since the early days of the republic and which did not admit of ready compromise.[90] Fear of nationalization inhibited state intervention on behalf of the locomotive builders. This fear was also responsible for the ridiculously low locomotive duties in the tariff of 1910, against which the locomotive builders were powerless.

Notwithstanding the French locomotive case, overall, the French and U.S. trade policy toolboxes were quite different. The U.S. toolbox was limited to the tariff, whereas colonial expansion and international lending were part of the French toolbox. Where U.S. export-oriented industries were left to their own (private) devices, French export-oriented sectors could draw support from their government. Finally, whereas the trade issue in the United States was absorbed into class politics, in France, politicians carefully kept it outside party politics.

The Executive

In order to make the government work for French industrialists, Parliament had to curb the autonomy of the executive. During the 1890s, France moved away from its role as the talented weaver of the international commercial treaty network. The Méline tariff eliminated the autonomy the executive previously enjoyed in negotiating commercial treaties. After 1892, French treaties did no more than extend the "minimum tariff" in exchange for most-favored-nation pledges; otherwise, the "maximum tariff" applied.[91] Rates for the minimum tariff were changed only through the regular legislative process. In each treaty, France reserved the right to withdraw with a year's notice. Agreements were concluded with almost all trade partners. The role of the executive was further marginalized by the establishment of a permanent tariff committee in the Chamber, which was responsible for investigating and initiating tariff revisions. In a sense, France retained a "bargaining tariff," with the caveat that the bargaining authority was no longer the executive but the Chamber of Deputies, and that commitments could not be guaranteed for longer than a year.[92] These qualifications were enough to make France a "taker"—slow to seize opportunities, whose negotiating cycle was determined by that of countries with long-term tariff commitments, especially Germany. Like Britain, France discovered that tariff independence had its diplomatic price.[93]

It is important to note that the Quai d'Orsay, France's Foreign Office, did not relinquish control over trade policy when there was a conflict with diplomatic goals. The policy of tied loans, for instance, called for the agreement of the Quai d'Orsay and thus was certain to be influenced by the diplomatic priorities of the time. For instance, France could treat neither Russia nor Japan with as heavy a hand as it did Rumania or Turkey.[94] The tariff assimilation of the colonies created additional points of conflict. The Quai d'Orsay, in charge of administering the Tunisian and Moroccan protectorates, regularly put forward binding conventions or considerations of *haute politique* to shelter these colonies from tariff abuse. Meeting the Quai on such grounds was not easy for trade interests. Hence, when the Franco-German accord of 1911 (in which France promised to follow an open door policy in Morocco) came before the Senate, Jules Méline opposed ratification, but in vain.[95]

Now and then, the Quai d'Orsay tried to curb the rise of protectionism. During the revision of 1910, the Quai was concerned about foreign reprisals against increases in French duties and their possible negative political consequences. The Quai's hand was stayed by the threat of xenophobic backlash, which depended heavily on a foreign country's own response to the French tariff. The Belgians threatened retaliation against wine from the Midi, but their legislature overreacted to such an extent that there was an anti-Belgium outcry in the Parisian press that rendered impossible any intervention by the Quai on behalf of Belgian export interests. In contrast, despite similar threats of retaliation, the German government's more discrete intervention paid off. Poidevin argues that the Quai was influential in cushioning the impact of the French tariff on Britain, Italy, and Switzerland—the first because Britain was France's alliance partner, the other two because the Quai feared they might fall into the German orbit.[96] How it did so, in the absence of public support, is unclear.

Like the U.S. State Department, the Quai endeavored to help French exporters by gathering commercial intelligence. In 1898, an agency was created in France—*the Office national du commerce extérieur*—equipped with special commercial agents. Eight years later, the institutional marriage of French commerce and diplomacy was consummated with the creation, within the Quai, of the *Direction des affaires politiques et commerciales*. The consular corps was in part made accountable to the Commerce Ministry, and various commercial agents and attachés were appointed.[97]

Policy Orientation

Pressure politics makes tariff rates a reflection of sector interests, which, in turn, are a reflection of organization (hypothesis 5.2) and the business cycle (hypothesis 5.1). There is no cross-industry analysis of tariffs available in the case of France for this period. The only existing evidence for hypothesis 5.2 is Villey's authoritative coverage of the revision of 1910. Having already referred to his study, I recall only his central claim here. Villey claims that demands formulated by the trade associations reflected the degree of prosperity in their respective sectors.[98] In most sectors, the commission's recommendations confirmed the wishes of the respective associations.

The French case should provide evidence of a strong correlation between the level of protection and the business cycle (hypothesis 5.1). Paradoxically, I am not able to document this correlation systematically, because the possible measures of the business cycle all fail to pass the most elementary tests of significance. Part of the difficulty arises from the fact that France had only one major tariff change in this period—the Méline tariff. Later changes were incremental and so product-specific that their effect seems to have been overwhelmed by other spurious factors picked up by our tariff proxy (the ratio of customs receipts to imports).[99] I must therefore fall back on a more qualitative account. The Méline tariff punctuated a period of economic slump for traditional industries—especially cotton—and for agriculture. The price of agricultural commodities in general fell sharply after 1882 and, unlike most industrial prices, remained depressed throughout the decade. The greatest gap between the two factors of production was recorded during the election year 1889, and in the following year.[100] These were the years preceding the expiration date of the treaties of commerce, when trade reform was high on the legislative agenda. Then, starting in 1895, there was a decline in protection, which leveled out in 1904 (see figure A2.3 in Appendix 2). The trend during 1895–1904 toward greater openness reflected the worldwide recovery, which, in France, began in 1894 and continued until World War I, with only two short interruptions, in 1902 and 1906. The general tariff revision of 1910 was not motivated by a change in the product cycle but by the need to patch the holes in the schedules of 1892, which were rendered obsolete by the appearance of new products and by the new tariffs adopted by France's main trading partners, especially Germany.[101]

Britain

Maturation of Party Politics

In Britain, the escalation to party politics did not occur during the depression of the 1880s, as it did in the United States, but was postponed until the twentieth century. The tariff issue was never dealt with squarely; nor was it taken up in Parliament between 1883 and 1903. The votes recorded in figure A3.3 (Appendix 3) during that period concerned trademarks (1887, 1894); duties on foreign prison-made goods (1897); and sugar bounties in India (1899)—all issues related to Tariff Reform, to be sure, but not, by any means, reducible to Tariff Reform. The data raise two questions: (1) Why was the tariff not at issue in Britain in the midst of the depression? Why did the tariff become a partisan issue in the prosperous decade 1900–1910? The answer is paradoxical. There was no mass support for protection in Britain, yet the Conservative party espoused protection, with the consequence that the party lost all the elections in which it pushed the issue. Although the electoral outcome is compatible with the present theory, the behavior of the Conservatives a priori is not, and needs to be carefully elucidated.

Convinced of the popularity of free trade, Gladstone, in 1881, challenged the Conservatives to take up the protectionist cause. Aware of the threat, leaders of the Conservative party waffled, leaving each MP to decide for himself. In 1886, the Liberal party split over Gladstone's Irish home-rule bill. The Liberal Unionists relocated to the Conservatives' camp, rebaptized Unionist for the occasion.[102] The Liberal Unionists were adamant free traders, and Conservative leaders were only too happy to oblige their odd bedfellows by shelving the trade issue. The Conservative front bench then imposed censorship, and the issue did not arise in Parliament again until 1890. The ban was lifted when the support of the Liberal Unionists became superfluous.[103] The Conservatives went into the election of 1892 tentatively committed to retaliation against unfair trade practices; but they lost. The leadership then reopened negotiations with the Liberal Unionists, which led to the creation of a single Unionist party. The party ditched the trade issue once again. Not until 1903 were twenty-seven protectionist backbenchers able to challenge the Conservative leadership and register a vote in favor of Tariff Reform. Joseph Chamberlain, mayor of Birmingham and a former Liberal Unionist, became head of the protectionist movement. By 1906, the Tariff Reformers had gained full control of the Unionist party. The Tories took up Gladstone's challenge, and party politics reached full maturity. But, as Gladstone had predicted, the Tories lost. They lost three elections in a row—1906 and 1910 (January and December). To anticipate the analysis below it was not until the 1930s that the Tories won an election under the protectionist flag, at which time another great depression lent them a hand.[104]

The Tories owed their misfortunes to the peculiar nature of their electorate. The Conservative party in the late nineteenth century counted within its ranks two important constituencies, the agrarians and the industrialists (and businessmen) who had fled the Liberal party, alienated by its pro-Irish, anti-imperial policy, or its social progressivism. Unlike their French and American counterparts, British agrarians were a spent electoral force. They were overshadowed by the working-class vote, not so much in terms of number, a weakness they could have made up for in geographical distribution and political organization (the farm bloc in the Commons was 176 strong in 1887) as in terms of electoral appeal: They were a captive constituency of the Conservative party.[105] The agrarians knew the limits of their power. They had wanted protection from 1881 onward but had refrained from asking for it. At a conference held in 1892, the chambers of agriculture set up a national lobby, yet decided on a waiting strategy. They would wait for the urban and industrial areas to declare themselves for protection and only then rally to the cause.[106] The second group, the protectionist industrialists (represented by Howard Vincent, in Sheffield, and Joseph Chamberlain, in Birmingham), had no electoral substance beyond their own local bases; but their minds were brimming with ideas about how best to attract support from the working class.

The Conservative protectionists faced a delicate task. They had to engineer a mass base for protection among workers without antagonizing the agrarian element of their party. Chamberlain came up with the most imaginative program, Tariff Reform, which was a mix of imperial preference and old-age pension, the latter to be financed through import duties. Ready to gamble on a program he believed might undercut both Liberals and the nascent Labor party, Chamberlain and his seventy-two followers stormed the Conservative party, achieving majority control by 1906 and complete control by 1910.[107]

There was a snag in the Tariff Reform program, however. Since Britain imported mainly foodstuffs from its empire, no preferences could be granted to the colonies without Britain first imposing a tariff on foodstuffs imported from other countries. The price of food would increase, a prospect over which British farmers rejoiced, although workers did not. From the very beginning, accusations of "dear food" and "stomach taxes" plagued Tariff Reform.

More importantly, the British working class was already well organized, and its leaders saw no advantage in an alliance with the Conservatives. To gain access to the government required them to ally with the Liberals, who, out of electoral necessity, had since 1867 shown greater sensitivity than the Conservatives to the social demands of the trade unions. The practice of electoral agreements between Labour and the Liberals developed as early as 1903, and in 1909, Lloyd George put forward the "People's Budget," the Lib-Lab response to Tariff Reform: free trade and old-age pensions financed through an increase in direct taxation, especially on land. The stance taken by British workers in support of free trade reflected the existence of a relatively advanced degree of class consciousness and organization. French and American workers, by comparison, were disorganized, still unable to view their own interests independently of the shops in which they labored.[108]

Maintaining Weak Lobbies

The British lobbying scene was highly similar to the one in the United States. Few industries exhibited a definite stance on the trade issue, although the lack of reliable official inquiry into these matters makes this fact more difficult to prove than in the U.S. case. From 1886 until 1903, the issue was removed from the political agenda; afterward, the very idea of such inquiry was a partisan issue. Unable to win over the free-trade opposition, in 1904, Tariff Reformers set up the Tariff Commission, an unofficial body of businessmen, to prepare a "scientific" tariff. The commission distributed questionnaires, heard testimony, and published reports on thirteen industries.[109] These documents must be viewed with caution, however. Free-trade interests were underrepresented, mostly because they did not wish to be associated with a protectionist body.

With this caveat in mind, it is still striking to consider how few trade associations testified before the Tariff Commission. Very few witnesses were listed as explicitly representing a trade association. The associations were the British Iron Trade Association, the British Tube Association, the Fine Cotton Spinners' and Doublers' Association, the Axminster and Brussels and Wilton (Carpet) Association, the National Glass Bottle Manufacturers' Association, the National Federation of Meat Traders' Association, the Nursery and Seed Association of Great Britain and Ireland, the Market Gardeners', Nurserymen's, and Farmers' Association, and the Horticultural Trades Association of Great Britain and Ireland. Five other associations appointed delegates, but no testimony was taken for them by the commission, and no report was published. These were the Paper Makers' Association, the India Rubber Manufacturers' Association, the Institute of British Carriage Manufacturers, the Timber Trades Federation, and the Musical Instrument Traders' Protection Association.[110] If the association that took no position on the trade issue (British Iron Trade) is subtracted from the list, there remain nine industrial and four agricultural trade associations that articulated a trade preference—though not necessarily in favor of protection. The Fine Cotton Spinners' and Paper Makers' associations, for instance, favored free trade.

Not only was the number of associations that took a stance on the trade issue small, but those that accepted the invitation to appear before the Tariff Commission represented only a narrow segment of British industry. Of the thirteen sectors studied by the commission, eight were not represented at the hearings by their trade associations: woolens, hosiery, lace, silk, flax-hemp-jute, engineering, pottery, and sugar-confectionery. Moreover, there were five sectors for which one or more trade associations attended the hearings—iron and steel, cotton, carpet, agriculture, and glass—but no trade association spoke for its respective sector as a whole. This despite the fact that, in at least three of them—iron and steel, cotton, and agriculture—a large majority of producers leaned in a definite direction. In sum, trade interests in Britain generally were not articulated by trade associations. In the few cases where the association articulated a position, it did not represent the position of its sector as a whole.

This fact is all the more significant because, by 1904, most industries or branches thereof showed a preference for one side or the other of the tariff controversy.[111] Most iron and steel masters, for example, leaned toward protection.[112] The collieries, almost unanimously, favored free trade. Among the engineering trades, textile machinery, shipbuilding, and marine engineering leaned toward free trade, while machine tools, agricultural machinery, electrical engineering, and, perhaps, motor cars were protectionist. Among the textile industries, cotton was resolutely on the side of free trade, while silk, flax, hemp, and jute were for protection. Only the woolens industry was divided, with the piece-goods and yarn sections stumping for free trade and the wool merchants and top makers favoring protection. Among chemicals, all alkali producers sided with free trade, whereas most dyestuff manufacturers leaned toward protection. Agriculture was overwhelmingly protectionist. Even chambers of commerce evinced an unusual degree of involvement. A resolution of the Association of British Chambers of Commerce on "Tariff Reform and Imperial Preference" found forty chambers in favor, thirty against, and only thirty-one abstentions.[113] In sum, during the early years of this century, Tariff Reform was a prominent issue, partitioning industry into identifiable trade interests; yet those interests were not articulated by trade associations.

As in the past, British trade associations were created for purposes other than tariff lobbying. Mostly, they were intended for price-fixing. The lobbies that articulated the trade cleavage did not have a sectoral base; rather, they were heir to the transsectoral organizations of the previous period. For the protectionists, the National Fair Trade League carried on until it disbanded in 1891, whereupon the torch passed to Howard Vincent's United Empire Trade League, which, for a while, advocated imperial preference. After 1903, the battle was fought by the Tariff Reform League for the protectionist side and by the Free Trade League, the Unionist Free Food League, and the Unionist Free Trade Club for the free-trade side. The protectionists tried to undercut the working class's allegiance to free trade by sponsoring the Trade Union Tariff Reform Association, a relatively unsuccessful endeavor that found support mostly among flint-glass workers.[114]

Lobbies served as agents for the parties. The Tariff Reform League, for instance, became a fundraiser for the Unionist party. The wealth of the protectionist lobby varied with the electoral fortunes of the party. The successive electoral defeats of 1910 took their toll, and the Tory leadership's repudiation of food taxes in the winter of 1912–13 dealt the final blow to the lobby. The decline in the League's income was so abrupt that in 1911 its leadership was suddenly willing to make public the amount and sources of its revenues—information the once filthy-rich lobby had until then carefully guarded. The League sought merely to trick the rival Free Trade Union, whose funds were much greater than the League's, into similar publication of its finances.[115]

Issue Contagion

A contagion effect, similar to the effect encountered in the United States, affected the trade debate in Britain. The decisive conflict in Britain, however, was not between farm and factory but between shop floor and management.

As we have seen, Gladstone effectively discredited the demand for "fair trade" in the early 1880s by associating it with the mercantilist practices of the past—Corn Laws, state interference, and war. Protectionists, unable to urge their preferences at the sectoral level and vulnerable at the more general level of ideology, were hard pressed to package a program with sufficient side-payments alluring enough to allow them to break out of their isolation. Because it appealed only to import-sensitive industrialists, retaliation, the dominant fair-trade theme until 1903, fell short of these requirements.[116] In contrast, Chamberlain's Tariff Reform program was much more ambitious and far-reaching; it provided something for every producer group.

To begin with, Tariff Reform extended protection to manufacturing in the form of a duty not to exceed 10 percent. Industry would also benefit from preferential access to imperial markets. Naturally, the consent of the colonies would be required; but in 1903, there were reasons to believe that the colonies would support the scheme in exchange for reciprocal treatment. The dominions, in fact, expressed their support for such a formula at the Colonial Conferences of 1894 and 1902. In 1897, 1898, and 1900, Canada tried to force the issue by unilaterally granting preferences to British goods; South Africa did the same in 1902, and New Zealand in 1903.[117] It was unclear, however, how far they would agree to expose their nascent industries to British competition. Still, the prospect of displacing German and U.S. competition was sufficiently appealing to smooth over preliminary differences.

After British industry, the second beneficiary of Tariff Reform was the colonies, which would gain free access to the British market for their products. Since the overwhelming proportion of colonial imports were foodstuffs, Tariff Reform provided for duties on colonial staples—corn, flour, meat, dairy products, wine, and fruit.[118]

British farmers would benefit, too, although the extent to which they would do so was unclear. Certainly food duties would benefit the farmers in the beginning, since colonial supply of foodstuffs in 1903 still fell short of British consumption. In the long run, however, there was the threat that colonial agriculture would expand to meet the whole of British demand. In any case, agrarians had little choice; no one else was offering them anything.

Last but foremost, Tariff Reform was designed to appeal to British workers. First, workers would benefit from the revival of British industry, lower unemployment, and higher wages—the classic claim for the "trickle down" effect. Second, workers would respond to the concept of a strong empire shrewdly espoused by Tariff Reformers. The concept was in keeping with the Unionist tradition, whose own principal manifestation was opposition to Gladstone's Home Rule Bill for Ireland. The Conservatives stressed that the Liberals had wanted to weaken the empire by giving home rule to Ireland and that they were about to repeat their mistake with the rest of the empire. The working class voted Tory in such cities as Liverpool, where the presence of an Irish

Catholic immigrant community kept reminding English workers of the Liberals' soft stand on the empire.[119] Third, the excess revenues from the tariff would allow a Conservative government to reduce duties on items popular with the working class, such as tea, sugar, cocoa, and coffee. Fourth, the excess revenues could be used to finance social programs such as old-age pensions. Chamberlain hoped to revive the nineteenth-century myth of "Tory democracy" while trapping the Liberals in the Cobdenite tradition of nonintervention.

Chamberlain presented his program at a time when he and his followers in the Conservative party were a minority faction. The remainder of the party was divided between two other factions, the "free fooders," wedded to free trade, and the retaliationists or Balfourites, who straddled the fence in the dispute. The hopes of the Tariff Reformers for a rapid takeover of the party were soon disappointed. Instead, the factions settled into a war of attrition that cost the party hundreds of seats in the election of 1906. That election decimated the ranks of the free fooders, and in 1907, Balfour endorsed fiscal reform. The last free fooder was expelled in 1909.[120]

The Liberals, therefore, enjoyed plenty of time in which to mount a counterattack. Their sole target was the working class. In 1906, they ran on a program of free food and social reform—old age pensions, sickness insurance, unemployment benefits, and a ban on "sweated labor." The Chamberlainites were outbid, the more so because, still engaged in intraparty warfare, they were constrained to place greater emphasis on imperial preference than on social reform. Once in power, the Liberals delivered. The Trades Disputes Act of 1906 reversed the Taff Vale decision that had been detrimental to the unions. The budget for 1908 featured a set-aside for old-age pensions. The budget for 1909 finally introduced the fiscal alternative to Tariff Reform: Pensions would be paid by a series of increases in death duties, on high incomes, and especially, on land.[121]

The Liberal measures effectively merged the trade issue with the social debate, realigning the former with the latter.[122] In May 1907, Austen Chamberlain—son of Joseph—warned, "Our danger now is not liberalism, but 'Labour' working with and through Liberalism."[123] The radicalism of Lloyd George's budget of 1909 confirmed the validity of this assessment. The two ballots in 1910 registered a realignment of preferences among Unionist backers. Despite the now complete conversion of the Unionist party to Tariff Reform, many free traders voted Unionist out of fear of socialism.[124] Free traders did not necessarily oppose the Liberals' social program, only the way it was financed—through direct taxation. To quote the Duke of Northumberland:

> Protection cannot be worse than socialism. . . . And as . . . Tariff Reform or Socialism are the only possible alternatives at the moment, I am quite prepared to swallow the former.[125]

Election results showed the switch of working-class areas to the Liberals—in the industrial north, in Lancashire and London. The Unionists did well in the south and rural areas, both areas where "middle- and upper-class influence predominated."[126] Tariff Reform failed to win the working class over to the Unionist party, turning this party instead into the party of the propertied.

By 1910, the trade debate had become an appendage of the broader class conflict. The Liberals espoused free trade because it meant free food for the workers, while the Unionists espoused Tariff Reform because it offered a regressive way of financing social reform. The new class dynamic commanded changes in the party platform. Because food duties antagonized the workers, Balfour, in 1910, ditched food duties and, with it, the imperial plank of Tariff Reform.[127] From 1910 to 1914, the Unionists were committed to a policy of tariffs only on manufactured goods.

In sum, the result was different from what Joseph Chamberlain had expected: The working class rallied behind the Liberals, whereas the free-trade industrialists, finding socialism even less palatable than protection, rallied behind the Conservative party. The trade debate was rewritten by the class debate.

Export-Oriented Industries Disfranchised

As it had in the United States, party politics in Britain simplified the toolbox (hypothesis 5.7) and disfranchised exporters. The policy that could have helped export-oriented industries maintain their share in protected markets was the threat of retaliation against unfair foreign-trade practices. Discredited under Gladstone in the early 1880s, this policy received the final blow at the hands of the Tariff Reformers. Before Chamberlain, the Unionist party harbored a large faction relatively favorable to retaliation. Unlike Tariff Reformers who supported an all-round moderate tariff, the "retaliationists," with Balfour as their leader, demanded steep specific duties to level the field between domestic and dumped foreign products.[128] The goal lay as much in deterrence as in retaliation. The retaliationist faction did not survive the Tariff Reformers' onslaught. Its membership soon sank to 98 by 1905 and to 49 after the 1906 election, until Balfour finally rallied to Tariff Reform in 1907.[129]

As in the United States (though to a lesser extent), exporters in Britain expressed disaffection with "partisan football" and longed for a party-neutral tariff-making process. Paradoxically, the first attempt at such a process, in 1903, took form as the British Tariff Commission. There is no point in denying that this unofficial body, which lacked the King's approval and which was financed by private sources, was conceived as the partisan instrument of Tariff Reform. Yet, as Marrison has argued, the protectionists expected no more from the Commission than a "scientific" assessment of the current trade policy.[130] In making their choices of commissioners and witnesses, the founders sought to achieve a fair representation of British industries. Their abridged questionnaire was mailed, whenever possible, to every firm engaged in the manufacturing of the products that the commission selected for the inquiry. Their attempt failed largely because the hardened free traders spurned the invitation.

The second manifestation of this longing for a neutral tariff-making process came from the Association of British Chambers of Commerce, a body no one would have suspected of harboring a protectionist bias. In 1911, the association submitted a memorial to the prime minister, asking for the appointment of a royal commission to inquire into the fiscal question, "so as to remove the matter from party politics."[131] This was probably the only proposal its members could agree on. Nonetheless, it suggests the irritation experienced by a majority of British businessmen over the turn the trade debate took after 1903. The Liberal government ignored the request.

The Executive

In Britain, as in other countries, business clamored for the state to lend a hand in promoting national trade abroad. The Foreign Office was asked to pay more attention to economic matters, to include trained commercial agents in delegations, and to help adventurous individuals set up business in tropical climes. At the same time, commercial state agencies were asked to join hands with diplomats to facilitate export trade. The Foreign Office created its first commercial unit in 1872 and began to appoint commercial attachés in 1880. Commercial intelligence was rationalized in successive steps. Special commercial agents were authorized in 1899, and the Advisory Committee on Commercial Intelligence was appointed in 1900.[132] By the turn of the century, this service was generally perceived as a public good that the state was expected to supply. It is interesting to note, however, that even this relatively inoffensive foray into the economy by the British state generated opposition from middlemen and from firms long established in distant markets.[133]

This increase in functions, however, was not accompanied by a parallel increase in executive discretion. On the contrary, the role of the state in formulating trade policy became marginal. The Foreign Office maintained its practice of signing only MFN agreements with major trade partners, going to the trouble of negotiating tariff agreements only when absolutely necessary and then only with such secondary countries as Egypt (1889), Greece (1890), Bulgaria (1905), Rumania (1905), Serbia (1907), and Japan (1911).[134] Furthermore, Britain refused to enter into a special agreement with the self-governing dominions, in spite of repeated invitations from the latter. Britain's unilateral free trade policy reflected both the domestic status and the ideological nature of the trade issue.

One exception to diplomatic apathy common to both France and Britain must be mentioned—the Brussels Sugar Convention of 1902. After two aborted attempts, in 1888 and 1898, this convention committed its European signatories to eliminate bounties on the production of beet sugar.[135] The convention was made possible in part by growing fear throughout Europe that the Conservative British government would impose countervailing duties on bounty-fed sugar in order to assist West Indian cane sugar. The fact that the British government was able to inspire such fear is indicative of a weakening of the partisan grip on the sugar issue. Blind to international factors, party politics usually has an adverse impact on trade leverage. The success of the convention was made possible in France by the overruling of the agricultural ministry and the beet sugar interests by a finance minister bitter over the extravagant cost of bounties. Pressure politics was displaced by considerations of a higher order. In sum, the Convention of 1902 would not have been possible had the British and French executives not been awakened to the need; yet, in truth, the convention was an isolated event.

The Private Toolbox

British export-oriented industries adjusted to their political disfranchisement by becoming self-reliant—they enhanced their private policy toolbox (hypothesis 5.9). Cartels were tolerated in Britain, not prosecuted, as they were in the United States. There was a brief, but not quite successful, movement toward amalgamation at the time of the Boer War. As an alternative to amalgamation, trade associations concerned mainly with price-fixing or the regulation of output became the standard mode of private business organizations. In 1918, these associations numbered five hundred or so, with nearly a hundred for the iron and steel industry alone.[136] It is unclear whether they were effective. In an open economy—especially in such sectors as steel, in which foreign dumping regularly demoralized the market—these combinations could not regulate prices, much less raise them. They could only cut down the volume or the cost of production by closing unprofitable plants. Additional associations were created to promote foreign trade abroad, and still others to organize a good showing for the industry at international exhibitions. None were political lobbies; rather, they were manifestations of industry' attempts to become self-reliant.

The export-oriented sectors adjusted by cutting wages. Wage rates in the coal-mining industry, for instance, moved up and down with the selling price of coal.[137] Potters and weavers were paid by the piece. Workers countered by organizing and staging industrywide strikes. Employers, in turn, organized; in 1914, the Board of Trade counted 1,487 employers' associations concerned with labor matters.[138] Typically, the government did not intervene in wage matters.

Export-oriented firms in traditional lines of business adjusted by redirecting their sales toward less developed markets. The machine tool industry, for instance, was more competitive in the empire, and in Latin America and Japan, than it was in Europe.[139] The most striking example was cotton, however. In 1896, India received 40 percent of British exports of cotton piecegoods, Latin America received 16 percent, and Europe and the United States together received only 8 percent.[140] Lancashire's long-standing interest in the Indian market had, in 1857, led the industry to support Palmerston's empire-building policy and oppose Gladstone's Irish Home Rule Bill, in 1886. Their interest had also led the weavers to establish the first Indian Famine Fund (1877) and support the remonetization of silver (1891), two measures designed to fuel Indian consumption of English piecegoods. This retreat to the Indian market was not the result of government regulation, as it was in the case of France with respect to Indochina. Lancashire did not need a policy of imperial preferences in order to sell cotton goods to India; continuation of the Liberals' open-door policy was enough. In India, as in Latin America and Africa, British bankers, shippers, and manufacturers conducted integrated operations in a way that undercut the open-door policy.[141] None of this, however, was official policy.

Finally, British industrialists adjusted by investing abroad. A handful of firms emulated American multinationals, opening production units on the continent or in the United States—BAT, J.&P. Coats, Courtaulds, Dunlop, English Sewing Cotton, The Gramophone Company, Pilkington, Reckitts, Royal Dutch Shell, and Vickers.[142] In most cases, however, British producers, unlike Americans, had no special skills to export; instead, they showed a marked preference for portfolio investments.

In both Britain and the United States, therefore, export-oriented sectors found themselves without an ally in the party system. Unable to secure help in the form of promotion policies, they developed their own export-promoting devices, individually in the United States and collectively in Britain.

The Trade Orientation

The theory predicts that (1) policy orientation in party politics reflects the profile of the party in power (hypothesis 5.3), and (2) the impact of the business cycle on the policy outcome is indeterminate (hypothesis 5.4). Both predictions have been observed. We know that, until World War I, British industry received zero nominal protection. British trade policy remained free trade until 1914, irrespective of the ups and downs of its economy.[143] The impact of the business cycle was visible only in the degree of mobilization of protectionist forces: The decline of the fair-trade movement after 1887 paralleled the arrival of an era of prosperity; and Tariff Reformers took over the Unionist party in 1907, during a year of economic crisis.[144] Nevertheless, the business cycle did not have the expected impact on the free-trade camp. Contrary to the predictions of business-cycle theory, the crisis of 1907 mobilized free trade-oriented workers behind the Liberals to the same degree that it mobilized protectionists behind Tariff Reform.[145] The reason for this unexpected consequence is to be found in the capture of the trade debate by the class conflict, which the crisis amplified. Since protection was a remedy requested by industrialists, class logic determined that protection was against the interests of workers. Moreover, as the crisis sharpened and broadened class identification, a larger proportion of workers were mobilized behind free trade, thus making it even more difficult for protection to become the law of the land. In a situation like this, pressure politics would have transformed the crisis into support for protection. Instead, party politics transformed it into opposition.

Summary

We can now better comprehend the contrast between the United States and Britain, on one hand, and France, on the other. The trade issue in the United States and Britain became a salient issue, popular with farmers in the United States and workers in Britain. It also became a divisive issue, pitting farmers against industrialists in the United States and workers against protectionist industrialists and agrarians in Britain. As party politics consolidated its grip on policymaking, accommodation between free traders and protectionists became impossible. Moreover, as trade was cannibalized by the farm-factory dispute in the United States and by the class conflict in Britain, trade coalitions crossing these cleavages (for instance, the free trade coalition between U.S. farmers and MNCs or that between British exporters and the working class) became impractical. The result was the disfranchising of industries whose preferences did not fit into the dichotomy of free trade protection (mostly industries depending on foreign markets). Firms operating in these industries had to become self-reliant, by forming cartels or by opening production units in protected markets abroad. They also tried to press their governments to remove the tariff from party politics.

In France, too, trade threatened to become a divisive, salient issue in the late 1880s. Yet, there, the dominant Republican party secured a corporatist agreement between primary and secondary producers, thereby keeping trade sheltered from the partisan debate. Trade became a nonsalient, consensual issue, yielding a policy process governed by logrolling and the universal accommodation of interests. A large number of interests were accommodated by the tariff or, whenever the tariff proved insufficient, by additional policies such as tariff assimilation and tied loans. As the French policy toolbox expanded, French firms had less need to become self-reliant than their Anglo-Saxon counterparts, and they had no desire to remove tariff-making from politics. Finally, in none of the countries did the executive play a specific role in defining trade policy; tariff-making had become an entirely domestic affair.

The crisis of the 1880s launched each country on a trajectory it maintained until the next great depression, that of the 1930s. Until then, interest realignments—France, 1892; the United States, 1888; and Britain, 1910—were not seriously challenged.

Nine

The First World War, 1914–18

WORLD WAR I created both constraints and opportunities that executives were able to use to pursue policies formerly forbidden to them. In France, the war allowed the state to regain the initiative over special interests and launch an institutional offensive aimed at perpetuating the primacy of the executive long after the armistice. In Britain, the war neutralized partisan bickering, allowing Tariff Reformers to enter the Liberal government and force protection on their allies both during the war and in its aftermath. In the United States, the outbreak of the war offered the President an opportunity to wrest trade policy from party hands and finally use it to expand American trade abroad. The viability of these schemes, however, depended on the continuation of executive politics, which was itself dependent on the war emergency. With the return of peace, these schemes collapsed.

The Advent of Executive Politics

Executive politics obtains whenever a country is confronted with an external threat that is military and inescapable (hypothesis 4.3). Although World War I was just such a threat, the *outbreak* of war did not establish the primacy of executive politics over trade policy; almost a year passed before the three governments realized they were not dealing with a traditional nineteenth-century engagement. At first, the war was expected to be short, an affair of admirals and generals, while the rest of the country could go on with "business as usual."[1] This was especially true in the case of the two nonbattlefield countries, Britain and the United States. In Britain, until May 1915, the Liberal government successfully maintained a free-trade, laissez-faire approach. Asquith resisted direct attempts to control armament production and promote the dye industry through duties.[2] The so-called McKenna duties, which provided for a 33.3 percent ad valorem tax on imports of luxury goods, including motor cars, were imposed solely to free cargo shipping space.[3] In the United States, the Wilson administration spent the first year of the war debating which side to support and two additional years debating whether and when to intervene.

Two factors combined to pave the way for greater executive initiative: the failure of the Allied blockade to starve the Central Powers, and the depletion of Allied shipping and stocks of ammunition. In all three countries, executive politics manifested itself—in two ways. First, the war and related economic issues, including trade policy, became a matter of bipartisan support, and thus the basis of national coalition government in the two parliamentary regimes, the *union sacrée* (France) and the "grand coalition government" (Britain). Second, the war allowed party leaders to pursue trade policies not in line with their party's traditional orientation. We consider Britain, France, and the United States, in turn.

The British "shell scandal" of May 1915 led to a public outcry that brought down the prewar Liberal government and thus made it possible for the state to assume direct control of the engineering industry. Nevertheless, although the new Asquith government discarded its initial business-as-usual attitude, it shied away from the comprehensive economic mobilization normally called for by war, lest a precedent be set that would favor protection. In 1915, Germany announced a *Zollverein* for postwar central Europe. In Britain, the debate crystallized around effective opposition to the proposal.[4] Concerned about German competition once the war ended, chambers of commerce throughout the country, including Manchester, asked for tariffs on postwar trade with Germany. Furthermore, the sectors that were part of the war effort—foodstuffs, clothing, heavy industry, and engineering—refused to respond to the government's invitation to speed up war production unless they received guarantees against the risks of excessive postwar production capacity. Unwilling to give up its antitariff stand, the Asquith government first argued that Germany was a "beaten nation," then appointed the Balfour Committee to consider postwar trade policy.

After the government fell (December 1916), to be replaced by a grand coalition government led by David Lloyd George, the British state took over shipping, imports, and food distribution. Lloyd George began directing the Ministry of Munitions to take over management of every aspect of the war economy, staffing the ministry with noncivil servant personnel, especially businessmen. He then took up the cause of businessmen and, though a Liberal, promised them postwar protection. On February 2, 1917, the Balfour Committee issued an interim report recommending the adoption of imperial preferences at war's end, a measure to which Lloyd George pledged the cabinet.[5] To enhance Britain's bargaining position with respect to Germany after the war, the cabinet gave its full support (and Asquith, reluctantly, agreed) to the Paris Resolutions of 1916. These resolutions endorsed a French proposal to set up an Allied trade bloc for the purchase and worldwide distribution of basic raw materials after the war. German access to the arrangement would depend on its territorial concessions at the peace negotiations. The British cabinet then provided itself with the necessary means to implement the program: (1) the 1917 Non-Ferrous Metal Industry Bill licensed access to the metal trade; (2) in July 1918, Britain renounced its commercial treaties and thus its obligation to honor most-favored-nation treatment agreements; (3) an amendment, in 1918, to the Trading with the Enemy Act banned German banks from trading in Britain. The government also proposed an import-export bill, designed to secure state control over British exports. Because of a free traders' row in Parliament, however, the bill was temporarily withdrawn, lest it become a partisan bargaining chip later.

Despite the unprecedented level of state interference, business-government relations remained good throughout World War I. And, in spite of state controls over the supply of raw materials and pricing, the armaments industry made colossal profits. Some observers inferred from this that "war socialism" was another instance of business control over the state, but it is easy to read too much into the situation.[6] Although industrialists profited directly from state intervention (a clear break with the past), they had little impact on running the economy. Once the government had committed itself to victory at any cost, industrialists cooperated lest the government make good on its pledge to take over British factories.

France achieved executive politics by different means. Unlike Britain, in France contingency plans were soon upset by wartime conditions. In one month the country lost possession of 60 to 80 percent of its heavy industry to the enemy. Disorganized and forced to flee to Bordeaux, the government delegated production of armaments to the *Comité des forges* (the steelmasters association), and it negotiated contracts for the production of chemicals with that industry's leading firms.[7] Unlike in Britain, in France close relations between state and industry were not innovations. Rather, the novelty in France was the increase in state control over industry. Once the initial panic was over, the state was better able to direct the economy, especially after the advent of the Clémenceau government in November 1917. The main rationale for state initiative, in France as in Britain, appealed to the popular fear of losing the war. Added to this rationale was the unrelenting pressure Britain put on France. France was dependent on Britain for the supply and shipping of foodstuffs and raw materials without payment. As Godfrey noted, the British government met French shortages, but not without insisting that "France demand of her industrialists the same degree of sacrifice that Britain demanded of hers." French bureaucrats, Godfrey continues, used British pressure "as a weapon for extending state control."[8]

The war emergency gave state officials the opportunity to reverse their traditional dependence on business for policymaking. In 1917, Etienne Clémentel, the minister of commerce, sponsored the creation of a consortium of private industrialists charged with allocating and regulating the price of raw materials.[9] Clémentel's idea was to regroup industry around the French state as the central unit of organization and perpetuate state-control of the economy long after the armistice. His plan was part of a broader plan whose ultimate aim was to give France a voice in the future economic development of Germany. Clémentel thus sought to perpetuate the wartime cooperation of the Allies in the form of a general economic bloc in which the Allies would be bound together by preferential tariffs and joint participation in a trade bloc. It would be the task of the trade bloc to allocate—and regulate—the price of raw materials. Eliminating conflicts over scarce raw materials would not only serve world peace, as the French minister claimed, it would also help rein in German revisionism. Implementation of this grandiose scheme would have had dramatic consequences for industry-government relations in France, since the management of world trade entailed the regimentation of French industry by a revamped Ministry of Commerce, a move considered necessary if France was to distribute supplies allocated to it by international bodies.

The outcry that greeted Clémentel's plan was testimony to its boldness. Most chambers of commerce—that of Bordeaux, especially, and the ANEE (an association of exporters)—denounced what they perceived to be unjustified state interference. Their criticisms were echoed by the *Journée industrielle* and *Le Temps*, two organs representing the views of the textile and mechanical industry and the heavy industries respectively. But the war emergency and the general unpopularity of particularist dissent allowed Clémentel to dismiss his critics and proceed with the plan.

In the United States, geographical immunity placed the government in a different situation. The immediate impact of the war was to emphasize to the administration the country's international economic status. Whether the United States intervened or not, the war offered the Americans the prospect of displacing German, British, and French commerce in Asia and Latin America. As the combatants entrenched themselves in eastern France, the Wilson administration contemplated the profits to be made by supplying the wartime needs of the Triple Entente and the postwar needs for the reconstruction of Europe. The opportunity was a godsend, and the Wilson administration endeavored to help international bankers and exporters realize it.

The administration, however, was a prisoner of its populist base. In his first year, Wilson had implemented a policy of antitrust and free trade that was resolutely antagonistic to business. He lowered the tariff, intruded into high finance, strengthened antitrust laws, and canceled the China consortium.[10] The only political space left open to big business was export promotion; in May 1914, thirty-five representatives of the largest banks and corporations in the United States formed the National Foreign Trade Council (NFTC) to press the administration for export-promotion measures.[11] Although Wilson (and even Secretary of State William Jennings Bryan) were committed to export promotion, they were constrained by the populist mandate of 1912. Already, in the midterm election of 1914, the Democrats had lost their overwhelming majority in Congress. Though still in control, there were more dependent on their agrarian constituency.[12]

The outbreak of the war in Europe led to a realignment of the U.S. electorate. As it became the country's most important issue, the war divided the electorate into neutralists and interventionists. Once the country entered the war, however, the war united the nation behind the imperative of victory. Skillfully riding these changes in the electorate, the Wilson administration gradually abandoned its efforts to balance the agrarian and industrial interests in the Democratic party and began to favor the latter. The first divisive debate in the electorate was over the appropriate U.S. stance with respect to the war. Agrarians were opposed to joining the Entente, either because they had nothing to gain from it or because, as in some parts of the South, they supported intervention against Britain.[13] Within the administration, the conflict was between Secretary of State Bryan, a staunch advocate of absolute neutrality, and Commerce Secretary Redfield and Treasury Secretary McAdoo, who defended the preference of exporters and financiers for intervention. For one year, Bryan succeeded in stopping New York bankers from extending credit to the Allies for the purchase of ammunition. As Wilson gradually adopted the preferences of the eastern business community, Bryan resigned, and the ban on loans was repealed.[14]

U.S entry into the war accelerated the realignment in the electorate, and by 1919, the Wilson administration was giving more active support to American export trade than had any previous administration. After 1915, the administration fully backed National City Bank in an overt attempt to displace British dominance in foreign-branch banking.[15] In 1916, the Federal Reserve Act of 1913 was amended to allow bankers to "combine" in opening branches abroad without fear of prosecution under the antitrust laws. Three years later, the Edge Act extended the same immunity to the pooling of banking resources. The goal of this act was to finance reconstruction in Europe. That same year, the Webb-Pomerene Act extended antitrust immunity to exporter combinations. A Tariff Commission was created in 1916 at the request of a majority of the business community. Finally, the Shipping Act of 1916 involved the government in a large-scale shipbuilding program, a measure long sought by exporters.

The war made it feasible to take the trade debate out of party politics. More effective at curbing imports than any tariff, the war reconciled protectionists to the Democratic administration. With the mutual consent of the government and representatives of each industry, prices were fixed. The war effort also converted the federal government into a promoter that distributed war contracts to all producers without regard for orientation on trade. Institutionally, the war led to the War Industry Board, a central corporatist structure flanked by sixty-odd "commodity sections" staffed almost exclusively by businessmen drawn from various industries.[16]

In all three countries, therefore, the war allowed governments to break with traditional, existing constraints and pursue policies of their own choosing. In France, where interests had ruled unopposed for several decades, the government regained the policy initiative. In Britain and the United States, where the government had enjoyed autonomy but within the ideological limits of party politics, party leaders broke free and pursued policies of national scope. This surge in executive autonomy everywhere, however, was dependent on the war emergency. Peace stopped the surge in its tracks.

The Demise of Executive Politics

Executive politics was displaced when the external challenge subsided (hypothesis 4.4). In all three cases, the demise was swift, for national executives had not taken advantage of the war to set up a trade treaty network that could have bound them long after peace was restored. Because they lacked proper securing to the international system, war-trade institutions collapsed as soon as they lost their domestic standing.

The debilitating effect of peace on executive autonomy and postwar planning was most evident in France. Clémentel's domestic scheme was viable only as long as his proposal for an interallied bloc remained possible. When the return of peace made continuation of the war alliance unworkable on the external front (Washington nixed the project), the French government lost its bargaining power on the domestic front. Clémentel fell back on the voluntarist option. Though still in the government in 1919, he sponsored the organization of the *Confédération générale de la production française* (CGPF), the response of business to the workers' *Confédération générale du travail* (CGT)—and hardly more cohesive. This consolidation of business interests arose from the need for French employers to designate representatives who would sit down with their CGT counterparts at the International Labor Organization. Although the Minister of Commerce had hoped the CGPF could play a role in the mediation of economic—and tariff—conflicts, the CGPF limited itself to those questions on which there was a reasonable possibility of industrywide agreement—which, in practice, meant only labor and social issues.[17]

The slowest to mobilize, the United States was the fastest to demobilize. Many industrialists, especially major figures in the steel industry, expressed a desire to continue the war service committee system beyond the armistice. They did not look forward to returning to the prewar system of party politics. In 1919, Commerce secretary Redfield obliged the industrialists by setting up the Industrial Board, a reincarnation of the wartime arrangement; but the experiment had to be abandoned for fear of antitrust litigation.[18] The fact is, the Wilson administration was no longer in a position to uphold the interests of big business. Wilson had used the war to shift the base of his power from the West and South to the East. But he could not expect to maintain such an awkward position after the war.

The war-induced identity of interests between free trade and internationalism ended. Agrarians, returning to their prewar isolationism, pushed for immediate disengagement from Europe. Bipartisan support evaporated, and the President lost the initiative—the loss of which was most apparent in the handling of European reconstruction. To pay back its war loans, Europe needed to rebuild the wartorn economy and import raw materials and equipment, mostly from the United States. For that, dollars were needed, and dollars could be obtained by exporting to the United States, provided the United States lowered its tariff barriers. Dollars could also be obtained through additional U.S. loans. U.S. bankers were willing to lend to Europe, provided Washington reduced the financial risk through guarantees or improved European credit worthiness by canceling U.S. government war loans. The Wilson administration, because of agrarian opposition, could not deliver these guarantees or cancel the war loans.[19] All it could do was grant a one-year extension (until September 1919) to the War Finance Corporation. The administration refused to raise the tariff, thereby giving the Republicans an opportunity to run on a protectionist/isolationist platform in the election of 1920. The Republicans also urged government withdrawal from international lending, arguing that the American export surplus would be financed by Wall Street lending.[20]

Deregulation of American industry proceeded rapidly in Britain as well.[21] Nevertheless, the postwar sweep of wartime legislation was not as clean as it was elsewhere. Although all controls over imports were lifted in December 1919, this abrupt decision was not an act of the government but the result of a court ruling that struck down the legal basis for controls. The McKenna duties, initially adopted to save shipping space, were renewed in 1919. The war-inspired recommendations of the Balfour of Burleigh Committee were implemented long after the war was over. In 1919, the recommendation to extend preferential treatment to British dominions was adopted; and the recommendation to penalize foreign dumping and protect "key industries" and strategic products was implemented by the Safeguarding of Industries Act (1921). The government was a coalition government, which justified each measure as a step toward greater preparedness for a national emergency. Had executive politics in Britain gathered enough institutional momentum to outlast the war?

It had not. The government coalition of Unionists and Liberals—and with it, wartime rhetoric—outlived the war because of the ongoing destabilization of the Lib-Lab coalition. The war led to an unprecedented mobilization of the working class, which threatened to make Labour the first party of the Left.[22] The Liberals split between the Asquith wing, which favored an alliance with Labour, and the Lloyd George wing, which opposed it. Fearing social troubles, the Unionists retained Lloyd George "as a man who could talk to the working class."[23] Therefore, the coalition government, though initially intended as a war machine, was revamped as a class machine on Armistice Day. Marring this conversion was the clash between Lloyd George Liberals—sensitive to free trade—and the Unionists—committed to Tariff Reform. The two sides worked out a compromise: They would implement only those trade measures agreed to in common before the armistice. This platform, while moderate, incurred the wrath of the Opposition, which advocated all-out free trade. In any case, the cohabitation was short-lived. No longer fearing a revolution, the Unionists, in 1922, dumped Lloyd George and his faction quickly dissolved. The election of 1923 marked a return to the prewar partisan dynamic in which trade cleavage closely overlapped class cleavage. In sum, after 1918, the trade policy of the coalition government was the policy of a hung government, one whose war rhetoric obfuscated changing electoral dynamics.

The disappearance of executive initiative in Britain, France, and the United States did not mean restoration of the prewar institutional setup. In all three countries, the war left the executive with extended jurisdiction over the economy. The war did much to improve business views on the efficiency of state intervention in the economy. National industries emerged from World War I with a greater number of trade associations. In a sense, the war paved the way for the transfer of trade policymaking to the executive branch when the next emergency struck in the 1930s. Relocation, however, differs from empowerment. Pressure and party politics can thrive equally in the legislature or the executive. As was true before the war, policymaking after the war strictly reflected the electoral context of the trade debate.

Ten

Tariff-Making and State-Building, 1919–39

THE INTERWAR PERIOD presents us with a combination of historical transformation and cross-national diversity. Historically speaking, the period registered two developments in state-society relations: the universal relocation of tariff-making from the legislature to the executive; and the simultaneous growth of institutional networks which linked organized interests to the state. Comparatively speaking, in the Great Depression, each of the three democracies followed one of two divergent policy paths. Either they tried to save their way out of the depression and were protectionist, or they tried to spend their way out of the depression and moved toward free trade. These two sets of developments—changes in the policy process and changes in the policy outcome—are addressed simultaneously.

A striking fact of the interwar period is the partial retirement of parliaments from formulation of the tariff. Parliamentarians and Congressmen alike responded to the growing complexity of tariff management by redirecting trade interests to the executive branch, while reserving the right to intervene periodically. These delegations of power varied in their timing and scope. In France, delegation came relatively early; most trade bills were simply deferred to the executive. In Britain, in 1932, Parliament delegated tariff-making, in part, to an independent agency—the Import Duties Advisory Committee—although Parliament retained the right to ratify each change in the tariff. In 1934—with the passage of the Reciprocal Trade Act, which transferred tariff-making to the State Department—the United States achieved a level of delegation comparable to that in France.

In conjunction with the trend toward delegation of parliamentary responsibility in trade policy, all three countries experienced a trend toward some form of corporatism.[1] As the market seemed to be losing its ability to regulate commercial intercourse, it was felt that there was the need for producers to join trade associations. After the onset of the Great Depression, hopes for industrial recovery were pinned to whatever self-organization a sector could achieve. At some point, the government explicitly encouraged the formation of trade associations, cartels, or price-fixing agreements in sectors that seemed incapable of collective action on their own. This twofold evolution—toward executive authority and corporatist intermediation—led to the decay of the past informal parliamentary representation of interests and its replacement by a denser, more systematic, network of trade associations and state agencies.

These institutional changes are indisputable; but their impact on policymaking is debatable. Did relocation of the process of intermediation sanction the "growth of private power and the twilight of sovereignty," as Maier argues? Or did it signify a rise in state autonomy, as students of state institutions argue?[2]

The present study suggests that the answer is neither. Institutional relocation per se had no significant impact on the relative degree of autonomy enjoyed by policymakers. Instead, relocation must be analyzed as delegation to the executive branch by a parliament no longer willing or capable of administering the tariff, but which remained intent on preserving unaltered the existing parameters of policymaking. In France, where the policy process consisted of pressure politics, the transfer of responsibility to the executive did not make the conduct of trade policy more coherent. It did, however, transform receiving agencies into arenas for mediation and thus attracted the attention of interest groups and parliamentarians acting as intermediaries. In Britain, where the policy process consisted of party politics, the new trade institutions conformed to party politics. Trade associations did not increase their control over policymaking; instead, the trade official acquired more autonomy than his French equivalent. In the United States, the New Deal made party politics safe for the Democrats by relieving Congress of the formidable task of bridging the farm-factory cleavage and by entrusting it, instead, to the executive branch. In all three countries, then, relocation reflected the exogenous challenge of the growing complexity of tariff-making in a world of monetary and electoral uncertainty. This change, however, was policy-neutral.

What, then, effected the change in policy? The variation in national responses to the Great Depression has elicited scholarly attention. The dominant explanation—successively developed by Thomas Ferguson and Peter Gourevitch—emphasizes the role of producer coalitions.[3] Ferguson argues that the initial downturn in trade increased the political influence of labor-intensive industries, turning them into the anchor for a ruling coalition that advocated adjustment through protection and fiscal retrenchment. In contrast, the subsequent upturn increased the political influence of capital-oriented sectors, turning them into the anchor for a coalition with labor under the banner of free trade and demand stimulus.

Gourevitch, while endorsing Ferguson's model, adds a necessary twist to encompass European national experiences: The propensity for labor to ally with farmers than with business was much greater; thus, the initial support for pro-labor policies could come only from farm groups, in the form of a red-green coalition.[4] Only in instances where labor and farmers cooperated, presenting industry with a fait accompli, would capital-oriented industries bite the bullet on the other issues and come out for free trade. Such was the case with the U.S. New Deal, as well as the Scandinavian "cow trades." Where no red-green coalition emerged—in Britain, for instance—or where this coalition was unstable—as it was under the *Front Populaire* in France—labor found no allies among industry.

Although quite attractive, the producer-coalition explanation encounters difficulties in the case of Britain. Ferguson's model cannot explain why the American free-trade experiment was not replicated in a country well supplied with export-oriented industries. Gourevitch's variant is unconvincing for a country in which workers were the dominant electoral force and in which the electoral redundancy of agriculture should, in fact, have made it easier for British labor to impose Keynesian and free-trade policies on business. The interpretation I propose in this chapter suggests that the key place to look for the explanation is in the policy process. The Great Depression of the 1930s made economic management so salient and divisive that, in every country the depression resulted in an electoral realignment against the party unfortunate enough to find itself in charge when disaster struck. As a consequence, the Left was discredited in Britain (and Australia); while the Right was discredited in the United States, France (and Sweden).[5] Where the Left took power, trade policy moved in the direction of free trade; where the Right took power, protection remained the dogma of choice. Business realignment followed, rather than preceded, electoral realignment.

Combining considerations of process and policy, this chapter argues as follows. Until the Great Depression of the 1930s, policy process and policy outcome for each country remained what they had been before World War I: party politics and protection in the United States, party politics and free trade in Britain, and pressure politics and protection in France. The Great Depression interrupted these processes and outcomes by making the trade issue universally salient and divisive. As a result, party politics was reinvigorated in both the United States and Britain; and the orientation of the trade policy switched to free trade in the United States and protection in Britain. In France, the crisis repealed pressure politics and promoted party politics, and, for the first time in fifty years, the regime recorded its first successful, albeit timid, inroads into protectionism.

As before, each case study in this chapter first analyzes the origins of the policy process, then surveys the consequences for lobbies, parties, and the executive. It concludes with a review of orientation and policy tools.

France

The Policy Process until 1936

The Méline tariff of 1892 compromise and the particularistic trade regime that ensued continued to underlie French policymaking, with the exception of a tentative realignment in 1936 under the Popular Front. French trade policy

TABLE 10.1

France: Agrarian Population, Rural Population, and Agrarian *Syndicats*, 1891–1936

	Working population engaged in agriculture (%)	Rural population (%)	Number of agrarian syndicats (%)*	Members of agrarian syndicats (%)**
1891	—	—	23	45
1901	—	—	27	40
1911	40	56	35	38
1921	39	54	38	35
1926	35	51	47	48
1931	33	40	51	51
1936	33	48	—	—

*as a percentage of all registered *syndicats*.
**as a percentage of all members belonging to a registered *syndicat*.
Sources: Barral 1968: 217; INSEE, *Annuaire statistique de la France, 1951*. 1952: 100.

owed its resilience to the continuing centrality of the farmers, whose support every government coalition actively courted. Farmers were sufficiently organized throughout this period to be able to rely on pressure politics. Farmers, in fact, represented 48 percent of all individuals belonging to a registered *syndicat* (see table 10.1).

The farmers appeared happy with the legislative status quo, despite a series of measures apparently adverse to them. From 1919 until 1928, new protection applied to manufactures but not to farm products.[6] The average tariff rate for agriculture fell from parity with industry in the 1900s to half of industrial protection in the 1920s. War legislation that prohibited the exportation of foodstuffs was not rescinded until 1926, in order to contain inflationary pressures at home. And, on several occasions, the executive secured foreign outlets for industrial products by negotiating reductions on farm duties. Indeed, French governments were able to adopt a more pro-urban position between the end of World War I and 1929 than they had in the past, precisely because French farmers basically were satisfied with the state of trade. The farmers owed their unique situation to the war. In Britain and the United States, the war had boosted farm output. In France, however, farm production fell by 40 percent. A smaller farming population and a diminished area of arable land combined to reduce the ratio of national sufficiency from 88 percent in 1913, to 63 percent in 1919. By 1930, the ratio was still only 75 percent.[7] French agricultural prices were systematically higher than world prices. Cattle, grains, and other staples were in demand and fetching good prices.[8] To be sure, farm organizations continued to press various requests on governments. But the troops were scattered and the electoral weapon buried. Until 1930, the Radical party—the farmers' party par excellence—was not well disposed toward protection.[9] As a result, the trade issue was not salient. The corporatist bargain of 1892 institutionalized in the Méline tariff, and confirmed by the tariff of 1910, continued to circumscribe the trade debate.

In 1932, domestic prices collapsed, and the state of affairs changed drastically. The farmers mobilized, rightist and fascist movements found support in the countryside, and the Radicals rediscovered the allure of protection. Unable to choose between the interests of the urban workers and those of the farmers, the Steeg government fell in January 1931. From 1932 until 1934, successive Radical governments, despite an official commitment to deflation, provided farmers with all the protection they wanted. The contradiction grew untenable, and in December 1934, the Flandin government utilized the threat of dissolution to persuade the Chamber of Deputies to abolish price guarantees on wheat.[10]

"Blum's Agrarian New Deal" [11]

The year 1936 was a turning point in French politics. The victory of the *Front Populaire* (a government coalition of Radicals, Socialists, and Communists) shattered the 1892 bloc and sketched the possibility of a realignment similar to that of the New Deal in the United States. The Popular Front was a response to the Great Depression, which polarized public opinion and emptied the Center of followers. The tardiness of the response reflected the delayed impact of the crisis, as well as a prudent steering of the crisis, that saved the Center-Right from the kind of political flop experienced elsewhere—the suspension of convertibility in Britain and the Smoot-Hawley tariff of 1930. The elections of 1936 did not register a realignment to the Left as much as they did a realignment *within* the Left. The Communists gained primarily at the expense of the Socialists, and the Socialists at the expense of the Radicals.

The Popular Front was the first French government to articulate the demands of the French working class.[12] Indeed, the Popular Front was fundamentally an urban, working-class government determined to keep the price of food reasonably low. With workers chronically unhappy about food prices, the labor movement consistently criticized the policy of protecting agriculture. As early as 1889, several Parisian unions had called for the free entry of wheat and flour.[13] However, the unions were a captive constituency of the extreme left (Socialist at first, Communist after 1919), which had never had the opportunity to influence government policies—that is, not until the advent of the Popular Front. With their party in power, blue-collar workers were likely to upset the arrangement of 1892 (hypothesis 4.1). As a condition of approving devaluation in the autumn of 1936—which would cancel the benefits labor had recently extracted from management in the Matignon Accords—the Communists asked that the government be empowered to lower import quotas and tariffs. The government thereupon availed itself of the new powers to reduce tariffs by 20 percent for primary products, 17 percent for semimanufactures, and 15 percent for finished goods; import taxes were lowered on certain agricultural products and several quota restrictions were lifted, mostly on food-stuffs.[14] Although these reductions constituted little more than "an earnest of good intentions" (for they certainly were not enough to balance the reevaluation of foreign currencies), yet they indicated a will to fight inflation, especially as it was reflected in high food prices.[15] Whether or not as a consequence of these measures, the volume of imports between 1935 and 1937 increased by 29 percent.[16]

The Blum government would not tolerate politicization of the trade issue, believing that to do so would antagonize the Radicals and split the red-green coalition. Instead, the government predicated its survival on its ability to engineer a Swedish-style quid pro quo in which workers consented to price supports for agriculture, while farmers agreed to social benefits for workers. Yet, Léon Blum was not very successful at keeping the coalition together but instead let his government adopt measures that upset the farm interests. He did not appoint a Radical as minister of agriculture, but rather a Socialist, Georges Monnet. Monnet applied himself to the task of getting Parliament to pass a Socialist plan for a state-run wheat office that would have the power to control wheat imports and exports. He also applied himself to the task of ensuring an adequately remunerative price for wheat—a measure which, at the time, had deliberate Socialist overtones. The bill touched off a sharp controversy over state interference, but managed to pass the Senate, still dominated by rural Radicals, only after the government accepted an amendment to confer price-fixing power on the wheatgrowers.[17] Through shrewd appointments, the government denied the agrarians full control over the wheat office. In response to Communist pressure, the government delayed until 1937 adjustment of the floor price of wheat to the devaluation of autumn 1936. Finally, intoxicated by its unexpected electoral success in 1936, among the peasants of central and southwestern France, the Socialist government tried to expand its agrarian base in the countryside by promoting social reforms in favor of tenants and farmworkers at the expense of landlords and farmers. The attempt failed because the measures were shelved by the Radical-controlled Senate. As Luebbert demonstrates with respect to Germany, Spain, and Italy, this procedure was unlikely to yield the type of corporatist agreement necessary to keep the Popular Front together.[18]

The farmers were unimpressed by the reflationary policies of the Left. They were also opposed to state intervention in favor of workers. In September 1936, the vegetable growers, themselves victims of the deflationary policy, staged a spectacular strike around Paris.[19] Radical support of the Popular Front was sharply criticized by agrarian delegates to the Radical Congress of October 1936.[20] In February 1937, more Radicals found it difficult to support renewal of the delegation of economic powers to the government, once it was understood that the delegation would be used to reduce protection for agriculture. Although a majority of Radicals in the Chamber of Deputies still favored the delegation, their colleagues from the more rural Senate voted it down. The same scenario unfolded in June 1937, when the Blum government once again requested full emergency powers (including trade), then resigned when the Senate Radicals failed to go along. By contrast, these powers were granted immediately afterward to the Chautemps government (Radical), which used them to repeal the liberalization of trade measures enacted by the Popular Front.[21]

This politicization of a consumer-primary producer cleavage, in which urban labor was pitted against farmers, contributed to (although it did not determine) the fall of the Popular Front. The consumer-primary producer cleavage, however, did not quite revolutionize tariff-making; because its very activation isolated the workers, whose parties could not make it on their own. As in Sweden and the United States, leftist rule required that the cleavage be controlled. Still, French politics was never the same after the *Front Populaire*. The political hegemony of the Center-right had been shaken and would be brought down at the Liberation.

Bureaucratization of Pressure

With the exception of the Popular Front, the electoral context of tariff-making in the period 1919–39 replicated the prewar lack of salience and the managed consensus of the trade issue. Yet, in formal terms, tariff-making underwent a major institutional change when it was moved out of Parliament and into the executive branch. The result was not a dual-track system, patronage-driven in the Chamber of Deputies and rational in the state; rather, the result was reproduction and perfection within the state of the prewar committee system.

The delegation of parliamentary power to the executive branch began in 1919, immediately after war controls were abolished. The reason was technical. The war had destabilized the gold standard, and many nations, including France, kept their currencies floating. Certain countries even engaged in "exchange dumping" (depreciating their currency to promote exports). Currency instability made tariffs ineffective, unless they were capable of rapid adjustment to meet the fluctuations of foreign exchange. The French Parliament, deeming itself unfit for the task, extended the war legislation that empowered the government to modify the duties by decree.

This delegation of power posed serious dangers. There was the danger that the government might take advantage of the new power to pursue policies that would unravel the delicate balance of interests reached in 1892, renewed in 1910, and very carefully reproduced in the composition of the Chamber Customs Committee. Even if the government had no such intention, there were interests that would, in any case, lose from the institutional relocation. The farmers, for instance, would find it hard to duplicate in the executive the control they had over Parliament—the Ministry of Agriculture was not the Senate. These technical difficulties were resolved in two ways. First, Parliament kept the government on a leash by consenting to short-term, specific delegations only, obliging the cabinet to return regularly to request an extension. Parliament used this leverage systematically to induce the government to steer the desired course. Second, the government surrounded itself with a formal network of trade interests which it consulted whenever it sought to modify the tariff. Allow me to develop each point.

The first check on governmental arbitrariness was Parliament itself. From 1919 on, the Chamber Tariff Commission ensured that the government would respect the requisites of pressure politics; otherwise, the Chamber of Deputies would withdraw its delegation. The early governments apparently did well, for two successive ministers of commerce, who resented the pressure to which their office was submitted, tried unsuccessfully to talk the Chamber into reassuming its tariff responsibilities. Instead, Parliament conceded three more extensions. Then, however, the cabinet, trying to take advantage of its new authority to contain inflation, negotiated reductions on foodstuffs with commercial partners. This diversion of trade policy to fulfill monetary goals was unacceptable to a majority of the Tariff Commission. Because the deal targeted mainly products of the soil, it alienated farmers. The farm bloc next mobilized its industrial allies; and by December 1922, the government could find no majority in Parliament to renew the delegation.[22] Parliament thus retrieved its prewar authority. Because the currency still was not stabilized, however, the Chamber Tariff Commission refused to concern itself with partial changes in the tariff, preferring instead to maintain the status quo until the franc had been stabilized. To do nothing was politically safer than to do something wrong. In fact, it was precisely the degradation of the franc that made the status quo bearable.

When the franc was finally stabilized in 1926, a new delegation of authority allowed the government to conduct negotiations with Germany. In the process, however, the farmers secured two concessions: repeal of the export prohibitions, and exclusion of farm products from the negotiations. This made possible the tariff of 1928, in which Parliament ratified the industrial duties negotiated by the executive and included the farm duties demanded by farm organizations.

The Great Depression struck, however, and in 1931, Parliament delegated to the executive branch the power to impose quotas on foreign imports, especially foodstuffs. With the crisis deepening, the government requested full powers over the tariff. As in 1922, it sought the right to reduce duties in accordance with its general policy of deflation. These powers were denied in 1933, but, owing to the intractability of the situation, full powers were approved twice in 1934. The compromise of 1892, now at risk, was ultimately ruptured by the Popular Front. The agrarian Senate retaliated by blocking Blum's successive requests for full powers over the tariff. As we have seen, the Senate correctly suspected Blum of contemplating serious cuts in food duties. They granted full powers to his successor, who used them to raise the food duties. Therefore, all along, Parliament was using its leverage to prevent the executive from using *its* trade powers to discriminate against agrarians.

The second check on governmental discretion was consultation. At one time or another, state officials invited all branches of industry to send representatives to attend specially organized advisory committees. Known as the *procédure consultative*, this institutionalization of interest representation in the state affected almost all aspects of state policy. With respect to trade policy, this development owed its existence to delegation of parliamentary responsibilities to the executive branch. To perform its task in accordance with parliamentary expectations, state agencies found it necessary to replicate—or even perfect—the links that the Chamber tariff commission had developed over the years with influential trade interests. Basically, to minimize parliamentary interference, administrative agencies needed independent access to trade information.

Consultation thus accompanied delegation. For instance, between 1919 and 1922, the administration of duty-multipliers, a device designed by the executive branch to neutralize the deleterious effects of exchange dumping, was entrusted to a *Commission spéciale* staffed, for the most part, by representatives of the trade associations. This commission could not modify a multiplier without consulting the interested trade association. A high official of the customs services provided the press with the following description of the decision making process:

> The interested parties are always consulted. Better, since this system has been in application, it works as follows: the *Direction des douanes* receives requests from industrialists and their corporate groups on the modifications to bring about in the existing custom rates. The revision committee reviews the requests, receives the delegates who expressed them, listens to their arguments, debates them if necessary, then performs a personal study of the points raised and finally writes up its report. The report is circulated to the departments responsible for the issue, which in turn review the case, come to an agreement and work out a decree that is submitted for presidential signature and parliamentary approval.[23]

The procedure followed in negotiating trade agreements provides another manifestation of consultation. To begin with, although the *Direction des accords commerciaux* was part of the Quai d'Orsay, the French Foreign Office, actual responsibility for negotiations was gradually transferred from career diplomats to experts detached from Commerce.[24] Once the minister of foreign affairs decided to open negotiations with a foreign government, the *Direction* would send a memo to the trade associations likely to be interested in the negotiations, asking them to submit their desiderata. Whenever possible, the government would gather together the representatives of interested industries in each country concerned. In the negotiations with Germany, for example, meetings of this sort were arranged for thirty-seven different industries.[25]

The generalization of quotas after 1931 reinforced the consultative process. The process was fragmented among sponsoring agencies from various ministries, with each agency responsible for fixing quotas in the area of its competence with little regard for others. Each agency was assisted by a series of *Comités interprofessionnels*, until 1934, staffed only with producers, and afterward with importers as well. The inclusion of importers had no pluralist implications, for they automatically received import licenses and thus had a vested interest in the proper working of the logroll.[26]

By the late 1930s, France had thus evolved its bureaucratic variant of pressure politics. This variant differed from the traditional parliamentarian variant only in location; otherwise, little had changed. After 1892, under the parliamentary variant, when Parliament began to deal with the tariff piecemeal, fragmentation characterized the tariff debate. Fragmentation was also typical of the new bureaucratic variant, in which each sponsoring ministry and direction set up an advisory body within its own jealously guarded jurisdiction. In both variants, moreover, the trade debate was parochial. In Parliament, the trade debate had been separated from the partisan debate. In the executive branch, trade policy was made at the ministerial level or lower, and its day-to-day management ran counter to many broader goals pursued by the government. Up to 1934, the protectionist orientation of trade policy remained unaffected by the government's policy of deflation. It was never affected by the Foreign Office's concern for trade openness. Only on rare occasions was the government capable of using trade policy to further goals of a diplomatic nature.

Finally, in either variant, political authority refused to challenge the trade associations' capacity to organize and represent their respective sectors of production; and public officials did not attempt to deal with firms directly. Throughout the period, the most important trade associations (responsible for representing their sectors) remained the privileged interlocutors of both Parliament and the administration.

The Executive

The Quai d'Orsay participated in the making of the tariff through negotiation of trade agreements. In these negotiations the Quai tried to bring the national interest to bear on the process. In some cases, the Foreign Office's notion of "national interest" included the preservation of French export interests abroad. For instance, the Quai regularly warned other ministries against this or that country's threat of retaliation against French protectionism. The Quai also designed various formulas for circumventing Parliament's ban on granting MFN treatment in exchange for concessions to French exporters. In other cases, the Quai became an outright advocate on behalf of foreign governments with which, for political reasons, it wished to maintain cordial relations. In still other cases, the Quai sought to impose trade sanctions against unfriendly governments.[27] Overall, the erratic nature of the Quai's interventions makes their impact on policymaking difficult to assess. Several bilateral trade agreements led not to reductions in duties but to increases. Such was the case in treaties signed with Italy (1923), Czechoslovakia (1923), Turkey (1924), Belgium (1925), and Germany (1927).[28]

It was when the Quai d'Orsay attempted to pursue a policy on a multinational front that the limits of its allowance of discretion show most clearly. Between 1925 and 1930, the Quai was involved in a large-scale offensive at the League of Nations on behalf of the liberalization of world trade.[29] French diplomats correctly perceived that France had to take a leading role in trade matters if it wanted to prevent Germany from turning the small East European states into satellites. However, the international drive for open trade pursued in the higher spheres of governmental power had no impact on French duties, which continued to be set within the sponsoring ministries at the ministerial level or lower.

The rise of the Nazis alerted the Quai to the need to consolidate its political relations with Eastern Europe. The Quai thus sought to reinforce its diplomatic ties with these countries by importing their raw materials and agricultural goods, especially wheat, in order to reduce the countries' economic dependence on Berlin.[30] The French market, however, could not accommodate any more primary goods without cutting into sales of domestic and colonial producers. The Quai's strategy thus met with the insurmountable opposition of all the domestic ministries concerned, especially Agriculture.[31]

The Policy Toolbox

The logic of pressure politics is one of accommodation. Whenever the tariff failed to fulfill its ecumenical responsibility, it was amended or supplemented by a new policy instrument (hypothesis 5.7). The response to currency instability and the development of the colonial market were the two most important policy spillovers of the period. By contrast, a renewed attempt to interest bankers in the fate of industry did not fare well.

The number-one economic constraint for the trade policy of France between the wars was the value of the franc. Weakened by debts incurred during and after World War I, France's currency started to slip in 1922 and took a dive in 1925–26. An unprecedented price explosion occurred, followed by currency stabilization (December 1926) at one-fifth the franc's prewar parity. As a result, the fear of reenacting the 1926 fiasco was so great that successive governments refused to touch the new parity until, after six years of depression, it had become indefensible. In the autumn of 1936, the franc was released from its gold anchor and allowed to depreciate, until it stabilized again in 1938 at about one half its 1926 parity.

Most of the changes in trade policy were intended to neutralize the impact of monetary vicissitudes on actual levels of protection. The effective levels of protection, decided in 1910, were maintained through a system of frequently adjusted duty-multipliers.[32] This system was in effect from 1919 to 1922. In 1924, the fall of the currency spurred exports to the point of depleting the supply for the domestic market, thus leading French industrialists to protest against price increases for standard commodities. At the request of the industrialists, the government prohibited exports of leather and skins, woolen cloth, cottons, seeds, lumber, charcoal, and so forth.[33] Conversely, the depression, along with the stubborn adherence to the gold parity of 1926, soon priced French products out of the market, obliging the government to erect an unprecedented wall of tariffs and quotas merely to maintain the effective rates of 1928. Because trade conventions froze most duties, the government resorted to quantitative restrictions. But it is doubtful that higher duties alone would have been sufficient.

The policy of quantitative restrictions had the drawback of discriminating against certain trade groups. For example, shipping interests, which now handled a much lower volume of trade, were seriously disadvantaged. Exporters who lost their foreign markets were also harmed. They were the victims of retaliation abroad and high production costs at home. The entire civic body of Calais, a port city with a large tulle and lace export-oriented manufacturing community, resigned in protest. In the autumn of 1932, exporters across the nation organized the Union française des industries exportatrices to fight quotas.[34]

Clearly, politicians had to do something. To appease the citizens of Calais, the minister of education promised to furnish all French schools with lace curtains. To meet exporters' complaints, the authorities imagined a way of turning quotas into bargaining tools. Starting in the fall of 1934, only 25 percent of the previous year's quota would be renewed automatically; the remaining 75 percent would be withheld pending negotiations with each exporting country for the granting of special concessions to French exports. The same rule governed the redistribution of unused quotas.[35] The results do not seem to have met expectations, however; only small countries were sensitive to this type of leverage. Britain, Germany, and the United States were capable of retaliating and causing further damage to the French export trade.

Colonial development, which replaced the simple, prewar tariff assimilation, is another instance of spillover. With the onset of the Great Depression, more and more producers availed themselves of the colonial outlet. For manufacturers of refined sugar, cotton fabric, cement, and groundnut oil, the colonial market was the almost exclusive recipient of exports—absorbing over 87 percent.[36] For many other sectors, too—including iron and steel products, metal tools, machines, automobiles, and chemicals—the proportion sold in the colonies increased substantially. Even traditionally export-oriented sectors, such as silk fabric, wool fabric, clothing, and leather goods, were able to redirect a greater part of their exports to the colonial market.

With more and more industries thus developing a stake in colonial purchasing power, the debate over the colonial tariff was bound to expand to include the larger issue of colonial development.[37] Interests slated to benefit from colonial development held that the colonies should develop resources to complement those of the metropole. Agrarians, however, correctly sensed that the complementarity sought by the industrialists implied large imports of colonial agricultural products by the metropole—trade being a two-way street. Indeed, when the crisis hit and primary products worldwide suffered a heavy drop in price, colonial exports found a refuge in the high-priced French market; they were exempted from the stringencies of the quota system that had been developed to protect metropolitan farmers against foreign dumping. In addition, the French government established price supports for hard-hit colonial crops at a level higher than world prices.[38] In 1937, colonial imports represented 69 percent of metropolitan imports of foodstuffs and 15 percent of their national consumption. In the period preceding the crisis, the corresponding figures were 34 percent and 8 percent respectively.[39] Finally, reversing thirty years of colonial, financial self-reliance, the ministry of colonies, in 1931–35, guaranteed a series of loans to finance public works in the colonies. Public investment would thus fill in for the now reticent private-sector investment. Not only did the crisis affect French colonies less than it did other developing parts of the world, but the changes in terms of imperial trade improved in favor of the colonies.[40]

French farmers resented being the only ones to bear the burden of imperial preferences. Yet, they did not try to take the issue to the electors, where presumably they might have enjoyed greater support. In any event, the farmers had a weak case. They had no sincere interest in the industrialization of the colonies and little interest in retaining the empire. Further, refocusing the debate on the question of the profitability of the empire was politically inopportune. Although the large majority of the French population had rarely cared one way or the other about colonial policy, the mere fact that, in 1938, the fascist governments of Germany and Italy requested a share of the French empire was enough to set off a nationalist reaction in favor of a "Greater France."[41] Not until after World War II did decolonization become a plausible option.

The third episode in the French government's attempt to promote exports was the creation of a bank to finance international trade. In 1919, bankers and public officials agreed to set up the *Banque nationale du commerce extérieur*, which would have a double purpose.[42] First, it would facilitate imports of raw materials by advancing the necessary credits; and second, it would facilitate the sales of French products in foreign markets by taking over the task of discounting foreign commercial paper. Bankers, however, resisted state intervention in an area of business they considered their own. Their support was conditional: The new bank could not open branches outside Paris, nor in countries already served by French banks. Nor could it accept deposits other than the annual public subsidy, a formula that effectively condemned the bank to insignificance. By 1922, the affair was widely acknowledged a failure.

Legislators next tried export guarantees. A law passed in 1928 gave the government the authority to insure up to 80 percent of the value of an exporter's sales. But the measure applied only to sales to foreign governments or their agencies with whom the Quai d'Orsay had an agreement. It was not until the Popular Front had nationalized the *Banque de France*—the central bank—that legislation extended the guarantee to private orders, as well as the remaining 20 percent. Finally, in 1939, tax enticements were adopted for banks engaged in the financing of exports.[43]

With due allowances made for export finance, it is reasonable to argue that, more than ever during the Great Depression of the 1930s, the ability of the French government to imagine bold, sophisticated policy techniques was exercised in the service of an unimaginative, conservative objective: maintaining the status quo among trade interests. Except during the government of the Popular Front, French farmers stayed "on board," thus allowing the compromise of 1892 to survive the turmoil of the depression.

Policy Orientation

France is a good example of pressure politics, in which the Popular Front was the exception. According to hypothesis 5.1 (about the business cycle), that cycle ought to be among the events most likely to determine the orientation of trade policy. (Hypothesis 5.2, about collective action, is not considered here because of the lack of data.) The results shown in table 10.2 only partially illustrate this hypothesis. While the Popular Front dummy is significantly correlated with a lowering of the tariff, the business cycle is correctly signed but fails to reach the 0.05 level of significance. There was a spurious factor.

Among the events that are most likely to have interfered with the expected relationship between business cycle and tariff level is the currency. We saw that French governments sought to maintain the extant level of real protection by raising duties when the franc rose and reducing them when it fell. If

TABLE 10.2
Determinants of the Tariff, 1919–39

	France		Britain		United States
	\multicolumn{5}{c}{*Dependent variable: log of the percentage of change in the duties-imports ratio.*}
	I	*II*	*III*	*IV*	*V*
Business cycle	−0.024	−0.012	−0.023		−0.029
	(−1.68)	(−0.87)	(−2.48)*		(−1.85)*
Party cycle			0.027	0.028	0.016
			(2.00)*	(2.00)*	(1.15)
Popular Front	0.060	0.055			
	(1.79)*	(1.84)*			
Price of FF in $		0.073			
		(2.42)*			
Price of sterling in FF			−0.072		
			(−3.12)*		
Price of $ in sterling					0.069
					(1.05)
Constant	0.022	0.024	0.005	−0.013	0.013
	(2.18)*	(2.56)*	(0.40)	(−1.21)	(0.75)
R-squared	0.22	0.45	0.54	0.17	0.41
Number of observations	20	20	20	20	20

* Significant at the 0.05 level.
Coding rules and data sources:

Changes in the nominal tariff: Logarithm of the yearly change in the average ratio of customs revenues collected to total imports. Source for Britain and France: Mitchell 1980: Series F1 and H5. Source for the United States: U.S. Bureau of the Census 1976: Series U-207 and Y-353.

Business cycle: Economic expansion or peak years were coded "1"; contraction or economic through years were coded "0." Sources: same as above.

Party cycle: This is the trade orientation of the governing party (or coalition thereof), with protectionists coded "1" and free traders coded "2."

Popular Front: Coded "1" for the year 1936, "0" otherwise.

Franc-dollar and sterling-franc exchange rates: Logarithm of the yearly change. I.N.S.E.E., *Annuaire Statistique*. 1951. 1952: 503.

Dollar-sterling exchange rate: Logarithm of the yearly change. *Statistical Abstract of the United States*. Washington, D.C.: U.S. Government Printing Office, various years.

that was indeed the case, we should observe a positive correlation between changes in nominal duties and variations in the currency. This high correlation is shown in the second equation (column II), which includes variations in the franc–dollar exchange rate. It should be noted, however, that interpreting the correlation is complicated by the presence of another spurious factor:

the fact that customs receipts were specific (the importer pays a fixed amount) rather than ad valorem (the importer pays a percentage of the value of the import). As a result, higher import prices due to a depreciation of the franc artificially yielded a reduction in the ad valorem equivalent of the tariff (which our proxy captures); conversely, lower import prices due to an appreciation of the franc caused a rise in the ad valorem equivalent of the tariff. The dependent variable reflects the combination of the two effects—the actual and the spurious—and greater precision is not possible. Instead, we must rely on qualitative accounts. Standard accounts of the policy of the period point to an increase in the tariff between 1920 and 1922, to another increase in 1928, sporadic increases in 1929, and, of course, to a surge in quotas after 1932, which was uninterrupted until 1936.[44]

The French case is worth comparing to the British case. In both countries, tariff-making was redirected to the executive branch; yet, in France, the executive branch was decentralized, penetrated, and distributive, whereas, in Britain, the administrative process was autonomous, centralized, and partisan.

Britain

Party Politics

In the case of Britain, the interwar period is not homogeneous; rather, it is characterized by the juxtaposition of two very different epochs whose dividing line was the crisis of 1931. The party dynamic of the prewar period continued unchanged throughout the 1920s. Still hopeful that they could appeal to the workers by means of Tariff Reform, the Conservatives actually helped sustain the Liberal-Labour coalition, whose dual leadership was content to use the trade issue to round up worker support (a paradoxical instance of hypothesis 4.1). In contrast, the 1930s prefigured the post-1945 dynamic, which was no longer governed by the cleavage between laissez-faire and protection but, rather, was informed by two radically different forms of collective management: self-help and state-run.

The tariff remained a sensitive electoral issue during the 1920s, mainly because Tariff Reformers persevered in the face of repeated electoral failure. Hopeful that the war had modified the basic outlook of many workers, in 1923, the Conservative premier, Stanley Baldwin, called for the electorate to endorse Tariff Reform without food duties. Once again, the Conservatives were trying to reconcile workers to the industrialists' demand for a tariff, one which, this time, would exclude foodstuffs. As before, the key electoral group in Britain was the working class. The farmers, a captive Conservative constituency, were neglected. Fixated on the workers' vote, the Conservatives disregarded the needs of the farmers—indeed, the Conservatives betrayed them. As a partner in the coalition government, which they dominated, Conservatives, in the spring of 1921, repealed farm price guarantees just as world prices began to fall; they did so just four months after they had gotten Parliament to pass an act that expressly required a four-year notice for repeal.[45] From then on, the main farming lobby—the National Farmers' Union (NFU)—pressed the Conservatives, unsuccessfully, to endorse subsidies for agricultural production. The endorsement did not come until 1932—that is, after the workers had abandoned free trade.

The election of 1923 thus revolved around the trade issue, as Conservatives advertised protection as a way to fight unemployment. As in 1910, election results were disastrous for the Conservatives, who lost their comfortable majority and relinquished power to the first Labour government ever formed in Britain. The Conservatives promptly forsook tariff reform, pledging themselves only to preserve the status quo of the pre-1923 coalition government. All in all, theirs was a very limited program which, by 1928, affected no more than 3 percent of British imports.[46] Only in November 1929 did the Conservatives again endorse the full Tariff Reform program.

World War I had not fundamentally modified the British workers' commitment to free trade. As early as 1917, the Labour party conference and the TUC voiced their opposition to the postwar protective schemes contemplated by the coalition government.[47] No dissidence among the unions was noted until 1928, with the insignificant exception of the motor workers of Coventry (1924) and the lace workers of Nottingham (1925).[48] The situation changed radically in 1928, when trade unions in the woolens and the iron and steel industries broke with the TUC and supported the protectionist proclivities of their respective sectors. The subsequent economic crisis generalized the change in policy preferences.

The line between Right and Left was momentarily redrawn in the trade debate of 1923. The fight for free trade reunited the Liberals and cemented a new Liberal-Labour alliance in Parliament. The two MacDonald governments (1924 and 1929–31) played the trade issue for all it was worth. To be sure, their emphasis did not necessarily guarantee electoral success, since, after 1923, the Conservatives downplayed the trade issue. Also, trade cleavage competed with class cleavage, with the latter, unlike the former, tending to isolate Labour from the Liberals. There is no doubt, however, that in the 1920s, free trade contributed to maintaining the Liberal-Labour alliance. The demise of free trade in the 1930s ushered in a decade of confusion on the Left and Conservative dominance on the Right.

The crisis of 1931 reshuffled the cards in a way reminiscent of 1910. The economic depression discredited free trade and generated in its stead mass support for protection. The impact on the party system was momentous. The Liberals were left without an issue, and the Labour party split. Since 1923,

Labour had accommodated an extreme left faction that repudiated both free trade and Tariff Reform on the grounds that both policies caused unemployment. The faction advocated, instead, import control and bulk purchase, measures judged too radical by a party dominated by older-generation free traders. As the Great Depression put an end to free trade, the party's center of gravity shifted to the Left. The unions withdrew their support from free trade but maintained their opposition to Tariff Reform. Faced with the twin specters of nationalization and state interference, the Conservatives, in alliance with Liberal and Labour defectors, became the champion of industrial self-help (belief in the ability of the private sector to organize itself out of the crisis).

In sum, dissolution of the free-trade bloc at the polls did not remove divisiveness from the trade debate; rather, it transformed the fight between free traders and protectionists into a fight between protection for capital and protection for Labour. For the second time in twenty years, the class issue had redrawn the trade debate.

Party Politics by Delegation

In Britain, relocation of the trade decisionmaking process to the executive branch took place in 1932 with the creation of the Import Duties Advisory Committee (IDAC). Both before and after 1932, lobbying was weak at the sectoral level; in neither period did policy outcome actually reflect the sectors' respective aptitude for collective action. Instead, trade orientation reflected the interplay of partisan forces.

We consider the period of the 1920s first. As we have seen, during and after World War I, the Lloyd George coalition government adopted a limited set of protective measures: the McKenna duties (1915);[49] the Dyestuffs Act (1920); under which organic dyestuffs were imported under license; and the Safeguarding of Industries Act (1921).[50] In 1919, the government also extended to the empire imperial preferences on most of these duties. Implementation of these measures during the 1920s fell victim to partisan alternation: cut by Labour, restored by Conservatives. The first MacDonald government repudiated the preferential arrangements with the dominions agreed to in 1923, repealed the McKenna duties, and allowed some safeguarding duties to lapse.[51] Back in power, Baldwin restored and expanded the McKenna duties,[52] granted safeguarding duties to new sectors,[53] imposed special duties on silk goods, and granted imperial preferences on most of these duties. The second MacDonald government allowed all the safeguarding duties up for renewal to lapse, and repealed the antidumping provisions of the Act of 1921.[54]

Even during the second Baldwin government, the relative success of firms in applying for safeguarding duties depended less on lobbying performance than on Baldwin's notion of political acceptability. Baldwin interpreted the defeat of 1923 as a clear rejection of his proposals for a general tariff; but he still considered that "for safeguarding we have a perfectly clear mandate." [55] As a result, duties were granted to relatively small, low-visibility sectors—lace, gloves, buttons, and so forth—but were refused in cases where they might have been perceived as a step toward a general tariff. Steel and woolens were excluded outright from applying. Agriculture was excluded, too, since in 1923, Baldwin had committed himself not to impose food duties.

Finally, among those sectors that qualified for duties, the protectionist bias of the Baldwin government often prevailed over other considerations. For instance, the report of the Lace Safeguarding Committee, assembled by the government to evaluate the lace industry's application, concluded that, by the standards laid out in the government's white paper of 1924, the industry did not deserve protection. Nevertheless, the committee recommended a duty. Protection for artificial silk yarn was opposed by one of the most powerful trade associations in the country—the Cotton Spinners' and Manufacturers' Association, as well as by the Joint Standing Committee of the Cotton Trade, which represented all sections of the cotton trade in Lancashire and adjacent counties—but to no avail. [56] In sum, sectors received or were denied protection for reasons exhibiting no apparent relation to the degree of sectoral organization.

Sectoral unity did not pay off; dissidence was rewarded. The steel industry is a case in point. The National Federation of Iron and Steel Manufacturers (NFISM) stayed out of the trade debate until 1931, months after the Federation of Business Industry (FBI), the main industry association, had recommended a tariff. The NFISM remained neutral, despite the fact that, as the decade came to a close, opposition to protection was confined to an economically insignificant section of the industry: the re-rollers and a few small firms which feared that removal of cheap imported steel would increase their dependence on larger firms. Even the South-Wales tinplate manufacturers and the British Engineers' Association, hitherto opposed to protection, came to side with the larger, heavy industry section. [57] Yet, as Tolliday writes, the re-rollers "formed an active lobby who were able to exploit the broad political problems raised by the tariff issue to exercise an influence in the debate out of all proportion to their economic weight." [58]

Not surprisingly, lobbying with respect to trade reverted to the prewar model: ad hoc, national organizations, established to stall or advance the fight for Tariff Reform within the Conservative party. The growing irrelevance of the FBI—the business peak association that grew out of wartime consensus—derived from the FBI's search for consensual issues in a highly divisive context. [59] On the protectionist side were the National Union of Manufacturers (1916), the British Empire Producers' Organization, the British Commonwealth Union (1916), the Empire Industries Association (1924), the Empire Economic Union, and the National Council of Industry and Commerce

(1930). On the side of free trade were the Imperial Commercial Association (1923), the Parliamentary Committee for the Defense of Free Trade (1923), and older organizations such as the National Association of Merchants and Manufacturers, the National Chamber of Trade, and the Chamber of Shipping. (This list is not exhaustive.) These organizations engaged in advertising campaigns and fundraising for their respective party candidates.

The Great Depression shattered the free-trade front and rewarded the protectionists' thirty-year-long campaign for Tariff Reform. The Import Duties Act of 1932 imposed a 10 percent import levy and created the Import Duties Advisory Committee to write a general protective tariff and amend it afterward as needed. The standard view of this period is that the tariff system and the IDAC were a great "encouragement to the formation of new, or the strengthening of existing associations." [60] Herbert Hutchinson, the assistant secretary of the IDAC, explained that "[the committee] did not refuse to consider representations from individual firms, but it lost no opportunity of encouraging the members of any industry or section of an industry to make a united approach, and so far as possible to settle any internal differences of view among themselves." [61] The post-1933 period did, indeed, register a relative increase in the formation of national and regional trade associations. [62]

It is important to note, however, that the industrialists' aptitude for collective action was not reflected in the IDAC's recommendations. The committee did not deliver protection to the organized, as would have been the case in pressure politics. Often, the committee did the reverse: It made the granting of protection conditional on organizational centralization. "[The committee] took this line," Hutchinson wrote, "not only for its own convenience and for expediting its work, but also because it believed in cooperation between firms as a means to the success and efficiency of an industry." [63] The IDAC was the implementing officer of the new Conservative ideological commitment to industrial self-help.

In some cases, protection preceded sectoral organization. Such was the case with steel. In October 1932, the IDAC renewed steel duties on the condition that the weak NFISM be replaced by a new central body with greater supervisory power over the sectional associations. The result was the British Iron and Steel Federation (BISF), created in 1934. In other cases, protection preceded the creation of a compact between organized producers and organized consumers. Hence, with respect to leather, fertilizers, and sodium nitrite, the IDAC required negotiation of price agreements between the Tanners' Federation and the Association of Shoe Manufacturers, between the Fertilizer Manufacturers' Association and the Farmers' Union, and between Imperial Chemical Industries, Ltd. and the Bleachers, Dyers, Printers and Finishers' Association.

The IDAC was endowed with an autonomous set of goals drawn from the Conservative government's antisocialist mandate. This mandate laid out a distinct pro-industry, class interest sufficiently broad to free the IDAC from sectoral pressures. The committee could evaluate cases on their respective merits, granting protection to those sectors that needed it most and attaching strings where appropriate. The first to learn at their own expense about the relative autonomy of the committee were the MPs who represented the wool and worsted industry of Yorkshire and whom the committee firmly declined to receive.[64]

The difference between the French and British cases is worth recapitulating. The administrative structure of each country closely reflected its respective quorum. Fragmentation of the French structure among a plurality of line agencies made it easier for industries to maintain access to the policymaking process. By contrast, centralization of the British structure into a single, independent, staff agency helped guard the partisan mandate from the taint of particular interests. Moreover, in France, each trade official was in charge of only one sector and was briefed by that sector alone. This official thus became the main lobbyist to the government for his respective sector. In Britain, by contrast, trade officials enjoyed sufficient programmatic autonomy to try to shape sectoral organization according to their own class vision of what was best for industry.

Consolidating Party Politics in Parliament

The IDAC was created, Hutchinson insisted, "to take the tariff out of politics." [65] By "politics," he, of course, did not mean party politics, but Parliament and the cabinet. Relocation of the tariff-making process to an autonomous agency did not weaken party politics, but instead strengthened it.

Taking tariff-making out of Parliament, in fact, could only strengthen party politics. By keeping the involvement of MPs to a minimum, the IDAC kept Parliament from becoming a forum for various special interests. Although Parliament had to vote on every tariff change, the procedure was expedited by allowing little debate and no amendment. Taking "the tariff out of politics" also meant placing it somewhere other than in a line agency, certainly somewhere other than in the cabinet. Government's input was kept to a minimum. Even though the IDAC had only an advisory role, it had all the trappings of an independent regulatory agency. "The Government [was] content to accept the Committee's recommendations without question as representing what was desirable in the interests of British industries in the home market," Hutchinson wrote.[66] The government reserved the right to modify the tariff only when negotiating trade agreements with Britain's partners.

Taking the tariff out of the cabinet mattered for another reason. For a year, the cabinet had been divided between free-trade Liberals and Conservative protectionists. Putting the determination of the rates in the hands of the

IDAC was intended to minimize recurrent conflict, in part, by allowing the "National Government" to downplay differences over protection and place the main emphasis on anti-socialism.[67] The trade rhetoric of the national government, however, was out of line with the actual content of the policy, which was Tariff Reform straight and simple. This rather unpartylike self-restraint reflected the fact that, in 1931, the Conservatives did not want to govern alone, but preferred to associate leading politicians from other parties with unpopular measures which, nevertheless, they wanted to enact. When the free-trade members of the cabinet resigned in September 1932, the National Government had, for all practical purposes, become a Tory government seasoned by inclusion of a few Labour and Liberal renegades.

Therefore, in France, relocation of tariff-making to the administration was intended merely to relieve Parliament from the technical complexity of modern tariff-making—the growing international economic uncertainty called for a flexibility Parliament did not have, whereas, in Britain, the shift was also meant to relieve Conservative MPs and ministers of the burden of confronting both the mass of particular interest groups and the ideological divisions among ministers. Relocation was meant to save pressure politics in France and party politics in Britain from the shortcomings of the parliamentary procedure, shortcomings that had been exposed by the new challenges of the interwar period.

The Executive

In Britain, as in France, the end of World War I relegated to the background the executive as an autonomous actor. Throughout the 1920s, foreign policy laid no special claim to trade policy except in an ad hoc, inconsistent way. Trade policy did not become an extension of diplomacy by other means, but remained very much a domestic affair. The policy of imperial preferences, for instance, made no diplomatic sense. The policy redistributed British imports of grain away from Eastern Europe—at a time when Germany was actively promoting its political and economic presence in the region—toward Canada, which was in no danger of falling into the German orbit. The Foreign Office objected to imperial preferences but was kept out of the policy process. It had almost no representation at the Ottawa Imperial Conference of 1932.[68] The Foreign Office tried unsuccessfully to reverse this policy, but imperial preferences were the party line; the electoral security of the government depended on it. Prime Minister Neville Chamberlain made it clear that "the political aspect must be recognized." "The Dominions must have a preferential position even if we had to pay for it." [69] And so Britain did pay. To compensate for the lost trade channels, the British government, in February 1938, created a "fighting fund" in the form of credits to be made available to selected strategic countries for the purpose of expanding British export markets. Rumania, Poland, and Greece benefited.[70]

The Nazi threat presented the British cabinet with a classic security dilemma, to which there was no more effective response than a flexible mix of deterrence and accommodation. Lacking both colonies and a convertible currency, Germany was dependent on Britain as its best client to acquire the currency needed to import raw materials. Germany's alternative was to pursue a policy of economic extension eastward and southward, through a mix of barter agreements and military intimidation, a policy that could lead only to an arms race with Britain and a possible crisis. Britain was thus faced with a choice: weaken the German economy through economic encirclement at the risk of accelerating German rearmament, or pursue a policy of economic appeasement in exchange for military guarantees. The British cabinet—first under Baldwin, then under Chamberlain—responded by mixing elements of both tactics, depending on Hitler's moves. On the one hand, between 1937 and 1939, the cabinet held open the possibility of talks toward the conclusion of an economic settlement with Hitler. The cabinet prolonged the clearings agreement that provided the German economy with the precious sterling until war broke out.[71] On the other hand, Britain sought to prevent Germany from establishing a trading monopoly with Eastern Europe by extending credits to Danubian states,[72] and Britain joined the anti-German network woven by Cordell Hull when it signed the Anglo-American Trade Act.[73]

The success of these dual tactics, however, was predicated on the British cabinet's ability to neutralize domestic interference on behalf of domestic producers injured by these policies. This the cabinet was not able to do. The difficulty was especially acute in the case of the Anglo-American Agreement.[74] When the Foreign Office tried to speed up signing of the agreement by reminding the Board of Trade of the political significance of the agreement, the board responded: "to lay upon [the negotiators] in their instructions the duty of considering the political aspect of the matter can do nothing but weaken their hands in doing the job which they are sent out to do, that is, to make a satisfactory trade agreement."[75] The Anglo-American Agreement took a year and a half to conclude, by which time it was drained of its strategic relevance.

More generally, one could argue that Chamberlain was unable to threaten economic sanctions as often or as strongly as he would have liked, because of the strong preference among industrial and imperial circles for economic appeasement.[76] In March 1937, the Federation of Business Industry opened up direct contact with its German counterpart, the *Reichsgruppe Industrie*, to plan for talks on an Anglo-German cartel that would cover every sector of production. The Anglo-German industrial conference opened in Düsseldorf on 15 March 1939, the day German troops moved into Bohemia. Whitehall immediately wired the FBI that the British government was to have nothing further to do with the negotiations. The head negotiator for FBI wrote, "We decided, that political difficulties have nothing to do with industrialists, and we are going to carry on our programme exactly as planned." [77] The conference was actually a success.

If trade policy did not become the continuation of diplomacy by other means in interwar Britain, some other form of diplomacy became the continuation of trade policy by other means—private diplomacy, that is.

"Industrial Diplomacy"

Whereas the logic of pressure politics is accommodation, the logic of party politics is exclusion: the deliberate (though temporary) exclusion of individuals with opposite interests to those in government, and the indirect (but permanent) exclusion of interests without a party to articulate their interests. As a result, there is no political incentive in party politics to find new policy tools; and policymakers cannot justify the creation of new tools by claiming the political necessity of accommodating excluded interests (hypothesis 5.7).

The shrinking of the choice set in Britain was all the more dramatic because the economic need for alternative instruments was strongly felt. The interwar period saw the relative decline of several British staple export industries: cotton, coal, iron and steel, and shipbuilding. Throughout the period, agriculture suffered from overproduction. Even international shipping could no longer hold its own in the face of subsidized national fleets. Many industrialists, bankers, and politicians believed that the old industries were in need of restructuring, either through coordination or through amalgamation.

Conservatives were convinced that tariffs and imperial preferences were the solution to the ailments of British industry. These measures, they claimed, would help not only industries selling in the imperial market but also firms selling in the world market. Exporters would benefit from London's novel ability to leverage access to foreign markets by offering reciprocal access to its protected domestic market and to the imperial market as well, since Britain would now have a say in the dominions' trade policy. The imperial market was consecrated by the Ottawa Conference of 1932–33, and Britain resumed its pre-1881 policy of signing bilateral agreements. Results fell short of expectations, however. The imperial market did not increase British leverage toward other nations, but rather reduced it, since London could not discuss the duties involved at Ottawa without first obtaining the consent of the respective dominions. The British balance of trade improved in relative (not absolute) terms in two cases only: first, in relation to countries with an inconvertible currency, for which the flow of trade was subordinated to debt collection—a fact bound to favor the country with a passive trade balance; and, second, in relation to the Scandinavian countries, who sold primary products to Britain and thus stood to suffer from the diversion of trade caused by imperial preferences. In other markets, tariffs and preferences did not help, but actually hurt, because these countries retaliated against British exports.[78]

The Conservative government also tried to reserve the colonial market for the Lancashire cotton industry. That industry had gradually lost the Indian market to local Indian spinners who won protection when India acceded to tariff autonomy in 1919. In 1934, the Board of Trade asked all colonies and protectorates to impose quotas on all foreign textiles, with the result that British shipments to colonies more than doubled.[79] As a market, however, Nigeria was no substitute for India.

What was needed—with respect to iron and steel before 1932 and to cotton textiles, shipbuilding, and coal all along—was a more direct form of state intervention. Were the British elites ready to resort to public subsidies? They had been willing at an earlier time, when the main debate was between free trade and protection. In 1915, for example, the Liberals had preferred subsidies to tariff for promoting the organic dye industry.[80] The Conservatives, too, after the disqualification of protection in the 1923 election, had for a while considered subsidies as an alternative way of assisting the steelmakers.[81] But the rise of Labour, especially its socialist wing, along with the twin threats of planning and nationalization, removed state injunction and public subsidies from both the Liberal and the Conservative repertoires, out of fear that these measures would provide an opportunity for the Left to realize its dreams of nationalization. The tariff controversy thus took place in the antechamber to the broader controversy over the role of the state in the economy. The latter debate was no less partisan than the former. Confined to the extreme left in 1919, debate over the state economy matured into a full-fledged partisan debate in 1936, when the socialist faction took over the control of the Labour party.

Trapped in their official discourse, Conservative governments began to address the pressing needs of British industries through unofficial methods. They engaged in private, covert negotiations with bankers and industrialists, a practice aptly termed "industrial diplomacy" by Richard Roberts.[82] Offstage, governments tried to come up with solutions that required no formal legislation or that required, at most, legislation that could not be construed as too coercive of industry or too generous toward it. A rather odd development, this development may be coded as a sophistication of neither the public policy toolbox nor the private one, but rather of some intermediate category of toolbox.

The first manifestation of industrial diplomacy was aimed at the iron and steel industry. In 1928, Steel-Maitland, minister of labor, suggested that the impetus for rationalization should come from the banks, as it did in the United States. The Joint Stock Banks' refusal to emulate J. P. Morgan prompted the Bank of England, under the leadership of Montagu Norman, to enter the field of industrial restructuring.[83] A privately owned institution, the Bank of England created two independent bodies, the Securities Management Trust (SMT), to advise on mergers, and the Bankers' Industrial Development Company (BIDC), to advance financial support. Norman created the two sister companies with more than the steelmasters in mind. One of Norman's first deals was to lend assistance to the Lancashire Cotton Corporation, created to amalgamate some 200 spinning mills. A similar deal in 1930 involved creation of the National Shipbuilders' Security, Ltd., a concern which, by the end of the decade, had purchased and scrapped one-third of British shipbuilding yards. The Bank also became involved in shipping, armaments, and, to a lesser extent, locomotives, film, automobiles, and small industries in depressed areas. In all of this, the government was not a passive player, just an unofficial one.

The rationale common to all these ventures was a political one. Intervention by the Bank of England was designed, by Norman's own admission, to "keep the government out of industry." [84] The advent of the second Labour government, in May 1929, put the concept to a test. Sir Oswald Mosley, on behalf of the left wing of the Labour party, called on the Labour cabinet to adopt an ambitious proposal to combat unemployment, including rationalization of industry through a state-controlled bank. Mosley's scheme was defeated by the rightwingers of the Labour cabinet on the ground, among others, that the Bank of England was already involved in industrial reorganization. Norman was vindicated. But the depth of the crisis and the tightness of credit made the issue moot, since even Norman's clout among City financiers was no longer sufficient to place the BIDC's new bond issues without a Treasury guarantee, a manifestation of state intervention that Norman would not countenance.[85]

With the Bank on the sidelines, the government faced renewed pressure to intervene, especially in the export trades, which stood to gain little from tariffs. Here, the government took the line that it would not offer help unless every single firm within a trade requested it. Getting a trade to reach the necessary level of coordination in a country with no tradition of sectoral lobbying in matters of trade, however, often required much informal arm-twisting, as evidenced by the case of the cotton spinning industry, whose trade association suffered from excess capacity but which was still incapable of collective action. The cotton industry contemplated the creation of a board equipped with statutory powers for the scrapping of surplus spindles; but the government refused to grant the authority unless a united industry officially requested it. The Joint Committee of Cotton Trade Organizations tried, but failed, to muster a majority. After years of behind-the-scenes discussion, the government managed to put together a formula on which 78 percent of expressed opinions in the industry could agree; the formula became the basis for the Cotton Spinning Industry Act of 1936. Schemes for centralized marketing in agriculture rested on the voluntary principle. The government created boards to centralize sales and regulate output at the request of interested producers—potatoes, milk, and wheat—and, whenever a food-processing industry was involved, at the request of compacts between growers and processors—pig and bacon, hops and brewers.[86]

The government breached the lines of its self-imposed restraint in the case of coal mining. The coal industry was in even worse economic condition than cotton, and it was more divided.[87] The mine owners were split between low-cost coastal producers and high-cost inland producers, while the unions, organized and strong, pursued an undisguised strategy of nationalization. Liberals and Conservatives sought to halt the threat of nationalization by emphasizing industrial restructuring—the common bane of owners and unions. All the parties could do, however, was force a cartel on the owners by threatening owners with compulsory amalgamation. The Conservative government's overt pressure on the coal industry turned out to be the exception that proves the rule. As far as the Conservatives were concerned, the danger was not that restructuring would lead to nationalization, but that the absence of restructuring would.

The incapacity of successive British governments to institutionalize consultation, as the French had, is all the more significant, since the principle of consultation seems to have been firmly established after the war. An advisory committee declared in 1918 that "government Departments should regard [trade associations] as the authoritative and accredited medium of communication upon all questions connected with [their] industries." [88] Another wrote of ". . . an obligation upon Departments to avail themselves of the advice and assistance of advisory bodies. . . ." [89]

Roberts suggests that civil servants shrank from official corporatist relations with business, because they feared that state intervention would undermine the "proper role of Parliament." [90] I suggest that constitutional integrity was a convenient, timeless principle seized on by pro-business politicians desperate to avoid the slippery slope of nationalization. Labour made definite threats to nationalize the flour-milling industry in 1929, the cotton industry in 1935, and the Bank of England, coal mining, and gas and electricity in 1937.[91] Paranoia ran high among industrialists. Collaboration between capital and labor was unworkable, even at the sectoral level, as shown by the protectionist steelmasters' reaction to the about-face of the steelworkers' unions in favor of protection in 1928: The steelmasters refused to join with the union in its request for a government inquiry into the distressed state of the industry for fear that such an inquiry was intended to "prepare the ground for nationalization of the industry as an election issue." [92]

In sum, business-government consultation developed in both Britain and France, but in rather different ways. Consultation was ad hoc and covert in Britain; it was systematic and institutionalized in France. Moreover, because the British government was in control of the public agenda, it also was in control of the nonpublic one. It was able to initiate consultation and choose interlocutors at will, bypassing existing trade associations in the process if it so desired. In France, by contrast, consultation became part of the administrative routine, and officials were denied the prerogative both of choosing not to consult and of choosing the interlocutors. The fact is, French trade institutions were designed to accommodate a broader variety of interests than were their British equivalent.

Policy Orientation

In party politics, the trade outcome should not necessarily reflect the degree of interest organization, as is the case in pressure politics. Indeed, Forrest Capie, who performed the only cross-sectoral study available for the period, found no such correlation. He regressed the effective rate of protection in 1935 against a selection of industry variables and found that "industries least concentrated by size got the highest level of protection." [93] Capie's results provide support for "the argument that the least concentrated by size would have been the most needy and therefore most likely to secure higher protection"—a result incompatible with pressure politics but quite compatible with a government of Tariff Reformers. This affirmative action-like rationale was used by the Import Duties Advisory Committee in its response to the Sheffield Cutlery Manufacturers' Association when the latter recommended a tariff on scissors but not on other cutlery, because of the existence of an international cartel agreement in regard to the latter. [94]

In party politics, the trade outcome should reflect the stand of the winning party. Tariff levels should reflect the party cycle (hypothesis 5.3), rather than the business cycle (hypothesis 5.4). A longitudinal test is performed in table 10.2, the results of which call for two remarks. First, the British case is in stark contrast to the French case, with respect to the relation between currency variation and tariff levels. In both Britain and France, there was a strong correlation between currency fluctuation and the tariff; however, the correlation ran in opposite directions in the two countries. Indeed, in Britain in 1931, there occurred a simultaneous realignment of four variables: (1) a crisis that caused (2) the slide of the pound, (3) victory of the Tariff Reformers, and (4) the rise of protection. Unlike in France, there was no attempt in Britain to neutralize the impact of the devaluation by freezing or reducing duties. Instead, devaluation and the tariff had a cumulative effect, well in keeping with Tariff Reformers' partisan design.

The second remark concerns the close correlation between the business cycle and the tariff. In normal times, this correlation would be interpreted as falsifying party politics (hypothesis 5.4). In the context of the Great Depression, however, the reverse is true. What is going on here is that the Great Depression (the business cycle) caused the single partisan realignment of the period, which, in turn, caused the change in the tariff. The business cycle modified the policy outcome through partisan mediation—a rare occurrence, yet one that, far from invalidating the party politics hypothesis, actually supports it. In sum, while hypothesis 5.3 (on the party cycle) is observed, hypothesis 5.4 (on the indeterminacy of the business cycle) is not confirmed, owing to the gravity of the Great Depression; thus it is without prejudice to the party politics hypothesis.

The United States

Stabilizing Party Politics

Just as before World War I, the tariff was a salient, deeply divisive issue after the war. In the 1920s, the farm-factory cleavage slipped out of alignment with the free trade-protection cleavage; so, once again, both parties were threatened by a split on sectional lines. Because farmers were the source of the threat, party politics was the only policy process capable of stabilizing the political scene. The period, therefore, can be analyzed as attempts by each party successively to salvage party politics in the face of deep sea-changes in rural areas. The Republican leadership first tried a "McKinley" on the farmers, seeking to anchor the farmers firmly to the Republican camp through generous extensions of the tariff to primary products. The ploy worked in 1921 but could not be implemented in 1930, for lack of partisan discipline among Republican congressmen. Next, the Democratic leadership proposed a federation of farmers and big business under the free-trade banner. Roosevelt succeeded where Hoover had failed by transferring the task of reconciling the two factors of production to the executive branch. That branch, he correctly figured, could be structured to perform the task more effectively than congressional committees. The policy process, therefore, except for a brief lapse into logrolling in 1930, remained party politics throughout.

As was the case in France and in the United States before the war, American farmers remained the keystone of trade policy. When the prices of farm commodities stumbled in 1920 and stagnated for three years, American farmers grew restive over the dominant trade policy. Farm organizations began to question the utility of free trade for agriculture, and the consumer-oriented policy of the Wilson administration no longer appealed to them. At first, they turned to the Republicans, who obliged them by passing the Emergency Tariff Act of 1921, designed to raise duties on agricultural products exclusively. The following year, the more general Fordney-McCumber Tariff Act made the raises permanent, and the Smoot-Hawley Tariff Act updated the raises in

1930. However, as we have seen, protection could do little to relieve the farmers. In the 1920s, protection helped truck farmers in the Northeast, farmers situated along the Canadian border, and fruit and vegetable growers in Florida and California. Nevertheless, protection was ineffective in bringing relief to the cereal producers of the Great Plains and the cotton planters of the South, who continued, as they had in the past, to grow more than the domestic market could absorb.

To make protection work for the farmers, their representatives propounded the McNary-Haugen Plan. Introduced in Congress on five occasions between 1924 and 1928, the McNary-Haugen Bill proposed to do publicly for agriculture what the U.S. Steel Corporation had done privately for the steel industry: create a government-sponsored corporation to purchase surplus crops on the domestic market, until domestic prices reached a target level equal to the world-market price, plus the amount of a protective duty. The purchased goods would then be dumped abroad at the lower world prices. To make good its operating deficit, the corporation would tax farmers according to their production—a tax that would, of course, be much lower than the "superprofits" afforded by the expected high domestic prices.

The existing policy process—party politics—proved unable to articulate the farmers' demand for price supports. The McNary-Haugen Plan, vehemently opposed by Wall Street, was vetoed twice, once by President Coolidge and once by President Hoover. The Democratic party was also reluctant to endorse the plan, since apparently it would make farm products more expensive all around, both for consumers of foodstuffs and for manufacturers of wool, cotton, and leather. Both parties were divided along urban-rural lines. The Democratic platform, for example, incorporated the demands of the farm bloc, but presidential nominee, Al Smith of New York, was reluctant to commit himself.[95]

Farmers' misgivings about free trade threw the parties into a crisis. With their core constituency drifting away from free trade, the Democrats felt a much reduced obligation to stand by free trade. Smith's endorsement of protection for industry, for example, was not simply idiosyncratic; it reflected a widespread attitude within Democratic ranks, as evidenced by the fact that the platform of 1928 advocated protection for "the maintenance of legitimate business and a high standard of wages for American labor."[96] On the Republican side, the nagging question of the relative balance between tariffs on primary products and tariffs on manufactures undermined the party's efforts to keep the farmers on board. The result was the breakdown of partisan leadership in both houses of Congress over the Smoot-Hawley tariff of 1930, when partisan discipline reached its lowest point in the period 1888–1940 (see figures A3.1 and A3.2 in Appendix 3). Debate over Smoot-Hawley was a replay of the battle in 1909 between Eastern establishment Republicans and farm-state Republicans. As in 1909, the agrarians lost and, as hypothesis 4.1 would have it, took their revenge in the next election. Farmers believed that industry had fared far better than agriculture in 1930. Further, a spree of retaliatory measures met American farm exports after Smoot-Hawley went into effect, and the utility of protection was soon much discredited in the eyes of farmers still burdened with surpluses.

Smoot-Hawley gave the Republican tariff a bad name. As an issue, free trade once again offered a unique electoral opportunity to the Democrats: trap the Republicans into assuming complete responsibility for the Smoot-Hawley legacy. FDR, however, would not be able to profit from the Smoot-Hawley fiasco unless he could reconcile the farmers to free trade. To do so, he would have to surmount the farm-factory split, which was, in fact, as destabilizing for the Democrats as it was for the Republicans. As was demonstrated in 1930, party caucuses in Congress were unable to contain the sectional conflict among their respective members. Roosevelt's genius consisted of streamlining tariff-making in Congress and absorbing into the executive branch that part of tariff-making responsible for the intrapartisan chaos in 1930—that is, setting individual rates. Relieved from this task, congressmen and senators were free again to indulge in broad ideological debates and cast highly partisan votes. Indeed, voting discipline on trade bills increased in 1934 and thereafter (figures A3.1 and A3.2). By tinkering with the formal institutions, the New Deal once again made party politics in tariff matters safe for the Democrats.

Although New Dealers were correct in claiming that the executive branch (not process) could be restructured to maximize cooperation between farm and factory on the tariff more easily than Congress could ever be, the experiment was not problem-free. Discord was built in, and the formal rules for decisionmaking were in a constant state of flux. At first, Roosevelt settled on an unlikely duet between the farm program administrator, George N. Peek and the representative of free-trade industrialists, Secretary of State Cordell Hull. Although these men agreed on the concept of export promotion through negotiation of bilateral reciprocity agreements, they strongly disagreed about the details.[97] Farm organizations were opposed to Hull's use of bilateral agreements to propagate free trade, and they disputed the inclusion of the unconditional MFN treatment clause in every agreement. The Reciprocal Trade Agreement (RTA) Act of 1934, however, sanctioned the principle of MFN treatment and made the State Department under Hull the exclusive site for rate-setting. Nevertheless, there were two penalties for the victory: the State Department was opened to outside influence; and crippling limitations were imposed on the department's capacity to negotiate in any sphere related to farm products. These limitations were expressly intended to keep the farmers on board, an aim even more important to the Roosevelt administration than free trade.

Not surprisingly, the limitations were not enough to turn the farm organizations into enthusiastic supporters of the RTA program. Not a single farm organization testified in its favor in 1934, and four organizations testified against it. In 1937, only a tobacco growers' association testified in favor of the renewal; whereas seven testified against it. Not until the renewal in 1940, did the two major farm organizations of the United States, the American Farm Bureau Federation and the National Farmers' Union, appear at congressional hearings to testify on the same side of the debate as the Roosevelt administration.[98] Nevertheless, the farmers stayed on board.

What role did the workers play in this debate? The answer is—none. The American Federation of Labor (AFL) had no collective opinion on the tariff. Since 1882, its affiliates had been free to promote the trade position of their respective industry. It was not until 1943 that the Congress of Industrial Organizations (CIO) took a stand in favor of the New Deal's Reciprocal Trade Agreement, and not until 1949 that the AFL followed suit, still hesitantly.[99]

Roosevelt succeeded where Cleveland had failed: He managed to reconcile the farm vote with the free-trade industrialists. In the 1930s, as in the 1890s, farm prices were plummeting. In both periods, the farmers' primary concern was not free trade but higher prices for farm products. Yet, in both periods, free trade was the winning card, the only issue capable of bridging the farm-factory cleavage. The farm-factory cleavage defeated Cleveland, but not Roosevelt, because Roosevelt was able to contain the cleavage by the delegation of rate-making to the executive branch.

Lobbies

Many aspects of tariff-making between the wars have been attributed to the lobbying of private interest groups. In this section, I review three instances of private lobbying—Hoover's "associative state," logrolling during the passage of the Smoot-Hawley tariff, and business support for the New Deal. These might be coded prima facie as instances of pressure politics; but, under closer examination, they fall readily into the category of party politics.

In the 1920s, Secretary of Commerce Herbert Hoover endeavored to draw industry and government closer together into what has been called an "associative state," in which state officials and representatives of organized business work in close cooperation. After a vain attempt to get Congress to approve a reorganization plan that would have made the Commerce Department the core of the association, Hoover worked to realize his scheme on a smaller scale, within the existing Bureau of Foreign and Domestic Commerce.[100] Under Hoover's direction, the bureau created seventeen commodity divisions, each headed by appropriate trade association appointees. The Foreign Division was strengthened to assist exporters by seeking new markets, establishing credit ratings, and helping untangle local laws and customs.

Did Hoover's program differ much from the French advisory system, introduced above as the epitome of pressure politics in a bureaucratic environment? If the two programs differed, it was not intentional. As Murray Rothbard writes: "Herbert Hoover's entire program of activities as Secretary of Commerce was designed to advance the subsidization of industry and the interpenetration of government and business." [101] Hoover believed that every industry should be organized into a trade association, and that trade associations should have permanent contacts with the state. Hoover also professed support for labor unionism and for active collaboration between unions and their corresponding associations in the management of their common trade. Had Hoover's vision of industrial relations and business-government relations been upheld, the parties could, no doubt, have retired from tariff-making. Hoover's ideas, however, were never taken seriously. Not only were they opposed by his colleagues in the administration, but party politics remained a strong deterrent to the effective sectoral organization necessary to make the program work. As a result, the seventeen commodity divisions created in the Commerce Department were never more than fact-finding agencies; they were never part of any decisionmaking process.

The second instance of private lobbying to be examined here is the passage of the Smoot-Hawley Tariff Act. Like many of his contemporaries, Schattschneider, struck by the irrationally high levels of protection yielded by the 1929–30 revision of the tariff, sought to explain the policy outcome as a case of pressure politics.[102] The procedure for tariff-making, he argued, made it impossible for congressional committees to formulate a coherent policy; instead, it privileged a pressure dynamic dominated by protectionist interests. The public hearings held before congressional committees, crowded and harried, provided little useful information. The poor quality of the evidence, Schattschneider argued, obliged Congress to set individual rates according to simplistic decision rules—"protection all around," "the right to protection," "uniformity," phrases typical of logrolling.[103] Congress was left to extend protection to any applicant who requested it unopposed. Furthermore, the process favored protectionists at the expense of free traders. Testimony in favor of increasing protection outweighed testimony opposing the increases, because, as Schattschneider noted, "[b]enefits [generated by an increase in a specific duty] are concentrated while costs are distributed." [104] Free traders confronted greater costs of collective action than did protectionists.

In response to Schattschneider's interpretation, it is important to note that the facts he points out as ideal or typical of pressure politics are also compatible with party politics. A Republican Congress, elected on a protectionist platform, was unlikely to be concerned about the quality of the evidence.[105]

Congressional committees adopted simplistic rules of decision, perhaps because the Republicans favored protectionism over free trade. Under the circumstances, the policy outcome was a foregone conclusion, and it is not surprising that free traders chose not to organize a plausible defense. Protectionists, however, still had to testify, for tariff protection was granted only to those who requested it and only at the rate requested. Hence, the poor showing by free traders in 1929 may be accounted for by organizational ineptitude or the presence of a hostile administration, or both.

Smoot-Hawley was not a pure case of pressure politics, however. The confusion derives from a misunderstanding of the role of interest groups and logrolling in the debate of 1930. These two factors are commonly held to be responsible for the collapse of partisan discipline during the tariff revision, whereas the reverse is closer to the truth. It is because partisan discipline collapsed that interest groups and logrolling found a way into the debate.

It all started when the presidential candidate, Herbert Hoover, promised to call a special session of Congress early in his administration to raise the tariffs on agricultural products alone. Once in office, Hoover honored his pledge and called Congress into session in June 1929. The legislative process, however, did not unfold as neatly as promised. The House Republican leadership caused the first wrinkle by drafting a bill to increase duties for farm products *and* several manufactured products. Following a party caucus, leaders redrafted the bill to include several more industries—a second wrinkle. When presented on the floor of Congress, the bill was rebuffed and was sent back to committee with instructions to include all industries. There was, however, no economic justification for a general tariff revision, since the economy was still booming. The bill reached the Senate and, there, what was left of partisan leadership evaporated.[106]

President Hoover's failure of leadership angered the farm-state Republicans. They began to reenact the fratricidal battle of 1909, between the Eastern establishment of the party and the Midwest "insurgents." While the bill was in committee of the whole in the Senate, farm-state Republicans, in alliance with their Democrat equivalents, endeavored to iron out all increases in the tariff rates for industry.[107] For the most part, they were successful. The overall ad valorem rate of protection was raised from 34.61 percent under the 1922 act to 43.15 percent by the House; it was reduced to 40.54 percent by the Senate finance committee, and then further reduced to 35.10 percent by the committee of the whole.[108] However, after two basic raw materials, oil and lumber, underwent the same surgery, the Republican-Democratic coalition started losing crucial members to the protectionist side. At that point, Senator Joseph R. Grundy from Pennsylvania, a protectionist, began to organize his infamous "sugar-cement-lumber-oil" logrolling coalition, raising the Senate's final figure to 38.99 percent. Because the conference bill did away with the remaining changes made by the farm coalition, the latter voted against the conference report. It is, therefore, *because* and *only after* partisan discipline stumbled over the farm-factory cleavage—the nemesis of both parties since the Civil War—that logrolling took over.[109]

Further evidence that Smoot-Hawley was not a pure case of pressure politics is provided by the fact that the bill was not orchestrated by congressional committees, as was then standard with "pork-barrel" bills. Rather, logrolling arose spontaneously on the floor of the Senate. Equally telling was the lack of popularity that greeted Grundy's logrolling achievements. Recall that logrolling functions well when the unit of interest aggregation is the sector. When the unit is the factor, logrolling generates distributive externalities that can no longer be passed on to an uninvited third group; it will only wreak havoc on the kind of summit negotiations that are required to stabilize factor politics.[110] In the partisan process of the 1930s, logrolling revealed gaping holes in party discipline and party leadership. Because the content of the bill changed as fast as alliances formed, the party's goals and the initial campaign promises were overlooked, an oversight that the Democratic opposition gladly called to the attention of American voters at the first opportunity.

The third instance of lobbying occurred under the New Deal. Thomas Ferguson has argued that the economic policies of the New Deal reflected the preferences of the most powerful bloc of industrialists and that membership in this bloc changed in accordance with the business cycle. Nationalists, therefore, dominated in 1933, and internationalists got the upper hand when the economy later recovered.[111] Although Ferguson's mapping of industrial support for the New Deal is probably correct, what his interpretation fails to consider is that the policy change may not have reflected business realignment, but may have occurred at the instigation of the administration, industrialists joining or opting out, depending on their capacity to bear the costs of the proposed policies.

Indeed, at first, the New Deal tried to be everything to everyone, legislating cartels for industries, cartels and price supports for crop growers, and a modern industrial relations system for labor. The impossible synthesis soon unraveled, and the main electoral supports of the New Deal were revealed with greater clarity—the regime rested on a red-green electoral compact in which labor accepted higher food costs in exchange for farmers' support of social insurance. These electoral supports dictated the choices of the administration: Higher food costs required a combination of protection and aggressive export promotion. Social insurance implied higher labor costs. As Ferguson has shown, not all industrialists could withstand the consequences of these policies. Import-sensitive and labor-intensive industries opted out. Those who chose to stay on board could have done without higher wage pressures; but they were still better off cooperating.[112]

In conclusion, none of the three cases disprove the primacy of party politics. The "associative state" never had a chance. When logrolling resurfaced through a break in party politics, Congress was effectively quarantined; and when the New Deal could no longer accommodate the contradictions of its election promises, businessmen had a choice between exit and loyalty.[113]

The Policy Toolbox under the Republicans

The policy instruments used during the 1920s were those of the past. The ideological confrontation between free trade and protection made export promotion a residual category (hypothesis 5.7). Successive Republican administrations did little for exporters and less for multinational companies. Of the three measures requested by exporters—a tariff commission, reciprocity, and tied loans—the Republicans took none seriously.

The idea of an independent tariff commission was a carryover from the earlier period. Then exporters expected such a commission to take over from Congress part of its tariff-making responsibility and to constitute an executive agency equipped with the expertise necessary to make rates "scientific." In 1910, Taft had established the Tariff Board, which failed. In 1916, the Tariff Commission was created but with no more than fact-finding authority. In 1922, Warren Harding agreed to give it another try: section 315 of the Fordney-McCumber tariff gave the President the power to modify rates by up to 50 percent on the advice of the Tariff Commission.[114] Section 315, however, also fell short of exporters' expectations. The commission immediately became embroiled in the very kind of partisan conflict it was supposed to overcome. The six-member commission was split between the three remaining Wilson appointees, who wanted to encourage fair competition, and the three new Harding appointees, who were staunch protectionists. Predictably, the commission's investigation into wheat led to two opposing sets of recommendations, one protectionist, the other status quo. The investigation into sugar, from which the three Wilson Progressives managed to exclude one of the protectionists, resulted in a majority report that recommended a reduction in the sugar duty, and a dissenting opinion that claimed the duty should be increased. As Progressives were gradually replaced by protectionists, the commission overcame its initial split, though not to the exporters' benefit.[115]

The failure of section 315 sealed the fate of section 317, a new attempt at reciprocity by the Republican leadership. Section 317, in combination with the unconditional MFN principle adopted in 1923, gave the President the authority to offer MFN treatment in exchange for similar treatment, and otherwise to threaten retaliation. However, without the bargaining chips afforded by rate reductions under section 315, gains were limited. Of the meager eight trade agreements the State Department had signed by 1929, only the one with Germany had any significance.[116]

Powerless with respect to the tariff, exporters tried to shift the issue of export promotion to export finance. Although the war turned European nations into massive dollar borrowers, massive foreign lending did not always benefit U.S. exporters. Most of the foreign loans floated by New York bankers were government bonds, and the proceeds went either toward the amortization of previous loans or toward the realization of public works on which only nationals could bid with any chance of success. In 1922, the National Foreign Trade Council—the lobby for "big business"—launched a campaign to include in all foreign-loan agreements a clause that would tie at least 20 percent of the loan to the purchase of U.S. goods. Sensitive to the needs of exporters, Commerce Secretary Hoover, in 1922, was instrumental in putting together a loan-control procedure such that each department with an interest in foreign loans could express its opinion of individual flotations before they were made public.[117] Worried that Hoover's scheme would make lending more difficult, U.S. bankers took the matter before President Harding and convinced him to abandon the plan. Hoover eventually created within the Commerce Department the Finance and Investment Division, an agency he intended to act as a link between bankers and manufacturers. But bankers turned down the invitation on the grounds that any successful collusion with the manufacturers would imply greater restrictions on foreign lending.

The inadequacy of the public toolbox encouraged private imagination (hypothesis 5.9). Some giant corporations continued to ship goods abroad on the basis of their own credit with the banks or on the basis of an agreement to accept payment in manufactured goods, which they could resell in the United States or elsewhere; others purchased or built producing units in Europe.[118] By contrast, small and middle-size exporters, who had to depend on bank credit to ship goods to Europe, had either to look for alternative markets or, more likely, withdraw from the export trade altogether.

The Policy Toolbox under the Democrats

The New Deal did more for exporters than had the previous Republican administrations. Having put an end to the secular ascendancy of New York private investment bankers—the House of Morgan, in particular—Roosevelt moved the federal government into the business of underwriting export trade. The Eximbank, for example, was chartered in October 1933 to make tied loans to the Soviet Union.[119] The second leg of export promotion was, of course, the RTA program. By January 1, 1940, agreements had been reached with twenty-one countries that accounted for 60 percent of U.S. trade. Concessions were granted on 1,014 tariff rates, and the ad valorem rate on dutiable imports into the United States declined from an average of around 50 percent in the 1930–34 period to about 37 percent in 1939.[120] Even though it is partially attributable to devaluation this was a substantial result.[121]

This refurbishing of the trade policy repertoire by the administration seems paradoxical. Only in pressure politics do politicians usually feel a need to develop new policy tools in order to deal with the broad diversity of interests (hypothesis 5.7). Operating on the basis of exclusion rather than accommodation, party politics allows politicians to function with a simplified toolbox. A blanket commitment to free trade in 1932 might have dispensed with the need for the administration to set up the Eximbank and the RTA; but the administration could not afford a blanket commitment to free trade, and it was faced with the additional problem of making free trade work for the farmers. As we have noted, farm organizations were not ready to condone unilateral cuts, multilateral negotiations, or even bilateral negotiations based on the MFN principle; they wanted barter agreements. Moreover, free trade would have wreaked havoc with the farm program. The gap between the farmers' position and that of the State Department tied the hands of the latter, forcing it to create new policy instruments.

The administration adjusted to its constraints in the French manner—by multiplying policy exceptions and imagining new policy instruments. Foodstuffs were among the exceptions; they were rarely included in the negotiations, an exemption that made agreements with Argentina and Peru impossible. Wool was placed off limits, and the pledge was renewed in the election of 1936, despite the fact that the renewal caused a trade war with Australia.[122] Goods most likely to muster support from key Democrats in Congress got an increase in protection. Sugar, for example, got strict quotas, with the result that trade agreements could not be signed with Nicaragua, Peru, or the Dominican Republic.[123]

State Department negotiators perfected several techniques intended to reconcile—at least, in appearance—export promotion with import protection. The most useful device was the quota. The introduction of quotas in trade agreements made it possible to decrease nominal tariffs without decreasing the actual level of protection. The only loser here was the Treasury—that is, the taxpayer. An agreement with Canada was made possible by including quotas on Canadian imports of dairy products, cattle, lumber, and potatoes. An agreement with Cuba included quotas on filler tobacco.[124] Cotton and crude and fuel oil (which were allowed to jump on the agrarian bandwagon on account of their impeccable Democratic electoral credentials) were also subject to quantitative limits. By 1939, in fact, one-fourth of all dutiable imports were subject to quotas.[125] Another technique used by the State Department was to confine its concessions to commodities that did not compete with American products to any appreciable extent.[126] Yet another technique was to circumscribe the concessions to commodities for which the other country was the principal supplier. This technique curtailed the generalizing of concessions on the basis of the MFN clause. A fourth gimmick reached similar results through systematic use of reclassification. The following illustration is borrowed from Diebold:

> In the British agreement we reduced the duty on canned herring, "packed in immediate containers weighing with their contents more than one pound each"; Norwegian herring of exactly the same quality continued to pay Hawley-Smoot rates since they were regularly packed in four- or six-ounce containers.[127]

Of the 1,014 reductions in tariff rates implemented through the tariff agreements, 436 involved reclassification.[128] A fifth technique, one that was destined to a bright future, was to include in the agreement an "escape clause," which permitted either partner to withdraw a concession from which a third party was deriving the major benefit.[129]

This proliferation of tools did not reflect an increase in state autonomy. Rather, it was a sure sign of the reduced margin for maneuver available to the administration in the trade arena. To be convinced of this fact, it is only necessary to look at the policy process set up by the RTA, in the State Department.

State's Lost Autonomy

The RTA transferred the nitty-gritty of rate-setting to what seemed a sanctuary in lobby-infested Washington—the Department of State—an agency traditionally alleged to care for the economic interests of foreign countries at the expense of U.S. economic interests. Moreover, after two years of belaboring the economic value of the RTA program—its contribution to exports, free trade, and economic prosperity—Secretary of State Hull began to emphasize the role of RTA as preserver of the peace.[130] He began to argue that the renewal of trade according to liberal principles would pull the world out of the depression and prevent the spread of war. As the actual risk of war rose, Hull sought to turn the RTA into a tool of foreign policy. His escalating reliance on in-house rhetoric—added to the fact that, of all the federal agencies, the State Department was probably the least attuned to domestic issues, should have given a boost to executive autonomy in the administration of the RTA. In reality, the converse was true; and Hull failed to keep the private economic interests at bay.

An autonomous executive who dismissed the special interests of farmers would have been incompatible with the political task tariff-making was expected to accomplish. The State Department was asked to accommodate the farmers' demands (and the demands of other powerful industries located in Democratic electoral territory, such as oil), at the risk of spoiling its "splendid isolation" from society. This change did not sit at all well with Hull, who, after all, in 1934, had opposed both holding hearings on tariff policy and publishing the preliminary list of items being considered for concessions every time negotiations with a trade partner were contemplated. Hull argued that these two procedures "would give away to foreign nations our ammunition." [131] The real reason was of a different nature. Deprived of these two means of access to policymaking, trade groups could be faced with a fait accompli, and their ability to influence the content of the trade agreements would be kept to a minimum. The pressure against Hull was too strong, however, and both the holding of hearings and publication of the list soon became standard operating procedures.

As an additional measure of insulation, the State Department, from the outset, had used the interdepartmental committee that held the hearings as a "buffer agency." Committee members who received the testimony of witnesses were not the officials who actually negotiated the agreements—and the names of the latter were kept secret. This, too, had to change. Carl Kreider, a student of the RTA, notes that "the history of trade agreement hearings since 1934 has been a story of gradual weakening of the executive's freedom of action." [132]

A good illustration is the negotiations of 1938 over the Anglo-American Agreement—the keystone of Hull's grand strategy. Despite the political importance of a U.S.–U.K. rapprochement, which Hull by no means underestimated, the American team set as its official target Britain's renunciation of imperial preferences, and kept harping on the point to get the best of the bargain, as they eventually did. Such petty intransigence is rather unexpected in a diplomat intent on reassuring Prime Minister Chamberlain of the reliability of the United States in case of war.[133] The fact of the matter, however, is that Hull had very few allowable concessions to bargain with and thus very little freedom in which to act. The overwhelming majority of testimony recorded by the State Department came from protectionists protesting against one or another of the proposed concessions.

> Approximately 80 per cent of the testimony presented orally was given by domestic manufacturers protesting against a proposed concession. About 10 per cent came from exporters asking for concessions from the United Kingdom, and less than 5 per cent came from importers asking for a reduction in the United States tariff on specific items.[134]

Because of agrarian pressure, the negotiations between the two countries almost did not even get started.[135] Britain required Australia's consent before she could proceed with the negotiations, and Australia would not consent, unless the United States reconsidered an earlier offer for a trade agreement that would concede free entry into the United States for Australian wool, butter, beef, mutton, and lamb. That earlier offer had been turned down, because Roosevelt had pledged high duties to U.S. wool. Australia retaliated, and United States exporters lost 20 percent of their Australian market, but the

United States had not changed its position. Faced with the double threat, however, Hull reopened negotiations with Australia in 1938. Nevertheless, the political pressure from the wool interest was such that, as Rowland notes, "the State Department took its final avenue of escape—to propose and then insist on a deal whose terms Australia could not—and did not—accept." [136]

A second reason for Hull's failure to jumpstart his trade program by plugging it into U.S. grand strategy was that there was no such strategy. Congress had imposed a policy of absolute neutrality on the executive regarding the prospects of a war in Europe. Under such conditions, trade policy could not serve as an adjunct to a U.S. alliance strategy that could not be publicly articulated, even assuming there was an alliance strategy. In any event, trade treaties were poor substitutes. Even Roosevelt seemed to have lost patience with Hull's program, confiding to Morgenthau: "Henry, these treaties are just too god-dammed slow. The world is marching too fast. They're just too slow." [137]

Policy Orientation

As in the case of Britain, it should be possible in the case of the United States to observe a correlation between the nature of the party in power and the orientation of the trade policy, and of course there is such a correlation. The Republicans raised the tariff, the Democrats lowered it. Table 10.2 tests the party-cycle hypothesis (5.3) in concurrence with the business-cycle hypothesis (5.1), as well as its converse, hypothesis 5.4. As was the case for Britain, in the U.S. case, the data bear out hypotheses 5.1 and 5.3, thus making it impossible to separate their impacts on policy orientation. This spurious correlation occurs because the business cycle—i.e., the Great Depression of the 1930s—caused the only partisan realignment of the period in both Britain and the United States. This result, however, in no way weakens the party-politics hypothesis; for, in party politics, the hypothesis acknowledges that the business cycle can effect the policy outcome, provided the business cycle is mediated by the party system, as was the case in the 1930s.

Note a difference between the results for the United States and Britain. The two countries differ in the impact of currency fluctuations on the tariff—positive in the case of Britain, negative in the case of the United States. The Roosevelt administration used the tariff to counter the inflationary consequences of a weak dollar.

Conclusion

More than any other, the interwar period shows the weakness of interest-group explanations. Throughout the period, the trade issue was a salient, divisive issue in Britain and the United States; it became so in France toward the end of the period. In all three countries, the Great Depression revitalized party politics, causing the orientation of trade policy to flip over. These similarities make a party explanation of national responses to the Great Depression a strong theoretical contender. The depression was so severe that economic policy, in all its forms, immediately became a partisan issue. The party associated with its occurrence was immediately discredited, while the party fortunate enough to be "out" was thrust into power. In countries such as Great Britain, the Left fell victim to the crisis, the worker vote was fragmented, the Right had a field day, and the outcome was orthodox adjustment and protection. In countries such as France and the United States, the Right suffered the blast, workers voted as a bloc for the Left, and a pro-labor response was improvised.

These tectonic changes in voter alignment delineated the choice set, foreclosing prior options, opening new ones. Protection was not a viable strategy in the United States; it was only weakly viable under the *Front Populaire*. Conversely, free trade was not a viable strategy in Britain. With the exception of France, where free trade was timorous and short-lived, businessmen adjusted to the best of their abilities, pursuing export promotion in the United States and exploring imperial opportunities in Great Britain.

In addition, the interwar period is a marvelous testing ground for standard institutionalist claims. The interwar period provides us with a unique way of assessing the role of the policy process as defined in this book, in direct competition with the broader institutional framework. Two central propositions of the institutionalist school were found wanting. First is the innovative character of state-building. There is no doubt, as students of state building argue, that the institutional change that took place during the period 1919–1939—in all three countries, in one form or another, and which one may characterize as a modern instance of state building—was a response to an environmental challenge. Currency fluctuations called for flexible tariffs and triggered the transfer of parliamentary responsibility to an executive agency in charge of monitoring. It is important to note, however, that the causal relation between the external challenge and the institutional response was neither direct nor unproblematic, but was mediated by political competition.

Hence, where pressure politics dominated, as it did in France, the familiar aspects of interest penetration, decentralization, and logrolling were replicated in the administrative arena. Lobbying was institutionalized as consultation; the old practice of appointing key industry deputies to the parliamentary Tariff Commission was reproduced by assigning industries to corresponding sponsoring ministries and turning the ministries into advocates of the industries within the government. The traditional concern for universal representation was zealously extended by multiplying the number of advisory committees. In contrast, where party politics obtained, as it did in Britain and the United States, the administrative process bore the marks of autonomy, centralization, and partisanship. Consultation with special interests was either avoided altogether or was conditioned by the rules of fairness and publicity. Centralization was a guarantee against sectoral clientelism, but not class favoritism. The British IDAC pursued its class policy goals, recommending greater protection for the unorganized than for the organized. Also, even though the U.S. State Department could not implement its policy choices freely, the department enjoyed ample discretion in determining the negotiating agenda, subject to the farm constraint.

The second institutionalist proposition not confirmed by events of the period concerns the relation between state building and political autonomy, a relationship which students of state-building generally believe to be positive. Institutional innovation, institutionalists usually argue, provides policymakers with additional policy tools and greater margin for maneuver and thus facilitates the task of adjustment. This line of reasoning is flawed, however. No more than the construction of more freeways can ease traffic jams in urban areas, can additional policy tools expand the margin for maneuver of public officials. Institutional innovation was not born of political autonomy, but of the lack of political autonomy. An autonomous policymaker is, by definition, confronted with fewer political demands than a policymaker who enjoys no political autonomy; the former needs fewer policy tools than the latter.

Among the three countries studied, the most institutionally innovative policymaker by far was France. There the administration reproduced on a grand scale the lobbying structure of the chambers, and trade policy spilled over to tangential policies, including colonial development. Such policy and institutional resourcefulness originated in the pledge exacted by Parliament from the executive to find a solution to the problems experienced by all organized special-interest groups, regardless of their trade or partisan orientation. Institutional muscle grew out of political flabbiness, policy diversification from the French polity's failure to cushion public officials from trade interests. In contrast, in Britain and the United States the policy process at any given time disfranchised one or several categories of trade interests, thus releasing public officials from the task of imagining new and official ways to rescue these groups. In Britain, this nonintervention principle led to such irrational outcomes that public officials worked on the sidelines with private industry to come up with private solutions. Meanwhile, the U.S. New Deal innovated perhaps more than its hypothesized share. It had to force the farm-factory cleavage to conform to the protection-free trade cleavage, so that party politics as a process could be sustained.

Eleven

Creation of the Cold War Trading Regime, 1940–62

U.S. trade policy has been the orphan
of U.S. foreign policy.
 (*Senator Russell Long*)

UNTIL WORLD WAR II, and with the exception of World War I, trade policy in
Britain, France, and the United States was essentially a domestic affair. Although the 1860 Cobden-Chevalier Treaty was in part the product of a trade-
security linkage, states generally refrained from using trade policy to pursue
security goals. World War II—and, more especially, the ensuing rivalry with
the Soviet Union—altered this state of affairs. Bipolar logic required free trade
with allies and neutrals, but restrictions on trade with the enemy. Trade became an international issue, one with visible security implications to be settled within a multilateral framework. Industries and parties lost control of the
orientation of their country's respective tariff policies. Tariffs came to be allocated by executives concerned about enforcing a modicum of multilateral discipline on their nationals.

The result was disqualification of the two classic tools of protection, tariffs
and quotas. By becoming a member of the General Agreement on Tariffs and
Trade, governments promised to forsake the unilateral use of quantitative restrictions and commit themselves to negotiating successive rounds of tariff
reductions. Moreover, by becoming members of the European Economic
Community, France first and later Britain agreed to reduce tariffs further for
EEC members while, at the same time, delegating their negotiating authority
to the EEC as a supranational organization. Finally, membership in the International Monetary Fund prohibited the use of currency devaluation to curb
imports and promote exports.

The regulation of tariffs and quotas, and the creation of supranational trade
institutions to administer them, did not make world trade significantly freer;
nor did it put rent seekers and political entrepreneurs out of business. Instead,
these developments motivated governments that could not afford to ignore
the performance of domestic industry to develop a new set of protective and
promotional tools beyond the reach of international regulation. Governments
explored several options characterized by varying degrees of state intervention. One, a minimalist option suggested retaliation for "unfair trade practices" and safeguards. Two, the development of nontariff barriers (NTBs)
could take one of two forms, which differed primarily in degree of state inter-

vention: (a) the negotiation of reciprocity agreements, either among private producers (international cartels) or between governments (voluntary export restraints—called VERs—or voluntary import stimulation); or (b) the manipulation of regulatory rules in related areas, such as public procurement policies, local content, foreign investment, and so forth. The third option was allocation of public subsidies to industry, either indirectly (tax breaks, regional development policy) or directly (planning, industrial policy). Because they targeted not the product but the production process, direct subsidies entailed the highest degree of intervention.

If a government could not afford laissez-faire because it needed to protect its domestic industry, and if, additionally, the same government found insufficient relief in GATT-sanctioned circumventions and lacked the market power to impose or negotiate favorable NTBs, the option that remained was direct intervention. The government could manipulate public policies with the potential to affect competitiveness—taxes, investment incentives, and access to public finance. Moreover, since the costs of generous wage contracts and of days lost to strike could no longer be passed on to consumers without loss of competitive edge, governments in countries with strong trade unions were forced to broaden the trade agenda and include an incomes policy. As a country thus enriched the panoply of its trade tools, the scope of the trade debate expanded considerably.[1]

Different countries selected different options. The United States, by and large, stayed within the GATT guidelines, resorting now and again to safeguards and VERs. As the world economic leader, the United States could afford free trade, at least until the early 1960s. Working within the GATT framework, the President brought the Cold War to bear on the domestic trade debate, using the security emergency to assert executive preeminence in policymaking and making openness the guiding principle. Although Congress often voiced the discontent of injured domestic interests, it did not question the link between security and trade.

France and Britain, on the other hand, could not afford openness. Their ailing economies called for strong medicine. During the 1950s, they found momentary relief in the use of exchange controls, GATT safeguards, and the maintenance of imperial preferences. In the long run, however, laissez-faire was the same as industrial capitulation; and both countries had to reach beyond the framework of the GATT (and, subsequently, of the EEC) to invest in interventionist tools. Doing so implied two consequences. First, working in the shadow of GATT meant carving out a new policy arena in which the executive would not be able to assert its preeminence on security grounds. This new policy arena was dominated by domestic forces. Second, the extent to which France and Britain were able to develop interventionist policies depended on the nature of the policy process specific to the new policy arena. In the determination of the policy process, the political balance between labor and capital was decisive. In France, where, after 1947, capital was politically dominant, the policy process was pressure politics. Business-government relations, therefore, grew close, and the trade policy turned resolutely interventionist. In Britain, where the working-class movement held capitalist political dominance in check, the policy process was party politics, interrupted now and then by failed attempts to remove trade policy from party politics by means of tripartite corporatist negotiations among business, labor, and government. Business-government relations, therefore, remained distant, and state intervention in British industry fell short of the French model.

The year 1962 marks a turning point in the postwar era; for that is approximately the time when the three economies began to feel the full impact of trade liberalization.

The United States

The Rise of Executive Politics

The post–World War-II era is accurately captured in the concept of U.S. economic hegemony. Not that the world in 1945 suddenly became unipolar; rather, in matters of trade and currency, the United States took the initiative in establishing a multilateral trading system.[2] A point less often emphasized is that this trading system experienced two successive foundings. The first founding corresponded with the signing of the Atlantic Charter in 1941, which, in turn, spawned the IMF, GATT, and the International Trade Organization (although the ITO was not implemented). The second founding coincided with the outbreak of the Cold War in 1946–47, and begat the Marshall Plan, the North Atlantic Treaty Organization (NATO), the European Coal and Steel Community (ECSC), and the EEC. This second founding forced the universalism of the first trading regime into a particularistic security framework. Other GATT members became the military allies of the United States, whereas Communist regimes were discriminated against. Thus the spirit, if not the letter, of the trading regime underwent a change. The source of the change can be traced to the electoral changes and partisan realignment that coincided with the onset of the Cold War.[3]

The outbreak of World War II conferred on the Reciprocal Trade Agreement the security status that Secretary of State Hull had tried to win for it since 1937. Indeed, the war transformed the policy process into a robust case of executive politics. During the debate over extension of the RTA in 1943, Cordell Hull warned that repudiation would send the wrong signal to the Allies; the RTA thus received bipartisan support. As the war drew to a close, however, the trade-security linkage frayed. All Hull could find to say in defense of an extension in 1945 was that curtailment of the RTA would undermine the U.S. delegation to the San Francisco conference on the United Nations. His appeal to universalism was insufficient to hold partisan politics in check. Roll-call votes on key RTA motions and amendments show that the percentage of congressmen voting with their party was over 90 percent in the House and over 70 percent in the Senate, although, for Republicans, the figures dropped to 80 and 50 percent in the final vote.[4] Partisan bias registered at even higher levels in the renewals of RTA (1948 and 1949), though, once again, Republicans to a greater extent broke with partisan discipline in the final votes. The postwar international economic regime was accurately denounced by some as an "application of New Deal economy on a world scale."[5] Early on, the foreign economic policy of both Roosevelt and Truman was partisan. Universalism, identified with the Democrats, was roundly denounced by Republicans.

When the midterm election of 1946 sent a Republican majority to Congress, the situation for the Truman administration became tenuous. Rather than risk Woodrow Wilson's fate, Truman decided to exploit the growing tension between the United States and the Soviet Union to foil the isolationists. The "Truman Doctrine" for Greece and Turkey fired the opening salvo in a grand strategy to contain communism worldwide and Republicanism at home. The Marshall Plan was linked to security in 1947, as was the RTA in 1948. The campaign succeeded beyond all expectations. Economic isolationism was discredited and fell into such disarray that the Republicans—prudently, it turned out—decided to eschew a frontal attack on the RTA during the renewal of 1948 and confine their attacks instead to procedural matters (peril points and the independent Tariff Commission).[6] In the presidential election of 1948, Truman scored the biggest upset victory in U.S. political history, and the Democrats regained control of Congress.

What was founded in 1947? Security became a bipartisan affair, and free trade was laid in the procrustean bed of security. The trade-security linkage, in turn, prepared the ground for the transformation of tariff-making from a partisan process into an executive politics process.

The change developed as follows. Traditionally, foreign policy was neither a salient nor a consensual issue. The president and officials of State Department, Defense Department, and Senate Foreign Relations Committee were the only active participants in the debate on foreign policy. The participation of the House Foreign Affairs Committee was inconsequential. Party loyalty took care of the remainder. On interwar issues such as disarmament, the Four Power Treaty, foreign loans, and foreign aid, Republicans in both houses of Congress tended to be more internationally oriented than were Democrats when a Republican was in the White House and less internationally oriented when a Democrat was president.[7] The process was not party politics, for all that; rather, party loyalty in Congress reflected widespread indifference. Few votes were to be made out of foreign policy back home. It was merely an easy way for members of Congress to please the executive wing of their party.

With the onset of the Cold War, however, foreign policy became a salient issue. The House Foreign Affairs Committee rose in popularity—by 1949 there were more requests for seats on it than on any other committee.[8] In addition, the Cold War caused prior partisan loyalty to be overhauled and foreign policy to be turned into a consensual issue. A transversal cleavage emerged which divided senators and congressmen into a majority of internationalists and a minority of isolationists. Since the Democrats had their man in the White House, and thus did not need more than partisan loyalty to support his foreign policy, the onus of rounding up support for the President's foreign policy fell on the Republicans—more specifically on Senator Arthur Vandenberg, the ranking Republican on the Senate Foreign Relations Committee. In April 1946, during debate over the loan to Britain, and then in 1947, during the debates over the Truman Doctrine for Greece and Turkey and the Marshall Plan for Europe, Vandenberg rallied support for the Democratic administration on the grounds that "if we do not lead, some other great and powerful nation will capitalize on our failure and we shall pay the price of our default."[9] Vandenberg's geostrategic rhetoric became the hallmark of Republican reasoning in all successive debates on foreign policy.

Aware of the new importance of trade in the fight against Communism, Vandenberg also applied his skills to defuse partisan conflict in the domain of trade policy. A severe test presented itself in 1947, when powerful Republicans on the Ways and Means Committee circulated the Jenkins Resolution, which would have limited future tariff cuts and most assuredly weakened the credibility of U.S. negotiators at the ongoing GATT negotiations in Geneva. Sensitive to the potential damage to the country's image as a world leader that was posed by the Jenkins Resolution, Vandenberg and his colleague Eugene D. Millikin worked out a compromise with the Truman administration, according to which congressional action on tariffs would be deferred until the end of the negotiations. In return, the administration would issue an executive order to establish a formal governmental mechanism for considering and acting on applications for tariff relief submitted by domestic industries injured by trade concession—a procedure known as the "escape clause."[10] With this agreement in his pocket, Vandenberg persuaded his Republican colleagues to drop support of the Jenkins Resolution. A similar scenario unfolded when the act came up for renewal in 1948. An intensely partisan debate in the House produced a bill opposed by Truman; again, Vandenberg was instrumental in engineering a compromise bill acceptable to both Congress and the administration.[11]

As a result of these negotiations, the trade debate lost its partisan content. In 1951, the Democratic leadership in the House lost control of the RTA legislation when a minority of Democrats crossed party lines to support several Republican floor amendments intended to reinstitute the restrictions of 1948. With the advent of a Republican administration in 1953, support for and opposition to free trade were transpartisan at first, and often bipartisan later on.[12] Thus, the fact that the midterm elections of 1954 returned a Democratically controlled Congress seemed to have no effect on Eisenhower's capacity to get his trade legislation accepted by Congress.

More important, as the trade cleavage lost its partisan flavor, it began to resemble the cleavage in foreign policy. Protectionists became isolationists, and free traders became internationalists. Evidence for this can be found in the Senate votes on the tariff, when tariff votes are regressed on votes cast on foreign policy, while controlling for partisan affiliation (table 11.1). If it were true that, during the Cold War, trade policy and foreign policy were produced by two-issue areas that partook of the same policy process and were decided in accordance with the same rationale, the political alignment of one policy area should mirror that of the other. That is, senators opposed to internationalism should also oppose further tariff cuts. The test covers the period from about 1900 to 1960.

The results indicate that, before World War II, voting on foreign policy had little in common with voting on the tariff. Partisan affiliation was the overriding factor, with a standardized coefficient hovering around 0.60. The war period 1941–45 saw a reversal of the pattern, with the foreign policy variable acquiring three times the punch of the party variable: 0.46 against 0.15. The postwar period saw a temporary return to the prewar pattern that lasted until 1949. Finally, after 1951, foreign policy consistently outperformed partisan affiliation, with respective coefficients of 0.56 and 0.16 in the last two years of the Truman administration, and 0.37 and 0.28 under Eisenhower. The Cold War hypothesis (an application of hypothesis 4.3 on security emergency) is confirmed, though with a three-year lag.

Hence, throughout the 1950s, openness was justified by security needs. The claim was repeated over and over that the national security of the United States necessitated the creation and maintenance of a free-trade area comprising the "free world." Even the Department of Defense saw a direct link between economic interdependence and the maintenance of a reliable U.S. alliance system.[13] Illustrative of this attitude is the following ruling in 1951, in which the Truman administration turned down a petition for relief submitted on behalf of the American garlic industry:

> There are many reasons for welcoming the increase in imports of Italian garlic. The United States has a stake in the strength and prosperity of Italy. We have recognized that fact in the aid we have given to Italy under the European Recovery Program and under the Mutual Security Act. Italy has done a good job with that aid. Her production has increased. The strength of her Communist Party has declined. But Italy needs to find ways of earning more dollars. . . . Every obstacle the United States puts in her way in these efforts is a step harmful to our mutual security and costly in the end to the consumer and American taxpayer.[14]

The president concluded with the following general statement:

> If we are restrictive in our trade with other countries, they must find other areas with which to trade. Cooperation in the economic field is fundamental to other forms of cooperation.

TABLE 11.1

U.S. Senate, Determinants of Tariff Roll-Calls, 1905–61 (ordinary least squares estimates)

Administration	Period	Partisan allegiance (Democrat vs. Republican)		Foreign-policy vote (interventionist vs. isolationist)		
		coeff.	t-stat.	coeff.	t-stat.	R-squared
T. Roosevelt, Taft	1905–13	0.52	5.87*	0.04	0.38	0.47
Wilson	1913–21	0.85	12.82*	–0.03	–0.39	0.79
Harding, Coolidge, Hoover	1921–33	0.61	6.36*	–0.20	–1.48	0.68
Roosevelt	1933–40	0.70	7.34*	0.14	1.21	0.61
Roosevelt	1941–45	0.15	1.21	0.46	2.96*	0.29
Truman	1945–50	0.55	8.00*	0.18	1.70	0.60
Truman	1951–53	0.16	1.70	0.56	4.82*	0.49
Eisenhower	1953–61	0.28	3.59*	0.37	3.75*	0.32

* significant at the 0.01 level.

Coding. The dependent variable is (or are) the Senate vote(s) on trade bills, coded "1" for protection, "0" for free trade. Partisan allegiance is coded "1" for Republican, "0" for Democrat. Foreign policy vote is (or are) the Senate vote(s) on foreign policy bills, coded "1" for isolationist and "0" for interventionist. *The two independent variables are standardized so as to make their coefficients comparable.* Results for the constant are omitted. The number of observations (one per state) varies between 43 and 50. Whenever possible, "announced" and "paired" votes were included in the "yeas" or "nays".

The roll-calls that were used for foreign policy are: Feb. 13, 1905, amendment to Arbitration Treaty with France; March 19, 1920, final vote on Lodge Resolution (League of Nations); March 24, 1922, Washington Treaties; Nov. 27, 1922, vote to recommit Liberian Loan; June 6, 1924, La Follette motion on German Relief; Jan. 27, 1926, U.S. adherence to the World Court; April 28, 1926, Czechoslovakian War Debt Settlements; July 21, 1930, London Treaty limiting naval armaments; Jan. 29, 1935, U.S. adherence to the World Court; Feb. 18, 1936, Clark amendment to Neutrality Act; Oct. 27, 1939, Neutrality Act, H. J. Res. 306; March 8, 1942, Lend-Lease, H. R. 1776; May 10, 1946, British Loan, S.J. Res. 128; April 22, 1947, Greek-Turkish Aid, final vote; Nov. 26, 1947, Interim Aid, Malone amendment; March 14, 1948, Marshall Plan, Taft amendment; Sep. 22, 1949, Foreign Military Assistance Act, George amendment; Aug. 31, 1951, Mutual Security Act (M.S.A.), Dirksen amendment; May 28, 1952, M.S.A., Long amendment; July 1, 1953, M.S.A., Case motion; Aug. 3 1954, M.S.A., Long amendment; June 2, 1955, M.S.A., Long amendment; July 24, 1956, Foreign Aid Appropriations, Ellender amendment; Aug. 27, 1957, M.S.A., Committee amendment; June 6, 1958, M.S.A., passage; July 8, 1959, M.S.A., passage; May 2, 1960, M.S.A. passage.

For roll-calls on trade policy: March 15, 1909, Payne-Aldrich tariff; July 22, 1911, reciprocity with Canada; Sep. 9, 1913, Underwood tariff; Feb. 19, 1921 emergency tariff; May 11, 1921, Second emergency tariff; Sep. 19, 1922, Fordney-McCumber tariff; June 12, 1930, Hawley-Smoot tariff; April 1, 1932, Collier trade bill; June 4, 1934, Reciprocal Trade Agreements Act (RTA); Feb. 25, 1937, RTA extension; April 5, 1940, RTA extension; June 14, 1943, RTA extension; June 20, 1945, extension, O'Mahoney amendment; June 19, 1947, Wool Supports, conference report; June 14, 1948, RTA extension; Sep. 15, 1949, RTA extension; May 23, 1951, RTA extension; June 24, 1954, RTA extension, Gore amendment; May 4, 1955, RTA extension; July 22, 1958, RTA extension, Johnson amendment.

Sources: Congressional Record; Congressional Quarterly.

The administration's trade policy was governed by two rationales. First, the vast purchasing power of the domestic market should be used to lure foreign countries into the American security orbit. Second, tariffs should be reduced to shift the burden of the foreign policy from the taxpayer (in the form of foreign aid) to the import-sensitive sectors (in the form of Allies' imports to the United States). No one even alluded to the old Democratic saying that without imports there would be no exports.

The Role of the Lobbies

One of the most disputed questions of postwar U.S. trade policy concerns the role played by American business in the formulation of U.S. foreign economic policy. Revisionist historians are quick to question the official, self-serving justification of U.S. foreign policy goals and point to the few particular and selfish goals that were disguised by the universalist, patriotic discourse of the public officials.[15] Essentially, the revisionists argue that the United States came out of World War II with a vast industrial surplus capacity that would have to be scrapped unless alternative markets were found. Large American corporations commissioned the Democratic administration to turn devastated Europe into a creditworthy consumer by means of various measures that included cancellation of British war debts, creation of a banker of last resort in the IMF, and promotion of exports through the Marshall Plan. These policies were biased against American labor.[16] David Eakins has advanced the provocative argument that this group of measures was a New Deal for free enterprise: Its large-scale compensatory spending was intended to prevent stagnation of the capitalist economy without taking the form of spending at home, a policy that endangered the free-enterprise system.[17] The evidence on which revisionists rely the most stresses the fundamental identity of goals and personnel of the U.S. multinational companies and the policy agencies in Washington.

The revisionists have a point when they argue that the American state pursued policies that corresponded to the long-term interests of the most advanced, concentrated sectors of its economy. The fact that openness met the interest of the multinational companies, however, does not mean that the policy was adopted for their benefit. This period poses the same puzzle as World War I. Why, after 1915, was Wilson able to pursue a foreign economic policy that favored the interests of American multinationals when he had not been able to do so in 1913? Similarly, why were the Roosevelt and then the Truman administrations able to achieve after World War II what Cordell Hull failed to achieve in the 1930s? The answer is the same for both questions: The Democrats were able to promote the interests of American big business when the transformation of the policy process to executive politics freed trade policy from class conflict and particular pressure. By rooting openness in the urgency to contain communism, in 1947, the executive was able to generate support for export promotion in the nation at large, a support group that transcended the smaller group of exporters. In support of the executive-politics argument, two sets of facts should be noted, facts which are at odds with the rent-seeking argument: (1) exporters never felt a need to organize a broad, permanent coalition of export interests; and (2) exporters adopted a long-term perspective toward trade policy. The following discussion revolves around these two points.

The policy of openness did not reflect the organized support of a broad, permanent, free-trade coalition. Lobbying was not active but reactive. Consider lobbying in Congress. In the tradition of Schattschneider's study of the 1930 tariff, I looked at the relative distribution of testimony at congressional hearings. Figure 11.1 summarizes the hearings that preceded adoption or discussion of a major piece of trade legislation between 1934 and 1987. Testimony was coded according to whether or not it supported the proposed trade legislation. Only testimony and written statements submitted by trade unions and trade associations were recorded.[18] Two measures were calculated. First is the ratio between the number of interests for and against the legislation, which records the feeling a committee member develops for where the average lies. The second measure indicates the number of times a claim in one sector was left unchecked by a counterclaim in the same sector, at the same level of representation by a rival organization. Despite their different shortcomings, these two measures closely parallel and validate one another.

The shape of the curve is most interesting. The correlation between lobbying activity and the policy outcome is the converse of what one would expect in a hypothetical case of pressure politics. Policy orientation did not reflect the preferences aired by the most active interests. Except for 1934, the date of its inception, the Reciprocal Trade Agreement received more support before and during World War II than after it. Protectionists put on the strongest show of opposition in the 1950s, when the policy of openness was most actively pursued. In all likelihood, these interests were reacting against the one-sidedness of executive policy, which peaked in that decade.[19]

The same imbalance in representation was noticeable in the administrative branch, although evidence here is scanty. Only 28 percent of the oral statements made during hearings held by the State Department in 1947 were favorable to the new liberal orientation.[20] It is not until 1953, the year a Republican returned to the White House, that big business became directly involved in policymaking. President Eisenhower appointed to his cabinet two prominent corporate leaders, George M. Humphrey and Charles E. Wilson—a "political audacity," in the editorial words of Fortune magazine, for the only appointment comparable to these two back to 1900 was that of Andrew Mellon, in 1921.[21] The Republican party, however, immediately fell prey to a bitter intraparty fight. Protectionists came close to overwhelming the executive, although the reason they failed had little to do with lobbying by free traders. Indeed, with the advent of a Republican administration, a spate of protectionist pressures were released, including those of textile interests in New England

FIGURE 11.1
Oral and Written Testimony at Congressional Hearings, 1934–87

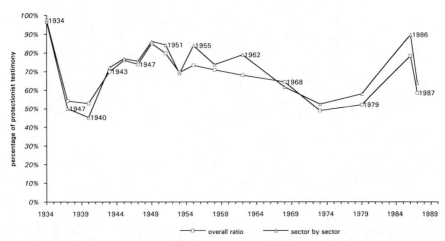

Coding: See main text and n. 18 (p. 335). For 1934–51, data include testimony before the House Ways and Means Committee and the Senate Finance Committee, interests appearing before both committees being computed only once. For 1953–87, data only include testimony before Ways and Means. Oral and written presentations are weighted equally. The observations number: 37 (1934), 24 (1937), 70 (1940), 30 (1943), 100 (1945), 88 (1947–48), 60 (1949), 69 (1951), 82 (1953), 45 (1955), 110 (1958), 144 (1962), 70 (1973), 46 (1979), 51 (1986), 41 (1987). Lower numbers for the 80's in part reflect the growing proportion of ad hoc coalitions, not included here, with no prejudice for the results; in 1987, e.g., the breakdown of ad hoc coalitions was 10 for protectionists, and 9 for free traders.

Sources: U.S. Congress, House Committee on Ways and Means, Reciprocal Trade Agreements (RTA), Washington D.C.: U.S. GPO, 1934; Extending Reciprocal Foreign Trade Agreement Act 1937; Extension of RTA Act 1940; Extension of RTA Act 1943; 1945 Extension of the RTA Act 1945; RTA Program 1947; Trade Agreements Program 1948; 1949 Extension of the RTA Act; 1951 Extension of the RTA Act; Trade Agreements Extension Act of 1953; Trade Agreements Extension 1955; Renewal of Trade Agreements Act 1958; Trade Expansion Act of 1962; Foreign Trade and Tariff Proposals 1968; Trade Reform 1973, Multilateral Trade Negotiations 1979; Trade Reform Legislation 1986; Comprehensive Trade Legislation, 1987. U.S. Tariff Commission, Digest of Testimonies Received on HR 10710, The Trade Reform Act of 1973, Washington D.C.: U.S. GPO 1974; Senate Committee of Finance, RTA, Washington D.C: U.S. GPO 1934; Extending Reciprocal Foreign Trade Agreement Act 1937; Extension of RTA Act 1940, Extension of RTA Act 1943; 1945 Extension of the RTA Act; Extending Authority to Negotiate Trade Agreements 1948; Extension of the RTA Act 1949; Trade Agreements Extension Act of 1951.

and the South, certain farm interests (minor crops), the mining industry of the mountain states, the oil interests of the South, the coal interests of Pennsylvania, and several railroads. Had all these interests applied pressure on Congress at once and in the same direction, the Eisenhower administration would have found itself in a serious predicament. The coalition, however, was plagued by sectional rivalry which pitted oil-consuming New England against oil-producing South. The traditional New England industries were willing to accept the more favorable escape clause procedure granted by the Simpson bill; but they did not want the bill at the price of an increase in energy prices, which the proposed oil quotas would entail. The imbalance of the bill—which granted quotas to oil, lead, and zinc but granted only procedures to textiles, leather, and other manufactured products—ensured its defeat.[22]

The opposition put up by the free-trade interests was so insignificant that a handful of export-oriented businessmen grew alarmed; after the dust had settled, they found it wise to organize themselves as the Committee for a National Trade Policy.[23] Hearings in 1955 saw an exceptionally high turnout of big corporations.[24] Once organized, however, the CNTP lost its momentum. The Eisenhower administration could not afford to give industrialists an opportunity to test the CNTP's combat skills. Instead, the administration engaged in a policy of preemption by means of side-payments. Offering strategic imperatives as a pretext, the administration launched a program of stockpiling for lead and zinc and instituted quotas for "industries indispensable to national security" (that is, oil). Inevitably, these measures had an unnerving effect on exporters. Whether for lack of strength or opportunity, the CNTP did not become the praetorian guard of the executive in the area of free trade. Instead, it suffered the fate of numerous think tanks created after World War II, whose research capabilities, at best, duplicated those of the administration.[25]

Undoubtedly, the evidence relied on here has its shortcomings. It captures only the visible part of lobbying, a part that may not be representative of what goes on behind the scenes. After all, the multinationals have an incentive to go public only when they are among the losers. This would be the claim of revisionists. Note, however, that this sub rosa version of rent seeking is insufficient to account for the sudden centralization of the trade-policymaking process in the executive branch after the war. This leads to my second point.

Rent seeking is a weak explanation for the shift in policy, since it cannot account for the sudden ability of officials and multinationals in the late 1940s to give up the pursuit of short-term, particular interest and, instead, aim for longer-term goals. The most striking feature of the policy of openness pursued by the Truman (and, later, the Eisenhower) administration is its long-term rationale—opening the world market was deferred to the indefinite future (actually, it took ten years). Rent seeking, however, does not allow participants to wait patiently for the future. Essentially, the logic of rent seeking forces it to be short-term: A firm that refrains from pursuing an immediate rent, on the grounds that the rent would be suboptimal in the long run, is likely to be worse off, since other firms will grab the rent and spoil the long-term calculation of the first firm. For this reason, regardless of the degree of competitiveness of the participants, optimal outcomes are never realized in the rent-seeking process. The very fact that, in 1947, multinationals could escape this dilemma—and contemplate the day when a fully rebuilt, politically stabilized, affluent Europe would welcome large flows of American imports—is evidence that the policy process was not pressure politics but, rather, was structured to rule out rent seeking.

Consider the example of the Marshall Plan. The plan was not designed or administered to rid domestic producers of unwanted economic surplus—at least, not in the short term. Initiated by the State Department and sold to the American people by the administration, the enabling legislation passed Congress with a minimum number of special interest provisions.[26] More important, the program was administered in such a way that little was conceded to special interests. The statutory goal of officials in the European Cooperation Administration was to get maximum European recovery from the minimum of American tax dollars, not to use American tax dollars to directly purchase U.S. exports. Very often, indeed, the two were incompatible. Good management of the ECA budget meant that European nations used the dollars they received for items they could procure only in the United States, while purchasing other items—such as coal, cotton, and farm products—from other countries. Good management of ECA also meant fostering a policy of import substitution, intended to reduce the need for U.S. exports. This developmental strategy was optimal in the long run, for it would enlarge the purchasing power of Europe and create a market for U.S. exporters. In the short term, however, the strategy did nothing to relieve the plight of those who most needed a boost and who happened to be influential in Congress.

Requests for special treatment for coal and oil producers, fruit growers, dairy producers, machine tool manufacturers, and small business were channeled by a congressional watchdog committee to ECA officials—all in vain.[27] The only special interests the ECA could not resist were the growers of wheat, corn, and tobacco, on whose behalf Congress was particularly adamant about special treatment. Except for wheat, corn, and tobacco interests, Arkes is right when writing that "the ECA was the despair of those people who were most apprehensive in their concern for American self-interest."[28]

Among other measures that discounted exporters' short-run interests was the State Department's decision to strengthen the sterling area and acquiesce in discrimination against U.S. goods by Commonwealth countries. In 1949, the same favor was extended to all European governments; Europeans liberalized their respective trade policies while maintaining restrictions against dollar goods.[29] Washington's support of this step, as well as further steps toward European economic unification, could not be justified on the grounds of free trade and export orientation, except by making a detour through the field of security. The readiness of the State Department to compromise the welfare of American exporters in order to maintain U.S. world leadership is best shown in the debate over the charter for the International Trade Organization. The draft, negotiated by diplomats, was condemned at home by both free traders and exporters, who judged it as too restrictive.[30]

In sum, the Marshall Plan was designed and administered with the long-term economic and military interests of the United States in mind. Because U.S. national interests overlapped with the defense and prosperity of Europe, the foreign economic policy of the United States, after 1947, took on the characteristics of a benevolent leadership. Revisionists add little to the argument by pointing to the convergence of interests between large multinational corporations and the executive's grand strategy. These corporations took advantage of—but could not be responsible for—the long-term dispositions of the administration. Left to themselves in a classic pressure-politics setup, the corporations would have been engaged in hopeless and trivial pursuit of quick, suboptimal rents. It was the mobilization of the American public behind a policy of anticommunism—a fundamentally popular policy—along with the linking of containment with reconstruction of Europe and establishment of a stable international trading regime, that allowed politicians to pursue the interests of the vanguard of American capitalism. Executive politics steeled policymaking against special interests, making it imperative for large firms to give up on rent seeking and focus their attention on the distant future.

In sum, the policy of openness did not reflect the existence of a triumphant coalition of MNCs and other free traders. Rather, the policy reflected the influence of the executive. The executive learned to divide the ranks of protectionists by means of deliberate manipulation of side-payments. Self-reliance gave the executive the freedom to employ foreign aid in pursuit of longterm goals, unhindered by the immediate needs of exporters. The executive would not have been able to disregard the preferences of exporters had it relied solely on their support to contain the protectionists in Congress.

The Defense of Congress

A literal reading of the RTA Act would suggest that the transfer of tariffmaking from political parties to the executive branch had been accomplished as early as 1934, that it was simply renewed afterward without major alteration. Yet, it would be inexact to infer functional identity from procedural continuity. Delegations in the 1930s differed from those in the 1950s, owing to a change in the nature of the principal. To be sure, in both cases, the immediate principal was Congress, but Congress acting in a different capacity. In the 1930s, the immediate principal was the Democratic majority, i.e., a partisan majority, whereas in the 1950s, the immediate principal was a bipartisan majority. As a result, the policy process was more exposed to specialinterest pressure after World War II than before it. Party politics in the 1930s excluded protectionists, with the exception of those situated in Democratic land (oil). Bipartisan politics in the 1950s could not exclude protectionists as easily. That is, the Congress of the 1950s could no longer count on partisan discipline to fulfill its gatekeeping role; instead, Congress had to rely on the concept of national emergency, a consensual (and thus weaker) principle. Consensus reduced the information content of tariff-making, making it easier for special interests to steal in. Therefore, there was a danger that Congress would be besieged by a coalition of the labor-intensive industries severely affected by tariff cuts (cotton textile, oil, coal, lead and zinc) and that eventually these industries would force the ultimate agent—the executive—to weaken or surrender its delegation.

Congressional leaders parried this threat by measures designed to divide the protectionists, should the latter decide to act together. Thus, Congressional leaders first adopted a series of administrative and quasi-judicial procedures that required the participation either of the Tariff Commission or of the courts: escape clause, antidumping duties, countervailing duties. Claimants were expected to exhaust these avenues before turning to Congress.[31] When, in 1953, these procedures failed to divert the coalition of oil, coal, lead-zinc, leather, and textiles, Congress requested the White House to make special deals with key protectionist interests, thus dividing the protectionist camp. The quasi-judicial procedures discouraged sectoral organization, whereas the special deals discouraged the formation of intersectoral compacts and log-rolling coalitions. From 1953 on, protectionists never again targeted the central orientation of the policy, which remained free trade; they merely sought exceptions. Instead of attempting to form a broad coalition to repeal free trade in Congress, protectionists went separately to the White House, where they promised individual support for freer trade in exchange for individual immunity.[32]

The institutional weakness of Congress obliged the President to "manage" bipartisan support. Whether he could do so and still minimize the exceptions to free trade is a question that received a different answer at different times. The concern was not serious until 1962. Between 1947 and 1962, the U.S. Tariff Commission completed 112 investigations, recommending action in 33 cases, only 15 of which were sustained by the President.[33] Special deals were cut—with oil, lead and zinc, and textiles. Still, when compared to the degree of liberalization achieved during that period, the number of exceptions granted against free trade was rather small.

The Executive

The U.S. executive was now firmly in charge of trade policy. Hot and cold wars had transformed the State Department into the most influential agency in Washington. Congress increased the negotiating authority of the State Department by 50 percent in 1945 and by additional percentage points afterward. Although the extensions came with strings attached, the economic superiority of the United States in the world provided State with a broad margin for maneuver. The country's trade policy was in the hands of diplomats who believed that tariff liberalization would enhance the prospects for "Pax Americana." For a while, trade truly was the continuation of diplomacy by other means, since the department, all too often, was prepared to sacrifice domestic interests in the pursuit of diplomatic ones. As a result, State became the favorite target of the isolationist *irréductibles*, who simultaneously accused the department of being soft toward the Soviet Union and staffed with Communists, of caring more about the welfare of the people in allied countries than of American taxpayers, and, in the domain of trade, of being more instrumental in opening the domestic market to foreign goods than opening foreign markets to U.S. goods.

Tool Kit and Policy Orientation

The U.S. trade policy tool kit conformed to expectations: It was simple (hypothesis 5.7); and it did not include subsidies (hypothesis 5.8). Although the United States had little use for provisional measures, when it did resort to them, its preference went to GATT safeguards (tariffs or quotas) and VERs, whose implementation did not require a close relationship between government and industrialists involved. It should be borne in mind, however, that the policy outcome was overdetermined, an outcome that reflected the dominant trading position of the United States.

With respect to tariffs, the present theory predicts that the policy outcome will reflect security considerations, embodied after World War II in the

TABLE 11.2

Pearson Correlation Coefficients between French, British, and U.S. Tariffs, and between Each Tariff and Corresponding Changes in the Business Cycle, 1946–79

	British tariff	French tariff	U.S. tariff
British tariff			
French tariff	0.35		
U.S. tariff	0.56	0.18	
British business cycle	0.14		
French business cycle		−0.02	
U.S. business cycle			−0.05

Coding rules and data sources:

Changes in the nominal tariff: Logarithm of the yearly change in the average ratio of customs revenues collected to total imports. For Britain, the customs revenues only bear on the official category "Protective Duties." Source for France until 1975: Mitchell 1980; thereafter, INSEE, *Annuaire statistique de la France*, various years. Source for Britain: Central Statistical Office, *Annual Abstract of Statistics*, various years. Source for the United States until 1970: U.S. Bureau of the Census 1976, Series U-207 and Y-353; thereafter, U.S. Bureau of the Census, *Statistical Abstract of the United States*, various years.

Business cycle: Economic expansion or peak years were coded "1", contraction or economic through years were coded "0." Sources: same as for the tariff.

GATT multilateral trade negotiations. In other words, the tariff of the three countries should evolve in tandem (hypothesis 5.5). This prediction accords with the actual evolution of the respective tariff rates of the three countries and is reflected in the shape of the tariff curves (figures A2.1, A2.2, and A2.3 in Appendix 2) and their mutual correlation. Table 11.2 (see p. 215) records the Pearson correlation coefficients between the national tariffs for the period 1946–79 (no reliable British data are readily available for before or after this period; see Appendix 2). The table also shows correlation coefficients between business cycle and tariff level for each nation. For each country, the external correlation is higher than the internal one.

With respect to the overall level of protection (not simply the part covered by GATT, measured in table 11.2), hypothesis 5.6 stipulates a reverse correlation between the level of protection and the economic stature of the United States relative to its allies. Two types of data must be combined: tariffs and NTBs. Figure 11.2 zooms in on the period 1950–84, both showing the tariff proxy and reproducing for NTBs the Magee, Brock, and Young's treatment of the Hufbauer, Berliner, and Elliott's data set.[34] Figure 11.3 provides a numerical count of three types of restraint: (1) tariff increase—usually a concession withdrawn by the United States after it was found to injure domestic producers; (2) global quotas—mostly under section 22, for which the United States needs a special waiver from GATT; and (3) bilateral agreements—which circumvent GATT procedures. Tariffs and global quotas begin to rise linearly in 1951 and peak in 1960, whereas bilateral agreements pick up in 1961. The three curves—tariff, tariff-equivalent

FIGURE 11.2
U.S. Tariff Rate and Tariff-Equivalent NTB Rate, 1950–84

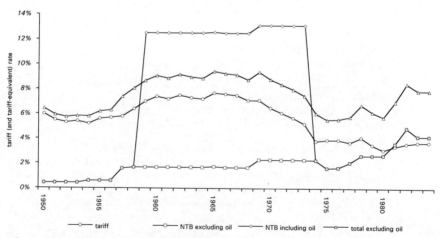

Source: Magee, Brock, and Young 1989: 262; Hufbauer, Berliner, and Elliott 1986: 3–5.

FIGURE 11.3

Number of U.S. Temporary Import Restraints in Existence in a Given Year, 1945–87

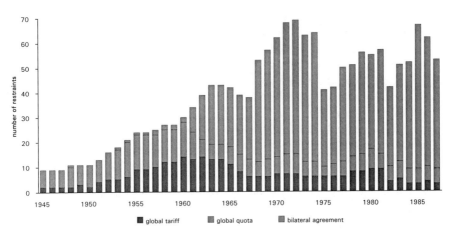

Coding: Restraints are global quotas (sec. 22 of the 1934 RTAA, actions in connection with "national security," and with "market disruption"), global tariffs (all withdrawn GATT concessions), and bilateral agreements (OMA, VRA, and VER). Not included: restraints resulting from investigations conducted under antidumping and countervailing statutes, sec. 337 of the 1930 Tariff Act, and sec. 301 of the 1974 Trade Act.

Sources: U.S. Tariff Commission (since 1974: U.S. International Trade Commission), *Operation of the Trade Agreements Program*, annual report, various years; U.S. President, *Annual Report on the Trade Agreements Program* (Washington, D.C.: GPO, various years); Hufbauer, Berliner, and Elliott 1986.

of NTBs, and number of NTBs—suggest that U.S. trade diplomacy exhibited its highest attachment to openness before 1950, and that protectionist measures steadily crept in afterward. The year 1950 marks the turning point of the U.S. world export share. From then on, U.S. trade hegemony is on the decline.[35]

France

From Party to Pressure

The Soviet threat was not felt the same way in France as it was in the United States. The threat, military and stable, was avoidable as long as France participated in the U.S.-sponsored international order—NATO, GATT, IMF. Membership in GATT gave the French executive the authority to regulate tariff- (and quota-) making but granted the executive no particular autonomy over the formulation of NTBs and planning, which fell outside the GATT jurisdiction and which France soon adopted. Therefore, except in applying the GATT-regulated policy tools, the French executive was unable to use the

Soviet threat to reconfigure France's trade institutions to its own advantage. Outside of GATT, the prevailing process for policymaking was domestic— party and then pressure.

World War II begat a novel political situation in which French labor was a full-fledged political actor. As we have seen, after years of evasion, in 1936, the class conflict broke into the policy process under the Popular Front. For the first time, the Communist party—including the affiliated *Confédération générale du travail*, the most powerful workers union—took part in policymaking. Although the Popular Front was short-lived, it set a precedent whose reprise was likely. Preparation for war and the period of the phony war (roughly, October 1939 to May 1940) may have eased labor-management relations, at least in the armament sectors; but the fall of France and the advent of the Vichy government revealed how deep-seated the class antagonism was. Although Henry Ehrmann is fundamentally correct in describing the Vichy regime as one controlled by trade associations, this orgy of pressure politics took place within a regime that was partisan at heart. By banning parties and trade unions, Vichy disfranchised both organized labor and farmers.[36] The Libération reversed these positions. Business was accused of acts of collaboration with the enemy, deprived of representation in a political arena now heavily biased toward the Left and Center, and dispossessed of its reliable press. Thus, for a while, organized business retired from the political scene.[37] The provisional government nationalized major firms: deposit banks, insurance companies, the electricity and gas industries, coal mines, and Renault (automobiles). The steel industry barely escaped the list, thanks to the moderating presence of de Gaulle and the Christian Democrats (MRP). These measures had a clear partisan content; they reflected the unusual strength of the Communist party (polling 29 percent of the electoral vote in 1946), as well as the great prestige of the Red Army.

The advent of the Cold War marked the end of France's experiment with Right-Left alternation. With the rise of the Soviet threat, the United States abandoned its political neutrality and in 1946 began to use economic aid to promote the French Right, then, in 1947, to exclude the Communists from the government. For the next thirty years, the political system reverted to its pre-1936 pattern, in which the most powerful trade union confederation, the Communist CGT, found itself without representation in the political system. Disfranchisement of the workers as a class restored the farmers, shopkeepers, and other middle classes to their traditional electoral preeminence. The Cold War made the French political system safe for business.

There are a few notable policy exceptions to this generalization. Membership in the U.S. bloc provided the French executive with opportunities in the form of Marshall aid and U.S. backing for European integration. Then, too, there was the German threat, whose recurrence in history had persuaded many people of its inevitability—although from a strict, structural perspective they were wrong. Combining the resources of the Cold War—American aid and backing for European integration—with the pervasive Germanophobia enabled enterprising politicians in the French Ministry of Foreign Affairs to acquire sufficient momentum to force on an unconsenting business community three remarkable pieces of legislation: the Monnet Plan, the Schuman Plan, and the Treaty of Rome. These measures were to have long-term consequences for France's trade future. The restrictive hypothesis 4.3 (on security emergency) cannot, technically speaking, predict these measures; yet their origin places them in a category with military threats. In all three cases, policy outcome proceeded from a policy process informed by a foreign-policy linkage.

We consider planning first. Two conceptions of planning competed for recognition at the Libération: the Socialist conception, best expressed in the Philip Report of July 1944; and the neo-Liberal conception, first expressed in the Courtin Report of November 1943, and toward which Jean Monnet, father of the first plan, inclined.[38] The Socialists got to try their idea first. In 1944, a planning division was created within the Ministry for the National Economy, under Pierre Mendès-France; but the office failed to function. Shortly thereafter, the new ministry was displaced by the Ministry of Finance.[39]

The neo-Liberals succeeded where the Socialists had failed because Monnet was able to tap the two dominant security concerns of the time: French Germanophobia and American anticommunism. The Monnet Plan was the Quai d'Orsay's answer to the question that had haunted France since World War I (it still does): how to prevent still another German invasion.[40] All along, from Clémentel and Poincaré to Monnet and Schuman, the answer was the same: "[T]he surest guarantee for the maintenance of peace," Hervé Alphand, an official of the Quai, declared in 1947, "will always consist in the limitation of the German steel potential."[41] American lack of support for Paris's neutralization of the Ruhr proposal left the French only with one alternative: persuade the Allies to allocate to the French steel industry a share of the coal and coke output of the Ruhr sufficient to stunt the development of a fuel-starved German steel industry. Through sheer reverse induction, the planning commission calculated the overall growth rate that would be necessary for the French economy to absorb the plotted increase in steel output. It then derived the impact of this growth on a selected number of basic sectors. When the Monnet Plan was made public, in March 1946, an agreement was reached under which the Allies would limit German steel output and increase German coal shipments to France.

While Germanophobia provided the rationale, anticommunism provided the financial resources. As Kuisel has convincingly shown, Monnet was able to tap the "American connection."[42] The First Modernization Plan (1946) was financed through a credit to be administered by the U.S. Eximbank and the World Bank (a creature of Wall Street) for the years 1946–49. In 1947, when these resources fell short of the plan's needs, the plan was revised and extended until 1952, which enabled France to receive Marshall Plan money.

In both cases, Washington's fears of a Communist takeover played an important role.[43]

The strategic origins of the Monnet Plan help explain why the plan escaped the Charybdis of bureaucratic politics and the Scylla of partisan controversy, as well as why it was accepted by a business community otherwise inimical to planning. The superior needs of French diplomacy allowed the Quai d'Orsay to overrule the objections of his colleagues from the Ministry of Finance, the Ministry of National Economy, and the Ministry of Industrial Production to the creation of a special agency directly responsible to the Prime Minister— the *Commissariat Général au Plan* (planning commission). The Finance Ministry was disqualified; because Washington did not want the funds to be used for current operations—that is, to finance the inflationary spiral that benefited the dominant interest groups at the time (peasants, trade unions, and military).[44] Higher politics also allowed the Quai to keep the plan out of the domestic ideological battle and to produce a blueprint acceptable to Washington, despite the fact that the plan had first been advanced by a coalition government in which the Communists were the largest party. Finally, the "American connection" in Monnet's idea of planning was very attractive to business. American sponsorship was a strong guarantee that the funds would not be used to foster objectives antagonistic to business. Indeed, the preparation of the plan offered organized business an opportunity to come out of its political isolation. Business leaders found the planning commission officials eager to hear about their respective investment projects and their needs for long-term financing.

The Monnet Plan failed to rein in German steel output, however. In 1947, the United States requested that German output be increased to the French level. Ironically, Washington's provision of Marshall aid to the French was made conditional on France's acceptance of the request. The Cold War called for an economically strong West Germany firmly attached to the West. The Quai, therefore, effected a tactical U-turn in May 1950, by proposing in the Schuman Plan, to place the Franco-German output of coal and steel under a common supranational organization, which would be open, as well, to other European nations.[45] Adenauer welcomed the French government's initiative, the United States applauded it, and four other European nations jumped on the bandwagon.

The French steelmasters, who had not been consulted, threw their weight against the Schuman Plan. They dragged in on their side the *Conseil national du patronat français* (CNPF), along with several other heavyweights from industry. Had the battle been fought by the rules of pressure politics, steel would have won. The Quai, however, pitched the debate at the level of principles, throwing off key the steelmasters' advocacy of their sectoral interest. The Quai called the tune, and the bill cleared Parliament by a plurality of 377 positive to 235 negative votes. Almost all of the negative ballots were cast for ideological reasons by the two political extremes: Gaullists and Communists. The

Socialists, the Radicals, and the Christian Democrats unanimously voted for the plan; 85 percent of the Independents (the party closest to the interests of big business) also joined the supporting chorus.[46]

The Schuman Plan was a mere dress rehearsal for the more audacious EEC. Negotiations over the EEC took place in Brussels, the proceedings shrouded in secrecy.[47] Trade associations were not consulted, nor was a systematic study made of the economic impact of the project on French industry. The CNPF and all the important sectors of French industry were opposed to the common market. Still smarting from their previous defeat, however, they carefully avoided overt confrontation with the government over the principle of integration—even more so since the Suez fiasco, the Soviet Union's condemnation of Euratom and the Common Market, and the Soviet crackdown on Hungary convincingly demonstrated the need for such integration. Business preferred, instead, to advance amendments that were unacceptable to France's international partners. Finding itself in the comfortable position of playing broker between its European partners and domestic industry, the Mollet government extracted just enough concessions from the former to defuse the organizing thrust of the latter.

The government's victory resulted from its ability to lift the debate above the interests and the parties. In the Assembly, Premier Guy Mollet opened the Euratom debate by recalling that the goals of European integration were to tie West Germany to the Western Alliance. The debate was not influenced by the business cycle; the continuing deterioration of France's trade balance in 1957 did not fuel protectionism but was turned by the government into further evidence of the need for integration. Nor was the debate held hostage to political instability; the European bill garnered broader partisan support than the Bourgès-Maunoury government under which the plan was brought to a vote.

Hence, the Fourth Republic took major initiatives in regard to industry. The source of its autonomy was not its institutions—which, by everyone's account were weak—but the international environment: Germanophobia and the Cold War. This autonomy, had no sustaining power, however. Germanophobia had produced the Monnet Plan, but it was of no help in ensuring implementation of the planning commission's projections. American funding and the strings attached to the plan helped Monnet resist the downward pull of special-interest and bureaucratic politics; but, as soon as Marshall Plan funds dried up and taxation took over, Monnet could not keep his offspring from sinking into the morass of domestic politics. The GATT assuredly was binding, its multilateral dynamic, no doubt, quite safely out of the reach of special interests. Planning, however, fell outside the GATT's jurisdiction. In the case of the Treaty of Rome, parliamentary ratification did not even guarantee implementation, since, in 1957, most observers believed that France would not be financially capable of taking the liberalizing measures scheduled to begin January 1, 1959. Indeed, no less than the threat of civil war, a constitutional crisis, and the rise to power of a war hero equipped with the most sweeping delegation of legislative power ever seen in peacetime was required before France could proceed with the scheduled liberalization.

In sum, by 1960, trade policymaking in France was proceeding along three parallel tracks. (1) The GATT track, dominated by executive politics, owed its origins to the communist threat. (2) The EEC track—including tariffs, price fixing in the steel and coal industry, and price supports for agriculture— was also dominated by executive politics. (3) The non-GATT, non-EEC track—including exchange controls, price policy, imperial preferences, and planning (starting with the second installment)—was mediated through party politics until 1947, and afterward by pressure politics.

The Capture of Planning

The consultative system, which business and government had established be- fore the war, was destroyed under the Libération and bypassed during the making of the Monnet Plan, the Schuman Plan, and the Treaty of Rome. Yet, far from disappearing, the system showed tremendous resilience, especially in capturing the new redistributive field of planning.

The consultative system reached a unique degree of achievement under the Vichy regime. Vichy reorganized the institutions inherited from the Third Republic along two lines. On the one hand, the law of August 16, 1940, eliminated the Parliamentary channels of interest representation and, with it, any prospect of mass-based producer groups playing a role. Second, the Vichy regime streamlined the bureaucratic channel of interest representation. In sec- tors deemed important, the three traditional actors—trade association, cartel, and advisory committee—were merged into one organization: the *Comité d'or- ganisation professionnelle*. The outcome was an authoritarian, "corporatist" re- gime that institutionalized the domination of business over labor and, within business, of large concerns over small ones.[48]

After a vain attempt to purge and use them, the Libération government dismantled the Vichy-born *Comités d'organisation*, entrusting to the trade asso- ciations the task of allocating scarce materials and awarding import licenses. After quantitative controls were lifted in 1951, the trade associations played an important role in administering the governmental price control policy.[49] More generally, the trade associations retrieved their prewar advisory role in the traditional domain of regulatory politics.

True to its external origins, the Monnet Plan bypassed the established con- sultative system. The content of the first plan did not reflect the usual interac- tion among competing interests as much as it reflected the planners' own priorities: rapid growth in basic sectors to permit these sectors to charge lower prices to the rest of industry. Moreover, since the definition of what consti- tuted a basic sector was broad, the planners' actual selection of sectors reflected mainly a concern about implementation. The planning commission thus sought to bypass trade association officials, who usually were not accredited to commit their membership, and, instead, establish direct agreements with industrialists. In addition, given the plan's sectoral focus, the planners unimaginatively favored concentrated sectors, in which the action of one or a few large companies would be decisive, at the expense of sectors in which production was dispersed among a large number of participants.[50] This accounts for the selection of coal, petroleum, electricity, cement, steel, fertilizer, and basic chemicals. In addition, two manufacturing industries were retained, because they were concentrated: shipbuilding and agricultural machinery. Sectors that were basic but which appealed to large segments of the population, agriculture and public works, were left out because they were too unwieldy. Sectors such as coal, electricity, and railways were favored over private sectors for the additional reason that, as nationalized industries, they were considered more obedient in implementing the targets of the Monnet Plan—a mistaken belief, as the future would show.

The first plan, however, was not typical of the French planning process or of the broader policy process. Once Marshall Plan aid ended, special interests repossessed the planning process with arresting celerity. The elements of business that had been denied Marshall Plan money, but which otherwise had enough clout to press their demands on the political system, were intent on seizing the first opportunity to lash out against the planning commission. That opportunity came in December 1949, when the Bidault ministry asked Parliament for authorization to levy taxes to cover part of the Marshall Plan's investments. Leaders of the CNPF and the CGPME (the small and medium-size companies confederation) complained that the nationalized sector had been unduly favored. The leader of the mechanical industries railed against *dirigisme* and socialism.[51]

The planning commission was able to fend off the attack, but not without political support from the trade associations that represented the sectors that stood to benefit from the plan. The lesson was clear: As soon as Marshall aid dried up and taxation took over, the autonomy of the planning commission to maneuver would dwindle. Either the Monnet office would be the prisoner of the interests it favored, and thus run the risk of becoming another sponsoring agency; or it would have to open the plan to a much wider array of interests, thereby restoring the procedural bases of pressure politics.

Furthermore, the planning process had one serious drawback, one that would become more serious if the planning commission lost its clout. Planning favored, if it did not positively sanction, collusion among producers of the same sector.[52] Bias was especially acute in the steel industry, where, by controlling the allocation of funds, the planning commission had been able to extract from the industry a commitment to restructure and modernize some facilities. However, the more detailed the investment projections agreed to by the planning commission and the industrialists, the greater the need for planners to help the steel industry overcome the uncertainty of its economic environment—specifically, in the determination of sales prices. Forming cartels might hinder specialization and efficiency, but it helped in the planning and implementing of the expansion in output. Therefore, in 1947, the steel industry obtained the right for its trade association and its marketing cartel to fix prices de facto.[53] Strong cartels also existed in the cement, chemicals, petroleum, and electrical equipment industries.[54] In 1949, Monnet responded to the problem by proposing an antitrust bill. Parliament stalled. It was at this point that Monnet produced the blueprint for what became the Schuman Plan.

By 1952, the planning commission had ceased to be an autonomous actor. The Second Modernization Plan diluted its focus among seventeen sectors, now including textiles, machine tools, mechanical and electrical industries, construction, and agriculture. In many of these atomized sectors, implementation of production targets was entrusted to the trade associations, which, of course, were without power over their members. Business was divided. The former critics of planning welcomed the priority accorded to manufacturing, with the consequence that former allies became critics. The steel industry found the plan's projections overly timid. Renault, a nationalized enterprise, paid no attention to the plan's production ceilings. For private industry, planning was bound to be less compelling, since private capital markets were being restored. Indeed, 70 percent of the second plan was scheduled to be financed by private funds. Tax incentives were not as selective as direct subsidies, and private firms would pay no heed to the plan targets unless they were in need of public assistance.[55]

Pressure politics required that discrimination among interests should be based not on some technocrat's assessment of economic desirability but on conditions of political necessity. State officials could not focus only on advanced, concentrated sectors; they also had to rescue traditional, declining industries from the torments of the market or, in hopeless cases, keep them on a life-support system and phase them out as painlessly as possible. The cotton textile industry belonged in the hopeless category. The outbreak of the war in Indochina cut the industry off from its largest single colonial outlet, an outcome that was disastrous for the industry. Foregoing all future investment, working with amortized machinery, and hiring cheaper female and immigrant labor, marginal firms engaged in the destructive practice of cutthroat competition, thereby denying larger firms the possibility of self-financing their investment.[56] The cotton industry trade association appealed to the government. In 1953, an ad hoc five-year plan was worked out with the planning commission. The planning commission wanted to impose restructuring on the cotton textile industry, as it had done with the steel industry four years earlier. Instead, the cotton trade association, dominated by small firms, pushed for a plan of conversion to the African market that would benefit all producers regardless of size. The association's proposal prevailed; the *Caisse de riblonnage* was created to purchase and scrap the machinery that was not adaptable to the all-African strategy. The government made available funds and part of the receipts from a tax on textile sales.[57] It also provided protection for the home and African markets, since all prior measures of openness had been repealed in February 1952. The Office of Exchange Controls was ordered to restrict the use of nonfranc currencies for purchases of foreign textiles. As Mytelka points out, the result of the textile plan was to preserve a "large number of small firms" and maintain a "sizable labor force" in the industry.[58]

This policy was replicated in the machine tools industry. The planning commission had tried to include the industry among its priorities in 1946, but had to give up the attempt when it became clear that the disorganization of the industry was such that basic market information was not available.[59] The industry was left to fend for itself—not, however, without benefit of high tariffs to protect its own products, even products it did not produce. The planning commission hoped thereby to entice machine tool builders to explore new development possibilities.[60]

The importance for trade associations to assume control over sectoral plans cannot be overstated. With the setting of tariffs, quotas, and other regulatory gimmicks now delegated to the GATT and the EEC, rent seeking came to center on subsidies. Unable to stop the French state from surrendering its regulatory terrain to international cooperation, the trade associations were faced with a vital task: Establish an outpost in Treasury's territory—a field of competition newly revealed by the Keynesian revolution and which the planners, on their own initiative, had been the first to explore. As we shall see when we turn to Britain, a similar attempt there by trade associations to raid the state budget met with failure. The French lobbies succeeded because the policy process was one of pressure politics.

On the Ideological Scene

Moving into the area of redistribution is risky business, because the matter is likely to stir passions on a class scale, much more so than the tariff. As we have seen, in prior decades merely mentioning the possibility of a state subsidy to a private industry was enough to elicit calls for nationalization from the Left. In Britain, the threat of nationalization froze trade associations in their tracks. In France, by contrast, the threat of the Cold War put consideration of nationalization on ice.

French governments were free to subsidize private industries directly. The French trade unions, weak and divided, had lost all political power in 1947. The exclusion of the Communists after 1947 discredited Popular Front-type alliances and, in turn, eliminated the possibility of a replay of the Matignon Accords of 1936, which had raised labor costs by 37 percent.[61] Business and government were not deterred from establishing a close working relationship, nor by the threat of retaliation in the form of nationalization by a government of the Left, nor by the need to buy out the unions through an income policy as in Sweden, nor by employee participation on corporate boards as in Germany.

French governments were capable of keeping partisan rivalry out of planning because all governments emerged from the moderate Center and partisan extremes were excluded. The realm of the possible was precisely defined. To be sure, political rhetoric knew no bounds; the phraseology that filled Parliament was consistently ideological, dogmatic, and cast at the level of moral principles.[62] Nevertheless, business and public officials knew quite well that actual policies were going to bear the mark of centrist realism despite the perilous extension of trade policy into highly controversial arenas, such as state sponsorship of trusts, public subsidies for private capital, and collusion between planners and private managers. Surely the gap between words and deeds did not help endear the institutions of the Fourth Republic to the voters (a fact that may explain why voters so readily withdrew their support in 1958, when the regime was confronted with the Algerian crisis). The gap was certainly a potential source of political instability, though not the kind of instability business might be expected to factor into their investment calculations; had it not been for the Algerian crisis, the Fourth Republic might still be the law of the land.

The Executive

The executive exercised authority over the aspects of trade policy that fell under the jurisdiction of the GATT. In addition, the Ministry of Foreign Affairs enjoyed a certain autonomy in formulating economic policy in matters linked to Franco-German security. This led to a string of impressive decisions—the Monnet and Schuman plans and the Treaty of Rome. The popular image of a Fourth Republic run by an executive branch dominated by a handful of technocrats such as Monnet, Schuman, and Massé, owes much to the Quai d'Orsay's postwar schemes. Yet, with the exception of these "coups," executive autonomy was not the dominant mode. Foreign policy coups had no impact on the management of the brand new areas of sectoral planning and public transfers to private industry.

Policy Tools

Pressure politics calls for a broad diversity of policy tools (hypothesis 5.7). The GATT disqualified tariffs and quotas but allowed the metropole to maintain imperial preferences at their prewar level. Moreover, the dollar scarcity actually led to effective reinforcement of imperial preferences, as exchange controls over the franc zone put an end de facto to the open-door policy that had benefited Morocco and the East African territories. The first policy response of French governments was one of colonial retrenchment. The proportion of French exports absorbed by the colonies was consistently greater than before World War II—from percentages in the low thirties in the 1930s, to percentages in the high thirties in the 1950s. Conversely, the metropole continued to absorb colonial staples, which enjoyed higher prices in France than elsewhere, thanks to a price-support system financed with taxpayers' money.[63] With decolonization just around the corner, however, colonial retrenchment had no sustaining power.

The second policy response was that of planning, a redistributive policy calling for collusion between planners and industrialists. According to hypothesis 5.8 (industrial policy), such collusion is sustainable only in a low-quorum situation, one that minimizes the political risk for industrialists. Indeed, the readiness of trade officials to resort to subsidies was high in France. We have already encountered ample evidence of this readiness in the discussion of planning. The contrast with the British case will drive the point home.

Policy Orientation

The French tariff was reduced in conjunction with those of other GATT members, as hypothesis 5.5 on reciprocity predicts (see table 11.2). But the tariff changes were nominal, because, until 1958, GATT's regime was overruled by exchange controls. By easing or restricting exchange controls with a trade partner, a government could automatically accelerate or check trade flows between the two countries. Instituted to preserve the balance of payments, exchange controls were adjusted according to the vicissitudes of the business cycle. Consider, for example, the yearly data measuring the average degree of freedom of currency exchange:

Date	Percentage of imports freed	Date	Percentage of imports freed
November 1949	50	November 1954	65
October 1950	60	January 1955	75
February 1951	75	September 1955	78
March 1952	0	January 1956	79
September 1953	8	April 1956	82
December 1953	18	June 1957	0
April 1954	53	December 1957	40
September 1954	57	December 1958	90
October 1954	63	January 1962	100[64]

The three periods of expansion and inflation—1950–51, 1953–56, and 1957—were accompanied by a freeing of exchanges. By contrast, the two periods of deflation, both imposed by a government concerned about an overheating economy, were accompanied by protection. Only the liberalization in December 1958 broke the pattern, when de Gaulle's government was able for the first time to impose deflation and openness simultaneously. Until 1958, the automatic correlation between the level of protection and the business cycle was not made to displease French industrialists. However, as I did not study the policy process behind the changes in the currency, it would be presumptuous to take the correlation as evidence of rent seeking. Hypothesis 5.1 is not testable within the limited scope of this study.

Britain

Party Politics

As in France, the focus of the trade debate in Britain shifted from tariff to subsidy. This change was not in the political interest of the Conservatives, whose electoral success in the 1930s had rested on their capacity to reconcile anti-interventionists of all stripes under the banner of Tariff Reform. But Washington, on whose financial support London was totally dependent, obliged his majesty's government to relinquish the tariff to multilateral negotiations (hypothesis 4.3). The strings attached to the 1945 U.S. loan, the Bretton Woods Agreement, and the GATT negotiations elicited little support in Britain, even among free traders, who found American haste unrealistic. Desirability bowed to necessity, however. Domestic opposition to the GATT after the war was confined to a small minority of imperialists.[65] With Tariff Reform sidetracked by the GATT, the choice set consisted of two radically distinct options: laissez-faire, which would clobber traditional sectors such as coal, steel, and shipbuilding; and French-style state intervention in the form of subsidies.

As it had in France, the end of the war in Britain ushered in a period of partisan confrontation. Nationalization, a popular but long-repressed demand of the unions, was the salient, divisive issue of the time (hypothesis 4.1). The victory at the polls of a Labour government committed to a program of nationalization marked the end of wartime executive politics and the return of partisan confrontation. The new Labour government proceeded to a series of nationalizations, some of which raised no opposition (Bank of England, civil aviation, cables and wireless, coal, railways); others inspired the opposition of the Tories (long-distance road transport, gas, and steel). Industry and the Labour government also clashed over the government policy of forcing on fragmented industries the creation of tripartite advisory bodies—called "Development Councils"—which would be authorized to raise compulsory levies. Four would be created in the sectors of cotton, jewelry and silverware, furniture, and clothing.[66]

Unlike France, party politics in Britain continued uninterrupted after 1947. Returned to power in 1951, the Conservatives denationalized steel and part of the road-transport industry. They also abolished the development councils in the jewelry and clothing industries. The dispute over steel continued into the 1960s. Britain's special trajectory after 1947 stems from the fact that, unlike its French equivalent, British policymaking offered no edge to the international environment. Labor was not affected by the Truman Doctrine, because of the unpopularity of communism among the working class, nor did Washington object to Marshall Plan aid being administered by a government of the Left. Moreover, because of Britain's geographic isolation, its traditional guarantee of inviolability, British governments felt no political need to promote European integration; nor was there any popular urging to do so. With the exception of British membership in GATT and IMF, which enjoyed the strength of a constitutional given, trade policy and policies toward industry in Britain were purely domestic, partisan affairs.

In the partisan conflict, organized labor was pitted against organized industry. Both labor and industry supported state intervention, but each supported a different kind. Industry supported a "profit-first" approach, which consisted of promoting investments and dividends first and allowing wages and welfare payments to catch up later. This approach was being successfully developed across the Channel. The trade unions, in contrast, preferred a "wage-first" approach, which would sustain demand through high wage settlements and welfare payments, while the state would rescue and help to modernize those sectors that proved unable to bear the wage burden. This was the Swedish model. Neither side could pursue its favored approach successfully without the cooperation of the other side. The profit-first approach required employees to refrain temporarily from pressing wage claims. The wage-first approach required industrialists to agree to reduce profit margins and not to pass on the costs incurred by wage increases to the consumer—since to do so would have the effect of canceling out wage increases. Since neither side could trust the other to cooperate spontaneously, the GATT's open regime would become policy by default—that is, unless capital and labor could engineer a corporatist pact covering the distribution of the costs and benefits of an interventionist trade policy. Precisely because of the partisan nature of the policy process, however, this pact was politically out of reach. Because the two sides could not agree on any approach, absence of agreement was tantamount to surrendering British industry to foreign competition.

Various explanations have been advanced to account for Britain's inability to reach a corporatist pact. Marxists have emphasized the political and financial power of the City, which, they alleged, imposed a sterling-first strategy on the government.[67] Here, they have mistaken cause for effect. It is precisely because labor and capital could not reach agreement on an income policy that governments of both Right and Left could curb the incipient wage-price spiral only by means of monetary discipline. The sterling-first strategy was not capital's first choice; it was the suboptimal equilibrium.

Institutionalists have looked for an explanation in the lack of centralized, comprehensive, and authoritative peak organizations capable of entering into a bargain and delivering on their promises.[68] This explanation is insufficient. Even if such peak associations had existed, it is hard to see how they could have escaped the suboptimal outcome to which they were condemned by the political dynamic. A pact cannot be concluded unless the signatories feel sufficiently confident that the existing conditions critical to the economy of the deal will obtain for the entire period covered by the pact. Among these critical conditions is the determination of who governs, whether it be the Left or the Right, and especially whether it be the moderate or the extreme wing of each party. Extremes never favor corporatist agreements; their constituencies—weak unions and small businesses respectively—are inept negotiators and are usually shortchanged. Incomes policies benefit the strong unions more than weak unions and big business more than small business. Subsidies to industry tend to go to large corporations, and higher wage increases accrue to strong unions. Weak unions thus tend to prefer nationalization to corporatism, whereas small business prefers laissez-faire to state intervention. Bevanites within the Labor party wanted nationalizations; the neo-Liberals within the Conservative party opposed tripartite consultation and the welfare state. Hence, in order for the Trades Union Congress and the Federation of British Industry to covenant nonviolent relations, each needed assurances that the government would remain in the hands of the moderate wing of each party. If an extreme wing were to take over leadership of the party, that wing would explicitly disavow the peak association and mobilize the rank and file against it.[69]

Party politics cannot ensure exclusion of extremes. The rise and decline of each extreme faction in each party depends on the electoral cycle; each defeat discredits the faction in charge of the orientation of the party before the election. Thus, the defeat of the Conservatives in 1945 discredited the neo-Liberals in the Conservative party, whereas the improved Conservative showing in 1950 and the subsequent three successive victories vindicated the moderates, until the defeat of the party in 1964. In the case of Labour, the victory of 1945 worked to the credit of the Bevanites. The crisis of 1947, however, brought a midterm reassessment that placed the moderates in charge. Defeat in 1951 brought the Bevanites back into power; but the defeat of 1955 sanctioned the return of the moderates.

In sum, the existence of hard-core ideologues in each party, combined with the intrapartisan dynamic of party politics, made corporatist agreements between TUC and FBI fundamentally unstable. Had both parties consistently been dominated by their respective moderate wings, it is conceivable (though not necessary) that the TUC and FBI might have taken advantage of such a partisan consensus to force a price-and-wage discipline on their members. However, the possibility—indeed, the certainty—that an election would alter the balance of power within the defeated party and bring extremists to the fore encouraged defection.[70]

Corporatism in Britain would have made sense as an institutional strategy if one party had become dominant and/or had developed an electoral interest in defusing the class cleavage. The only cases of stable corporatist bargain are to be found in Scandinavian countries, where the working-class movement achieved political hegemony between the wars. In such a setting, industrialists were deterred from defecting, lest defection bring trouble to them in the form of statutory controls and artificially tight labor markets.

The Collapse of Sectoral Consultation

Britain emerged from the war with a fully developed panoply of consultative bodies, through which private interests could press special claims. However, these bodies were unable to articulate the new, challenging issues of the postwar era.

The war gave a boost to the organization of trade associations. The state delegated control of exports and allocation of raw materials to the trade associations.[71] In addition, since the state controlled every aspect of the economy, firms found it useful to join trade associations in order to gain access to various government departments. Trade associations developed privileged relations with their respective sponsoring departments, which, in turn, were responsible for protecting their interests in policy negotiations with other departments.[72] World War II placed a premium equally on organization in industrial relations and on the requirement that employers settle wage disputes through collective bargaining. From the workers' perspective, the unions were much attractive because wartime full employment had strengthened the bargaining position of the unions, as well as making a privileged partner of government; tripartite representation was the organizing principle of most wartime advisory committees. Britain thus ended the war in possession of a dense, comprehensive system of industrial organization.

It is equally interesting that the Labour government that took office immediately after the war did not dismantle the wartime system of business-government consultation. This decision to continue the "business-in-government" system reflected both Britain's need to perpetuate for a time the economic controls of wartime and the desire by the new government to conciliate business. In 1947, the British Employers' Confederation (BEC), the Federation of British Industries (FBI), and the Trades Union Congress (TUC) were each represented on thirty or more committees, whereas most industries had their own advisory councils. When the government finally retired statutory war controls, in 1947, it sought to institute voluntary agreements instead and found the consultative network very useful to that effect.[73]

Was Britain equipping itself with the institutions of pressure politics? Had business-government relations, by 1947, become similar to those in France between the wars?

The answer to both questions is No. The cooperation that organized business offered the Labour government was tactical. Industry resented the bureaucratic restraints that paralyzed business during wartime—such as building permits, import and export licenses, and the allocation of scarce materials. Neither trade associations nor the consultative system was a weapon for the conquest of the state; rather, they were the first line of defense against a powerful, overbearing state machine. In 1944, the Federation of British Industry was already warning its members that unless they organized into tightly knit trade associations, the government would devise its own methods of administration, an outcome the FBI had worked to prevent.[74] The FBI's exhortation to its constituency, to preempt the organizational vacuum, was reiterated in a report published in 1946.[75] Collaboration with the government served to subvert war controls; substitution of "voluntary" for compulsory controls was merely to be a first step toward the elimination of controls altogether. As FBI president Sir Frederick Bain told his members in 1948:

> A frontal attack on controls will not be successful, but if we can prove that Industry is sufficiently responsibly-minded to be trusted to control itself within broad limits laid down by the Government, we may be able to shift the basis from detailed Governmental control to internal industrial administration, and that is the most promising method of tackling the problem.[76]

The tactic worked. Indeed, most statutory controls were "tackled" in the years 1947–8, thus dispossessing the Labour government of its wartime powers. By 1949, industrialists felt confident that they could launch an open attack on the government and ask for the end of controls to move toward a more liberal economy. The battle raged over Labour's steel nationalization bill. "By 1949," Stephen Blank writes, "the Government's whole program of economic policies was under attack from industry, and conflicts took place at almost every point at which the two came into contact."[77] The second Churchill government terminated all controls.

In sum, the network of consultative links with industry was useful as long as Britain maintained its war controls, whether they were statutory or "voluntary." As these controls were phased out, and since no new policy tools took their place (Britain did not adopt the French form of planning), the advisory bodies ran out of things to advise on. In the 1950s, business-government relations in Britain reverted to the informality of the predepression era. Few trade associations enjoyed a clientelistic relationship with their sponsoring depart-

ments. The Board of Trade was not dependent on trade associations for industrial information, nor even on the FBI, which, Blank argues, never managed
to "capture" it.[78]

The decay of the consultative system reflected the basic mistrust that existed between the business community and a government that could not be
relied on to pursue the interests of business. This unreliability definitely characterized the Attlee government, as well as successive Conservative governments, owing to their chronic electoral dependence on the working-class vote.

The Failure of Factorwide Consultation

From the end of World War II until 1962, the Trades Union Congress and the
Federation of Business Industry made three attempts at corporatist bargaining,
with no real success. The unions viewed corporatist bargaining unenthusiasti-
cally; they were wary of controls that might interfere with collective bargaining.[79] The unions had consented to self-restraint during the war (they had
successfully resisted wage-fixing), but they were loath to continue it afterward,
since, "for the first time in history those who do the manual work are in short
supply."[80] Neither did the unions aspire to a managerial role in industry. The
idea of workers' control—that is, the appointment of workers' representatives
to boards of directors—received no attention even in the nationalized industries. Finally, as long as favorable wage settlements could be obtained, the
steelworkers' unions were not even united on the desirability of nationalizing
the industry.[81]

The first attempt at a tripartite agreement took place at the initiative of
Labour chancellor Cripps. Following the convertibility crisis of 1947, Cripps
relied on the FBI to press industry to limit dividends, and on the TUC to press
the unions to restrain their wage claims. Still in its voluntarist phase, the FBI
agreed; but it took great effort on the part of the government to convince the
TUC. A bargain was finally reached in March 1948, which lasted about a year,
until the second devaluation. The TUC took the initiative in asking for another round of restraints but fell prey to a full-scale revolt and had to withdraw
from the bargain.[82] The FBI held firm on its dividend commitment for another
year but, in the face of mounting inflation, finally gave it up.

Unable to bring the two sides to an agreement, successive chancellors preferred to relinquish interventionism and retire to the macroeconomic heights
of Keynesian demand management. This retreat to the abstract consensus of
Keynesian economics had definite electoral advantages. For one thing, it kept
the government out of the face-to-face, no-win confrontation of industrial
relations, while moving it into the more rewarding business of distributing
welfare payments and creating full employment. Inflation ensued, however.
Soon the Conservative government sought a pact from the TUC and FBI to
restrain wages and prices. These associations made their agreement dependent

on satisfaction of demands which, in the last analysis, were incompatible. The incompatibility thus obliged the government to side with industry; and TUC withdrew. Once again, the only alternative was macroeconomic—deflation. The upshot was an economy caught in a suboptimal "stop-go cycle" that discouraged investment.

The third attempt at corporatism led to the creation, in 1961, of a planning apparatus nicknamed "Neddy."[83] This time, the proposal came at the behest of powerful FBI members who blamed the government for continually changing interest rates without a coherent plan and, thus, for throwing off firms' investment plans. Uncertainty could be reduced, business argued, if, one, business, unions, and the Treasury were provided with hard information on investment expectations, and, two, if they could agree jointly on a growth rate for the next five years. The FBI's purpose was to confront both politicians and unionists with the tangible facts of economics. Though well disposed to French-style planning, the Conservative chancellor, Selwyn Lloyd, believed (rightly) that, unlike in France, long-term real growth was not to be achieved in Britain without short-term wage restraint. Lloyd thus tried to broaden the agenda to include an incomes policy based on the Scandinavian model. This third attempt failed because the TUC, distrustful of the government, refused to discuss incomes policy. Indicative planning proceeded without a target for wage increases, and growth fueled a wage-price spiral, which, because of the upcoming election of 1964, the Conservatives did not have the nerve to curb.

It should be noted, incidentally, that the illusion that Neddy might "deliver" prompted each of the two peak associations to reassess its internal organization with an eye to making it more corporatist. Although such efforts yielded nothing concrete on the TUC side, on the business side, they led, in 1965, to the merger of the FBI with two other major business organizations—BEC and the National Association of British Manufacturers (NABM)—into the Confederation of British Industry (CBI). Organization is more likely to follow strategy than strategy is to follow organization.

In sum, even though Britain ended the war with a broad array of consultative bodies through which private interests could press special claims, these bodies failed to articulate the new, challenging issues of the postwar era. The decay of consultation at the microlevel reflected the failure of consultations at the macrolevel. As a result, consultation continued to be limited to the regulatory measures of the past (export credits, trade marks and patents, commercial intelligence, enticement to research, and tariff classification). Consultation did not extend to state intervention in industry, such as income policies, nationalization, monopolies, cartels and price rings, and financial and credit policies; the initiative for those measures remained with the ministers.[84] Nor could consultation be applied to industrial restructuring and modernizing, which were kept outside the scope of public intervention during the period under consideration.

"Butskellism" and Ideology

"Butskellism" is the collective term for the similarities in the policies of the 1950s pursued by Hugh Gaitskell, the last Labour chancellor, and R. Butler, the first Conservative chancellor. The term is apt, since the policies shared a principal feature: The budget remained the main instrument for managing the economy, regardless of the government's partisan orientation. Butskellism, however, was a reflection less of the end of ideological conflict between the two parties than of the limited content of Britain's policy toolbox. Labour as well as Conservative chancellors had to accept that planning was not feasible. Because raising taxes was not feasible either, especially before an election, the only two instruments of economic regulation left were the budget deficit and the bank rate. This stripped-down panoply proved workable, thanks to the unusually benign environment of the 1950s. Britain was able to tap the worldwide rise in demand stimulated by the Marshall Plan and the Korean War, and the otherwise favorable conditions of the 1950s, without incurring the shock of foreign competition at home. The only crises Britain confronted were of its own making.

The second source of policy uniformity was the electoral necessity for both parties to expand the welfare state. Welfare programs had long existed, but in the past their scope had varied with the business cycle, expanding in times of affluence and contracting when most needed. Now that Keynes had justified their countercyclical use, welfare programs ceased to be, in Lowi's terminology, a "redistributive" policy tool that pitted the needy against the rich. Instead, welfare programs became actual "distributive" tools that could be targeted to benefit all electoral groups, while deferring the tax burden to unspecified, future generations.[85] This aspect of the Keynesian revolution brought in its wake a dramatic change in the capacity of political parties to organize public opinion. Instead of targeting large, general producer groups, such as farmers, workers, and small business (as they had done before the war), the parties were now able to pinpoint more specific targets, groups such as old-age pensioners, newly married couples, servicemen—that is, "consumer groups," to use Samuel Beer's terminology.[86] Thus, as parties one by one peeled off the outer layers of the proletariat and the bourgeoisie, in effect, they increased the floating vote, intensified centripetal competition, and led to the formulation of very similar electoral manifesto.

If a uniformity in policies characterized the 1950s, there was no comparable uniformity of attitude. Not only did the parties remain distinct, well-disciplined machines, they each continued to harbor a core of ideologues merely biding their time. The collapse of corporatist consultation, I argue, was directly attributable to the parties. Also, the impact of party politics, with regard to the selection of industries for nationalization, was felt directly at the microeconomic level. For instance, when the Iron and Steel Board—set up in 1951 by the Conservatives after they had denationalized the industry—requested the statutory power to force rationalization on the industry, its proposals were never discussed by the government. Keith Ovenden argues that the proposals were rejected by the Conservatives for political reasons.[87]

> Convinced that the promise of renationalization of iron and steel was an electoral millstone around the neck of the Labour party, [the Conservatives] were not anxious to institute a reform that would bring the industry under such a close degree of public supervision as to provide Labour with an opportunity "to slip the noose" and repudiate its commitment to renationalization.

Furthermore, the issue of nationalization ensured the continued supply of cash to the Conservative party, which, between 1945 and 1966, received substantial campaign funds from the steel industry.[88]

In short, the decade of the 1950s resembles the period 1886–1903. Just as Tariff Reform in an earlier period smoldered under the censorship of a Conservative leadership unconvinced of its electoral potential, so, in the 1950s, party leaders carefully avoided the issue of industrial policy, preferring to entrust the fate of industry to management of macroeconomic demand. In the 1950s, as in the 1880s, external competition remained mild enough and the world economy clement enough for political parties to avoid the issue.

The Executive

Except for issues covered by the GATT, the autonomy of the executive was governed by partisan considerations. Trade issues outside GATT were domestic concerns with no apparent link to international exigency. The implication of these conditions is that the British government's approach to trade agreements, such as the ECSC and the EEC, was purely instrumental. Britain would not join these groups without the approval of major domestic forces. In the event of domestic opposition, the cabinet could overcome it only by extracting side-payments for domestic groups from other governments. Under these circumstances, Britain had little negotiating leverage. This point requires some elaboration.

When, in 1963, the Macmillan government applied for British membership to the EEC, the EEC turned down the application on the grounds that the "Six" were not able to grant the required side-payments. The Macmillan government was caught in a dilemma.[89] On the one hand, it was necessary for Macmillan to rally public opinion in support of the EEC, in order for the Six to consider Britain a credible applicant. (Previous governments had rejected two earlier offers from the Six to negotiate with them—once, in 1950, over the formation of a coal and steel pool, and a second time, in 1955–7, over membership in the Common Market.) On the other hand, if Macmillan staked his political reputation at home on EEC membership, he would have a weaker bargaining position vis-à-vis the Six; they would see him as bound to accept whatever conditions were offered. In the end, Macmillan decided to strengthen Britain's hand by allowing domestic opposition to EEC membership to grow unchecked, a tactic that rebounded on him when the Labour opposition decided to join the fray. The issue turned partisan: Labour championed the causes of British sovereignty, British farmers, Commonwealth producers, and world peace; whereas the Conservatives consolidated behind Macmillan. Labour's opposition made it unlikely that the government which emerged after the next election (at the time, Labour's prospects were good) would consider itself bound by Macmillan's engagements to the Six. Britain's lack of bargaining flexibility was directly attributable to the domestic and partisan nature of British trade institutions; de Gaulle's veto of British membership merely underscored the British government's bargaining weaknesses.

Macmillan's inability to extract side-payments from the Six stands in marked contrast to Mollet's success in extracting side-payments for French farmers and French colonies from his five Common Market partners in 1956–57.[90] At home, Mollet, like Macmillan, faced serious domestic resistance from France's colonies, from half the political spectrum—Communists, Gaullists, Poujadists, Mendesists—and from the business community at large.[91] However, the two leaders differed in the credibility of their commitment to the construction of Europe. Whereas in Britain, Europe was an economic project whose desirability was measured directly by the scope of the side-payments Britain could extract from partners, in France, Europe was a political project. The principle of European union was rooted in France's needs for international security, a need that was salient among the French people.[92] Only the economic modalities of the union, its scope and timing, were left open to negotiation. The French commitment to Europe had two important consequences for France's bargaining leverage. First, Mollet was a credible negotiator who held a popular mandate; France's future governments could be expected to honor the engagements he made. Second, Mollet could use the resistance of special interests to strengthen the bargaining position of the French negotiator at the Brussels Conference. In short, Mollet could simultaneously be a credible negotiator and tough bargainer, whereas at any given time Macmillan either had to sacrifice toughness to credibility and get a bum deal, or sacrifice credibility to toughness and be left with no deal.

Policy Tools and Orientation

Given the partisan nature of the policy process, the toolbox in this case should be simple (hypothesis 5.7) and include no subsidies (hypothesis 5.8). These are stringent requirements, however. Socially and politically, the British government could not afford to allow its industry to deteriorate without intervening; yet the partisan nature of its trade institutions meant the government could not afford to grant direct subsidies either. Both Labour and the unions objected to outright subsidies to private industry; the party's left wing would not agree to socialize the losses without socializing profits, too.

The upshot was a compromise. Subsidies were granted, but where there was the least resistance. Some subsidies reached industry by means of para-public institutions to assist in financing industrial projects, such as the Industrial and Commercial Finance Corporation (ICFC) and the Finance Corporation for Industry (FCI). Both were founded in 1945 by the Bank of England jointly with the private London clearing banks and did not come under Treasury control.[93] These subsidies were part of the nonpublic (though not quite private) toolbox, which should be well developed in a high-quorum setup (hypothesis 5.9).

Other subsidies, while strictly public, were allocated by means of a detour through regional development. In 1934, regional development as a policy began to channel funds to selected areas afflicted by high levels of unemployment. The funds were used for sewage systems at first and, after 1936, to construct factories and provide loans and tax inducements to local firms.[94] The policy was resumed after the war, although its use slowed down in the early 1950s, when unemployment disappeared. The policy received high priority again after 1958, when the conjunction of secular obsolescence and a low point in the business cycle hit traditional industries very hard.

After 1958, regional policy became the government's main tool for intervention in industry. The regional emphasis may be accounted for by pointing to the historically high level of geographic specialization in British industry. The traditional industries that suffered the most from foreign competition—coal, shipbuilding, and textiles—were all located in small, circumscribed areas, thus making functional equivalents of support to area and support to industry. This virtual identity of sector and region, however, was insufficient in itself to account for the government's consistent choice of regional over industrial policy. The determining factor was, in fact, political. Regional policy drew support from both ends of the partisan spectrum. Industrialists still received the monies, but the process of allocation was indirect and acknowledged the special needs of labor. A derelict region thus offered an ideal meeting place for Britain's major producer interests: The policy provided for a discreet curtain between government and private business, while providing sufficient accommodation of labor's interests.

In a handful of cases, aid to industry avoided the circuitous regional channels and was given directly to industry. Military considerations, for example, justified direct aid to the shipbuilding and aircraft industries.[95] Another exception involved the cotton textile industry after 1959, where labor and management, both members of the Cotton Board, collaborated to urge the government to extract VERs from India, Pakistan, and Hong Kong and to urge Parliament to subsidize curtailment of excess capacity.[96]

TABLE 11.3

Assistance to Private Industry in Britain and France

	Britain (1960–61)		France (1966)	
	million £ (%)		million FF (%)	
Subsidies				
aid to firms	22	79	750	88
aid to areas	6	21	97	12
total	28	100	847	100
Loans				
aid to firms	15	25	3,024	95
aid to areas	45	75	143	5
total	60	100	3,167	100

Sources: Britain: Grove 1962: 265; McCrone 1969: 145. France: *Ecole Nationale d'Administration* 1973.

A final exception, which actually proved the rule, involved the steel industry. In 1960, the Macmillan government was bold enough to offer a loan to two steel mills—one of them still nationalized, the other privately owned—to finance new construction of two continuous-strip rolling mills. Although the mills were to be located in two areas with high unemployment, the loans aroused considerable partisan controversy. The Conservative right wing contended that the money should be raised on the open market, and the Labour opposition called for the nationalization of the private company or at least part of the profits to be generated by the new mill.[97] Macmillan's offer thus fired the steel issue back into the full glare of the partisan arena.

How much weight should be given to the evidence that confirms hypothesis 5.8 on industrial policy and how much to the evidence against it? A comparison with France, a case of pressure politics, is helpful in that respect. In terms of subsidies, the pattern in France was the reverse of that in Britain. Before 1968, aid to French industry was allocated directly to private firms; the relative amounts of subsidies and subsidized loans channeled through regional policies were insignificant in comparison. Not until 1968 did the subsidy amounts granted by regional development policy begin to show a continuous increase.[98] For evidence of this, see table 11.3, which provides British data for the year 1960–61 and French data for the year 1966 (no earlier breakdown could be found). If the subsidies and loans are added up (keeping in mind that the subsidy equivalent of a loan is much lower than the amount shown under the heading "loan"), regional policy represented 58 percent of aid to private industry in Britain, but only 6 percent in France.

The policy orientation of Britain was similar to that of any other GATT member. As hypothesis 5.5 would predict, changes in the tariff reciprocated mechanically every concession of tariff reduction (see table 11.2 above). By the end of the period, the cross-sectoral structure of Britain's tariff was very similar to the U.S.'s.[99] Unfortunately, British performance in the NTBs dimension is impossible to evaluate for lack of appropriate data.

Conclusion

The postwar era confronted Britain, France, and the United States with a military challenge (the Soviet Union) and an economic challenge (construction of an international economic regime to guard against a repetition of the interwar anarchy). The responses of the three countries exhibited elements in common, as well as dissimilarities. All three, for example, joined the multilateral trading system promoted by the United States. In the main, however, the United States worked within the GATT framework, whereas Britain and France supplemented their participation in GATT with state intervention in the form of indirect subsidies to industry in Britain and direct subsidies to industry in France. If the outcomes for the three are mapped on the general-particular axis, the United States turns up on the general side, France on the particular side, and Britain somewhere in between.

The policy process, by its very nature, was responsible for this outcome. In the United States, the Truman administration, from its outset, sought to link the trade debate to the foreign policy debate, by equating free trade with peace and tariffs with war. Ultimately, the United States established this improbable identity when it was able to name an enemy: communism. After 1947, the policy of containing communism abroad assisted the containment of special interests at home. Together, salience and bipartisan consensus led to the creation of a policymaking context in which producers could, with a fair degree of confidence, expect to see their common general interest implemented with a minimum of exceptions.

Britain went through a similar experience, with the difference that the constraining factor was not so much the Soviet Union as the United States. At the end of World War II, Britain, at the financial mercy of Washington, was in no position to stick to Tariff Reform. The dismal condition of British industry mandated the pursuit of a third way: public subsidies to private industry. The party system turned public aid to industry into a conflictual issue, which would be adjudicated only as part of a larger settlement including wages and prices. The extreme wing of each party, however, made it impossible for moderates to extract the necessary wage and price agreements from the labor and business peak associations. Leftist calls for nationalization led business to adopt a rigid arm's-length attitude toward successive governments, which muddled their way through the policy dilemma by resorting to an heterodox combination of macroeconomic management and aid to regional development.

France, too, was at the financial mercy of Washington and was in no position to snub the U.S. invitation to join the new international trading regime. Nevertheless, ostracization of the Communists and a return to centrist politics made it possible for industrialists, first, to take part in the state-run planning experiment, then, to capture it. The state made direct subsidies available to sectors, which accepted them happily with no fear of electoral retribution. In this way, France earned world recognition for her bold venture in that perilously flirtatious partnership between state and industry, and for which Harry Truman bore a greater responsibility than Colbert and the two Napoleons combined.

Twelve

The Rise and Fall of Industrial Policy, 1963–1989

[R]emember Caligula, who wished the Roman people
had one neck, so that he could cut it off . . . the safest
posture for an industry confronted by socialism would
be not to have an organization or spokesmen at all.
(Enoch Powell, *The Director*, February 1965)

FOR THE THIRD TIME in a century, a world crisis challenged existing alignments
and undermined extant trade-policy tools. The crisis unfolded in two stages.
At first, in every country, the 1973–82 crisis swelled the ranks of producers
who could no longer adjust to market forces and who sought relief through
politics. Governments responded by resorting to the usual Keynesian countercyclical panoply: After reflation proved self-defeating, they shifted to deflation, combined with price and wage policy in Britain, and a series of measures
to shore up employment—selective industrial policies, increased social transfers, and so forth. In the second stage, when these policies failed to help national economies out of the crisis, the economic debate polarized. The Left
asked for greater state intervention, while the Right advocated state retrenchment. The Right won—if not politically, at least in substance. The outcome
was the disqualification of state intervention in all aspects of the economy,
including trade policy. The crisis discredited the two pillars of industrial policy, sectoral targeting and national champions, previously adopted to promote
competitiveness at the industry and firm level. This general turn toward orthodoxy was spurred by a shift of the electorate to the right. Many of the
middle classes—taxpayers in the United States, independents and small business in France and Britain—rebelled against further state intervention, providing the Right in each country with its first natural mass base since the days
of fascism.

The impact on trade policy was brutal in France and Britain, but minimal in the United States. In France and Britain, the policy swung from involvement to disengagement. The turning point for Britain came in 1979
with the victory at the polls of the Conservatives under Margaret Thatcher.
In France, policy swung twice in the direction of disengagement: in 1978
under Valéry Giscard d'Estaing, in 1983 under François Mitterrand. In the
United States, the switch from the Carter to the Reagan administration,

though dramatically felt in most policy areas, did not translate into greater laissez-faire in the trade arena. The change, if any, was in the direction of greater protection. In light of the French and British experiences, how U.S. trade policy steered clear of the liberal renaissance constitutes the central puzzle of this period.

The solution is not to be found in the intensity of the crisis, which was equally felt in all three countries. Nor could it easily be teased out of social and electoral realignments, which were real but which were pretty much the same in all three countries. Nor could the variation be imputed to any difference in political or state institutions. If anything, it was the well-entrenched French state that should have ridden out the crisis with the greatest ease.

In all three countries the crisis led to a general partisan realignment. Where the trade policy process was pressure politics, it became party politics; where the process was already party politics, the party in power was disqualified, along with its policy repertoire and orientation, and the opposition was thrust into power. And where the trade-policy process was linked to the security issue, it escaped the effects of realignment. Therefore, policies that fell under GATT's jurisdiction (tariffs and unilateral quotas) were left untouched, whereas policies outside of GATT were vulnerable to partisan realignment. Depending on the proportion "in" GATT to that "out" of GATT, the trade policy of a country either steered clear or was engulfed by the partisan storm. In the United States, where the trade policy process remained firmly anchored to the bipolar structure of the Cold War, and thus was relatively sheltered from partisan agitation, the impact of the partisan realignment was minimal. However, in France and Britain, where the policy process was overextended into subsidies, and thus became exposed to partisan outbreak, the impact was brutal.

In both Britain and the France of the 1980s, party politics dominated the making of industrial policy. Party politics was not new in Britain, although, in the 1970s, there were so many attempts to depoliticize incomes policy—first, by means of statutory rules under Edward Heath, and then by tripartite negotiations under Harold Wilson and James Callaghan—that some real hope existed for a time that policy toward industry might revert to an institutional format more acceptable to private business. The crisis of the 1970s ended twenty years of repeated, though vain, attempts at corporatist bargaining in Britain.

In contrast, party politics was new in France. Industrial policy obeyed the rules of pressure politics until the election of 1978, when the Giscard-Barre government opted for a more selective, neo-liberal view of the state's role in the economy. The Left articulated the preferences of the "losers," angry workers, small business, the unemployed, and traditional sectors—all of them in need of state assistance and all alienated by the collusion that had characterized industry-government relations throughout the postwar era. The statist policies pursued during the first two years of Socialist rule completed the polarization of the industrial debate, rallying the Right behind a French version of Thatcherite conservatism articulated by the *Rassemblement pour la république* (RPR).

France

Salaried versus Self-Employed

In the years 1978–81, the policy process shifted from pressure politics to party politics. Those responsible for the politicization of the trade process were the workers and salaried classes, who were unable to pursue their preferences through pressure politics and who began to petition the parties (hypothesis 4.1). The switch reflected the conjunction of two underlying changes: reorganization of the Left under non-Communist leadership, and the long-standing inability of the workers and employees (the salaried classes) to push their trade preferences via pressure politics.

The reorganization of the Left is exogenous to the model and can only be described. The rise of the Socialists to a position of preeminence on the Left put an end to the political isolation of the working class, which, until then, had been closely identified with the ostracized Communist party. Initially, the Communist grip on the Left was loosened by demographic changes. The decline of the working class, the rise of the salaried class, and the growth of non-Communist unions provided a social base for the non-Communist Left. Then, under Mitterrand's leadership, the Socialists successfully challenged the Communist party's claim to federate the Left, thus providing workers and salaried employees with the partisan option they had been denied since 1947. With the signing of the *Programme commun*, in 1972, the reorganization of the Left was complete.

The displacement of the Communist Left was a necessary—but insufficient—condition for the articulation of worker trade preferences within the party system. Another necessary condition was the existence of worker grievances over the policy of business-government collusion, which fueled the partisan fire (hypothesis 4.1). This partisan fire threatened to destroy state intervention in industry by igniting an alternative base of support for the liberal creed among small business and the self-employed. The history of the transformation of French industry-government relations, from the collusion of the precrisis years to the distant and adversarial relations of the 1980s, had two stages: the conversion of the big business elite to liberalism, in the late 1970s; and the rallying of middle-class groups to liberalism in the early 1980s.

The conversion of big business to liberalism stemmed from the Giscard-Barre government's *libéral-interventionnisme*, a phrase coined in 1976, to cap-

ture the tension between the government's neo-liberal discourse and its dirigist practice.[1] Confronted by an economic crisis and an expanding Left, Giscard sought to shore up his electoral future among workers and employees—
who, until then, were the only distinct, mass base of the Right—by safeguarding jobs and local employment. The government tried to weather the crisis by
opening the state coffers to all those who were in need of assistance. Measures
were taken to aid the shoe, leather, clock and watch, and machine-tool industries. Long-term convalescents, such as the steel and shipbuilding industries,
as well as the Boussac group—the largest employer in the textile industry—
were put on life-support systems. In 1974, a *Comité interministériel d'aménage-
ment des structures industrielles* (CIASI) was created to help medium-size firms
in financial straits. Local aid agencies were set up for smaller firms.

This classic response by pressure politics in a period of crisis was similar to
the logrolling of the 1930s. The government did more than generalize financial transfers, however; it also requested its big-business allies to bail out the
government politically. In 1975, Premier Chirac asked the steel firms not to
declare any redundancies but to engage in countercyclical investment.[2] The
government also asked the other large firms to abstain from laying off workers.
In 1974 and 1975, the government forced the *patronat* (employers) to consent
to procedures to make collective layoffs more difficult and costly, including
redundancy payments of 90 percent of past salary in the first year.[3]

Big business grew restive, however. It had been promised liberalism, but was
treated to *dirigisme*. Big business had no choice. The government drew its
uncommon leverage from its electoral insecurity; for the alternative to Gis-
cardian liberal *dirigisme* was the Left's sweeping program of nationalization.

Paradoxically, the unexpected victory in 1978, as well as the good showing
of Giscard's party at the European elections of 1979, erased the government's
leverage—evidence that the process was not yet fully partisan. Pressed by their
most efficient corporate backers to implement a more selective economic policy, Giscard and Barre began by reducing assistance to the basic-steel industry.
After becoming majority stockholder in the two steel groups, the state announced a plan of modernization that involved the lay-off, by 1981, of 20,000
workers in the North and in Lorraine. The government also pulled the plug on
the Boussac group, which had been on public aid since the late 1960s. Then,
in September 1979, Giscard announced a new industrial policy. His declared
goal was to assist the most efficient firms in selected growth industries in which
France had a comparative advantage. Initially, six priority areas were chosen:
underwater exploration, automation of office procedures, consumer electronics, robotics, bio-industry, and energy-saving equipment (aeronautics and
computers were dealt with in other plans).[4]

The policy lost much of its selectiveness when the government declared the
textile industry to be of "strategic importance" and added it to the list of
recipients. In many other respects, however, the policy was a break with the

past. Price controls were abolished; unemployment was allowed to rise; profits were permitted to increase; investments were allowed to increase; and the movement toward relocation of productive units in the Third World was given the go-ahead. For the first time since 1970, governmental rhetoric began to favor profitable, self-reliant (and thus concentrated) business, thereby breaking with the century-old tradition of accommodating special interests.

While the Center-Right government of Giscard emphasized the need for the French economy to abandon traditional sectors to foreign competition and, instead, specialize in areas of growth, the Socialists took the opposite stand. They made defense of the traditional sectors part of their economic program, arguing that "there are no condemned sectors, there are only obsolete technologies." While the Giscard government was in the process of phasing out mines, metal works, and shipbuilding yards, the Socialists promised to make these sectors competitive, to expand capacity and maintain employment. Instead of specialization, they favored import substitution, even if it meant accepting some protectionism.[5]

A second feature of Socialist policy was the nationalization of the top twelve industrial groups and the top thirty-six investment banks. The main reason was a partisan one. The Socialists sought to penalize these groups for having financed losses by means of public subsidies, while keeping profits private. The advent of Socialist rule reflected the displacement of a process dominated by interest groups by one dominated by partisan considerations. Liberalism became synonymous with rule by the Right, whereas state intervention became identified with the Left. The Socialists won the elections of 1981 and set out to implement their economic policy.

In 1983, the Socialists negotiated a sharp turn. The economic priority was shifted from lower unemployment to greater competitiveness, a historic turnaround motivated by the deterioration of short-term economic conditions. Nevertheless, the turn did not defuse the partisan debate. Whereas the Socialists were drifting back toward the center, the Right moved sharply to the extreme. As early as 1981, Chirac had endorsed several of Ronald Reagan's favorite themes and had criticized Giscard for raising taxes and hiring too many public officials. By 1984, he had cast off all remnants of the Gaullist patrimony—social Catholicism, statism, planning, and national populism—and was maneuvering the RPR, and, along with it, the smaller parties of the Center-Right, into the antistatist estates of "liberal conservatism."[6] By privatizing industry, defending management's right to lay off workers, dismantling planning and the Ministry of Industry (all ultraliberal themes), the Right gained a new rallying cry. Industrial policy and state subsidies to industry were deemed illegitimate.

Although the lasting quality of this sudden conversion of the French Right to a market economy may be questioned, it nevertheless struck a powerful, responsive chord in the voters on the Right. The situation appears paradoxical, given that the core of this rightist electorate consisted of peasants, shopkeepers, crafts, small business, and independents—the traditional or endangered producers who, a priori, have little to gain from dismantling state protection and unleashing market forces. In fact, a large proportion of public resources was spent by reelection-minded governments under Pompidou and Giscard, on Malthusian policies that sheltered these groups from competition.[7] The paradox is resolved if one takes into account the change in policy process. After 1981, small businessmen and independents were threatened not with just some long-term, hypothetical extinction, as before, but with an immediate and tangible cash shortage. The Socialist government had raised taxes, increased the employer's share of social security payments, raised the minimum wage, and tightened the labor market through reflation—thereby making survival for small and unprofitable businesses more uncertain than for larger and more solid firms. The Left's inflationary policies cut into savings across the board, hurting small, inefficient asset owners first. Given the choices, even sectors otherwise condemned by long-term market trends managed to find the prospect of a free market economy—along with a freeing of the labor market—a comforting thought.

Party dynamics reinforced polarization of the debate. Mitterrand's turnaround in 1983 forced the ultraliberals to annex new issues—such as privatization of firms nationalized by de Gaulle himself, subcontracting of prisons to the private sector, l'école libre, and deregulation of higher education.[8] The Right also effected a U-turn on the issue of European integration, coming to subscribe fully to the pursuit of the European single market.

The realignment of farmers and small business on the Right is not temporary. It is the outcome of a process of reclassement of the middle classes that dates back to the Popular Front, when the Radical party began its historic right turn.[9] Where once it had been the guardian of the "republican synthesis," the Radical party became the victim of the class cleavage. This cleavage separated the indépendants (farmers, shopkeepers and small merchants, small business, craftspeople), who drifted toward the Right, from the salariat (engineers, technicians, clerks, state employees, middle management), who inclined to the Left.[10] By the time of the legislative election of 1978, voting estimates for the Left were 25 percent among farmers; 31 percent, small merchants; 43 percent, crafts, and 24 percent, professions; but 62 percent among middle management and 66 percent among clerks.[11] The Socialist "experiment" consolidated the trend.[12] Data for the legislative elections of 1978, 1984, and 1988 show voting estimates for the Left, respectively, of 27 percent, 25 percent, and 16 percent among farmers; 37 percent, 30 percent, and 35 percent among the independent middle class; and 53 percent, 53 percent, and 55 percent among the salaried middle class.[13]

In sum, the advent of party politics in contemporary France reflected a belated redrawing of the class cleavage between, on one side, a Left representing primarily the interests of both blue- and white-collar employees, and a Right representing primarily the interests of employers, the self-employed, and upper management. By anchoring the left, the salaried classes allowed the Socialists to displace the Communists. The success of the Left ticket in 1981 expropriated the rents that farmers and small and big business collected from the state. As we shall see, the direct consequence of the realignment was the decay of industrial policy.

Champions and Lame Ducks: Two-Tiered Lobbying, 1963–78

The years 1963–74 in France provide the most articulated version of industry-government collusion encountered in this study. (The background forces are sketched in chapter eleven). The postwar international trade regime made tariffs and quotas unavailable for domestic purposes, thus forcing the government to use subsidies. Throughout the 1950s, this necessity was tempered by the use of exchange controls and a retreat to the colonial market. The shift to currency convertibility in 1958, however, and the decrease in intra-EEC tariffs and the removal of all but agricultural quotas in 1962 made industrial policy and the attendant redistributive conflict the main ingredients of business-government relations. The complete transformation of trade policy from a regulatory tool to a public-subsidy issue led to the reorganization of the existing pressure-politics process away from a logic of decentralization toward a logic of centralization.

The center for decisionmaking in the administration shifted from the traditional sponsoring departments to that guardian of public funds, the Finance Ministry. The sponsoring departments were still requested to provide an analysis of the technical feasibility of the investment; but the study of the financial feasibility and desirability of the investment was to become the domain of the Treasury. As Erhard Friedberg and Dominique Desjeux have shown, however, the incessant flow of financial applications to the Finance Ministry created a problem of severe overload. The Finance Ministry coped by adopting strict rules of procedure: addressing each application in chronological order of submission, preferring to process applications, rather than meet with applicants, and basing decisions on strict criteria for legality and financial soundness rather than on a preestablished, clearly defined policy for the sector.[14] Ezra Suleiman reports being told by an official in the Ministry of Finance that the real function of the ministry "is not to have ideas. It is to oppose ideas."[15] The bureaucratic obstructionism practiced by the ministry had the perverse, though expected, effect of increasing centralization. Firms or sectors that were unable to obtain aid from the Treasury, but which had sufficient political clout, would appeal to the higher governmental levels: ministerial cabinet, ministers, the prime minister, and sometimes the President.[16]

In a development parallel to the centralization of pressure politics, a shift from no subsidies to out-and-out subsidies effected a concentration of aid among a very selective group of private interests. The logic of this inegalitarian dynamic is to be found in the way subsidies were used. Unlike regulatory measures, whose scope is either universal or restricted by market rules operating outside politics, subsidies to industry call for the government to pick winners directly—an illegitimate action from the standpoint of both the liberal Right and the anticapitalist Left. Wanting to shield themselves from criticisms of "playing politics," public officials demonstrated great concern over the "efficient" allocation of these subsidies. Officials typically preferred subsidies to go to recipients who were the most likely to show a result, either because they were dominant within their sector or because their connections with key public officials and their stake in absorbing the flow of *pantoufleurs* (civil servants shuffling to cushy positions in the private sector, often to drift back to public employ) made them more reliable than firms without such connections. In consequence, most of the subsidies distributed by the government were distributed to large firms, with the express purpose of increasing the dominance of those firms in their respective sectors. Trade policy thus became tantamount to the promotion of "national champions."

The national-champion strategy was begun under de Gaulle. On the pretext of equipping France with a policy panoply adequate to its international stature, the governments of the 1960s promoted products that involved French technology. The Gaullist state supported the research and development of a French nuclear reactor (graphite-gas), a French large computer, a French supersonic jet, a French launcher, and a French telephone switching center.[17] Along with this policy came the creation of national champions— which might be a public research center, such as CEA in atomic energy or CNES in space exploration; a public corporation, such as SNIAS and Aérospatiale in civil aviation; a semipublic firm, such as CII in computing or Elf-Aquitaine in oil exploration; or a private firm, such as Dassault in military aviation.

The strict emphasis on national technological independence turned out to make little sense and was abandoned during Pompidou's presidency. The promotion of national champions, however, continued. Only the public justification changed, from technological stunt under de Gaulle, to the need for firms to reach the size necessary to be considered a significant player in the world market. Numerous mammoth mergers took place in the years 1969–72. In 1972, 66 percent of the assets thus transferred came under the control of eight groups.[18] For all practical purposes, the target of the Fifth Plan—the creation of one or two corporations with an international size in each sector—had been attained by 1972.[19] State aid favored these groups; from 1973 until 1976, half of public aid to industry went to six corporate groups employing only 10 percent of industrial manpower.

Specific instances of business-government relations throughout these years often were based on explicit contracts. The first contracts were signed in 1959–60 between the ministries of Finance and Industry, on the one hand, and individual steel companies, on the other. The government provided loan guarantees in exchange for private investments commonly agreed upon. *Contrats de stabilité* were introduced in 1965, to replace the previous strict control of prices. These gave way to *contrats de programme* (1966), *contrats anti-hausse* (1971), and so on. *Programmes d'action concertée* were specified in joint action by industrialists and the state, to modernize and rationalize certain sectors around key firms in return for government grants. Beneficiaries included steel, data-processing (*plan calcul*), engineering, industrial electronics, furniture, and toys. Beginning in 1974, *contrats de croissance* were made with expanding firms which agreed to an investment program in exchange for soft loans. By 1977, about thirty of those had been signed.[20] In 1979, a version called *contrats de développement* went further than growth contracts, spelling out any additional state action to be taken to help the firm.[21]

More important than the written word was the spirit that infused business-government relations. None other than Jacques Ferry, leader of the steel industry and a prominent member of the CNPF, put forth a concept for a new relationship between state and private firms. At a CNPF general assembly, in June 1962, he set out the respective obligations of the parties. On the one hand, he declared, the state should renounce ad hoc intervention and grant to firms autonomy in implementing state-aided investment programs. On the other hand, a private firm might accept a "service contract with the state (whereby) it carried out certain tasks that do not use profitability as the decisive criterion." Ferry declared that "the employer no longer has the right to go bankrupt." He urged the state and his business colleagues to "deliberately accept the call of convention and contract."[22] Ferry's approach was sanctioned by the Fifth Plan, which encouraged industrialists to play a more assertive role in industrial policy, and by the *Plan professionnel* of 1966, approved by the Council of Ministers; according to the latter, individual steelmasters agreed to implement a detailed plan of reorganization and modernization of the industry in exchange for state subsidies.[23]

The correlate of the centralization of the institutional process, and the concentration of aid to a few recipients, was the weakening of the prewar mode of interest mediation—that is, of the tandem procession of trade association and sponsoring ministry.[24] There were several reasons for this weakening. First, specialized ministries, as we saw, were displaced by the Treasury. Second, the compartmentalization by sector of the trade associations (which was matched almost one to one on the bureaucratic organization chart) created divisions too narrow for large corporations, whose response to international competition was to diversify lines of production vertically or horizontally. Third, trade associations were poorly equipped to arbitrate the inevitable conflicts provoked by the movement toward greater concentration within the associations' own sectors. Offspring of the tariff, the associations offered a product-by-product approach to trade policy which conveniently overlooked the basic conflict between small and large producers in a given sector. The raison d'être of the trade association was accommodation of various interests, not playing off one faction against another. As in the case of the cotton textile trade association, in 1953, the reflex action of each trade association in this circumstance was to press for modernization as an alternative to concentration and restructuring.[25] Finally, trade associations were ineffectual at gathering investment information. Industrialists were not in the habit of sharing investment decisions with their trade association; and, with the state now in the business of financing investments, such information was crucial.

There were three exceptions to the tendency to weaken the trade associations. First, the *Chambre syndicale de la sidérurgie française* (CSSF), heir to the *Comité des forges*, managed to position itself as the necessary mediator between the state and the individual steel firms until 1978, although the state signed contracts directly with the firms.[26] The CSSF owed its exceptional position to the role it played in the planning process after the war, to cartelization of the sector, and to the high level of concentration of the sector. Second, the state decided to implement regulatory policies other than tariffs and quotas— such as price controls—at the administration of which trade association excelled.

A third, and more significant, exception derived from the constraints of contractual policy. The technocratic bias that was built into the contractual dynamic could not accommodate the interests of sectors that were highly decentralized, even though they might be politically powerful. When the spokesmen for these sectors called on the government, the latter responded by creating a new mechanism for aid to the sector that differed from those already controlled by the Finance Ministry. These new mechanisms reinvested in the old coupling between trade association and vertical agency some control over the public policy toward the sector. An example of this occurred in 1966, in the cotton textile industry. The *Centre interprofessionnel de rénovation des structures industrielles et commerciales de l'Industrie Textile* (CIRIT) was created to fund the restructuring of the textile industry. It was decided that the CIRIT would be ruled by a board dominated by the trade association and the textile office of the Ministry of Industry; the Ministry of Finance received only the right of veto.[27] French industrial policy thus developed a second tier, which was reserved for declining sectors and which was administered by the sector's trade association (and with respect to which bureaucrats felt a lesser urge to extol a quid pro quo, probably because these sectors usually were large and in a predicament). The second tier provided a useful corrective to the otherwise exclusive emphasis on champions, which disturbed the balance of access among interest groups.

In sum, the period 1963–73 in France marked the triumph of industrial policy and pressure politics. Industry-government relations were close and were often stabilized by means of explicit contracts. Both sides worked toward the concentration of French industry in the hands of the largest and most powerful business concerns. Big business and the state partook of common networks administered by the *grand corps* and staffed by means of *pantouflage*.[28] This idyllic relation lasted until the mid-1970s, when the economic crisis and a growing political uncertainty made continuation of the relationship both onerous and politically unwise.

French state-industry contractual relations soured in the 1970s, because neither party was able to live up to the terms of the agreement any longer. On the one hand, the economic crisis had made noncompetitive industries more dependent on state aid, thus tilting the balance of power toward state control. The need to rationalize aid in a budget crunch led the government, in 1979, to centralize all aid in a single agency—the *Comité de développement industriel* (CODIS)—chaired by the prime minister, and thereby short-circuiting the second tier of industrial policy made up of trade associations and sponsoring departments.[29] Trade associations, especially in the cotton textile industry, strongly objected to the CODIS.[30]

On the other hand, the rise of the Left as a plausible political alternative meant that the government was dependent on that fraction of business that was competitive. Giscard and Barre requested that their large business allies refrain from layoffs. The result was *dirigisme*, a category of business-government relations marked by mutual distrust. More and more, the government substituted its own judgment for that of industrialists, whom it regarded as either inefficient or uncooperative. And less and less industrialists welcomed government's intervention, which they no longer found to be beneficial. The Communist threat was both the cause of, and the reason why, many industrialists tolerated *dirigisme*.

The End of Business-Government Collusion: 1981–83

The 1980s were to be a decade of contrasts, as one extreme yielded to another. In ten years, industrial policy shifted from nationalization to privatization, from *dirigisme* to market discipline, from centralization of policymaking in the state to its delegation upward to the Brussels Commission and downward to the regions, and from a strong Minister of Industry to a weakened and resourceless one. The reason for these dramatic changes lay in the shift of the center of electoral gravity to the right. What remained constant during this decade was the incapacity of industry and government, Left and Right, to restore the prior levels of cooperation. The overarching dynamic of party politics condemned industry and government to behave like foes who must fight or strangers who must pledge noninterference.

The Socialist victory terminated thirty years of strong, uninterrupted business-government relations. The massive nationalization program implemented in 1981 "internalized" de facto the first tier of the industrial policy network inherited from the earlier period. Although the main rationale for nationalization was ideological, nationalization made sense from a strictly policy perspective. The leftist government needed the cooperation of large firms and industrial groups to implement its interventionist social and industrial policies; it would not otherwise have acquired that cooperation, short of nationalizing industry and appointing new management.

This full state control over large firms could also be used to sharpen the impact of subsidies, since the productive impact of a subsidy on the activity of a streamlined national(ized) champion was less likely to be diverted from its initial purpose than if it were given to a couple of private groups with subsidiaries operating in the most diverse sectors.[31] Fully state-owned firms could also be expected to be more malleable. The Ministry of Industry and the nationalized firms signed *contrats de plan* in which the ministry committed the state to a certain level of funding in exchange for a commitment from the firms to implement the goals of the Ninth Plan.[32] In effect, within the nationalized sector, Socialist policy was deliberately *dirigist*. Profitable public enterprises were asked to help the government find solutions to problems that were external to their respective managements. In 1983, for instance, the banks, Elf, and CGE were asked to spend their profits to keep ailing companies in business.[33]

Having committed itself to the rescue of all sectors, the Left extended the second tier of industrial policy considerably. Between 1981 and 1984, sectoral plans were conceived for toys, steel, chemicals, textiles, leather goods, machine tools, cars, furniture, and electronics. Rescue operations were mounted to bail out such bankrupt companies as Peugeot, Michelin, Creusot-Loire, as well as smaller firms, all through the intermediary of the CIASI (rebaptized CIRI). The textile industry found socialism significantly more generous and less dirigist than Barrism.[34] Finally, the industrial policy of the Socialists toward private firms that were not lame ducks seems to have had mixed success. Aid to private firms was usually contingent on their avoiding layoffs, a condition that had the effect of deterring applications for aid.

Disengagement and Privatization: 1983–90

In 1983 the Socialist government negotiated a sharp turn. Day-to-day meddling in the management of nationalized enterprises was discontinued. Economic priority was shifted from lower unemployment to greater competitiveness. Despite warmer relations with business, government did not resume the industrial policy of the past but carried on with the disengagement that had been initiated under the Giscard-Barre government and that was continued by the Chirac government of 1986–88. The two-tiered apparatus of industrial policy was progressively dismantled. Rather than create new aid agencies, the (Socialist) Fabius government pursued efforts to strengthen the financial markets. New financial mechanisms were created to increase savings, develop risk capital, and make investment in stocks more attractive. Quantitative restrictions on bank lending were abandoned in 1987 with the result that alternative sources of financing grew considerably, reducing the state's capacity to steer investment. No new sectoral plans were adopted after 1983. Creusot-Loire was allowed to go bankrupt. The shift in emphasis away from the firm and toward its financial environment was reflected by a shift of power in the state administration from the Industry Ministry to the Finance Ministry.[35] The managers of public enterprises established direct contacts with the Ministry of Finance, bypassing the Ministry of Industry. The pursuit of European integration expanded the jurisdiction of the Brussels Commission over industrial policy instruments. Regionalization of aid to industry, though still in its infancy, partook of the same trend toward the disengagement of state policy from industrial policy.[36]

The policy of the (conservative) Chirac government accentuated these trends. The very concept of industrial policy was dropped from the official discourse. The goal of the government was to privatize all public industrial enterprises. The Finance Ministry was entrusted with implementing privatization. About half the program (thirty out of sixty-five companies) was realized before the crash of October 1987 dried up the stock market. The government abandoned the right to allocate credit within the economy. Although the return of the Socialists under the Rocard government registered voter reaction against the extreme liberalism of the Chirac government, the "*nouvelle politique industrielle*" initiated in 1988 by the new Socialist Minister of Industry, Roger Fauroux, hardly broke with the trend toward disengagement. The new strategy was to give large firms the financial means, whether private or public, to buy themselves a "critical size" in the world market. In exchange, these champions were given the responsibility for lining up a network of small and medium suppliers, for defending them against hostile foreign takeovers and modernizing and making them competitive.[37] This new strategy, which somewhat resembles the German and Japanese models, delegated the task of structuring and modernizing the sectors to the largest firms and banks.

How do we account for the fact that the Socialist government initiated this reversal toward market discipline and decentralized networks? It seems paradoxical that a government committed to intervention could so easily reverse its course. The paradox deepens if we recall that Premier Barre, in the late 1970s, had not managed to restore market discipline, despite his proclaimed intention to do so. The paradox disappears if the question is divided in two parts: first, about the decision to switch course and, second, about the capacity to enforce the decision. With respect to the first question, there is little doubt that the Socialists would not have given up intervention had they not been forced to do so by the unequivocal failure of their economic policy during the first two years. Once the decision to ditch interventionism was taken, however, the capacity of the Socialists to restore market discipline was much greater than that of Barre or any other conservative government. After all, the state under Giscard and Barre was not autonomous, but was embedded in a dense array of corporate and sectoral interests that restricted the state's room to maneuver. The only time the government was able successfully to pressure its corporate friends was before 1978, when a leftist victory was perceived as imminent. At that time, however, the goal then was to curb layoffs, not promote market discipline. In contrast, the victory of the Left had an effect similar to that which Mancur Olson attributes to upheavals and invasions: It broke up the networks of bureaucrats and rent seekers and disbanded the "distributional coalitions."[38] Nationalization put the cream of French management out of business and wreaked havoc on the half-public, half-private corps-bank-industry fraternity.

This fraternity was not re-created afterward. To be sure, the Socialists also established networks, especially after 1983, when curbing state action sent Socialist high officials looking for more lucrative and challenging positions in private industry, banks, and public enterprises.[39] But the partisan alternation and the fragmentation of the Socialists into rival factions interfered with the reemergence of state-industry ties comparable to those of the past. Moreover, expropriation of the "monopolists" did not reconcile the state to the *petits patrons*, but paradoxically made communicating with them more difficult. As Suzanne Berger argued, the nationalizations led to "the removal of many of those business leaders who had previously mediated between the small and medium firms and big business, and between the private sector and the State."[40]

In sum, industry-government relations in France went through five phases: contractual (1963–74), dirigist (1975–78), liberal (1979–80), dirigist (1981–82), and liberal (1983–90). The first phase was characteristic of pressure politics, the other four of party politics.

Party and Industry

Party politics channels business-government relations through one or several parties of the Right or Center-Right. Profitable when the party of business is in power, this exclusivity can be disastrous when that party is in opposition. Notwithstanding Enoch Powell's advice (see the epigraph at the beginning of

this chapter), the traditional response to partisan mediation has been the creation of a national peak association in order to provide business with a cushion.[41] Trade and local associations were seen as unfit to perform this new task
because of the general nature of the issues that usually drive business-government relations in party politics. But if party politics made the business peak
association the center of attention, party politics also made that association
the center of internal tensions. The discussion typically revolved around the
proper distance and degree of neutrality that the peak association should observe toward the parties of the Right. Should the CNPF openly support the
Right, or should it play the role of a broker sufficiently neutral to invite consultation with a leftist government? In the latter case, how critical (or unsup-
portive) of the Right's policies for industry could the peak business association
afford to be?

In light of the framework used here, let me state the type of working relationship that one should observe between a rightist party and a peak business
association in the context of party politics. The two options offered to the
business peak association, partisanship and neutrality, appeal differentially to
small and large firms. Small business is generally less favorable to close industry-government relations than big business, because of the former's lesser organizational capacity to gather the spoils. This built-in discord is amplified when
the Left is in power, because of the greater economic vulnerability of small
business to the employee policies of leftist governments. Given that parties of
the Right tend to overrepresent size calculated in numbers, whereas the business peak association is likely to overrepresent size calculated in assets, the
peak business association can be expected to be pulled toward the right when
the Right wins power, but to gravitate back toward the center when the Right
loses power. In the case of Britain, a country with a long tradition of party
politics, the model is applicable verbatim, as we shall soon see. In the French
case, the model accounts for the underlying reality, though not for all of it,
since the organizational transition to party politics is recent and incomplete.

Basically, French business is split by the familiar small-big cleavage. Small
business holds individualist, antistatist views. It applauded the "*charte libérale*,"
a liberal manifesto officially adopted by the CNPF in 1965, which denounced
planning and *dirigisme*. Presidents of large companies, in contrast, disasso-
ciated themselves from the chart.[42] Two idiosyncrasies complicate the basic
picture. First, a large chunk of small business in France is not part of the
CNPF, but of the CGPME (a confederation of small and medium-size companies) and, since 1977, the SNPMI (*Syndicat national du patronat moderne
indépendant*, a splinter group). Second, big business is split between "ancients" and "moderns." The moderns correspond to the standard image of big
business; they are the new generation of managers of public and private firms
operating in new, highly concentrated sectors. These managers shifted from a

pro-rightist position before 1979 to a neutral position afterward. The ancients are relics from the not-so-distant collusive past. They are the wealthiest trade associations, representing traditional sectors—iron and steel, construction, public works, foodstuffs, and so forth. In control of the CNPF from the year of its creation in 1945, leaders of the top ten trade associations developed very close relations with the Conservative personnel, especially the Gaullists. They were, and still are, pro-right. The debate about the proper political attitude of the CNPF, therefore, was mainly between the two factions of big business— the managers and the associations.

The main stages of this rivalry were as follows. Until 1981, the associations dominated the CNPF. The threat of a Socialist victory in the late 1970s led the peak association to a close alliance with the Right. Its leader, François Ceyrac, officially sided with Giscard in 1981. The latter's defeat, along with the Socialist nationalizations, brought down Ceyrac's faction. The new president, Yvon Gattaz, a self-made businessman and representative of the provincial, small business base, was hostile to the Left.[43] After a year of confrontation, however, Gattaz endorsed the managers' apolitical approach and engaged in a policy of dialogue with the Left. The advent of the (conservative) Chirac government, in 1986, effected a dramatic realignment, because Gattaz's belated rallying to the cry for privatization allegedly cost him the leadership of the CNPF.[44] The new leader of the CNPF since December 1986, François Périgot, though himself a manager, has shown greater sensitivity to the politically induced switches in the balance of power within his membership. Under his leadership, the CNPF openly supported the Right under the Chirac government (1986–88). However, although the CNPF openly opposed Mitterrand's candidacy at the 1988 presidential election), it subsequently sought to distance itself from the Right under Rocard's Socialist rule (1988–91).

In France since 1978, therefore, the peak association has switched roles from partisan supporter to apolitical broker according to the party cycle. This dynamic is a direct reflection of the partisan nature of the policy process.

Another stake in party politics is the managerial control of former champions. The nationalizations of 1981 turned large concerns into socialist spoils. The privatization implemented by the Chirac government in 1986–87 turned them into conservative (not just private) spoils. Indeed, the rightist government appointed the heads of denationalized and newly privatized firms and allocated a large part of the "*noyaux durs*" to businesses with good connections to the RPR. (The *noyaux durs* are the stable nuclei of private shareholders holding a blocking minority on the board of freshly privatized corporations, a measure that it justified by the claim that it prevents premature foreign takeover.) The Chirac government created, according to Bauer, a "new economic technocracy close to the Gaullist party."[45]

Nationalization versus Privatization: The Ideological Discourse

Partisan mediation brought with it considerable simplification of the political debate, reminiscent of the prewar era. Disqualification of the Keynesian synthesis brought the partisans of liberal economics face to face with the tenets of Marxist-inspired policies. Until 1983, the initiative came from the Left; pledged since 1972 to a widespread program of expansion of the public sector, the Left proceeded to the realization of the program in 1981. Then, in 1984, the RPR and the UDF (Giscard's party) endorsed the concept of privatization and, once in power (1986), implemented a large part of their program. Many Socialist leaders, then in opposition, pledged the unmaking of several privatizations.[46] An early victim of politicization of the ownership question was the concept of mixed ownership (public-private), which had been standard practice until 1981 but which afterward became the bastard no one dared claim. The ban on mixed ownership ended up hurting state-owned companies most. Since they were forbidden to dilute their public capital, they could not tap the financial market—the most affluent source of cash since 1983.[47] At any rate, the ownership issue became so divisive for the Left that, after his reelection in 1988, Mitterrand unilaterally imposed a truce: no more privatizations and no more nationalizations, or "ni-ni" (neither-nor), as the French clerks dubbed it. The appointment of the Center-Left Rocard government further clouded the issue. For the last two years (1988–90), industry and government have maintained unnaturally civil relations. Banks and industries seem to have almost unanimously supported the "*nouvelle politique industrielle*" of the new government, a policy of internal aggrandizement and foreign takeovers conducted by national champions in preparation for the creation of a single European market after 1992.[48]

The Executive

The executive as autonomous agent played no new role in the formulation of trade policy. The executive maintained a firm commitment to the GATT and the EEC, a reflection of its postwar engagements. Tariffs, quotas, VERs, and antidumping remained out of bounds to partisan escalation.

It is interesting to note, however, that France's membership in the EEC came very close to becoming embroiled in the partisan battle in June 1982 and again in March 1983, when several members of the Mauroy government raised the possibility of withdrawing from the European Monetary System, at a time when the Communists were asking for withdrawal from the EEC altogether. Had Mitterrand heeded their advice, France's commitment to European economic integration would have immediately become a partisan issue. Among the reasons behind the President's refusal to give in to protection, the disinclination to question a pillar of France's postwar grand strategy must have figured prominently. Since then, Mitterrand and Jacques Delors, his ex-finance minister whom Mitterand soon after promoted to the directorship of the Brussels Commission, were instrumental in deepening France's commitment to the Common Market. The conservative Right jumped on the bandwagon with such undisguised enthusiasm that it provided Le Pen's extreme Right with the edge over the issue of nationalism, an issue still popular with middle-class voters.

Policy Tools

Hypothesis 5.8 states that pressure politics is more conducive to a targeted industrial policy than are party or executive politics, because of the close industry-government relations that characterize pressure politics (hypothesis 5.8 is the specification of hypothesis 5.7 for the postwar era). Consequently, one possible observation is that precrisis France resorted to direct subsidies to a greater extent than Britain, the United States, or postcrisis France. Summary data for aid granted to industry in the three countries for various years are provided in table 12.1.

French aid throughout the 1970s was channeled mainly through general and special grants to industry. Aid to regional development was small, while adjustment for workers looking for a new job was left to the labor market. Britain offered a contrasting picture, distributing a greater part of its assistance to industry in the form of regional development and aid to the labor market. The United States distributed the most aid to industry in the form of research and development funds, especially through the Department of Defense. Another interesting observation is the change undergone by the French breakdown in the 1980s, precisely toward a greater emphasis on the labor market.

Another important change in French policy toward industry, one that does not appear in the table, was the abandonment of sectoral policies after 1983. The state continued to pour billions of francs into specific industries, either as a result of past engagements, especially with traditional industries, or to consolidate the assets of nationalized—and, in 1986, about-to-be-privatized—companies. No new sectoral plans have been pursued since 1983, however. The practice of targeting sectors was over as of 1990.[49] French industrial policy has moved out of the firm, whether public or private, and has been operating instead in a more general financial, tax, training, and research environment.

TABLE 12.1
Breakdown of Public Transfers to Industry in France, Britain, and the United States (Postwar)

I. Public transfers including grants, equity capital, loans, and guarantees

	France				
	1970	*1973*	*1977*	*1983*	*1987*
Sectoral	64%	61%	49%	40%	42%
General investment	6	6	7	15	5
R&D civilian	3	3	4	4	5
R&D defense	na	na	na	na	16
Export	15	22	36	53	23
Region	11	8	4	2	2
Employment, training	na	na	na	5	7
total (in million FF)	3,807	5,750	11,129	39,039	88,013
total (as % of P.I.B.)	0.49	0.52	0.59	0.98	1.71

	Britain		
	1969–70	*1972–73*	*1976–77*
Sectoral	17%	27%	15%
General investment	51	21	8
R&D civilian	3	3	2
R&D defense	na	na	na
Export	2	24	28
Region	16	13	24
Employment, training	10	13	22
total (in million £)	1,418	1,493	2,915
total (as % of GNP)	3.01	2.34	2.31

	United States			
	1959	*1969*	*1980*	*1983*
Sectoral	0%	0%	0%	0%
General investment*	2	1	12	6
R&D civilian	11	38	21	12
R&D defense	80	55	49	69
Export*	6	6	17	12
Region	1	na	na	1
Employment, training	na	na	na	na
total (in million $)	4,652	9,322	18,268	21,090
total (as % of GNP)	1.1	1	0.7	0.6

* Figures represent the total of direct and guaranteed loans divided by three to estimate the subsidy equivalent.
na: datum not available. Column percentages were calculated as if *na* were equal to zero.

TABLE 12.1 (*cont.*)
Breakdown of Public Transfers to Industry in France, Britain, and the United States (Postwar)

Sources: France: for 1970, 1973, and 1977: BIPE 1983: 53. For 1983, *Les Notes Bleues*, 329 (May 3, 1987), 3. For 1987, *La Tribune de l'Expansion* (September 6, 1988). Britain: for 1969–70 and 1972–73, Corden and Fels 1976: 124. For 1976–77, Maunder 1979: 132. United States: general investment (small business): for 1959, Budget of the U.S. Government for the FY ending June 30, 1960, GPO, Washington, D.C.; O.M.B., *Special Analyses: Budget of the U.S. Government*, 1971, p. 72; 1981, pp. 148–49, 169–70; 1984, p. F-18. U.S.: R&D: National Science Foundation, *Federal Funds Research and Development Budget*, FY 1959, 1960, and 1961, p. 52; *Federal Funds for Research, Development, and Other Scientific Activities*, FY 1969, 1970, 1971, p. 118; FY 1980, 1981, 1982, p. 26; FY 1983, p. 26; FY 1987–89, p. 118. U.S.: regional aid: Benjamin Bridges, Jr., "State and Local Inducements for Industry," *National Tax Journal* 18:1 (March 1965), 1–14; Elliot Schwartz, *The Federal Role in State Industrial Development Programs*, C.B.O. (July 1984), 66–68.

II. *Public transfers including grants, tax concessions, equity capital, loans, and guarantees*

	France			Britain			United States
	1981–86 *	1986–88 **	1986–89 ***	1981–86 *	1986–88 **	1986–89 ***	1986–89 ***
Sectoral	56%	62%	35%	48%	50%	3%	0%
General investment	11	9	6	4	12	34	64
R&D civilian	2	6	12	7	7	10	10
R&D defense	na	na	na	na	na	na	na
Export	21	18	29	10	7	24	24
Region	4	5	24	14	24	24	10
Employment, training	6	na	12	18	na	5	3
total (as % of PIB)	1.5	1.1	na****	1.5	0.8	na****	na****

* Six-year average, excluding transportation, agriculture, and fishing; EC Commission 1989.
** Three-year average, excluding transportation, agriculture, and fishing; EC Commission 1990.
*** Four-year average, OECD Press Division 1992.
**** The OECD did not reveal absolute amounts.

Policy Orientation

TARIFF

The French tariff was decided on by an autonomous executive exchanging reciprocal concessions within the GATT multilateral framework and the EEC (hypothesis 5.5). The impact of these negotiations on the French tariff is visible from the mid-1960s onward (see figure A2.3, in Appendix 2; see also, table 11.2, for a test covering the 1946–79 period). Cross-industry studies of tariffs offer a sharper picture of alternative hypotheses and a better tool with which to assess them. Cross-industry studies have been used to prove (or disprove) the standard claim of political economy, that tariff levels reflect the preferences of those sectors best able to organize for political action. This hypothesis (5.2) assumes a case of pressure politics, and thus is incompatible with the case made here. (Remember that, since 1946, the tariff is set within the GATT, that is, by executive politics.) Hypothesis 5.2 has not been confirmed. A cross-industry study of the 1974 French effective tariff by Messerlin found no significant relation between tariff levels and industry characteristics, except for an unexpected negative relation to the degree of sectoral concentration.[50] Needless to say, the fact that French tariffs are set at the community level introduces considerable noise in the data.

NTBs

Unlike tariffs, NTBs work more or less on the margin of the GATT, and thus of executive politics. With tariffs declining, NTBs should rise to compensate. France since 1947 has developed planning and developmental agencies for that purpose. The speed and nature of this rise should reflect a pressure dynamic until the mid-1970s (hypothesis 5.1) and a party dynamic afterward (hypothesis 5.3). Although our qualitative understanding of French programs fits with these hypotheses, there hardly is any systematic evidence. NTBs are very difficult to measure. There is no longitudinal data set, only sporadic forays. A cross-national study showed that French NTBs were the most extensive among OECD countries in 1983. It was calculated that 57 percent of French imports were affected by "visible" NTBs—that is, quotas, VERs, decreed prices, monitoring, or antidumping or countervailing duties (not including subsidies).[51] Equivalent data were 43 percent for the United States and 14 percent for Britain. A cross-industry study of NTBs yielded meager results. Messerlin's study of NTBs (1974) found that the NTBs reflected the number of employees (a measure of the industry's size).[52] The systematic evidence is inconclusive.

Because of the complexity of postwar trade policy, the split of the policy process into multiple parallel tracks, and the lack of reliable estimates, the test of any hypothesis on policy orientation is rendered inconclusive.

Britain

Britain: The Revolt of Small Business

The impact of the oil crisis on British politics was similar to the impact of the Great Depression of the 1930s. It hurt the Left and disqualified the existing policy repertoire. As in France and the United States, the crisis in Britain triggered a switch of the median voter to the right, thereby benefiting the Conservatives—and more precisely the right wing of the Conservative party, which had long advocated a departure from the Keynesian tools of management in favor of monetarism and retrenchment. Also, as in 1930, the switch of the median voter to the right resulted from a two-step process. First, the unions were alienated by the pragmatism of the party's leadership, and they became radicalized, demanding greater state intervention in the economy (hypothesis 4.1). The unions became a repellant for otherwise unorganized strata of independents, small business, and so forth, which moved abruptly to the right, pulling the median voter along and allowing the Conservatives to resume power.

The period preceding the realignment of 1978 can be described as a repetition of the stop-go dynamic of the 1950s, with the added condition that manipulation of the bank rate could no longer check inflation (or reduce unemployment). Rather, the rate had to be propped up by either voluntary or statutory collective discipline. The partisan nature of policymaking discouraged mutual restraint between the unions and industry (see the discussion of Britain in chapter eleven). Consequently, voluntary restraint was forthcoming in periods of "stop" only, when there was hardly any need for it, not in periods of "go," when it was most needed. The result was that the government had to step in and impose a universally unpopular statutory freeze. From 1964 on, this scenario repeated itself three and a half times. In December 1964, the Wilson government had the TUC and CBI sign the "Declaration of Intent," in which the two organizations declared their common intention to reach a solution on inflation.[53] Because the two peak associations would consent only to voluntary, noncredible restraints, wage pressure continued unabated. Pressed to freeze wages by U.S. and foreign creditors, in September 1965, the Labour government persuaded the TUC and CBI to submit wage and price increases to regulatory review. Nevertheless, a one-year freeze had to be imposed during the sterling crisis of July 1966, with incessant Conservative attacks finally forcing the Labour party to abandon its incomes policy, which opened the way for the wage explosion of 1969–70. The new Conservative government took the offensive, regulating the right to strike, penalizing unofficial actions, and threatening eventual violators with sanctions enforceable by the courts.[54] But the unions were not deterred. After another round of unsuccessful tripartite talks, in 1972, Heath reverted to statutory controls, starting with a five-month pay freeze. The TUC withdrew its support, and a confrontation with the miners brought down the Conservative government. The subsequent Labour government under Wilson, and then under Callaghan, once again tried the voluntarist approach. In 1975, the government and TUC signed a "social contract" restricting wage increases. The policy was quite successful by British standards, lasting three consecutive years, until the economy began to emerge from the recession and the need for further wage restraint became important.[55] Pay settlements remained moderate for another year; but, in July 1978, the

TUC ended cooperation, throwing Britain into a "winter of discontent," which cost Labour the election.

The social contract was the swan song of incomes policy. The Thatcher government did not resort to it but tackled inflation instead through pre-Keynesian methods—the tight control of money supply and a tolerance for high levels of unemployment. This reversal to liberal orthodoxy reflected a 180-degree change in the number-one macroeconomic priority, from full employment to price stability. This reversion to the prewar agenda reflected two parallel changes in the party structure: (1) a polarization of the partisan debate, and (2) a shift of the center of gravity toward the right. Each of these points is developed below.

Both the Labour and Conservative parties have always harbored extreme wings; but, until the 1970s, the influence of the extremes within their respective parties was limited. The extremes typically asserted some influence in periods of opposition, especially after an election had removed their party from power and weakened the centrist wing. However, economic difficulties specific to Britain, and the 1973–82 economic crisis sharpened redistributive battles and, at the same time, cut into the budgetary slack needed by the leadership to keep its extreme wing in line when the party was in power. The balance of power in both parties during this period tipped toward the extreme wing. In 1973, the Labour party conference adopted a program widely perceived at the time to be the most radical statement in the party's history—to be outdone only a decade later by the manifesto of 1983. Among other things, the latter called for a new extension of public ownership, withdrawal from NATO and the EEC, and protection.[56] The Conservatives, in contrast, took a right turn in February 1975, when they elected Margaret Thatcher to succeed Edward Heath as leader of the party; their 1979 manifesto was a reactionary document.

The depletion of the centers of both parties, however, did not have the same effect on the electoral chances of the two parties. Whereas the Tory right wing was set up by the election to govern for more than a decade, the Labour left wing was abandoned by its moderate wing in 1981 and, after 1983, was gradually removed from positions of influence in the party under the leadership of Neil Kinnock. Along with the polarization within each party, the British party system as a whole experienced a shift in center of gravity to the right, a shift also experienced by the French and American party systems. As in France and the United States, this shift reflected a greater readiness on the part of the middle classes—the traditional troops of the Right—to experiment with policies of state disengagement in a broad range of issue areas. Shopkeepers, foremen, and self-employed businessmen not only voted overwhelmingly Conservative in 1983, they were found by a survey to be "the most right-wing of all" on the privatization issue.[57]

This change in British attitudes is particularly observable among small business. The fact that party politics was not favorable to establishment of a close working relationship between state and industry did not prevent the three governments from pouring millions into major industries. Small business, among the first to object, tried to use its privileged access to the Conservative party to put an end to the practice. At the Conservative party conferences of 1956 and 1962, speakers for small business complained about the undue burden laid on them by large government expenditures and the consequent rate of taxation and inflation.[58] Throughout the 1960s, they complained about Labour's selective interventions in industry, which tended to favor large concerns. Pressed by small business, who were heavily represented at the constituency level, the party conference of 1968 declared prices and incomes policy "at complete variance with the basic Conservative principle of free enterprise."[59] In 1972, Heath's disregard of this wish led a committee of backbench MPs to create the Small Business Bureau within the party in 1973. Mrs. Thatcher, "who comes from a family small business background," Wyn Grant writes, "has shown a particular concern for the interests of small businessmen whom she sees as playing a key role in Britain's hoped for economic revival."[60]

The opposition of small business to subsidies was not mere ideological penchant. As a leader of the Association of Independent Businesses, a small-business peak association, put it: "Our members have done badly from state subsidies in the last decade. Little wonder that we support cuts in corporation tax and an end to state subsidies."[61] Accordingly, the Thatcher government proceeded to tighten regional and selective subsidies and expand tax cuts. In 1981, fourteen tax-free enterprise zones were introduced, in conjunction with loan guarantee and business start-up schemes.[62] To be sure, what is good for small business is not necessarily bad for big business. Big business alone, however, was powerless to promote electoral liberalism, and its interest in change was less pronounced, since it tended to accommodate itself to interventionism better than did small business. The CBI's move toward a strong pro-Thatcher line followed, rather than preceded, the Conservatives' victory.[63]

As in France, the rallying of a majority of British small business around ultraliberal economics occurred during the economic crisis. The success of the rally amplified the inability of the Heath and Callaghan governments to contain wage pressure. The extremism of the Labour party after 1979 kept small firms in the Conservative camp. In Britain and France, therefore, small business and the middle classes at large provided the electoral support that ultraliberals needed to rollback the interventionist state. For the first time since the war, rightist governments were able to pursue pro-business policies openly and unapologetically, and at a minimal cost in side-payments to nonbusiness groups.

Industry-Government Relations

Industry-government relations at the micro-industry level took one of three forms: (1) dirigist, characterized by unilateral (uninvited) state intervention in industry; (2) voluntarist and contractual, characterized by attempts to institute tripartite consultation and corporatist compromise; or (3) liberal, characterized by an emphasis on state retrenchment and arm's-length relations. Industry-government relations in Britain went through five phases: dirigist (Wilson 1964–70), liberal (Heath 1970–72), dirigist (Heath 1972–74, Wilson-Callaghan, 1974–75); contractual-tripartite (Callaghan 1975–78); and liberal (Thatcher 1978–1991).

A move from one form of relations to the next reflected a combination of two factors. A move reflected, first, the identity of the party in government— Labour inclined to state intervention, and the Conservatives to liberal retrenchment. A move also reflected the type of industry-government relations in force at the macrolevel, because the micro- and macro-levels were so closely connected. Indeed, until the realignment of 1978, industrial policy in Britain was conceived of as a tool to fight unemployment. Tripartism at the macrolevel would encourage tripartism at the microlevel, whereas a turn toward *dirigisme* at the macrolevel would ruin participation at the micro-level. When viewed in light of these two rules of thumb, the evolution of British business-government relations after 1963 becomes intelligible.

The Labour government in 1964 was committed to state intervention. Planning was taken away from NEDO, which was outside Whitehall, and given to the Department of Economic Affairs (DEA), a new ministry whose minister ranked second only to the prime minister in the cabinet hierarchy.[64] Both the CBI and the TUC resented this displacement of the tripartite apparatus. Furthermore, the displacement triggered an official protest from the business peak association, in December 1965, when the chairmanship of the NEDC was removed from the Treasury and given to the DEA.[65] The negative reaction of the peak associations to this centralization of planning reflected their fundamental distrust of the state. Tripartism enjoyed the favor of the peak associations, their respective leaderships, and those members from whom the leadership was drawn: large unions in the case of the TUC, big business and the City in the case of the CBI. Tripartism offered these groups the opportunity to neutralize governmental initiative. Like all governments in party politics, the Wilson government behaved like an autonomous actor. It came into power with its ideas already formed about the type and orientation of policy to be implemented, and it had the capacity to confront producer groups, including those among its supporters, with faits accomplis. Understandably, the aim of the producer groups, both supporters and opponents of particular economic policies, was to force the government to negotiate these policies. Moreover, tripartism offered the ideal setting for such negotiations, because it brought two additional actors, TUC and CBI, into the policymaking process and thus reduced the government to the role of moderator.

Note that the same desire to force the government to consult with industry had motivated the creation of the advisory committee system between the wars. In the 1960s, however, this system was considered inefficient. The committees were commonly derided as mere "talking shops rather than a body where policies could really be hammered out round a table."[66] The centralization of subsidies further discredited the fragmented advisory system. A CBI pamphlet explained that "[o]nly the NEDC provides an opportunity of discussing major national problems in an atmosphere comparatively free from departmental pressures and in a wider economic context."[67]

The sterling crisis of 1966 hastened the end of the experiment in indicative planning and opened a period of uninvited direct state intervention in the economy. Two measures in particular were regarded by business as dirigist. The first was the Industrial Development Act of 1966, which overhauled investment incentives by substituting grants for existing tax allowances, thus introducing an element of ministerial discretion into the allocation process. The Conservative opposition denounced the act as a source of uncertainty for industry.[68] The second measure was the creation of the Industrial Reorganization Corporation (IRC) to promote mergers and rationalization schemes through either consulting or direct equity participation. The scheme was heavily criticized by the Conservative opposition, the CBI, and the Association of British Chambers of Commerce (which represented small business).[69] The Wilson government disregarded the objections of business. Pressed by events and unable to wait for the hypothetical results of tripartite consulting, the Wilson government legislated for itself the means to force an industrial policy on a reticent business community.

Dirigism implied bypassing what Young and Lowe call the "bottleneck" constituted of trade associations, consultative mechanisms, planning councils, and so forth, in order to establish direct links with individual firms.[70] The rationale for reaching the individual firm was the same as in France: Firms were the units of decision in matters of investment and thus the obvious interlocutors for a government intent on pursuing an industrial policy. The reason the practice of targeting individual firms in Britain was regarded as *dirigisme*, whereas in France at the time the same practice was mutually agreed upon, was that the organized-business community—the CBI, as well as the TUC—was opposed to it. The CBI was opposed to firm-targeting lest a Labour government directly influence the decisions of boards of directors by applying financial aid or pressure. The TUC shared the CBI's fears, for two reasons. First, it feared that the firm might seek to negotiate redundancies directly with the government; and second, the TUC feared that such agreements would enhance the power of shop stewards.[71] The Wilson government could overlook the opposition of the CBI and, more important, of the TUC, by drawing support from the party's electorate at large; the government could also draw support from the shopfloor and from the weakest TUC members. Shopfloors and weak unions generally lacked the TUC's enthusiasm for tripartite agreements, since the agreements were usually consummated behind their backs and rarely to their advantage.[72]

Wilson's emphasis on firm-targeting incensed small and medium business. As it had in France, this policy favored large firms and concentrated sectors. Small and medium firms did not benefit from selective state intervention, because they could not threaten massive layoffs. The Conservatives won the election of June 1970 on a platform promising retrenchment. Responsive to the complaints of small business, the government abolished the IRC and the investment grants.[73] Less support was made available for the promotion of profitable enterprises, and help was denied to lame ducks.[74] The government also intended to do away with the tripartite apparatus, but it abstained from doing so in the face of insuperable opposition from the CBI.[75] Liberalism in the domain of industrial policy lasted until 1972, when Heath made employment the government's first priority. Growing impatient at the incapacity of peak associations to agree to anything, Heath decided to use the resources of his office. He declared a freeze and a statutory wage and price policy at the macrolevel and adopted a panoply of selective tools to stimulate firms' investment at the microlevel. The Industry Act of 1972 provided for direct grants to individual firms and for the taking of equity holdings in assisted firms. The CBI denounced the uncertainty affecting the allocation of the new investment grants, making a plea instead for detailed criteria and an appeal procedure. Concerned principally about stimulating employment, the government rejected the plea on the grounds that this would lead to inflexibility and delay.[76]

The failure of the Heath government's policy of *dirigisme* provoked a left-wing backlash within Labour,[77] and Labour returned to power committed to very dirigist measures, whose two central features were the National Enterprise Board (NEB) (a replay of the IRC) and "planning agreements."[78] The planning agreements were to be signed between public officials and firms, with no sectoral mediation. The point was made with great clarity by Alan Williams, a junior minister:

> [O]ur attempted planning and industrial guidance has foundered at [the] sectoral level because decisions are not taken at that level . . . one must break from the sector to the key firm that can make the decision . . . that is the role that we wish for the Planning Agreement.[79]

Although constant reference was made to the French *contrats de programme*, the planning agreements were a statutory, coercive tool. As initially drafted, agreements were designed to channel all assistance—including tax allowances and public procurements—through company plans agreed to by the government, and the top manufacturing enterprises would be mandated to disclose information and negotiate agreements with the government. The CBI fought the bill tooth and nail and obliged the Labour government, which was a minority government, to expunge the compulsory obligations from the bill. The CBI maintained its opposition to the formula, pointing to the "real dangers of bureaucratic delay, unfair competition and breaches of confidentiality which would weaken the commercial position of the companies involved."[80] In the end, only two such agreements were signed, one with Chrysler (UK), when the government rescued that company from bankruptcy, and the other with the National Coal Board, a public agency. The TUC was lukewarm toward the concept all along, and the unions, which were party to the agreement with Chrysler, considered themselves committed to no part of it, not even to those provisions they had negotiated directly with Chrysler's management.[81]

The Labour government soon abandoned *dirigisme*. Taking advantage of the referendum on EEC membership (June 1975), whose favorable outcome routed the left wing, the government engaged on a tripartite experiment, known as the "Chequers strategy," or "industrial strategy."[82] The "industrial strategy" was the most successful corporatist experiment ever attempted in Britain. Lasting three years—from 1975 to 1978—it combined a relatively successful incomes policy at the macro-level with fruitful discussions and unofficial agreements at the sectoral level. Within the context of "Neddy," TUC and CBI organized sector working parties (SWP) to be held in each sector by trade associations (and/or by large firms in concentrated sectors), by trade unions, and by government representatives. Information was exchanged on a consensual basis, any agreement remained unofficial, and government aid was debated. Each sector operated at its own speed and under no planning constraint from the center. Industries with an interest in protection and subsidies took advantage of the opportunity to engage in direct lobbying of the government. In the few cases where unions and firms, large and small, could speak with one voice, deals with the government were struck.[83] The experiment came to an end in 1978, when the TUC withdrew its cooperation.

The collapse of the tripartite experiment caused (or revealed) a backlash among CBI members. The business peak association took the view that "poor profitability was related to an imbalance of bargaining power between employers and unions, which favored the unions."[84] One year later, Margaret Thatcher became prime minister. She implemented a systematic policy of state disengagement from the economy. All subsidies to industry, except for high-tech and R&D, were either reduced or phased out and replaced by tax allowances.[85] In 1988, she dismantled the sponsoring divisions of the Department of Trade and Industry and weakened NEDO, thereby destroying "the apparatus that would be required by any future interventionist government."[86] The CBI leadership at first revolted against the extreme aspects of Thatcherism—in 1980, the director general, Sir Terence Beckett, spoke of a "bare-knuckle" fight with the government—but he rapidly fell in line under the pressure of CBI's membership.[87] The break with the past was completed when a CBI-TUC draft agreement on the introduction of new technology was opposed by CBI's rank and file. "Many employers," according to Grant and Sargent, "were glad to see unions on the floor, and there was the view that profits could get up off the floor—where they were, too—and leave the unions down there."[88] As in the past, industry-government relations under Thatcher remained at arm's length.

Party and Industry

We saw in our review of the French case that party politics made it difficult for the business peak association to define a consistent role for itself. The French CNPF continued to alternate between the roles of partisan supporter and apolitical broker, depending on whether the Right or the Left was in power. This alternation was even sharper in Britain, where the business world was split between big and medium-small business, with the former generally preferring accommodation with the Left and the latter being opposed to it. This divergence in outlook corresponded to a difference in representation. Influence in peak associations tended to overrepresent wealth, whereas influence in the Conservative party tended, relatively speaking, to be more reflective of numbers. Big business was better represented in the peak association than in the party. In 1972, for instance, CBI drew 80 percent of its revenues from large individual firms, whereas 12 percent came from trade associations that represented medium and small business.[89] The fact that the latter controlled over 40 percent of the seats on the council could not by itself compensate for this discrepancy. It merely ensured, the Devlin Report remarked, that the CBI "does not operate through majority decisions imposed on minorities. . . . Policies must accommodate big companies if they are to be workable."[90] Conversely, surveys for 1973–78 indicated that the majority of large enterprises did not make any contributions to the Conservative party.[91]

In contrast, small business had more voice in the Conservative party than in the CBI. Small firms were well represented among the membership of the local party associations.[92] The Conservative party and the business community were formally linked through the Private Enterprise Consultative Group, which represented primarily small business. The rise of the "economic radicals" in the late 1960s, and their triumph in the late 1970s correlated with a reaffirmation of the importance of small business in Tory economics. By contrast, the CBI's rally behind Thatcherite economics was late and lukewarm; its resistance manifested itself variously and successively as support for proportional representation at the conference of 1978, criticisms of high exchange rates, in 1979 and Sir Terence Beckett's promise of a "bare-knuckle fight" in 1980.[93]

The leadership of the peak association thus was generally torn between its most influential members and the rank and file. Depending on which party was favored by electoral circumstances, the CBI played the neutralist card or the partisan one. The CBI typically acted as ideological sounding board under a Conservative government, when the influence of small business was at its height, and as nonpartisan broker under a Labour government, when that influence was nil.

Finally, as in France, the nationalization issue reemerged full-fledged in 1969 among the British Left, with one minor difference from the postwar debate: The Labour party conference was now calling for public ownership of specific firms rather than of whole industries.[94] In 1973, the party published a report calling for the takeover of the leading twenty-five firms.[95] The defeat of the Labour party's Left in the May 1975 referendum on EEC membership led to the implementation of a much-diluted version of the initial proposal, in the form of the NEB, a state-holding company, which ended up being used to rescue British Leyland and Rolls Royce from bankruptcy. The real source of polarization this time, however, came from the Right. With their neo-Liberal manifesto of 1983, the Conservatives engaged in systematic dismantling of the public sector.

Executive

The British executive maintained a firm commitment to the GATT. Britain's commitment to the United States, which many English since World War II have regarded as the key to their country's continuing status as a world power, guarded them against the temptation of protectionism. With one exception, trade policy, strictly defined, was not subject to partisan dispute: From 1979 to 1983, Labour's left wing displayed a staunch anti-Americanism, advocating both the withdrawal from NATO and the violation of GATT strictures against unilateral tariff increases. Even the CBI experienced the shock of protectionist ideas; at the annual conference of 1979, rank-and-file members rebelled and supported a protectionist motion put forward by the British Footwear Manufacturers' Association. This momentary slip was corrected at the next annual conference, when a large majority resolved against protection.[96]

Britain's commitment to the EEC is more problematic than its commitment to the GATT. From the outset, the issue was partisan; and it has remained so. The Labour Left strongly opposed entry into EEC. When its momentum within the party was strong, it could tip the balance in the party against the issue. Hence, the same Wilson who applied for entry in 1967 opposed a similar move by the Heath government in 1971, because the left wing was weak in 1967 but strong in 1971. Back in power, Wilson finally solved the conflict internal to his party by renegotiating the terms of entry and holding a referendum.[97] The defeat of the left wing of the Labour party over the issue definitely removed EEC membership from the agenda—until it was resurrected by the right wing of the Conservative party, under Thatcher. Capitalizing on the basically nationalist feelings of the masses and the discontent of small business because of European competition, Thatcher made EEC-bashing a staple of her government. In contrast, under the leadership of Neil Kinnock, the Labour party came to defend European integration.[98]

Thatcher's nationalist stand hurt her credibility among EEC members. In consequence, at first Britain had a hard time renegotiating its contribution to the EEC budget; and it had little if any voice in the shaping of the institutions. France and Germany were ready to go ahead with the Single Act, for example, with or without Britain's support.[99]

Policy Tools and Orientation

POLICY TOOLS

The content of the British tool kit reflected a compromise between Britain's economic need to rescue firms and industries from bankruptcy and its political incapacity to devise a stable, consistent industrial policy. British governments took a circuitous path around the dilemma, such as regional development and aid to the labor market. The contrast between the British and the French breakdown of public transfers to industry for the 1970s is sharp. It confirms hypothesis 5.8, which posits an inverse correlation between the quorum and the degree of disaggregation of public transfers. Table 12.1 shows that the proportion of subsidies channeled through direct subsidies was much lower in Britain than in France. Britain could not emulate French planning and industrial policy during that decade, because the parties found it futile to try to make the party system safe for tripartite agreements.

TARIFF

As hypothesis 5.5 would have it, the logic of the Western Alliance and the European dynamic led to the reciprocal elimination of tariffs between Britain and its trade partners (see table 11.2 in chapter 11 for a test covering the period 1946–79). Note also that Oulton's cross-industry study of British 1968 nominal and effective tariffs could not find explanatory factors that accounted significantly for inter-industry variation.[100] Instead, the author concludes that the cross-industry structure observed in 1968 is best explained as a reflection of prewar influences—a finding compatible with the hypothesis that reductions in the tariff since then have essentially been driven by rules of reciprocity.

NTBs

NTBs play a greater role than tariffs, yet one that is difficult to appraise. In the absence of longitudinal series, the party cycle hypothesis (hypothesis 5.3) cannot be tested. Qualitative sources report that the overall level of subsidies was reduced under Heath and Thatcher. The only study I have come across is Cable and Rebelo's cross-sectoral analysis of 1978 NTBs.[101] It found NTBs in those sectors that were afflicted by unemployment or in sectors in which developing countries enjoyed the comparative advantage of unskilled labor— hardly a discriminating result, since it applies universally to countries of the West.

The United States

Hegemonic Decline

Like Britain and France, the United States took a right turn with the election in 1980 of Ronald Reagan as president. This rightward shift was confirmed by the Democratic party's move toward the center after Mondale's defeat in 1984.[102] Had the policy process been party politics, as it was in Britain and as it became in France, the trade policy of the United States would have registered a decline in state intervention. In a country devoid of industrial policy and relying essentially on regulatory policies and bilateral international negotiations, state retrenchment would have meant a decline in managed and regulated protection. Instead, tariff barriers in the 1980s remained constant, while nontariff barriers increased.[103] The reason for this nonevent lay in the executive nature of the U.S. policy process which, until 1990, cushioned trade policy against the vicissitudes of domestic politics.

Explaining the continuity of the policy process by linking this process to the security imperative may seem an impossible task, given that the security imperative underwent serious revisions in the early 1960s and the 1970s. The concept—and, to some extent, the practice—of détente subverted the security imperative. Irrespective of whether the calming of the rivalry between the two superpowers was real or illusory, this question became a political issue that affected all the policies that were spinoffs of the Cold War. For instance, the debate on the military budget, a debate which, until then, had escaped partisan rivalry, became a proxy for the ongoing battle between those who wanted to increase social transfers and those who wanted to crowd social transfers out.[104] The remarkable point, however, is that détente did not subvert the GATT. The thawing of the Cold War may have justified a slowdown in defense procurements, but it did not justify scuttling the Western Alliance, of which the GATT was a pillar. The world remained bipolar and the policy process remained executive politics (hypothesis 4.3).

What changed was the part played by trade openness in the U.S. containment strategy. Whereas intentional trade self-discrimination was critical during the first decade of containment, its necessity faded once Europe and Japan became economic powers in their own right. As long as openness remained the pillar of the Western security alliance, there was no reason for the United States to assume more than its share of the burden, especially now that its postwar economic hegemony was dissipating. In fact, some began to argue that self-discrimination cut into U.S. security, for it undermined America's economic power in the long run. Such, in part, was the rationale for the Nixon administration's request, in 1971, for trade concessions from its allies. The so-called New Economic Policy was more than the "end of Santa Claus," as George Shultz was reported to have put it. It was instead, to use the words of a French editorialist, a "Marshall Plan in reverse."[105] Hence, while the Soviet threat kept trade tightly linked to security considerations, the rise of alternative economic poles in the alliance opened up new options for the United States in the determination of its trade orientation.

Congress, and not the State Department, was primarily responsible for taking advantage of these new options. The strategic redefinition was forced by Congress on a foreign agency often believed to place its bureaucratic interests above the national interest. The State Department suffered from a distinctive "trained incapacity" to appreciate the importance of economic factors, an incapacity that blinded it to the need to reassess the meaning of openness in view of the country's continuous economic slippage. Senator Russell Long summarized the situation with dramatic accuracy when he said that "U.S. trade policy has been the orphan of U.S. foreign policy."[106] Consequently, Congress withdrew guardianship of trade policy from the State Department and looked for acceptable foster parents. In 1962, negotiating authority was transferred to a newly created agency, Special Representative for Trade Negotiation (STR, later rebaptized USTR), which was placed under the President.[107] Organizationally, the STR office was (despite several upgrades, remains) a big head with a slim body. On the one hand, the STR conducts trade negotiations with GATT partners and chairs a cabinet-level interagency whose role it is to coordinate trade policy and advise the President. On the other hand, STR heads an agency which Congress purposely made weak in order to oblige it to rely on existing line agencies for information and analysis and thereby make it receptive to their respective institutional interests. It is often repeated in congressional hearings that the STR is the "honest broker" between various trade interests. The STR was institutionally designed to pursue a trade policy that, by and large, emphasized a fair distribution of the costs of free trade among its allies.

Congressional tampering with free trade and grand strategy did not reflect Congress's sudden interest in foreign policy. Rather, it stemmed from the logical working of executive politics in a representative system. Trade policy was still run according to the terms of the arrangement made in 1947: The President kept control over formulation of trade policy in return for consideration of congressional requests for the compensation of injured domestic interests. As the number of injured domestic interests surged in the 1960s and 70s, Congress often found itself vulnerable to protectionist influence and in serious need of executive help to keep special interests at bay. Congressional vulnerability was a consequence of executive politics, an institution that reinforced the hand of the executive, but which also stripped the popular assembly of all autonomy. Congress could not rely on partisanship to keep the interests at bay, nor did it share in the autonomy enjoyed by the President. Instead, Congress multiplied its requests for the White House to help by distributing side-payments and special treatment to special interests—mostly protectionists—who were threatening. Because the executive was dependent on congressional complacency for most legislative action, the executive could not afford to remain indifferent, but was constrained to renegotiate the scope of its trade authority at more or less regular intervals. Those renegotiations occurred principally during the passage of legislation that either authorized U.S. participation in a multilateral round of negotiations (1962, 1974, and 1986) or ratified the results of such negotiations (1967 and 1979). Congressional pressure made it impossible for the executive not to rethink the role of the trade variable in the security equation.

This second period of executive autonomy showed protectionist interests playing a larger role than during the postwar years, when U.S. industry was still unchallenged. This evolution is a direct consequence of the relative economic decline of the United States (hypothesis 5.6). Yet, as the next section is about to show, the overarching policy process evinced few characteristics of pressure politics.

Second-Tier Lobbying

The "national security" discourse is a consensual discourse. As such, it is a less effective means of gatekeeping than a partisan ideology would be. Consensus underproduces information and thus demobilizes voters. The policymaker can take advantage of the wider zone of voter's rational ignorance to engage in the practice of supplying rents, a product for which the demand considerably increased in the 1960s and 70s because the commercial superiority of American industry slipped away. Indeed, special interests have played a greater role in the definition of U.S. trade policy since 1962 than they did earlier. Using Congress as a sounding board, they acted to dispossess the State Department of its prerogatives in the trade area, because they found that department unresponsive to their demands. However, it would be a mistake to infer from the rise in rent seeking that there was a complete displacement of executive politics. Special interests remained so heavily mediated and interest competition so tightly regulated that, in the end, their impact on the policy outcome has remained circumscribed. Rent seeking thus did not fully displace executive politics; it developed as a pocket. Rent seeking was neither supreme nor free, but subordinate and regulated. These points will be developed, first, with respect to import trade, then to export trade.

IMPORT TRADE

The subordination of rent seeking to the main orientation of the trade policy is first observable in the practice of lobbying in Congress. Visible lobbying did not target the central orientation of the trade policy, which has remained freer trade; it merely sought exceptions.[108] I have already pointed to this trait in my survey of attendance at congressional hearings in the 1950s (see figure 11.1). Throughout, active lobbying in Congress was essentially reactive, and it reacted against the policy orientation. Besieged by protectionists in the 1950s, when the policy of openness was most actively pursued, hearings before the Ways and Means Committee attracted more free traders when the initial liberal orientation began to soften in the 1960s and 70s. Protectionists crowded Congress again in the early 1980s, in reaction to the rise of the dollar and the subsequent surge in import penetration.

The same pattern is discernible with regard to lobbying in the executive branch, where most of the lobbying was done by protectionists against the passage of legislation authorizing the executive to negotiate. The passage in 1962 of a bill that expanded the executive's negotiating authority resulted in the negotiation of special protection for five industries: cotton textiles, carpet, glass, lumber, and oil.[109] In 1974, during passage of another expansion, the administration negotiated policy exceptions with representatives from textiles, steel, ceramic dinnerware, certain types of ball bearings, stainless and alloy steel, nonrubber footwear, color TV sets, industrial fasteners, CB radios, and petroleum.[110] In 1979, ratification of the results of the Tokyo Round coincided with the conclusion of a second, domestic round of negotiations with the dairy, textile, nonrubber footwear, color TV set, and bolt, nut, and screw interests.[111]

Lobbying was reactive, for the reason that the market for rents was not free but was tightly regulated by the executive. As Finger, Nelson, and Hall have shown, protection is "administered."[112] It is subdivided into several "tracks," depending on the relative openness of the tracks to political influence. The "lower track," which includes antidumping and countervailing duty regulations, is governed by precise rules. The "higher track," which includes the escape clause, is more open to political influence. The higher track thus handles the cases that are too politicized for the lower track. In addition to these two tracks, there is a third, by means of which sectors strike an individual deal with the executive. Instead of attempting to form a broad-repeal coalition in Congress, protectionists go separately to the White House, promising support for freer trade in exchange for immunity from such liberalization.[113] Throughout the Tokyo Round, the USTR was flanked by a series of advisory committees, each staffed by concerned industrialists; these committees were concerned merely to add the finishing touches to the machinery destined to keep Congress a sanctuary, clear of sparring and lobbying.

The main rationale behind the administration of protection, as Finger, Nelson, and Hall argue, is to channel protectionist pressure away from Congress, while minimizing intrusions on to the executive's commitment to liberalization.[114] The executive is torn between, on the one hand, the need to defuse particular pressure on Congress through direct distribution of rents, and, on the other, the fear of allowing the awarding of those rents to undermine the substance of the liberal mandate. Channeling rent seeking into administrative and quasi-judicial procedures helps the executive to legitimize violations as well as to regulate the growth of the rent-seeking market.

The recent surge in antiprotectionist activity might be construed, however, to falsify this interpretation of the extant policy process.[115] Indeed, if the market for rent were as regulated as it is argued here to be, then producers who stand to lose from these rents should not organize antiprotectionist coalitions, but should rely instead on the executive to contain rents. When the executive concedes a rent to a particular sector, however, the executive can no longer be relied on to defend producers who are taxed by the rent. Indeed, this surge in antiprotectionist activity has taken place within the limited scope of product-specific debates, which have emerged in response to the sidepayments offered to protectionists by the executive on condition that they forego logrolling. With regard to the general trade debate, however, nothing has changed; there still is no free-trade lobby. Free traders, generally prompted by the executive, continue to organize on an ad hoc basis.

EXPORT TRADE

Exporters as a whole benefited considerably from the liberal orientation of the executive, but exporters as particular individuals did not. The administration of the Marshall Plan revealed in chapter eleven the intention of the executive to pursue goals that were long-term and general, and that offered little edge to the maximization of particular profits. As expected, exporters sought to capture short-term gains by reducing the State Department's voice in export promotion. Multinationals and bankers consistently pressed for the multilateralization of aid in the hands of the World Bank, whose presidents were carefully chosen from among Wall Street bankers and their regional equivalents.[116] By 1973, MNCs and bankers had obtained the multilateralization of 26 percent of total American aid, against 2 percent in 1965.[117] In addition, exporters sought to tie parts of the aid package to their particular needs. In 1954, the farm community got Congress to pass P.L. 480, a law providing for the sale of unwanted agricultural surplus in exchange for local, inconvertible currencies.[118] In 1959, all economic assistance was tied to American exports. Throughout the 1960s, the agricultural community sought the institutionalization of food aid programs for the relief of hunger in Asia. Throughout the 1970s, wheat producers sought to take advantage of détente to open the Soviet domestic market.

Over its lifetime, the Eximbank has been transformed from an instrument of foreign policy into a tool for export promotion—"Boeing's bank." Although export promotion was the Eximbank's mandate when it was created in 1934, from 1939 until the late 1950s, it was an instrument of foreign policy, lending successively to non-Axis powers in Europe, to mineral-rich Latin American countries, to non-communist countries in Europe, and then to LDCs.[119] Only in the late 1950s, under competitive pressure from Europe and Japan, did the Eximbank return to its initial purpose: export promotion. An amendment in 1971 sanctioned this reorientation by expressly directing the bank to provide financing that was competitive with the financing offered by the governments of foreign exporters.

From the perspective of the Department of State, these developments were double-edged. On the one hand, privatization of parts of the foreign assistance budget helped the State Department to muster a constituency for its foreign-aid program and thus slow down the isolationist trend that developed as soon as Congress grew weary of the strategic argument. The first ripple from that direction appeared as early as 1952, when the Republican party, committed to balancing the budget, won the White House and began to substitute hard loans, private investment, and larger imports for grants. The only remaining supporters were the public interest groups, whose leverage was virtually nonexistent.[120] Because the Cold War was abating and foreign aid was without a reliable domestic constituency, the State Department had to go along with the desire expressed by agricultural organizations and exporter groups to tie aid to the concurrent realization of specific domestic goals.

On the other hand, tying aid to exports curtailed the discretion of the State Department and, later, AID. Economic aid that comes with strings attached is less efficient than aid without strings. Moreover, the domestic constituency thus gathered is not reliable. For example, a decrease in the U.S. food surplus in the mid-1960s led farmers to lose interest in P.L. 480, precisely at the time when there was a sudden need for P.L. 480 for the relief of millions of victims of famine. In 1973, the Department of Agriculture withdrew its support altogether.[121] Having financed 26 percent of total agricultural exports in 1962,

P.L. 480 financed only 4 percent in 1973. In addition, the multilateralization of aid considerably limits the control the executive has on how funds are spent.

Still—and this is the point that deserves to be emphasized—exporters and multinationals could not afford to cut their ties with the State Department, because they needed the department to act as a bulwark against Congress's recurrent outbursts of protectionism. The State Department's fundamental commitment to a liberal order was the MNCs' only firm mooring in the unfriendly protectionist winds. Severing export promotion from foreign aid might have resulted in a backlash and served only to open the door to protectionist influence.

Exporters were aware of the danger. The recurring debate over centralization of trade-related functions in some upgraded version of the existing Department of Commerce continually found exporters on the defensive. They agreed with protectionists about the need to curtail the State Department's influence in the policy process, but not to the point of giving foreign trade up to the exclusive authority of an independent department—one similar to the old Board of Trade in Britain or MITI in Japan. The institutional outcome of this debate so far has been the dispersion of trade policymaking among a dozen or so agencies, including the Department of State, which are coordinated by the USTR.[122] MNCs recently revealed their basic anxiety during discussion of Senator William Roth's proposal in 1979 for the creation of a trade department to serve as the main vehicle for export promotion. The senator's proposal met with only cautious enthusiasm among the exporting community, who feared that such a department might become a captive of protectionist forces.[123] The Reagan administration endorsed Roth's proposal in June 1983; once again, however, the lineup for and against the proposal cut right through the export-import community.[124]

The ambivalence of exporters toward the existing policy process is further evidence of the executive nature of the process. On the one hand, exporters have been unhappy with the uncertainty of policy that derives from the trade-security linkage. On the other hand, they are afraid that severing this link would bring about pressure politics, a change certain to favor protectionists. The nagging desire of exporters to improve the status quo within the framework of the executive politics process is held in check by their fear of damaging that process beyond repair.

Executive Trade Leverage

The executive played a decisive role in the formulation of trade policy during this period. Since U.S. trade policy consisted essentially of regulatory measures (tariffs and quotas), which fell under the authority of the GATT, U.S. trade policy, unlike the British and the French, remained wholly the province of the executive. Furthermore, because the bipolar logic linked the survival of the GATT with that of the Western bloc, the executive did more than serve as a transmission belt between domestic trade interests and other GATT members. It also actively sought to keep trade policy in line with grand strategy. This was simply the continuation of the postwar setup.

What changed was the direction of trade policy. As the United States lost its trade advantage over its commercial partners, the link between security and unilateral free trade became tenuous. Congress pressed the executive for side-payments and special protection for certain industries, and the executive found itself obligated to extract trade concessions from countries whom it could not afford to antagonize, for security reasons.

This change in direction manifested itself in several ways. First, authority over trade was moved to the USTR, an agency evenly sensitive to security and commercial concerns. Second, the executive sought to renegotiate the international trade regime to its own advantage. Less able than other countries to resort to NTBs, the executive sought to expand GATT jurisdiction during the Tokyo and Uruguay rounds to include nontariff barriers (NTBs), such as subsidies, targeting, government procurement, and administrative protection. The executive also resorted to direct bilateral negotiations in order to safeguard domestic producers injured by imports. Although the United States has been the most frequent user of GATT article XIX, it has resorted primarily to bilateral export restraints, a less cumbersome discriminatory trade practice.[125] This is clearly demonstrated by figure 11.3, which computes the number (for want of dollar figures) of restraints enforced during a given year.

The United States has shown a distinctive preference for the negotiating table. Whereas Britain and France responded to the challenge of an open international economy not by inviting negotiations but rather by evolving (or at least trying to evolve) industrial policy means, the United States responded by resorting to VERs far more often than other countries did.[126] Even the EEC Commission seemed to prefer to deal with the Japanese challenge by means of regulation—antidumping, local-content and origin rules—though not exclusively.[127] Part of the explanation for the United States' propensity to negotiate stemmed from the unique configuration of the policy process—executive, with a pocket of pressure. An active trade diplomacy derives from a subtle mixture of credibility and inflexibility. On the one hand, the executive must be sufficiently free of domestic pressure to demonstrate to its negotiating partners a commitment to the success of the negotiations; on the other, there must be some domestic constraint which prevents the executive from negotiating away the interests of national producers. Congress played the constraining role in the United States by making the President's negotiating authority dependent on special concessions to injured domestic producers. The President was forced to extract concessions from the United States' trade partners in order to remain at the center of the trade policy process. Although Congress did not reduce trade policy to the status of a domestic issue, it did provide a counterweight that allowed the executive to focus on diplomatic activism on behalf of trade. U.S. trade leverage since the 1960s can be interpreted as the result of the executive process operating in a context of relative economic decline.

"Strategic Trade"

The duality of the policy process—on the first tier, the USTR pursued liberalization; on a lower tier, the International Trade Commission (ITC), Treasury, and Commerce handed out special protection—is reflected in the duality of industry trade "preferences." In their dealings with Japan, Europe, and certain Latin American countries, many U.S. firms have adopted a "strategic" approach.[128] Strategic trade is the translation of the GATT reciprocity principle to the level of the sector. Basically, it means that whether an American firm stands for free trade or protection is determined by what its Japanese counterpart does. The concept is very popular with all types of firms, because it subverts the distinction between free trade and protection—much as did the late-Victorian notion of "fair trade." Unlike Britain, where Gladstone struck down the concept, fair trade in the United States is very much alive. It owes its existence to the duality of the policy process, in which Congress is pitted against the President and the President against foreign governments, thereby placing the President in the advantageous position of extracting concessions from U.S. trade partners to avoid irrational behavior on the part of Congress. Were the policy process to revert either to pressure politics or to party politics, this constitutionally sustained balance would disappear. The administration's trade policy would then reflect the preferences of *one* dominant coalition (free trade or protectionist), and firms would have to choose their camp.

Failed Attempts at Partisan Mobilization

The policy process displayed very few traits of party politics. A look at the evolution of partisan bias in congressional votes on trade measures (see figures A3.1 and A3.2) confirms the thesis that policymaking was not party politics. The rise of the index in the 1980s should not be interpreted as a manifestation of partisan articulation. Another interpretation is more plausible: The rise reflects the fact that the presidency was in the hands of a Republican, whereas the majority in Congress was Democratic. Since Democrats tend to be more responsive than Republicans to the plight of workers displaced by Japanese competition, the institutional cleavage artificially reinforced the partisan cleavage.

The fact that trade has remained a nonpartisan issue can only be explained through the existence of a trade-security linkage. The comparative disadvantage that the United States shares with other Western European economies in labor-intensive sectors has made the party of the Democrats and of labor highly vulnerable to protectionism. In the 1950s, the cotton-producing South was the first to drift away from the free-trade consensus, when Southern politicians grew sensitive to the economic plight of the textile and oil industries. Then came the postwar alliance between big labor and big business, which crumbled in the early 1970s after the AFL-CIO endorsed the Burke-Hartke bill. That bill would have imposed mandatory quotas on all competitive imports, as well as a serious fiscal burden on the foreign investments of multinationals.[129] The bill did not get beyond hearings, but labor's new protectionist stance manifested itself in the Democrats' vote on the Trade Act of 1974. The unions' next major offensive against MNCs was the proposals in 1982–83 for establishment of domestic-content requirements. This UAW-backed legislation would have required a very high percentage of the value of motor vehicles sold in the United States to be attributable to domestically produced parts.

The Democratic leadership consistently resisted the protectionist onslaught. The reason is electoral. Protection was an irresponsible policy on security grounds. Had Democratic leaders endorsed the demand for protection, they would have condemned themselves to a position perceived by a majority of the voters to be particularistic, for favoring the interests of a factor against the interest of the nation. Unwilling to lose the median voter but unable to ignore the plight of organized labor, the Democratic leadership sought alternative policies. One way was to try to deflect the protectionist onslaught by means of subsidies. The McDonald proposal in the mid-1950s and the Trade Adjustment Assistance (TAA) program of 1962 were the first steps in that direction. In 1953, David McDonald, of the United Steelworkers (CIO), proposed the creation of a program of federal subsidies to firms, workers, and communities injured by foreign imports. The idea underlying the proposal was revolutionary: by socializing the cost of import-liberalization, the executive would abate protectionism at home. In 1962, the AFL-CIO made the legalization of the McDonald proposal its condition for further support of trade liberalization. The Democratic administration obliged and included the TAA program in its bill to Congress.

This proposal immediately moved the trade debate outside its traditional boundaries and into the broader issue of state intervention. Four groups crystallized around this development. Both the AFL-CIO leadership and the CNTP—the business group the most committed to trade liberalization—supported the administration bill. The rest of industry, whether import-sensitive or export-oriented, was opposed to it. Unions in import-sensitive sectors were willing to support TAA only in addition to protection, not as a substitute for it. The legislative outcome was in the form of a compromise. TAA was retained, but the criteria for eligibility were so tightly written that between 1962 and 1969, not a single trade-displaced worker actually got aid—and after the interpretation of eligibility was loosened in the early 1970s, only 48,314 workers won benefits from 1970 through 1974.[130]

Protectionism threatened to engulf the party once again during the oil crisis. In 1981, a new generation of Democrats became convinced that industrial policy could help bridge its internal party divisions.[131] Like adjustment assistance, industrial policy would substitute governmental subsidies for protection. The subsidies would help ailing industries, workers, and communities adjust to import competition. Protection against imports would also be granted, but only temporarily and only if the recipient was able to submit a plausible restructuring plan—similar to those submitted by Lockheed, New York City, and Chrysler, when Congress bailed them out in 1971, 1975, and 1979, respectively. In that regard, industrial policy was much more ambitious than adjustment assistance, for it gave the government a reasonable say in the way assistance could be used. The political goal of industrial policy, however, was the same: to reconcile import-sensitive labor to foreign competition and, in so doing, to make short-term assistance acceptable to export-oriented business.

Democratic initiatives eventually converged on the House Banking Subcommittee on Economic Stabilization which, under the leadership of its chairman, John LaFalce, held lengthy hearings on two bills, H.R. 4360 and H.R. 4361.[132] The bills aimed at institutionalizing three principles: targeting, conditionality, and tripartite representation. Targeting was soon dubbed the government's ability "to pick winners and losers." Its main vehicle was to be a bank. Conditionality—or quid pro quo—referred to the strings the government could attach to assistance. Tripartite representation referred to the composition of the supervising agency; state officials and representatives from both the unions and business would be collectively assigned the function of coordinating the policy.[133]

The legislative drive, and with it, the doctrinal synthesis, soon fizzled out. Both bills were reported but not acted on before adjournment. The partisan voting that resulted in mark-up did not go beyond the committee. Industrial policy became neither a rallying cry for the Democrats nor a focal point for the presidential campaign of 1984. The concept did not take off because, as the hearings made clear, the bills offered few prospects for reenacting the old New Deal alliance between Big Labor and Big Business. In only one industry, steel, did both labor and management agree on the concept of industrial policy. However, in sectors such as the automobile, machine tool, and aerospace in-

dustries, where management had coped with foreign competition by out-sour-
cing production, industrial policy received support from no one. Management
was opposed to it, and labor refused to consider it as a substitute for protection,
which was, in their eyes, the only measure capable of checking the export of
jobs.[134]

The failure of the concept of industrial policy reflected the inability of
Democratic leaders to stem the tide of the party toward protectionism. The
failure came at a time when Republicans seemed to be reversing their own
position on protection. Nevertheless, as already noted, the rise in partisan bias
in trade votes throughout the 1980s owed more to the institutional tension
between executive and legislature than to partisanship. After all, the Carter
presidency was not more protectionist than the Reagan presidency. In contrast, the recent breakdown of the Soviet bloc is bound to weaken the trade-
security linkage, dilute the national support for free trade, and perhaps make
the factor the decisive electoral force.

Policy Tools and Trade Orientation

POLICY TOOLS

According to hypothesis 5.7, high quorum correlates to a simplified toolbox.
Indeed, the United States did not augment its panoply of protective measures
(tariffs and NTBs) with subsidies to producers. The only subsidies distributed
were in the form of R&D, mainly through the Department of Defense (see
table 12.1). Whether or not D.O.D. subsidies constituted a camouflaged industrial policy will not be considered here; all we need to note is that, even if
the D.O.D. did proceed to a massive transfer of public funds to private firms,
including to the manufacturers of $435 hammers and $15,000 sofas, these
subsidies were essentially indirect—cloaked in, but also mediated by, the "national security" rationale. No comparison with the French case is warranted.

TARIFFS (NOMINAL AND EFFECTIVE)

According to hypothesis 5.5, in executive politics, changes in the tariff reflect
international negotiations. This fact is demonstrated in table 11.2. Yet, the
United States has received uncommon attention from political economists
intent on showing (by means of cross-industry comparisons) the relevance of
the rent-seeking (pressure) thesis. These cross-industry studies, however, have
failed to yield the promised results. The only economic variable that has consistently shown significant levels of association with high tariffs, whether
nominal or effective, is unskilled-labor intensity, hardly a discriminating finding, for it is common to all Western economies.[135] Several other economic
variables have shown expected results, but the results are not consistent.

Among those is the industry's growth rate—fastest-growing industries have the lowest duties—but the results are inconsistent from one study to the next.[136] Similarly, in some studies, but not others, the degree of industry concentration is found to be associated positively with tariff rates.[137] The consumer-goods ratio is associated with nominal tariffs, but not with effective tariffs, a result incompatible with collective action and thus with rent-seeking postulates.[138]

Lavergne found that, among the thirty or so variables he tested for four different years from the 1960s and 70s, the best explanation for the tariff structure at that time was the structure of the Smoot-Hawley Tariff.[139] Assuming that this variable does not pick up omitted (and still unknown) variables, "which influenced tariff levels in 1930 and continue to do so today,"[140] the most compelling interpretation for this surprising result was advanced by Finger:

> In essence, [Lavergne's] finding is simply that most of what was going on was a scaling down of the tariffs with very little change in their structure. The logic of the negotiating process ... suggests that variations from the 'scaling-down formula' mostly resulted from negotiators sticking with their reciprocity criterion, and were not due to the susceptibility of negotiators to interest-group pressures.[141]

Finger's interpretation is identical to hypothesis 5.5.

NONTARIFF BARRIERS

Unlike tariffs, NTBs work on the margin of the GATT and thus of the executive. With tariffs declining, NTBs should rise, to compensate. They should reflect the expansion of the pressure pocket itself—in turn, a reflection of the declining international stature of the country (hypothesis 5.6). The actual results are mixed. Different studies have yielded different results. Cross-industry regressions on NTBs exhibit a strong sensitivity to unskilled-labor intensity,[142] yet to capital intensity as well.[143] Concentration is also correlated, though at times positively[144] and at times negatively.[145] One study found the consumer–goods ratio to be significantly associated with NTBs.[146] Overall, it is hard to come to a definite conclusion with respect to NTBs. The approximate quality of the data also throws much doubt on the results.

The ITC activity has provided students of NTBs with a more reliable, albeit incomplete, source of data. Several findings stand out. First, there is incontrovertible evidence that petitioning and ITC activity (not outcomes) reflect variations in the business cycle,[147] as well as cross-industry variables[148] and the long-term decline of the U.S. economy from its postwar competitive supremacy.[149] Second, with respect to outcomes, several variables of pressure politics—size of the industry, political connections, poor performance—were found to correlate with ITC rulings.[150] Finger, Hall, and Nelson even found confirmation for their dichotomy between the "technical track" and the "political track," large, visible cases being more likely to end up on the political than on the technical track.[151]

VOTING PATTERNS OF CONGRESSMEN

Finally to be noted is the existence of a collection of studies that have successfully regressed specific congressional trade roll-calls on constituency-interest variables, such as industrial makeup, union campaign contributions, unemployment, as well as partisan affiliation.[152] These findings clearly confirm the idea that Congress is highly responsive to domestic factors, much more so than the executive.

What emerges from this pounding of beta coefficients and t-values can be more than a trifle unclear. The rising use of NTBs makes it inordinately difficult to reach a conclusion. All in all, it seems that tariffs are best explained by multilateral negotiations, whereas NTBs seem to be more responsive to factor and industry demands, a finding that reflects the general bifurcation of trade policy since the war between the GATT track and the track(s) that circumvents the GATT. Although NTB results are compatible with the present theory, the results regarding NTBs are also compatible with the standard political economy approach, which assumes the universality of pressure politics.

Conclusion

The post-1962 period perpetuated the trade-security linkage with respect to GATT for all three countries and, in the case first of France and then of Britain, with respect to the EEC. Tariff-making in all three countries remained the domain of international multilateral negotiations, and thus the province of the executive.

A major discontinuity between this period and the immediate postwar era concerns the fate of industrial policy. Adopted in France after World War II to circumvent the GATT-imposed ban on tariff manipulation, after 1966, the public practice of assisting private firms and entire sectors became a fixture of French trade policy. Successive British governments attempted to emulate the French. Despite the volatility of party politics and the fragility of CBI-TUC relations, they succeeded in developing their own system of allocation, albeit a less direct, less precise, and less stable one than the French system. These sophisticated policy appliances, however, did not survive the two oil crises. Feasible in moderate amounts, the subsidizing of industry became financially untenable. Alienated by taxes and untouched by transfers, traditional middle classes found attractive the antistatist discourse of the liberal Right. The demise of industrial policy coincided with the advent of party politics in France and with the end of corporatist trials in Britain.

A second, though more incremental change from postwar policy, was the rise in influence of the sectors in the United States. This reaffirmation of domestic forces did not displace executive autonomy, as it did in France or Britain; for it took place within the GATT framework. In the absence of support for industrial policy, successive administrations coped with the relative decline of U.S. competitiveness by working within the GATT margin of tolerance (escape clause, antidumping, countervailing duties, unfair trade practices) and the GATT silence (voluntary restraints). Since the GATT was the province of the executive, and since implementing most of the measures of special protection required bilateral diplomacy, the U.S. executive remained in charge. It did so, however, at the expense of furthering the growth of a rather extensive subarena of pressure politics.

EPILOGUE

COLLAPSE OF THE SOVIET UNION AND THE FUTURE
OF EXISTING ARRANGEMENTS, 1990 TO THE PRESENT

The collapse of the Soviet bloc in 1990 knocked away the security-issue foundations of the postwar trading system. Governments can no longer justify the existence of the GATT to their respective populations by invoking the need to keep the West united against the Soviet threat. The retirement of the nation from the field of trade policy leaves class as the largest potential mass constituency to be mobilized around the trade issue. In these circumstances, what is the future of executive politics in formulating the trade policy? The discussion that follows pertains mostly to the U.S. case. In Britain and France, pressure politics and party politics since World War II have structured the chief components of the trade debate—the allocation of subsidies. Only in the case of the United States does trade policymaking remain closely tied to the international multilateral trading regime. The additional question (the role and future of the EEC in the two European cases) is beyond the scope of this work.

A first line of argument is that a security risk—a diffuse fear of global annihilation—continues to exist. As a result, national electorates may be expected to penalize governments responsible for upsetting the status quo. Although this argument cannot be refuted on the basis of historical precedent (due to the unprecedented nature of the nuclear factor), it is nevertheless not a plausible argument. Precisely because nuclear war is unacceptable, the threat of a chain reaction from trade war and regime meltdown to military action is incredible. To be sure, there is always the possibility that a nondemocratic government may engage in risky tactics, but the link with trade is tenuous—too tenuous to expect French, British, and American voters to believe it. The threat to security seems to be gone for good; the trade agenda is thus freed from the gravity of strategic considerations.

We are left with three options: (1) pressure politics, (2) party politics, and (3) default, or maintenance of the existing institutional setup.

Lobbies alone are not capable of dismantling the executive process. Recall the tribulations of the protectionists in the early Third Republic, who had to wait twenty years for repeal of the international trading obligations contracted by the preceding regime. The most recent sixty years of multilateral trade negotiations have entangled the policymaking process in a web of international commitments. Moreover, dismantling the GATT is beyond the capabilities of any logrolling coalition, for two reasons. First, the policy process has the support of groups with general preferences, groups that enjoy an organizational advantage over special interests within the existing policy process.

Many producers who, in a different context, would pursue their own special interest, are unwilling to give up a process that allows them to pursue their general interests. Second, the present process offers alternatives to protectionists: antidumping and the escape clause, as well as other procedures which are easily accessible.

Only a political party is capable of dismantling the existing trade institutions of the executive process and restoring the conditions of pressure politics. And only a dominant party would have an interest in restoring pressure politics (hypothesis 4.4).[153] This would be the case, for example, if the Democrats were to become dominant and if they endeavored to reconstitute the New Deal alliance between big labor and big business for the support of a program of free trade plus subsidies. This eventuality seems somewhat implausible at the present juncture, given the financial impracticality of subsidies.

The requirements of party politics are less stringent than those of pressure politics. All that party politics would require is that the Democrats articulate the protectionist creed. Organized labor has been urging this course for quite a while, yet without success. Although they are a mass-based trade group, American blue-collar workers are no longer a median electoral force; and they are unlikely to become one in the future. The trade cleavage currently cuts center-left, splitting the Democrats down the middle. However, it is not unthinkable that a severe economic slowdown could make a protectionist of the median voter.

Short of such eventualities, the most plausible prediction is continuation of the existing setup. The process is sufficiently flexible to accommodate all sorts of interests, interests that range from exporters seeking access to Japan, to domestic producers battered by cheap competition from Asia. But how long can executive politics live on its own momentum? Continuation of this process implies that the United States must keep two irons in the fire: the discussion of liberalization measures with Japan and the European Commission, and the extraction of specific concessions from these same trade partners. It is difficult to see how the White House can reconcile these two activities for very long, now that the Red scare no longer provides the glue that held postwar institutions together.

Thirteen ─────────────────────────────────

Conclusion

> Sovereign is he who decides on the exception.
> (*Carl Schmitt, Political Theology, 1922*)

THIS BOOK OFFERS a general theory of trade policymaking. My concern has been, first, to integrate existing models of policymaking into an overarching framework capable of specifying the boundary conditions for each model, and second, to identify the rules of transformation that are capable of explaining shifts from one model to the next. The voters are the keystone of the framework, since, in an electoral democracy, it is the voters who determine the structure of the policy process and the changes in that process. In this chapter, I summarize the main themes of this book.

A Theory of Electoral Control

The central theme of this book is electoral control. Traditionally, such control was conceived of as the capacity of the electorate to choose policies directly. Although this ideal form is approximated when policy is made through party politics—that is, when different parties champion different policies and ask the voters to arbitrate—it is not universal, but rather is contingent on the presence of two electoral conditions: high salience and divisiveness. In this book, I offer an alternative way of thinking about electoral control, one that is more general and less restrictive than party politics alone. Voters control policymaking because elections provide policymakers with incentives to reproduce within their institutional microcosms the parametric structure of the electorate. Voters signal to their elected representatives the balance between particular and general goals that they wish to see struck by the legislative process. Voter control is indirect, since voters do not choose the outcome; rather, they create the incentive structure that motivates politicians to legislate in accordance with voter concerns. In short, if electors do not necessarily choose policies, they *do* choose the decision rules by which lawmakers make policies.

Institutional Slack

A first corollary of the electoral-delegation argument is the argument of institutional slack. Institutions are made up of layers loosely connected, which provide politicians with room for maneuver. The actual quorum and voting rule, the rules that determine the balance between particular and general policy goals, are not specified by a body of formal rules. In any event, it is difficult to imagine how a constitution could instruct a lawmaker to ignore particular pleas and focus exclusively on the general interest.[1] Institutional slack, indeed, is not a source of anarchy; instead, it provides within the system the very flexibility needed to make electoral control possible.

The strongest evidence for the existence of institutional slack is to be found in the interwar period, when devising a tariff was transferred from the legislature to the executive in all three countries, with no significant impact on policy process or policy outcome. Where it was once allocated by a decentralized committee system (as in France), the tariff came to be allocated by a decentralized system of sponsoring ministries. In contrast, where it was once in the hands of party leaders (Britain and the United States), the tariff came to be located within a central administrative agency.

The institutional-slack argument is at odds with traditional institutionalist explanations which posit the electorate as a source of policy instability that must be curbed by stable institutions capable of "inducing" stable policy equilibria.[2] The present study leads to the opposite conclusion. I argue that institutions created to induce equilibria are suboptimal, because (1) they unnecessarily remove a source of the slack which politicians, in bids for reelection, compete away; and (2) they are undemocratic, because they would remove the only consistent, reliable source of electoral control. Finally, institutions that induce policy equilibria are fragile constructs, because they attract the resentment of the losers.

Economic Indeterminacy

The second corollary of the electoral-delegation argument is that of economic indeterminacy. The economy does not determine trade preferences for a large majority of producers. Manufacturers seek a rent for what they produce; but they seek competition for what they consume. Further, their choice is not specific to the trade issue but has universal relevance: The choice is between maximizing particular versus collective interests. There is, as well, an intertemporal choice between short- and long-term payoffs. Economic indeterminacy is not a source of policy indeterminacy, because producers take their cues from the policy process. Typically, they seek rents in pressure politics—

that is, when the issue is not salient with the electorate; whereas they are more likely to seek a socially optimal outcome in party politics or executive politics—when the issue is salient with the electorate.

The idea that trade preferences are informed by politics has received ample confirmation. For instance, in the United States after the Civil War, we saw that Eastern manufacturers had a choice: press for lower tariffs in order to wipe out the excess war-induced production capacity of the West; or endorse the demands of Westerners for high tariffs and secure, in turn, a compensatory tariff on their finished products. The Eastern manufacturers endorsed tariffs, because the Democrats were no longer the party of free trade. By the end of the century, under Cleveland's presidency, U.S. exporters favored free trade, yet they did equally well behind subsequent Republican tariff walls by concentrating, dumping, and turning multinational. In 1881 and 1892, French industrialists were in a similar economic situation—choosing free trade in 1881 because they did not want to pay duties on their raw materials, but choosing protection in 1892 because a deal could be worked out with the agrarians. In the 1970s, when the process was pressure politics, French business supported industrial policy but opposed it in the 1980s, when the process became party politics. Even primary producers are sometimes open to several options: A standard demand of agrarians in both France and the United States in the 1880s was for free trade for everyone or rent for everyone (the rent being silver for U.S. farmers and protection for French farmers).

The economic-indeterminacy argument is at odds with the argument of Chicago political economists, who posit that the electoral process is faulty and the political system is a source of inefficiency.[3] Because voters are ignorant, have little incentive to get informed, and are vulnerable to ideological manipulation, argues Stigler, politicians end up doing pretty much what they wish—distributing rents to wealthy capitalists in exchange for cash, and thus generating mountains of dead-weight losses. As a mechanism of value allocation, therefore, democratic politics pales in comparison with the market, the only true process, says Stigler, for allowing "participation in proportion to interest and knowledge."[4] In this book, I question the critique of the economists. Economic indeterminacy yields the paradoxical result that ignorant voters are more instrumental in shaping the policy outcome than are resourceful industrialists. Moreover, although Stigler is right to blame rent seeking on voter's ignorance (rent seeking reflects the conditions of low salience and low divisiveness), the same ignorance is also capable of fueling an idealistic attack on rent seeking in defense of laissez-faire.

Systemic Indeterminacy

A third corollary of the electoral-delegation argument is the systemic indeterminacy argument. The modalities of physical survival, the ultimate end of foreign policy, are not always specified by the international system. Survival acquires a consensual and widely shared meaning only in exceptional circumstances, such as when a nation is aroused by a security threat. Short of this, the diplomat must root the foreign policy in a shallower soil made up of special and class interests. Diplomats pursue the national interest only when the nation is on their side; the rest of the time, they promote special and class interests.

The strongest evidence for the plastic nature of the national interest was found in wartime. During World War I, for example, President Wilson was able to rely on voters' urge for victory as justification for shedding his initial populist inhibitions and helping American industry extend its world-market share. The onset of peacetime immediately brought these achievements into question. In 1917, Clémentel, the French commerce minister, capitalized on popular intolerance for military setbacks to justify circumscribing the power of industrialists within the state. The end of the war, however, brought a rollback to all wartime changes. Similarly, in Britain, Lloyd George overcame the free-trade principles of his supporters at a time when such principles would have hampered the domestic war effort and made coordination with their French ally more trying. Peace returned the debate to the forefront and overturned the coalition government. Again, in Britain, World War II brought about the hammering out of a truce in industrial relations not equaled since. The end of the Cold War is about to open the gates of policymaking to a series of special and class interests which, until now, were restrained by the strategic imperative of the universal Red scare of the 1950s.

This argument conflicts with the realist and neorealist traditions, which equally discount the role of voters in foreign policy. The realists have long portrayed democratic governments as ineffective. Voter participation through parliamentary control, they argue, has made the conduct of foreign policy capricious, volatile, and unpredictable.[5] The neorealists claim that the systemic constraints are such that differences in domestic regimes do not translate significantly into differences in the conduct of foreign policy. This claim complements the realist view to the extent that it makes voter participation redundant.[6] The present work questions both strands of the realist tradition. Nondemocratic regimes are but the institutionalization of rent seeking in favor of the privileged. The governments of such regimes are more likely to entertain policies that are costly for the majority of the population and that have long-term disadvantages for the nation as a whole than are governments in democratic regimes, where elections provide the rest of the population with effective control over the scope and time frame of the policy goal.

Generally, the larger the support base, the better the approximation of a policy to the nation's interest. This proposition is observable even within the subcategory of democratic regimes. The preceding foray into the history of three countries confirms the hypothesis. Free trade, the only trade orientation in peacetime capable of approaching the common good, more often was the choice of factors than of sectors. Free trade drew greater support from the masses, whereas protection drew greater support from particular industrialists. Free trade was synonymous, first, with free food and then with anticapitalism (Britain), with trustbusting and then anticommunism (the United States), and with cheap bread and then socialism (France).

Realists assert that, because nations are selfish, they are prone to expansion, conflict, and war. If we assume that individuals are selfish, as this work does, is this assumption enough to make nations acquisitive? One way to think about this is to ask whether foreign policy has costs that are not borne by the people who mandate the policy. If the costs of war for a government are borne by disfranchised or misinformed nationals, a low expected booty might be enough for that government to start a war, because gains accrue to the minority and costs are spread among the majority. If nationals are included in the policy process, however, the expected booty must match the overall costs, since each voter makes his or her own cost-gain analysis. Wars that generate net overall gains are rare in a world where nations are keen on avoiding large-power imbalances.[7] Therefore, selfish individuals do not necessarily make nations bellicose.

The micropolitics behind the hypothesis that democracies are less prone to engage in wars than authoritarian regimes is logically sound.[8] It is as sound as the logic behind the hypothesis, that democracies are more likely to pursue free trade, stabilize currencies, and respect the environment than are nondemocracies. Of course, democracies will not always do such nice things; it is a probabilistic statement. Indeed, quite often, as the present study of trade has made very clear, they do not. Nevertheless, democracies are equipped with political institutions capable, now and then, of raising their aim above selfish, short-term targets set by small groups and, instead, taking aim at making the world a bit better and safer for its citizens.

"Sovereign is . . ."

Institutional slack, economic indeterminacy, and systemic indeterminacy are essential to the working of electoral delegation. To paraphrase Schmitt's definition of a sovereign—"Sovereign is he who decides on the slack and the indeterminacy." If there were indeed no institutional slack, or if that slack were entirely in the hands of some agenda-setter, there would be no room for popular sovereignty. If policy preferences were fully specified by the economy, then it would be difficult for the general interest to prevail over particular interests without risking an authoritarian backlash from excluded powerful minorities. If the international system structured foreign policy choices, then nations would knock together like mindless billiard balls. Voters are sovereign because institutional, economic, and international structures are loose.

Appendixes

Appendix One

Mathematical Appendix to Chapter Two

THIS APPENDIX completes and clarifies the assumptions and propositions offered in chapter two.[1] Closely following the outline of chapter two, the appendix sequentially develops the generic industrialist's lobbying calculus, the parties' calculus, the impact of the parties' decisions on the policy process, and ultimately on the industrialist's lobbying decision.

The Industrialist's Calculus (First Step)

Imagine a French firm engaged in the production of woolens. Assume that this firm is doubly import-sensitive: It consumes imported input (English yarn), and produces import-sensitive output (woolens). This firm can increase its profit in one of three ways: (1) invest in production, (2) lobby for a tariff on its output, woolens, and (3) lobby for free trade on its input, yarn. More generally, the profit-maximizing industrialist has three variables over which she is maximizing: (1) the quantity to produce Q, (2) the sum to spend on lobbying for a rent R generating negative externalities (tariffs, quotas, particular subsidies), and (3) the sum to spend on lobbying for a general policy measure G reducing negative externalities (free trade, general subsidies). G and R are not mirror images: more R does not entail less G, and a drop in corporate contributions does not automatically yield a greater G. The two lobbying strategies involve different policies, different externalities, different organization strategies, and different marginal costs.

The firm tries to maximize profit, that is, the difference between revenues and costs. Revenues are a function of both price and quantity produced. I assume that the firm is not a price-taker, but that, because of concentration, cartelization, or tacit collusion with the other firms in the sector, the product price instead is a function of the quantity produced Q.[2] The product price is also a function of the tariff on output R; for example, a rise in the tariff raises the price of the product and thus, under normal price-elasticity conditions, increases total revenues. Costs are of two types, production and lobbying. The marginal cost of production C is assumed to be increasing; it is a function of Q. The marginal cost of production C is also a function of the general policy G, because a lower tariff on inputs lowers costs of production. A second type of cost is the cost of lobbying, which is a function L of the resources expended on the general policy G and on the rent R. In notational form, the industrial-ist's maximizing calculation is thus:

$$\max_{Q,\ G,\ R} \pi = P(Q,R)Q - C(Q,G)Q - L(R,G) \tag{1}$$

with Q, R, and G the industrialist's decision variables.

Note that the specification of the maximization calculus would look differ-ently if, instead of involving tariffs, the policies R and G targeted subsidies to the firm. The variable R would drop out of the price function P, because subsidies leave usually product prices unchanged (unless they are financed through an excise tax on the very product that receives the subsidy); R would instead reappear in the cost function C, because subsidies reduce production costs.

Industrialists choose the profit-maximizing level of each of the three vari-ables Q, R, and G simultaneously while holding the other two constant; that is, they calculate the three respective partial derivatives of (1), setting each one equal to zero:

$$\frac{\partial \pi}{\partial Q} = P + Q\frac{\partial P}{\partial Q} - C - Q\frac{\partial C}{\partial Q} = 0 \tag{2}$$

$$\frac{\partial \pi}{\partial G} = -Q\frac{\partial C}{\partial G} - \frac{\partial L}{\partial G} = 0 \iff \frac{\partial L}{\partial G} = -Q\frac{\partial C}{\partial G} \tag{3}$$

$$\frac{\partial \pi}{\partial R} = Q\frac{\partial P}{\partial R} - \frac{\partial L}{\partial R} = 0 \iff \frac{\partial L}{\partial R} = Q\frac{\partial P}{\partial R} \tag{4}$$

In this book, I am interested only in the relative marginal efficiency of lobby-ing for a general policy to lobbying for a rent. This is given by the ratio of (3) over (4), that is:

$$\frac{\dfrac{\partial L}{\partial G}}{\dfrac{\partial L}{\partial R}} = -\frac{\dfrac{\partial C}{\partial G}}{\dfrac{\partial P}{\partial R}} \tag{5}$$

Equation (5) states that, in equilibrium, the relative marginal cost of the two lobbying strategies (left side) is equal to the relative marginal profit ex-pected from the two policies (right side). The first ratio is determined by the policy process; different policy processes entail different relative lobbying costs. In contrast, the second ratio is the product of technology and individual consumer preferences; a change in the tariff effects production and demand differently depending on extant market elasticities. In what follows, I take the ratio of marginal profits as given, and focus my attention, instead, on the determination of the ratio of marginal lobbying costs.

The Parties' Calculus

Relative marginal lobbying costs are a reflection of the policy process. The policy process, in turn, is a reflection of the electoral campaign; it is argued in chapter two that the amount of effort parties devote to the trade issue on election day both reveals and finalizes voters' expectations about how trade policy will be made after election day. I formalize the parties' campaign calculus; I then derive the impact on the policy process, and last the impact of the policy process on the relative marginal lobbying cost.

The setting of a party's campaign agenda under conditions of voters' rational ignorance can be analyzed as a spending game. The calculation according to which a party ranks issues in order of importance is analogous to the decision to allocate a given budget between various issues based on the party's assessment of the worth of each issue. The hypothesis developed in chapter two, according to which "parties are more likely to stress the trade issue on poll day if it is salient than if it leaves voters indifferent, and if it is divisive rather than consensual," can be derived from a mobilization model featuring two parties that each articulate one of two policy choices (free trade versus protection) and that expend "*effort*" to mobilize voters who would not otherwise be motivated to vote. Effort is a generic term encompassing cash, time, and voluntary human resources. The model allows us to predict how much effort each party will spend on promoting the trade issue, depending on the salience of the issue, its degree of divisiveness, and corresponding spending by the other party. Salience and divisiveness are determined exogenously.

There are two parties, indexed $i = 1,2$. The strategies are efforts. Party 1 and party 2 simultaneously choose their respective effort level x_i. The probability that party 1 will win is a function of how much effort it spends promoting its stand on the trade issue as well as how much the other side spends. Assuming the value of holding office for each party to be V (a constant) and setting the value of losing at 0, the payoffs to each party for promoting the trade issue are equal to the probabilistic benefit minus the cost:

$$\pi_1(x_1,x_2) = V f(x_1,x_2) - k_1 x_1 \tag{6}$$

$$\pi_2(x_1,x_2) = V [1 - f(x_1,x_2)] - k_2 x_2 \tag{7}$$

with $k_i \geq 1$.

The parameter k_i captures a party's spending efficiency. If $k_i = 1$, party i is relatively efficient at mobilizing voters on the issue, while, in contrast, if

$k_i > 1$, it is less so, for it magnifies the impact of cost x_i. The parameter k_i is useful in simulating the parametric conditions of salience and divisiveness: salience comes from the (inverse) size of the k_i's, while divisiveness comes from equality between the k_i's. Four cases are conceivable, depending on whether salience and divisiveness assume a high or low value. The combination of high salience and high divisiveness (case I) corresponds to the case in which both parties are very efficient at mobilizing voters in support of their side of the trade issue. That is: $k_1 = k_2 = 1$. Conversely, a case of low salience and high divisiveness (case III) is captured by the settings that satisfy the condition: $k_1 = k_2 > 1$. Consensus corresponds to a case in which one party— say, 1—is disproportionately efficient at mobilizing voters behind its trade stand. Consensus combined with high salience (case II) corresponds to the following settings: $k_1 = 1$, $k_2 > 1$. In contrast, consensus combined with low salience (case IV) corresponds to: $k_1 > 1, k_2 > k_1$. Before we can proceed to such simulations with numerical examples, we must first solve the game.

For simplicity, I assume that parties choose their strategies simultaneously and solve for the unique Nash equilibrium. Each party's problem (How much to spend?) can be written as

$$\max_{x_1} \pi_1(x_1,x_2)$$

$$\max_{x_2} \pi_2(x_1,x_2)$$

Using the ratio of party effort to total effort for each party's probability of success, $f(x_1,x_2)$ and $1 - f(x_1,x_2)$, the payoff functions are

$$\pi_1(x_1,x_2) = V \frac{x_1}{x_1+x_2} - k_1 x_1 \tag{8}$$

$$\pi_2(x_1,x_2) = V \frac{x_2}{x_1+x_2} - k_2 x_2 \tag{9}$$

Party i's reaction function specifies party i optimal effort for each fixed effort level of its opponent. If the π_i are differentiable and strictly concave, we can solve for these reaction functions using the first-order conditions. Let $x_1^*(x_2)$ be 1's best reply if 2 chooses x_2. $X_1^*(x_2)$ solves the following first order condition:

$$V \frac{x_2}{[x_1^*(x_2) + x_2]^2} - k_1 = 0 \tag{10}$$

By symmetry, the first-order condition for party 2 is

$$V \frac{x_1}{[x_1 + x_2^*(x_1)]^2} - k_2 = 0 \qquad (11)$$

The intersection of the two reaction functions $x_1^*(x_2)$ and $x_2^*(x_1)$ is the Nash equilibrium—that is, the pair spending levels (x_1^*, x_2^*), such that neither party can gain by a change in effort, given the effort level of its opponent. The Nash equilibrium satisfies $x_1^* = x_1^*(x_2^*)$ and $x_2^* = x_2^*(x_1^*)$. Using (10) and (11),

$$\frac{x_2^*}{x_1^*} = \frac{k_1}{k_2} \qquad (12)$$

Using (12) to solve (10) for x_1^* and (11) for x_2^*, we obtain the following results:

$$x_1^* = \frac{Vk_2}{(k_1 + k_2)^2} \qquad (13)$$

$$x_2^* = \frac{Vk_1}{(k_1 + k_2)^2} \qquad (14)$$

Equations (13) and (14) can be used to generate numerical examples with different exogenous values for parameters k_1 and k_2.

TABLE A1.1

Numerical Simulation of Variation in Salience and Divisiveness

	Assumptions				Results			
					Effort spent			Probability of winning	
Case	Salience	Divisiveness	Settings for k_1 and k_2	Numerical Simulation	by 1	by 2	total	for 1	for 2
				k_1 k_2	x_1^*	x_2^*		f	$1-f$
	high	high	$k_1 = k_2 = 1$	1 1	25	25	50	0.5	0.5
	high	low	$k_1 = 1, k_2 >> 1$	1 9	9	1	10	0.9	0.1
	low	high	$k_1 = k_2 >> 1$	9 9	2.8	2.8	5.6	0.5	0.5
	low	low	$k_1 >> 1, k_2 >> k_1$	9 18	2.5	1.2	3.7	0.67	0.33

$V = 100$

What is the impact of salience and divisiveness on spending? The more salient (cases I and II) and the more conflictual (cases I and III) the trade issue is, the more effort is spent on it.

Impact of Parties' Ranking of Trade Issue on Policy Process

The policy process is specified by the quorum and the decision rule. Quorum q is the minimum number of voters who, duly represented by their elected officials, allow the officials to make policies. It is expressed as the ratio of the total number of represented voters to the number of voters:

$$q \equiv \frac{\text{number of represented voters}}{\text{total number of voters}}$$

The quorum is a function of the salience of the trade issue on election day—that is, a function of the parties' combined spending x, that is, a function of their spending efficiency (the opposite of k_i): the higher the parties' combined spending efficiency (the lower the k_i's), the higher the quorum. A possible specification is

$$q = \frac{2}{k_1 + k_2} \tag{15}$$

with $k_i \geq 1$, and $0 < q \leq 1$.

The decision rule r can be either majority or unanimity; it is a function of whether the trade issue is divisive or consensual. The decision rule can be expressed as a function of the relative values of k_1 and k_2: the greater the spending efficiency differential, the more consensual the decision rule is. A possible specification is

$$r = \frac{\left| k_1 - k_2 \right|}{2(k_1 + k_2)} + \frac{1}{2} \tag{16}$$

with $k_i \geq 1$, and $0.5 \leq r \leq 1$ (note that in chapter two, r is restricted to the two extreme values, majority—$r = 0.5$—and unanimity—$r = 1$; this simplification follows from the reduction in chapter two of the policy process space to four types).

The Industrialist's Calculus (Second Step)

The argument is made in chapter two that the relative marginal cost of rent seeking to the marginal cost of pursuing a general policy $(\partial L/\partial R)/(\partial L/\partial G)$ is an increasing function of the quorum q and a decreasing function of the decision rule r. As the quorum increases, the cost of private lobbying increases, whereas, if the decision rule is majoritarian as opposed to consensual, more information is made available to the voters, thereby reducing the attractiveness of rent seeking to both politicians and industrialists.

Note, finally, that quorum and decision rule are, in turn, a function of the spending efficiency of the parties, which are in turn a reflection of the degrees of salience and divisiveness of the trade issue in the electorate. The industrialist's choice between investing in production, rent seeking, or pursuing a general policy measure is determined by the two electoral parameters, salience and divisiveness.

Appendix Two

Tariff Levels

THE AVERAGE nominal tariff calculated here is the ratio of customs revenue to imports. Although it is a standard way of measuring protection, the limits of this measure as an indication of a nation's trade policy cannot be overemphasized. In addition to recording changes in the degree of tariff protection, this measure reflects long-term changes in revenue tariffs (duties on tea and spices, low rates across the board, etc.) and short-term variations in import flows. Moreover, since World War I, the tariff has ceased to be the only form of protection and is, admittedly, a misleading approximation of relative levels of protection since the mid-1960s. The data for Britain after World War II are particularly deceptive, as the customs receipts until 1964 include several revenue tariffs. The time series for British customs revenue stops in 1964, as customs revenue was no longer reported separately after that year. From 1946 until 1979, however, the *Annual Abstract of Statistics* detailed the revenue generated by "Protective duties," whose ratio to imports is represented in figure A2.2.

FIGURE A2.1
U.S. Tariff, 1850–1987

FIGURE A2.2
British Tariff, 1850–1987

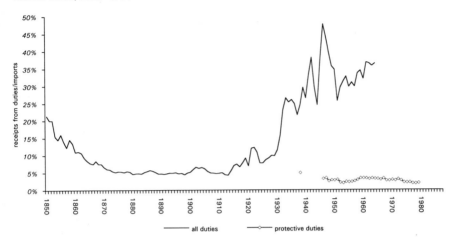

FIGURE A2.3
French Tariff, 1850–1987

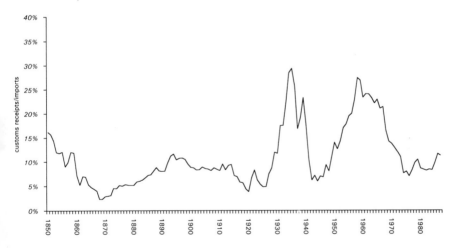

Sources: Source for Britain and France until 1975: Mitchell 1980: Series F1 and H5; thereafter: INSEE, *Annuaire statistique de la France,* various years. Central Statistical Office, *Annual Abstract of Statistics,* various years. Source for the United States until 1970: U.S. Bureau of the Census 1976: Series U-207 and Y-353; thereafter: U.S. Bureau of the Census, *Statistical Abstract of the United States,* various years.

Appendix Three

Partisan Bias in Voting on Trade Bills

THIS APPENDIX presents an indicator of party politics. The index of partisan bias calculated here is a chi square run on the two-by-two table representing the percentage of "yea" and "nay" votes for each party. In the U.S. case, the two parties are the Republicans and the Democrats. In the British case, the parties were reduced to two coalitions: Conservative-Unionist, on the right and Liberal-Labour, on the left. The chi square is halved so that it varies from 0 (no partisan discipline) to 100 (maximum partisan discipline). The use of the chi square is analogous, and the result is not intended to have any statistical significance. Except for a few notable exceptions, votes bearing on specific sectors or pertaining to specific countries or areas were not retained. Whenever several votes were available on a bill, the most representative was selected.

Several caveats must be noted. First, in the case of Britain, the index loses its significance after 1931, when the Liberal party allied with the Conservatives behind a protective platform. Second, the index could not be used in the case of France, because of the multipartisan nature of the party system. Table A3.1 reports the raw data. Third, the index could not be used systematically after World War II, because these two countries mostly relied on nontariff policies for which it is very difficult to find parliamentary roll-calls.

FIGURE A3.1
House of Representatives: Partisan Bias in Voting on Trade Bills, 1867–1988

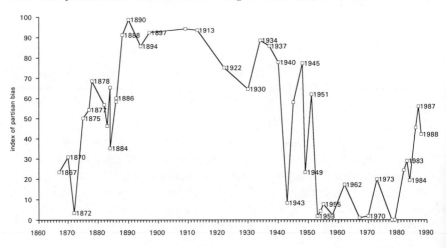

FIGURE A3.2

U.S. Senate: Partisan Bias in Voting on Trade Bills, 1867–1988

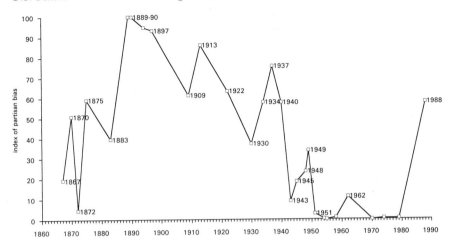

FIGURE A3.3

House of Commons: Partisan Bias in Voting on Trade Bills, 1846–1938

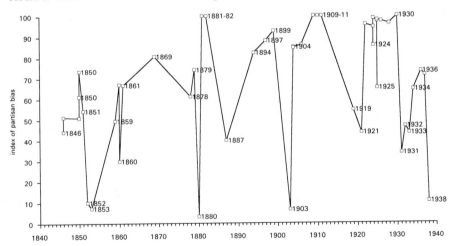

TABLE A3.1

Vote Breakdown on Selected Trade Issues—France, Chamber of Deputies

	Brame Interpellation Jan. 28, 1870		Feray Proposal Jan. 19, 1872		Tax on Raw Materials July 16, 1872	
	Protection	Free Trade	Protection	Free Trade	Protection	Free Trade
Extreme Right			19	8	8	20
Bonapartist	13	155	3	13	2	14
Right			97	56	61	67
Center Right			90	63	67	59
Center Left	12	31	37	71	55	45
Moderate Republican	3	18	28	82	75	27
Union Republican			3	53	24	21
Radical						
Other	4	8	20	21	17	8
Total	32	212	297	367	309	261

	Treaty with Italy June 7, 1878		Tariff of 1881 (Rouvier amend.) April 2, 1881		Tariff of 1892 (final vote) Dec. 29, 1891	
	Protection	Free Trade	Protection	Free Trade	Protection	Free Trade
Extreme Right					16**	18**
Bonapartist	20	54	47	23		
Right	45	3	51	3	117	5
Center Right						
Center Left	23	28				
Moderate Republican	94	87	190*	98*	183	27
Union Republican	20	26				
Radical	16	19	2	48	52	48
Other	7	3	10		18	5
Total	225	220	300	172	386	103

* Opportunist bloc.
** Boulangists.

TABLE A3.1 (*cont.*)
Vote Breakdown on Selected Trade Issues—France, Chamber of Deputies

	Berry proposal July 15, 1903		Oleaginous seeds duty Nov. 3, 1909		Tariff of 1910 (final vote) March 29, 1910	
	Protection	Free Trade	Protection	Free Trade	Protection	Free Trade
Independent	26	3	5	18	24	1
Liberal Alliance	41	1	29	27	50	4
National Republican	34	16	2	9	5	5
Progress Republican	75	7	7	16	17	7
Republican Union			16	20	26	4
Democratic Union	73	8	10	26	30	7
Democratic Left			9	18	26	3
Radical	58	11	45	42	83	7
Socialist-Radical	62	20	82	43	117	11
Extreme-Left Radical	13	10				
Parliamentarian Socialist	9	30	3	22	19	4
Revolutionary Socialist						
SFIO	0	12	0	52	11	35
Other	22	4	5	0	2	1
Total	413	122	213	293	410	89

	Tariff of 1928 Feb. 28, 1928		Delegation to Executive of right to modify tariff Feb. 16, 1937	
	Protection	Free Trade	Protection	Free Trade
URD	114	7	56	0
Independent Republican			64	9
Popular Democracy			13	0
Republican Left	76	7	38	1
Democratic Left			13	10
Radical	16	6		
Socialist-Radical	117	5	22	79
Independent Left			0	18
Republican Socialist	19	6	0	27
Socialist	26	6	0	147
Communist	0	21	0	72
Other	7	2	0	1
Total	375	60	206	364

TABLE A3.1 *(cont.)*
Vote Breakdown on Selected Trade Issues—France, Chamber of
Deputies

	Schuman Plan (confid. motion) Dec. 12, 1951		Rome Treaty July 10, 1957	
	Protection	Free Trade	Protection	Free Trade
Poujadist			35	1
Gaullist	116	2	16	0
Peasant	11	29	4	10
Independent	8	44	2	81
Overseas	0	10	0	6
MRP	0	87	0	74
RGR/dissident Radical			2	23
Radical	1	71	19	25
UDSR-RDA	0	17	1	20
SFIO	1	105	0	100
PCF/Progressive	101	0	149	0
Other	2	11	7	2
Total	240	376	235	342

Sources: Roll-calls were found in Chambre des députés, *Débats*. Partisan
affiliations were found in Adolphe Robert and Gaston Cougny, *Dictionnaire
des parlementaires français*, 5 vols. Paris: Bourloton, 1888–91; and Jean Jolly,
editor, *Dictionnaire des parlementaires français*, 8 vols. Paris: Presses Universitaires de France, 1960–77.

Roll-calls from the U.S. House of Representatives

Except when otherwise indicated, the vote selected is the one on the first
passage of the bill: Wells Bill, 28 February 1867; Tariff Act, 6 June 1870; Tariff
Act, 20 May 1872; Bill for the protection of the sinking fund, 23 February
1875; Mills Resolution, December 1877; Wood Bill, 5 June 1878; Eaton Bill
to create a Tariff Commission, 6 May 1882; Mongrel Tariff, conference report,
3 March 1883; Morrisson Bill, 6 May 1884; Converse Bill to increase the
duties on wool, 7 April 1884; Morrisson Bill, 17 June 1886; Morrisson Bill, 18
December 1886; Mills Bill, 21 July 1888; McKinley Tariff, 21 May 1890; Gorman Tariff, 1 February 1894; Dingley Tariff, 31 March 1897; Payne-Aldrich
Tariff, 9 April 1909; Underwood Tariff, 8 May 1913; Fordney-McCumber
Tariff, 15 September 1922; Smoot-Hawley Tariff, conference report, 14 June
1930; Reciprocal Trade Agreements Act (RTA), 29 March 1934; RTA extension, 1937; RTA extension, 1940; RTA extension, 13 May 1943; RTA
extension, 26 May 1945; RTA extension, 26 May 1948; RTA extension, 9

February 1949; RTA extension-Simpson amendment, 7 February 1951; RTA extension, 15 June 1953; RTA extension, 11 June 1954; RTA extension, 18 February 1955; RTA extension, 11 June 1958; Trade Expansion Act, 28 June 1962; Bill restricting imports from low wage areas, 28 September 1967; Trade Act, 19 November 1970; Trade Reform Act, 11 December 1973; Trade Adjustment Assistance, 8 September 1978; Trade Agreements Act, 11 July 1979; Automobile Domestic Content Requirement, 15 December 1982; Automobile Domestic Content Requirement, 3 November 1983; Trade Remedies Reform Act, 26 July 1984; Omnibus Trade Bill, 22 May 1986; Trade Bill, first vote, 30 April 1987; Trade Bill, first vote, 21 April 1988.

Roll-calls from the U.S. Senate

Wells Bill, 31 January 1867; Tariff Act, 6 July 1870; Tariff Act, 30 May 1872; Sinking Fund, 2 March 1875; Eaton Bill, May 1882; Mongrel Tariff, 20 February 1883; Allison Bill, 22 January 1889; McKinley Tariff, 10 September 1890; Wilson-Gorman Tariff, 2 July 1894; Dingley Tariff, 7 July 1897; Payne-Aldrich Tariff, 8 July 1909; Underwood Tariff, 9 September 1913; Emergency Tariff, 16 February 1921; Second Emergency Tariff, 11 May 1921; Fordney-McCumber Tariff, 19 September 1922; Smoot-Hawley Tariff, conference report, 12 June 1930; RTA, 4 June 1934; RTA extension, 1937; RTA extension, 1940; RTA extension, 14 June 1943; RTA extension, 20 June 1945; RTA extension, 14 June 1948; RTA extension, 15 September 1949; RTA extension, 23 May 1951; RTA extension, 24 June 1954; RTA extension, 4 May 1955; RTA extension, 22 July 1958; Trade Expansion Act, 19 September 1962; Trade Act, Long motion, 18 December 1970; Trade Reform Act, 13 December 1974; Trade Agreements Act, 23 July 1979; Trade Bill, 1988.

Roll-calls from the British House of Commons

Repeal of the Corn Laws, 15 May 1846; Tariff on sugar, 28 July 1846; amendment to Queen's address, div. no. 2, 1 February 1850; Disraeli's motion for a committee on agricultural distress, 21 February 1850; motion declaring injust the equalization of sugar duties, 31 May 1850; Disraeli's motion on agricultural distress, 13 February 1851; Palmerston's amendment, 26 November 1852; Hume's motion to repeal the import duties, 3 March 1853; repeal of wood duties, 3 March 1859; Du Cane's motion, 24 February 1860; vote of address approving treaty of commerce with France, 9 March 1860; repeal of misc. duties, 9 May 1861; treaty with France, 18 June 1869; wine duties, 1 March 1878; Indian duty, 4 April 1879; one-sided free trade, Wheelhouse's motion, 13 February 1880; foreign treaties, Richtie's motion, 12 August 1881;

Richtie's motion, 24 March 1882; Merchandise Marks Act, 27 January 1887; Foreign Goods Bill, Vincent's amendment, 2 May 1894; Foreign Prison-Made Goods Bill, 13 May 1897; Indian sugar bounties, 15 June 1899; corn duty, Chaplin's motion, 22 June 1903; Morley's amendment, 15 February 1904; Pirie's motion, 9 March 1904; Kitson's motion, 13 March 1906; Tariff Reform, Chamberlain's amendment, 19 February 1909; Chamberlain's amendment, 24 February 1910; Chamberlain's amendment, 9 February 1911; imperial preferences, Benn's amendment, 7 May 1919; Safeguarding of Industries Act, 7 June 1921; Simon's amendment, 4 December 1922; McKenna Duties, Baldwin's motion, 13 May 1924; imperial preferences, Baldwin's motion, 18 June 1924; Benn's amendment, 17 December 1924; McKenna duties, Sinclair's amendment, 9 June 1925; imperial preferences, clause 8, 12 June 1925; Safeguarding, 16 December 1925; Thomas' amendment, 8 June 1926; Dixey's motion, 1 May 1928; Baldwin's motion, 19 July 1930; Abnormal Importations Act, 19 November 1931; Import Duties Bill, 25 February 1932; Acland's amendment to address, 28 November 1933; retaliatory import restrictions, 26 June 1934; Key Industry duties, 9 June 1936; Anglo-Canadian trade agreement, Foot's amendment, April 1937; McKenna duties, 22 June 1938.

Sources: For the United States: *Congressional Record* (various years); *Biographical Directory of the American Congress, 1774–1927*, Washington, D.C.: U.S. Government Printing Office, 1928; *Congressional Quarterly Almanac* (various issues). For Britain: *The Hansard Parliamentary Debates* (various years); F.W.S. Craig, *British Parliamentary Election Results, 1832–1885*, London: Macmillan 1877; various issues of the *Liberal Magazine*; and A. Lawrence Lowell, "The Influence of Party Upon Legislation in England and America," *Annual Report of the American Historical Association for the Year 1901* 1 (1902) 319–542.

Notes

Introduction

1. The seminal contribution is Waltz 1979. On trade, see Krasner 1976; Gilpin 1987; and Lake 1988.

2. The U.S. watch industry in the 1950s and 1960s justified its call for protection in terms of that industry's contribution to national defense.

3. This paragraph and the rest of the book draw from the literature on public choice. For a stimulating treatment of policies of expansion along analogous lines, see Snyder 1991.

4. The partition of the field of international relations into different levels of analysis is useful, but it should not be allowed to evolve into a competition between levels of analysis. The unitary level of analysis is no more a rival approach to the study of the international system than rational choice is to the study of economics. Microanalysis in any field is useful to check the logical soundness of macroaggregates. The former provides the foundations for the latter, not an alternative. Nor are systemic theories any more exempt from examining their assumptions than Keynesian theory was. The claim that bad assumptions will be weeded out through empirical testing is poor methodology; given the chronic dearth of case studies in international relations, such a methodology is wasteful and improbable. (A similar criticism has been levied in a different form by students of process-tracing. See Aggarwal 1985; George and McKeown 1985.) The field is not split into levels but into mutually exclusive clusters of mutually reinforcing micro- and macropropositions.

5. Schattschneider 1935.

6. On collective action, See Olson 1965. On rent seeking, see the Chicago Political Economy School of Regulation: Stigler 1971; Posner 1974; Becker 1983; Peltzman 1976; also Krueger 1974. On applications to the tariff, Pincus 1977; McPherson 1984; Rowley and Tollison 1986; Magee, Brock, and Young 1989. In political science, studies using one form or another of the rent-seeking model alternatively focus on sectors: Schattschneider 1935; Kurth 1979; Gallarotti 1985; Cassing, McKeown, and Ochs 1986; W. Hansen 1990. On factors of production, Rogowski 1989; or both Gourevitch 1986 and Ferguson 1984.

7. On institutions and trade policy, see Katzenstein 1977; Krasner 1977. See also Pastor 1980; Hody 1986; Rogowski 1987; Haggard 1988; Finger, Hall, and Nelson 1982. Recent institutionalist work concentrates on congressional delegation: Goldstein and Weingast 1991; Lohmann and O'Halloran 1991.

8. On trade and ideology, Kindleberger 1951, 1975; Ruggie 1982; Goldstein 1986, 1988; Rohrlich 1987.

9. For a schematic illustration of the notion of cycling majority and appropriate references, see chap. 2, note 27.

10. This is the central concept of the structure-induced equilibrium literature, a subfield in itself. See Shepsle and Weingast 1981.

11. Riker 1980: 444–45.

12. Downs 1957.

13. For instance, Schattschneider 1935; Magee, Brock, and Young 1989; and many others (for a complete list, see chap. 12).

14. For instance, Katzenstein 1976; Zysman 1977; Schmidt 1988.

15. For instance, Platt 1968; Stewart 1978.

16. Assuming a one-dimensional, left-right axis, the *median voter* is defined as the voter situated at the median. In a policy process in which voters directly decide policy, the policy outcome reflects the preference of the median voter. See Downs 1957.

17. Another problem with the social-science-qua-deductive mode of presentation is that its greater (abstract) added value seriously reduces its scrap value whenever the added value dissipates.

Chapter One

1. The value of an endogenous variable is explained by and determined within the model, whereas the value of an exogenous variable is predetermined or determined outside the model. For instance, z is an endogenous variable in the model (x, y, z) if the value assumed by z is partly or fully dependent on the values assumed by x or y. Conversely, z is exogenous if its value is fixed independently of the values assumed by x or y (for instance, rainfall, in econometric models).

2. See introduction, note 6.

3. Krasner (1977) and Katzenstein (1977) point to cross-national differences in the respective roles played by special interests and state officials. Lake (1988) links the ability of state officials to prevail over special-interest groups and parties to their country's relative international power.

4. On ideology and interest, see introduction, note 8. On the impact of the issue scope on coalition-building, see Lowi 1964. On the impact of institutions on coalitions, see introduction, note 3. Finger, Hall, and Nelson (1982) show the impact of different simultaneous U.S. institutional setups on the policy orientation. See also Marks and McArthur 1990. John Mark Hansen (1990) shows the impact of the tax constraint on the size and nature of coalitions.

5. The median-voting model was first offered by Downs (1957). For a useful contrast between rent-seeking and median-voting models, see Mueller 1989: chaps. 10–11. For an application of the median-voting model to trade policy, see Mayer 1984; O'Halloran 1991.

6. Schattschneider 1960.

7. "Revisionist" historians also have sought to reduce every aspect of American politics to rent seeking. They have succeeded only insofar as they have trivialized the concept of rent seeking.

8. "Path dependency" means that the range of institutional and policy choices offered to actors at any given time is constrained by the choices made at an earlier time. On path dependency, see North 1991; Krasner 1984. Katzenstein (1977) stresses the importance of historical legacies. See also Skowronek 1982; March and Olsen 1989. On parties, see Lipset and Rokkan 1967.

9. It is the absence of such slack that makes authoritarian regimes dependent on particular policy coalitions. The most striking instance of this was Bismarck's Germany, a regime built on a tariff coalition between agriculture and heavy industry. In

authoritarian regimes, every policy debate can potentially degenerate into a constitutional debate; see Wehler 1985. For a forceful argument that stable democratic institutions do not, or should not, preempt the policy outcome, see Przeworski 1991.

10. For a brilliant elaboration on this theme, see Schattschneider 1960.

11. This literature is listed in the introduction, note 8.

12. On the specific factors and Heckscher-Ohlin models, see Stolper and Samuelson 1941–1943; Magee, Brock, and Young 1989; Rogowski 1989: 16–20.

13. Magee, Brock, and Young 1989: chap. 18.

14. On this, Bhagwati 1972.

Chapter Two

1. For an exposition of this debate, consult Pitkin 1967: 144–67.

2. See chap. 1.

3. The classic contribution is Alchian and Demsetz 1972.

4. On congressional delegation, see Kiewiet and McCubbins 1991; Goldstein and Weingast 1991; Lohmann and O'Halloran 1991; McCubbins, Noll, and Weingast 1987.

5. The use of the word *rent* in this context derives from the economic concept of *monopoly rent*, which the government can help generate in favor of a firm. I use the concept in a broader sense to designate any political measure that the government can take to favor a firm that is in violation of market competition.

6. An externality occurs when the adoption of a policy intended for an industry has an unintended impact on the utility of other industries or individuals. The externality can be either negative or positive. See Mueller 1989: 25. The definition of "positive" or "negative" is not self-evident, but depends, in turn, on the definition of the social goal. If wealth maximization is the social goal, then free trade is a policy that generates positive externalities. But if security is the social goal, free trade produces positive security externalities with allies but negative ones with enemies. The prior question, therefore, is who defines the social goal; I argue in chap. 5 that the voters do.

7. See chap. 1, the section on "Trade Preference Formation."

8. Downs 1957.

9. The reader may wonder why the parties clash on the trade issue rather than articulate the median voter's preference. The fact is that parties must be consistent, for rationally ignorant voters penalize politicians who change their positions too often. As a result, partisan cleavages are rigid (Lipset and Rokkan 1967).

10. *Webster's Ninth New Collegiate Dictionary* 1989.

11. Schattschneider 1935.

12. The principal-agent terminology is borrowed from agency theory. It refers to a model of information asymmetry, in which one party, called the "principal," hires a second party, called the "agent," to perform some task. The agent knows something that is relevant to but unknown by the principal, usually pertaining to the moral qualities and competence of the agent. The problem is to design a contract that maximizes the principal's utility. This model is sufficiently universal to be applied to political relations of the types voter-representative, lobby-policymaker, and legislature-executive.

13. Lord Derby, *London Times*, 2 December 1887; cited in Brown 1943: 18.

14. As Rouvier, a politician of the Third Republic, put it: "Protéger tout le monde, c'est protéger personne" ["To protect everyone is to protect no one"]. Cited in Augé-Laribé 1950: 232. For a formal demonstration of the instability of oversized logrolling coalitions, see Riker and Brams 1973.

15. This example is borrowed from Yandle 1989: 29–53. Another example in the trade area is the marriage of convenience between multinational corporations and the Committee to Strengthen the Frontiers of Freedom, whose purpose was to increase foreign aid programs in America in 1959 (and increase U.S. sales abroad); see Rice 1963: 184.

16. We will see in chap. 4 that the difficulties that a concentrated interest lobby faces in associating with a public majority vanish if the lobby can convince the lawmakers that it speaks on behalf of that majority.

17. The "contagion effect" is borrowed from Schattschneider (1960: chap. 1).

18. "Shirking" describes the behavior of the agents of agency theory, whose relationships with their respective principals are typically fraught with cheating. Agent shirking is made possible by the fact that monitoring is costly to the principal in ordinary conditions of limited information. See note 12.

19. The word "stacked" is from McCubbins, Noll, and Weingast (1987).

20. Ferguson (1983) takes an extreme position on this issue. Magee, Brock, and Young (1989) take an intermediate position, granting a priori as much importance to cash as to votes.

21. Note also that the propaganda effect is ruled out of the analysis by the assumption of voter rationality.

22. Ferguson 1983. See also Edelman 1960: 702. Note the similarity of the take-over hypothesis to the argument presented by Williamson (1987): a firm that is engaged in a risky and costly contractual relation can reduce its exposure by means of vertical integration, that is, by substituting internal organization to market contracting.

23. The takeover may in fact inadvertently increase field costs, since the policymaker is perceived to be the agent of a special interest and voters penalize politicians who cater too much to private interests. This is the "distortion effect" modeled by Magee, Brock, and Young (1989: 39).

24. A commentator on an earlier draft of this book suggested that verticalization in the Williamson (1987) model does not imply the integration of the consumers, and thus, should not include the voters in the present analysis. Although the point is well taken, it confirms the limits of the verticalization solution in the realm of rent production. The voters are a critical link in the chain of events that begins with the lobby's contribution and ends with the actual passage of the rent: lobby-agent-voters-rent. Integration cannot go beyond the agent; only the costs specific to the lobby-agent relation (shirking) can be internalized. The costs pertaining to the agent-voters relation (field, choice set) cannot.

25. Magee, Brock, and Young 1989.

26. The increase in the quorum alters the linear relation between cash and rent postulated by the Chicago school, replacing it with an S-shaped curve, representing a threshold effect and decreasing marginal returns. I owe this insight to Jason Cawley. This finding is not specific to electoral politics; for a similar argument in the field of regulatory politics, see Noll 1983: 399.

27. To see this, first consider the standard cycling situation: three voters (1, 2, and 3), three choices (A, B, and C), and a simple voting cycle (1 prefers A to B to C, 2 prefers B to C to A, and 3 prefers C to A to B). The winning issue depends on the voting procedure: A wins if the voting procedure pits B against C, and then B, the winner of this contest, against A (Procedure I); B wins if the voting procedure first pits C against A, and then C against B (Procedure II); and C wins if the voting procedure first pits A against B, and then A against C (Procedure III). A prior vote on the procedure to use would yield the very same cycling effect as voting on the issues themselves (Riker 1980: 444–45). No cycling of this kind plagues the delegation model presented here. Indeed, if voter 1 believes that issue A is more salient than B and issue B more salient than C, and voter 2's rank ordering is B-C-A, and voter 3's is C-A-B, then neither A nor B nor C is salient, since an issue is salient only if at least two out of the three voters rank it first. The same reasoning applies to divisiveness. Consider again the voting cycle just described: voter 1 prefers A to B to C, voter 2 prefers B to C to A, and voter 3 prefers C to A to B. There is no cycling possible here, because this is an unequivocal case of divisiveness, whereas consensus would require the three to share the same preference ordering.

Chapter Three

1. On these models, see Stolper and Samuelson 1941–1943; Magee, Brock, and Young 1989; Rogowski 1989: 16–20.

2. On the security effects of trade, see Gowa 1989.

3. On electoral uncertainty in comparative and historical perspective, Silberman 1993.

4. The best account still is Lipset and Rokkan 1967, which argues that all party systems in the nineteenth century reproduced the farm-industry cleavage, and then the workers-employers cleavage, either as realignments of the existing parties, or as new parties.

5. On two-party systems, Schattschneider 1960; on multiparty systems, Luebbert 1986.

6. See Kirchheimer 1966; Habermas 1973; Crozier, Hungtington, and Watanuki 1975; Beer 1982.

7. See Kindleberger 1975; Rohrlich 1987.

8. This does not mean that the party leader can arouse that support merely by restating general, long-term goals; specific promises are always needed. The role of such promises is less to commit leaders to the implementation of a particular program than to convey the party's ideological message. Ramsey MacDonald reminded his Labour party fellows in 1928 that "the production of a mere list of items of a programme, after the manner of the Newcastle Programme, was not the right way to go about the business." The program is "meaningless" unless it leads the voters to see "that, for example, when you say 'pensions' . . . you convey to the minds of your audience not merely a money payment, but a new system of society which is going to do justice to the weak, the needy and the abandoned." Cited in Beer 1965: 137.

9. Fiorina 1974.

10. Schattschneider 1960: chap. 1.

Chapter Four

1. Olson 1965.
2. Schattschneider 1960: 39–40.
3. Hansen 1991.
4. On the importance of reputation, see Dougan and Munger 1989. Students of party systems have consistently been struck by the small number of existing cleavages and their longevity. Lipset and Rokkan (1967) have reduced the complexity of European party systems to four cleavages: center-periphery (ethnic and linguistic), religious, urban-rural, and class. Especially puzzling has been the durability of the so-called "pre-industrial cleavages": center-periphery and religious. In comparison, industrial cleavages (urban-rural and class), although more recent, have not held as steady. I suggest that part of the explanation has little to do with socioeconomic and environmental factors, but simply derives from both voters' and policymakers' preferences for stable cleavages, the former out of a concern for politicians' accountability, the latter out of a desire to lock in broad segments of the electorate and turn voters into stable sources of support whenever the cleavage is reactivated.
5. The example is from Yandle (1989); see chap. 2.
6. For a study of incredible threats on the part of local party organizations, see Tsebelis 1990.
7. On the concept of corporatist agreement, see Schmitter 1981.
8. The phrase is from Herman Lebovics (1988).
9. These cases are developed respectively in chaps. 8, 11, and 12.
10. Schmitter 1981.
11. Lehmbruch (1979: 155) made the opposite argument—corporatism is a response to the inability of modern party systems to steer the economy. Short of making a functionalist argument, however, it is hard to see how a competitive party system could lay the foundations for peak associations to short-circuit that system.
12. Another example of corporatist bargain designed to secure a partisan coalition behind free trade is found in Sweden; see Pontusson 1992. For a more general statement, see Lehmbruch 1986.
13. Waltz 1979.
14. There is no need to assume that security is always a matter of executive politics. Like any other issue, security may be articulated by party politics or be captured by special interests. But in a situation of external emergency, defined as a threat that is both military and inescapable, the security issue becomes ipso facto an executive matter, drawing the trade issue in its wake.
15. Waltz 1967: 9.
16. This point is developed in chap. 10.
17. On overpriced toilet seats and coffeemakers, see *Wall Street Journal*, June 23, 1987, p. 31. The Eisenhower Administration unabashedly granted quotas to the oil industry to maintain an adequate domestic supply of petroleum in the event of war, "a remark calculated to elicit uproarious laughter at the Petroleum Club," Stigler (1971) rallied.
18. On capture, Bernstein 1955; Kolko 1963. On rent seeking, Stigler 1971; Posner 1974; Peltzman 1976.
19. The present critique draws from a wide literature, including, among others, Noll 1983; Weingast 1984; Fiorina 1985; and McCubbins, Noll, and Weingast 1987.

20. McCubbins, Noll, and Weingast 1987; also Messerlin 1983. Consult Yandle and Young 1986 for a typology of regulatory agencies into "captured" and "uncaptured."

21. The broad definition of institutional interest is offered by Pastor (1980). The narrow definition has not been applied to trade; the seminal work in policy areas other than trade is Niskanen 1971.

Chapter Five

1. For an example of this paradoxical combination of assumptions, i.e., that voters are rational ignorant, yet prefer free trade, see Magee, Brock, and Young 1989.

2. For the sake of simplicity, this point was omitted from the initial presentation in the flowchart of fig. 2.1. The corrected flowchart is offered in fig. 5.1. Note that this correction only applies to the variable "orientation"; for the variable "tools," the initial formulation is still valid.

3. For instance, business's response to the rise of the working-class movement could not be effectively handled by sector associations, but led to the creation of factorwide employers' organizations.

4. The point was made by Bauer, Dexter, and Pool (1963: 332–40).

5. On the business cycle, Gallarotti 1985; Cassing, McKeown, and Ochs 1986.

6. Lipset and Rokkan 1967.

7. Rogowski 1989.

8. Here is the demonstration that, under the assumption that parties lose power every time the economy slows down, the business cycle and the party cycle are bound to fall out of phase. Assume that the party advocating free trade is in power. The economy slows down, and the protectionist party is thrust into power; so far, the two cycles reinforce each other. The economy recovers, then stumbles again. This time, the free trade party is returned to power because it claims that protection is responsible for the downturn; the two cycles work at cross purposes. The effects of the business cycle are canceled by the dynamic of partisan competition.

9. The argument could be made that the cycle most likely to be felt in executive politics is the electoral cycle. The head of state is led to favor domestic interests over international interests every time her mandate or that of the members of her party comes up for renewal.

10. On longitudinal variations, see Maier 1975; Ruggie 1982; Goldstein 1986.

11. The usual attribution is to Tinbergen 1967, chap. 3.

12. On contagion, see Schattschneider 1960; also chap. 2.

13. The prediction that pressure politics is a requisite to industrial policy conflicts with standard accounts of industrial policy. The current (institutionalist) literature associates industrial policy with "strong states," an institutional reality thought to make room for decisional autonomy on the policymaker's part. In contrast, so-called "weak states," the closest institutional rendition of pressure politics, are considered unable to establish an industrial policy. See Katzenstein 1976; Zysman 1977.

Chapter Six

1. For earlier examples of states operating as parties, see Gramsci 1971: 227.

2. For the period 1860–1914 see, for example, on the United States, Beard and

Beard 1927; Beale 1930; on France, Smith 1980; on Britain, Tolliday 1984 and 1987; Semmel 1960; Rempel 1972; on all three countries, Gourevitch 1986. For the interwar period, on the United States, see Ferguson 1984; on Britain, Capie 1983; on all three countries, Gourevitch 1986. For the postwar era, on the United States, see Kolko 1972; Magee, Brock, and Young 1989; on France, Messerlin 1982.

   3. See Villey 1913.

   4. McCormack 1978; Lipset and Rokkan 1967.

   5. Lowi 1964; Pastor 1980: 83; Hody 1986: 172; Haggard 1988; Nelson 1989.

   6. Maier 1975; Middlemas 1979.

   7. Katzenstein 1976; Zysman 1977.

Chapter Seven

   1. Beard and Beard 1927: vol. 2, chap. 20; Beale 1930; Moore 1966: 130.

   2. Taussig 1931: 174.

   3. Dewey 1903: 203; Pitkin 1940: 409.

   4. Taussig 1931: 159n.

   5. Brown 1949: 41–44.

   6. Taussig 1931: 159; Tarbell 1911: 3–4.

   7. Taussig 1931: 174.

   8. Letter to Henry Wilson, cited in Coben 1959: 71.

   9. Summers 1953: 67; Coben 1959: 69, 73.

  10. Galambos 1967: 16.

  11. See the testimony of New England ironmasters in U.S. Tariff Commission 1882: 2250, 2457; U.S. Congress, House Committee on Ways and Means 1890: 11–33.

  12. Detzer 1973: 198.

  13. Terrill 1973: 189; Perry 1887; Miller 1929: 145.

  14. Johnson 1978: 65–66, 70.

  15. Deflation, which began years before the depression of the 1870s, was fueled by the Treasury's postbellum currency policy of zero growth, which was pursued in order to resume gold payments at prewar parity.

  16. The reader may wonder why the first section on the origins of the policy process is incomplete (divisiveness is not developed). Recall that the framework presented in part 1 offers hypotheses about the origins of pressure politics but does not permit greater specificity about the variant—competitive or logrolling—of pressure politics. Information specific to the case must first be introduced.

  17. Pincus 1977: 3, 48.

  18. Pincus 1977: 48.

  19. Pincus (1977: 71–72) mentions one instance.

  20. Pincus 1977: 5.

  21. Brown 1949: 83–107.

  22. Brown 1949: 123–24, 138.

  23. The American Iron Association was founded before the Civil War, in March 1855, but there is no direct evidence that it was ever engaged in lobbying for a protective tariff. The association ceased operating in 1859. Consult Tedesco 1970: 18.

  24. Coben 1959: 73–74.

25. Tedesco 1970: 38, 55, 81–82; Tarbell 1911: 86.

26. See George H. Ely's statement at the McKinley Tariff hearings in 1889: U.S. Congress, House Committee on Ways and Means 1890: 1–2.

27. The 1882 Tariff Commission heard statements by delegates from the following associations: the American Paper Makers' Association; the Silk Association of America; the American Flax and Hemp Spinners' and Growers' Association; the National Association of Wool Manufacturers; the National Association of Wool Growers; the United States Malsters' Association; the Manufacturing Chemists' Association; the American Iron and Steel Association; the American Pocket Cutlery Association; the American Window Glass Manufacturers' Association; the United States Potters' Association; the Association of Dealers in Pottery in the United States; the Tobacco Clay Pipe Manufacturers; the Silk Hat Manufacturers of the United States; the American Straw Goods Association; the Corset Manufacturers' Association of America; the Morocco Manufacturers' National Exchange; and the Sumac Manufacturers' Association.

28. U.S. Tariff Commission 1882: 139, 209, 287.

29. Brown 1949: 22–28, 142, 293–95; Coben 1959; Taussig 1931: 199.

30. Interestingly enough in 1867, the woolen manufacturers' only political support came from the two senators from Massachusetts, the very state where the NAWM was headquartered. These senators voted against the Wool Bill, but the woolen manufacturers could not overcome the coalition of western senators put together by the NAWM.

31. Brown 1949: 187, 199, 210, 247, 293, 356.

32. Ibid., 123–24, 183, 187.

33. Since low transportation costs made Lake Superior ore invulnerable to foreign competition, the only good reason for the perpetuation of the tariff on ore seems to have been the loss to maritime shipping the railroads would have incurred if Congress had remitted the duty. As a matter of fact, since 1872, many railroads had discovered a community of interests with AISA's protectionist members; they were indifferent to the prospect of high duties on rails as long as the consumer could absorb the costs, especially if the duties gave a boost to an industry in which the directors of the railroads were involved.

34. This paragraph draws from Tedesco 1970: 42, 61–62, 64–65, 141–42, 198, 223; U.S. Tariff Commission 1882: 1083–92, 1485, 1882, 2248; Summers 1953: 67; Taussig 1931: 271–72.

35. On this, see Hansen 1990.

36. This paragraph draws from Brown 1949: 29–39, 170–76; Tarbell 1911: 174–75; Tedesco 1970: 162.

37. Tarbell 1911: 137.

38. The Ways and Means Committee was controlled by the Republicans from 1865 until 1875 and from 1881 until 1883. Between 1865 and 1875, Republican leaders moved four tariff bills through Congress (the Wool and Woolen Act of 1867, the Schenck Act of 1870, the Tariff Act of 1872, and the Dawes Act of 1875) by relying mostly on their own protectionist forces. Between 1881 and 1883, they got the 1883 Tariff Act through Congress with the support of the Democratic protectionist minority.

39. Terrill 1973: 78, 80–81; Brown 1949: 427–28; Tedesco 1970: 143–44.

40. Gallarotti 1985.

41. Baack and Ray 1983. The 1870 rates reflect both the war increases and the Wool Act, as well as, in part, the 1870 Tariff Act, which was passed in July.

42. See Taussig 1931: chap. 3.

43. Competitiveness underlies the application of the theory of hegemonic stability to Britain; see the introduction, note 1. Consensus is emphasized by Kindleberger (1975), Rohrlich (1987), and Platt (1968).

44. Maddison 1982: 212.

45. Krasner 1976: tables 2 and 3, diagram 1.

46. Fuchs 1905: 13n.

47. Brown 1943: 4, 140–41.

48. See Royal Commission on the Depression of Trade and Industry 1886, esp. *Final Report*, 128.

49. Zebel 1940: 161–85.

50. Gaston 1975: 46; Platt 1968; Fuchs 1905.

51. Chamberlain to Dilke, 23 April 1881, cited in Gaston 1975: 250. Chamberlain did not become a protectionist until 1903.

52. Gaston 1975: 128, 274. More than a third of the responses (twenty-five chambers of commerce out of fifty-seven, and nine trade associations out of thirty-two) to the questionnaires of the Royal Commission of 1886 emphasized the need for Britain to take the necessary diplomatic steps to open foreign markets.

53. Gaston 1975: 221, 254, 262.

54. Brown 1943: 60, 78.

55. Ibid., 59–60.

56. This commission of inquiry was the Royal Commission, whose reports are analyzed below.

57. Zebel 1940: 173.

58. The inquiry had two parts: the first consisted of an examination of state officials and witnesses in four industries only; the second was more systematic, recording the responses to questionnaires mailed to "the Chambers of Commerce and other Associations representing the interests of the trading and industrial classes," to the trade unions, and to the diplomatic and consular officers. Unfortunately, the questionnaire sent to the trade unions contained no reference to trade policy: see Royal Commission 1886, in three reports, plus a final report.

59. Bradford, Dublin, Leith, Ipswich, and Swansea.

60. London, Liverpool, Newcastle, Belfast, Greenock, and Newport.

61. The four chambers in favor of free trade were Hartlepools, Nottingham, Oldham, and Walsall; the eight protectionists were Birmingham, Dublin, Exeter, Hull, Newark-upon-Trent, Ossett, Portsmouth, and Wakefield.

62. Carr and Taplin 1962: 119–22, 254–55; Kirby 1977: 11.

63. Allen 1970: 16–17.

64. Brown (1943: 52) gives a list. This paragraph draws from Brown 1943: 29–57 and the Royal Commission 1886: Second Report, appendix, part 1, 395.

65. Brown 1943: 46.

66. Fuchs 1905: 195–96.

67. This paragraph draws from Gaston 1975: 58, 67, 71, 79.

68. Fuchs 1905: chap. 2; U.S. Tariff Commission 1922; Platt 1968: 152.

69. See Irwin 1992.

70. Weill 1912: 266; Lhomme 1960: 91.

71. Consult Dunham 1930; Rist 1956.

72. The object of the vote was a law abolishing duties on the importation of raw materials, a domain not covered by the treaty yet a measure that all manufacturers could be expected to lobby for, since protection for their manufactures had been lowered.

73. Priouret 1963: 160–69.

74. On the mobilization of textile workers, see Fohlen 1956: 410; Priouret 1963: 184–86. On the Brame interpellation, see appendix 3, table A3.1. The Ollivier government did not leave the textile manufacturers completely empty-handed. On 9 January 1870, the government abolished the temporary admission of foreign yarn and cloth, a system under which semifinished goods could enter France duty free if the goods were to be finished in France and reexported. The measure antagonized the textile printers. See Fohlen 1956: 435.

75. In 1861 there were 282 charcoal furnaces and 190 coke furnaces; in 1870 the proportion was reversed to 82 and 184 respectively. See Gille 1968: 241.

76. Fohlen 1956: 293; Dunham 1930: 150.

77. In 1872, the Thiers government negotiated new conventions not due to expire until 1878. In August 1878, however, the parliament voted to extend the treaties six months beyond the general tariff. In 1881, a new series of conventions was negotiated with eight European governments, excluding Britain, to whom a law extended merely the benefit of the most-favored-nation clause. These new treaties were scheduled to expire on 1 February 1892.

78. The Société des agriculteurs de France (SAF) was founded in 1867. According to Golob (1944: 43), it was essentially "a club of distinguished landowners, members of the old nobility or conservative upper bourgeoisie who had acquired estates." In 1878, it counted 3,662 members.

79. For a description of the complex chain of legislative events that sealed Thiers' failure, see Arnauné 1911: 275; Levasseur 1912: 560–64; Dunham 1930: chap. 15; Smith 1980: 37.

80. This and the following paragraphs draw from the excellent study of the 1881 tariff by Smith (1980: chap. 4).

81. Smith suggests that "perhaps (the industrial deputies feared) the wrath of their urban and working-class constituents" (1980: 172, 174). If so, why did they behave differently in 1892? In fact, the concern for the workers' plight was residual: this plight came to matter, simply because the protectionists were too divided to impose a solution on their respective deputies. Note, however, that the role of the working class is unclear; Herman Lebovics (1988), for instance, argues that the social goal of the 1891 tariff was to calm the wrath of the working class.

82. *The Association de l'industrie française* (AIF) was organized in March 1878 and counted 128 members from mining, metallurgy, textiles, and shipbuilding: Smith 1980: 59. On the SAF, see note 78.

83. The reader may be reminded at this point that the members of the Senate were elected by a pool of electors that included local deputies and other directly elected local officials. In the Senate the rural areas were overrepresented and the urban areas, underrepresented.

84. Golob 1944: 54.

85. This paragraph draws from Gille 1964: 209–49, 221, 230–34; Gillet 1973: 140; Priouret 1963: 69–71; and Ratcliffe 1978: 61–138, 77.

86. These paragraphs draw from Gille 1964: 241; Rust 1973: 33; Smith 1977: 297; Priouret 1963: 183–84; Fohlen 1956: 435; and Gillet 1973: 140.

87. For a similar opinion, see Priouret 1963: 241–43.

88. The eight trade associations were the *Syndicat central de la tannerie*, the *Comité des forges*, the *Union des fabricants de papier*, the *Syndicat des raffineurs d'huile de pétrole*, the *Comité des distillateurs*, the *Comité central des fabricants de sucre*, the *Chambre syndicale du commerce d'exportation*, and the *Société des agriculteurs de France*.

89. Smith 1980: 90–114. See also appendix 2.

90. The very definition of "party politics" demands that the party or parties that make the trade policy be committed to one or the other side of the trade debate; the commitment of peripheral parties is of little relevance.

91. Data for the 1891, 1903, and 1910 vote breakdowns can be found in table A3.1. On the evolution of the Radicals' trade doctrine, see Elwitt 1975: chap. 6.

92. Smith 1980: 40, 171. Only the size of the farm bloc is known: 200.

Chapter Eight

1. Gourevitch 1986: chap. 3; Smith 1980; Lebovics 1988; Ferguson 1983.

2. Clarke 1971; Burnham 1981; Sundquist 1973.

3. Krasner 1976; Lake 1988.

4. There are other possible explanations, such as the degree of institutional strength, the nature of economic ideology, and geostrategic location; see Gourevitch 1986. To my knowledge no one has tried to apply these other explanations comparatively.

5. Lipset and Rokkan 1967.

6. Taussig 1893: 114.

7. Deflation began earlier than the Great Depression in the United States as a result of the Treasury Department's currency policy of zero growth, which was needed after the price explosion of the Civil War in order to resume gold payments at prewar parity.

8. This paragraph draws from Terrill 1973: chap. 5.

9. The Randall faction was the protectionist faction of the Democratic party; see chap. 7.

10. The content of the bill is discussed in Terrill 1973: 130–35, and Stanwood 1903: 234–35.

11. U.S. Congress, House Committee on Ways and Means 1890: 523, 681, 1046, 1362–65.

12. The reasons for the temptation of the worsted manufacturers are developed in Brown 1949: 23, 397–98, 417, 447.

13. The woolens segment managed to organize the Wool Consumers' Association in 1890 and then the Carded Woolens Manufacturers' Association in 1909.

14. Baker 1941: 77–78, 97.

15. Tarbell 1911: 325.

16. These paragraphs draw empirical evidence from Ingham 1970: 198–99; U.S. Tariff Commission 1882: 1485; Tedesco 1970: 201, 205; and U.S. Congress, House Committee on Ways and Means 1893: 295.

17. Taussig 1931: 384, 260.

18. This paragraph draws from Detzer 1970: 198–203; Fitch 1933: 216–17; Tedesco 1970: 250; and Taussig 1915: 269.

19. Chandler 1977.

20. Summers 1953: 167.

21. Four Democrats voted against the Mills Bill in the House of Representatives.

22. Stanwood 1903: 164–66.

23. For an analysis of the working of the reciprocity policy, see the section on the executive.

24. Tarbell 1911: 201.

25. Stern 1964: 11–24.

26. This paragraph draws from Stern 1964: 53; Sundquist 1983: 148; and Buck 1920: chap. 12.

27. More precisely, the 1896 Republican platform declared in favor of international bimetallism, which held that the U.S. government would remonetize silver only after having secured a similar move from its trade partners through an international agreement. But, in effect, this position amounted to gold monometallism, for Britain opposed such a move: Nichols 1933: 576, 584.

28. This paragraph draws from Hechter 1940: 86, 92, 105; and Stephenson 1930: 180.

29. Detzer 1970: 200.

30. Johnson 1978: 168–69.

31. Cited in Allen 1954: 351.

32. Link 1956: 192.

33. See Chandler 1959: 256; 1977.

34. See Wills 1913; Wright 1930.

35. Wiebe 1962: 90–91; Kenkel 1962: 30; Becker 1982: 79.

36. Becker 1982: 81.

37. Bidwell 1933: 41n.

38. Laughlin and Willis 1903: chap. 8.

39. David Lake has argued that the Democrats' program for free raw materials, though different from the Republicans' bilateral reciprocity policy, was also an export-promoting measure. Indeed, since Cobden, market liberals have constantly made the argument that low tariffs and expanding imports are the best means to promote exports. In that respect, Republicans and Democrats shared identical long-term goals. The means, however, were different. As Lake explains, the allocating mechanism in the Republican scheme was the state, while in the Democratic scheme it was the market. Lake's contention "that both parties adopted the same strategy despite their partisan differences is strong support for a systemic explanation of trade strategy," is limited. All it means is that Republicans tried to show some concern about export-oriented industries; Democrats had done so all along, especially before the Civil War. It says little about the difference with regard to the means, or about the parties' actual ability to deliver on their promises. In view of the failure of the reciprocity policy, it is hard to

agree with Lake's contention that "the tariff was 'internationalized,' or reconceptualized as an instrument of both protection and export expansion." Lake 1988: 108.

40. Steigerwalt 1964: 26.

41. For details see Laughlin and Parker 1903: 270–82, 312; and Lake 1988: 125.

42. Becker 1982: 95–96, 106, 114, 116.

43. Wilkins 1974: 159–60; Becker 1982: 105.

44. Corey 1930: 247, 319, 353, 446, 449.

45. Leach 1965: 218.

46. Parsons 1910: 13. The rest of this paragraph draws from Viner 1923: 89; Holt 1906; and Taussig 1915: 180, 203.

47. Tarbell 1911: 294–95.

48. Holt 1906: 8029; Parsons 1910: 72.

49. For cases of competitive firms asking for protection, see Ashley 1903: 96–97; Taussig 1915: 197–98.

50. See Conybeare's "Equation 8" 1991: 77.

51. When comparing the percentage change between 1870 and 1910, and between 1910 and 1914, Baack and Ray (1983) also found that the fastest-growing industries suffered the greatest tariff reductions, a finding compatible with my interpretation of the antitrust effect (as well as with about any line of argument).

52. The reason for using dutiable imports as opposed to all imports is the slightly greater sensitivity of the dutiable imports to partisan orientation than to the fiscal constraint.

53. Golob 1944: 152; Ashley 1920: 322–21.

54. Golob 1944: 86, 96; Smith 1980: 200; Barral 1974: 422.

55. Golob 1944: 162; Barral 1974: 424.

56. Golob 1944: 170.

57. The drawback system allows manufacturers to recover the tax paid on the raw material when the finished product made from this raw material is exported. The compensatory duty granted on the finished product is aimed at compensating the manufacturers for the duties they had to pay on the raw materials used in the fabrication of the finished product.

58. Golob 1944: 197–98.

59. The details of the debate can be found in Arnauné 1911: 287–300; and Smith 1980: 151–81.

60. In the case of hides, opposition came from the Paris leather manufacturers in alliance with port interests, such as Deputy Félix Faure, from Le Havre.

61. Golob 1944: 43.

62. Until then agriculture had been nominally part of the Ministry of Commerce and Agriculture: Barral 1968: 37, 39, 82.

63. Ibid., 110–13.

64. See table A3.1.

65. Barral 1974: 422–24.

66. Villey 1913: 129n.

67. The producers of the interior wanted the system of temporary admissions à l'équivalent, while the North and Meurthe-et-Moselle wanted the system à l'identique. The latter was a drawback—the pig iron to be transformed and reexported could be

imported duty free. The former differed in that the iron of which a finished product was composed did not need to be the same iron that was imported. See Rust 1973: 46–60.

68. This antiprotectionist organization found its main support among the members of the chambers of commerce of Paris, Bordeaux, Lyon, Marseille, and Reims. After the Chamber of Deputies had passed the bill, labor leaders and men of arts and letters joined the antiprotectionists in a *Comité de défense de l'exportation française et de l'alimentation nationale*; Golob 1944: 205.

69. Barral 1974: 426.

70. Arnauné 1911: 338–39. On farm duties, see Golob 1944: 234–35.

71. Augé-Laribé 1950: 246–52. For the party vote breakdown on the Berry Proposal of 15 July 1903, see table A3.1.

72. Smith 1980: 235.

73. Villey 1913: 133–36n.

74. Cited in Bézard-Falgas 1922: 159.

75. Smith 1980: 209, 224.

76. Hara 1976: 210.

77. On the party breakdown on the Tonkin votes in the Chamber of Deputies, see Schmieder 1966: 183–85.

78. Although in 1906 French exports to the empire represented only 11.4 percent of total exports, for most of these products the share was above 50 percent. See Marseille 1984: 51.

79. Facts and data supporting these statements can be found in Girault 1916. For an attempt to calculate the amounts spent, see Bobrie 1976.

80. Meynier 1981: 52; Sémars 1905: 189–92. In 1912, shipping to and from the colonies represented one-third of the total activity of the French merchant marine: see Girault 1916: 169; Schmieder 1966: 198.

81. Laffey 1969: 80.

82. On 1892, see Brelet 1923: 115; Pinot 1909: 508, 510; Garanger 1960: 35. On the 1910 revision, see Garanger 1960: 35; Pinot May 1909: 262n; Rust 1973: 291.

83. See Crouzet Winter and Spring 1974.

84. Poidevin 1971.

85. Poidevin 1969: 547–48.

86. Bouvier 1970: 358–62.

87. Although the commercial impact of the tied-loan policy was mixed, the impact on Schneider and French exports of field artillery was significant: see Crouzet Winter 1974: 64. In the case of equipment goods, such as road construction, railroad equipment, harbor installations, mining equipment, building construction, urban transportation, electrical networks, and telephones, however, the impact was less significant.

88. On the resolution of 16 January 1900, see François-Poncet 1927: 119–20. On the 1909 appeal, see François-Poncet 1927: 161; Brelet 1923: 119n.; Crouzet 1977: 190–92.

89. Rust 1973: 190. For the Socialists, nationalization would not only deal a blow to finance capital but would also prevent momentary unemployment in the locomotive and rolling stock industry.

90. Rust 1973: 202 argues that the builders were so alienated that they decided to take their case to the electors in 1914. Unfortunately, I possess no information about what actually happened.

91. Augier 1911: 34.

92. The concept of bargaining tariff is developed in U.S. Tariff Commission 1918: 506–8.

93. Arnauné 1911: 361.

94. Scores of examples can be found in Poidevin 1969. See also Thobie 1968; Rust 1973: 254–75.

95. Girault 1916: 151–55. In a resolution adopted on 19 May 1913, the *Association de l'industrie et de l'agriculture française*, the protectionist organization still headed by Méline, demanded that the policy of tariff assimilation be extended to all colonies.

96. This paragraph draws from Poidevin 1978; and Borrelly-Bitsch 1978.

97. Levasseur 1912: vol. 2, p. 370; Poidevin 1969: 804; Lauren 1976: 163.

98. Villey 1913: 133–36n.

99. For a discussion of this, see appendix 2.

100. Golob 1944: chap. 2.

101. The parliament wished to increase the gap between the general tariff and the minimum tariff, the latter being granted to governments extending preferential treatment to France. Specializations were introduced to limit the liberalizing impact of the most-favored-nation clause. Germany had inaugurated this feature in its 1902 tariff, with the effect of drastically reducing French imports.

102. Lubenow 1988.

103. Brown 1943: 65.

104. The Conservatives were not out of power, nor did they lose all elections between 1906 and 1931. They won twice, in 1918 and 1923, after downplaying the issue of protection.

105. Thomas 1939: 13–15.

106. Brown 1943: 151.

107. For detailed accounts of this period, see Fraser 1963; Gollin 1965; Rempel 1972; and Sykes 1979.

108. To be sure there were exceptions, at least in France: Paul Lafargue's *Parti ouvrier*, for example. Also Lebovics 1988: 92.

109. Report of the Tariff Commission 1904–1907.

110. Marrison 1983: 163n 98.

111. This paragraph draws from Marrison 1983: 159. See also Semmel 1960: 100; Rempel 1972: 97.

112. A substantial minority of steel manufacturers opposed protection: see Carr and Taplin 1962: 255.

113. Ilersic 1960: 155–56.

114. Brown 1970.

115. Coetzee 1986: 843.

116. The theoretician of retaliation, referred to at the time as the "Policy of Industrial Defence," was Ashley 1903.

117. U.S. Tariff Commission 1918: 505.

118. Sykes 1979: 54.

119. Clarke 1971: 37; Pelling 1967: xxiv, xxv.

120. Blewett 1968: 96, 120.

121. Semmel 1960: 152.

122. This paragraph draws from Brown 1970; Murray 1980; Scally 1975; Clarke 1971, 1972; and Blewett 1968, 1972.

123. Cited in Sykes 1979: 133.

124. This was true even in Manchester; see Clarke 1971: 100.

125. Blewett 1968: 121.

126. Sykes 1979: 207.

127. Ibid., 238.

128. Coats 1968: 195.

129. Amery 1932: vol. 6, p. 693; Blewett 1968: 96.

130. Marrison 1983.

131. Ilersic 1960: 156.

132. Gaston 1975: chap. 3; Platt 1968: 108.

133. Platt 1968: 117.

134. Fuchs 1905: chap. 2; U.S. Tariff Commission 1922.

135. This paragraph draws from Allain 1978.

136. This and the following paragraph draw from Clapham 1963: vol. 3, p. 316; Jeans 1903: 36; and Political and Economic Planning 1957: 9–10.

137. Kirby 1977: 14.

138. Clapham 1963: vol. 3, p. 317n.

139. Saul 1962–1963: 40.

140. Calculated in volume. Evidence on cottons was drawn from Farnie 1979: 91, 107, 121; and Semmel 1960: 137.

141. Parrini 1969: 26–27, 43n.

142. Stopford 1974: 316–17.

143. The proxy for the average tariff level used in fig. A2.2 (customs receipts/imports) is not zero, nor is it flat. Tariffs still existed, but their purpose was to raise revenues. Note also that the proxy picks up a host of factors other than protection. See appendix 2.

144. Zebel 1940: 180.

145. Sykes 1979: 193.

Chapter Nine

1. According to Asquith's celebrated formula.

2. Eichengreen 1982: 28.

3. Plowden 1971: 110.

4. This paragraph and the next draw from Cline 1982: 162, 170–73.

5. Lowe 1942: 38–39.

6. Hardach 1977: 107.

7. François-Poncet 1927: 169; Pinot 1919; Hardach 1977; Hennebicque 1917.

8. Godfrey 1987: 64, 77.

9. Mérigot 1943: 54. This paragraph and the next also draw from Trachtenberg 1977; Kuisel 1981: chap. 2; and Godfrey 1987: chaps. 3 and 4.

10. Mayer 1987: 39–40.

11. The NFTC asked that firms and banks be allowed to form export cartels and combine in opening branches abroad, that the federal government subsidize the creation of a merchant marine, and that Congress adopt a flexible tariff.

12. Sklar 1959–1960: 31.
13. Bensel 1984: 105–28.
14. Mayer 1987: 68–69; Abrahams 1967: 60–69; Lewis 1938: 534; Houston 1926: vol. 1, chap. 9.
15. Mayer 1987; Abrahams 1967: 50–51.
16. Rothbard 1972.
17. Lefranc 1976: 59; Villey 1913: 144n.
18. Rothbard 1972.
19. Abrahams 1967: 135–44.
20. Dulles 1926: 45.
21. See Tawney 1943; Armitage 1969; Snyder 1971: 39, 80.
22. The Liberal-Labour ratio of seats in the House of Commons shifted from 272/42 in the 1910 election, to 161/73 in 1918, and to 116/142 in 1922: see Butler and Sloman 1975: 189.
23. Ramsden 1978: 132.

Chapter Ten

1. Maier 1975; Middlemas 1979.
2. Maier 1975: 9; Pastor 1980: 83; Hody 1986: 172; Haggard 1988.
3. Ferguson 1984; Gourevitch 1986. Rogowski (1989) also emphasizes the role of producer coalitions but does not try to derive a trade policy outcome.
4. Admittedly this may be a simplification of Gourevitch's argument, which is more intricate and open-ended. On red-green coalitions, see also Esping-Andersen 1985; Katzenstein 1985; Rogowski 1989; and especially Luebbert 1991.
5. The German case is somewhat more complicated. Although the Social Democrats were not in power, they did play a critical role in maintaining the Weimar Republic, whose survival was not a given, as in the other countries, but which was embroiled in the partisan debate. Socialists, Liberals, and Catholics supported the republic, whereas the conservatives and nationalists did not. The crisis discredited the republican institutions, as well as the parties that supported those institutions and the policies they advocated.
6. See Augé-Laribé 1950: 389, 395, 405; Rosenstock-Franck 1939: 224.
7. Sauvy 1984: vol. 2, pp. 51–53, 65, 71.
8. Angelini 1932: 26.
9. Bernstein 1978: 76–77.
10. Soulier 1939: 380; Margairaz 1972: 79–80.
11. The expression "Blum's agrarian New Deal" is from Wright 1964: 64.
12. On the socioeconomic basis of the electoral success of the Popular Front, see Kolboom 1986.
13. Conseil supérieur du commerce, de l'industrie et des colonies 1889–1890: 92.
14. For an analysis of the measures, see Le Temps, 4 October 1936.
15. This was Haight's opinion 1941: 181.
16. Sauvy 1984: vol. 3, p. 338.
17. Wright 1964: chap. 4.
18. Luebbert 1991.
19. Margairaz 1972: 139; Cleary 1989: 85; Barral 1968: 254.

20. Bernstein 1978: 87.

21. Sauvy 1984: vol. 2, p. 151.

22. Augé-Laribé 1950: 399; Gignoux 1933: 41.

23. Statement to *Le Soir*, 7 January 1922, cited in Goujet 1922: 76.

24. Naudin 1928: 78. The CGPF made strong representations to that effect: Villey 1913: 210.

25. Naudin 1928: 87, 89–91; Lasserre 1933: 42.

26. Sauvy 1984: vol. 2, pp. 144–45.

27. Illustrations for each of these cases can be found in Guillen Spring and Winter 1978.

28. Naudin 1928: 213–16, 238–39.

29. Lasserre 1933: 49–51; Sauvy 1984: vol. 2, pp. 139–40.

30. Kaiser 1980: 200.

31. Empirical illustrations can be found in Kaiser 1980: chaps. 8 and 11.

32. Ogburn and Jaffé 1929: 546.

33. Guillen 1978: 64.

34. Haight 1935: 79–81.

35. Haight 1941: 173–77. French experts went as far as to sanction the application of the most-favored-nation treatment to quotas; the Franco-British Agreement of June 1934 bound the French government to accord the U.K. its mathematically attributable share.

36. Marseille 1984: 51.

37. Such an issue had already flared up twice before the war, in 1900 and 1910, and once after the war, with the 1921 *Plan Sarraut*, an ambitious empirewide scheme of public works that fell victim to the fiscal crisis of the early 1920s: Sémars 1905: 163; Girault 1916: 98; Roberts 1929: 612–18. The Great Depression revived the debate over colonial development.

38. The two exceptions, sugar and wine, are due to the political power of the beet sugar producers and the winemakers: see, respectively, Hoffher 1939: 59; and Barral 1968: 228.

39. Haight 1941: 264; Barral 1968: 226; Royal Institute of International Affairs 1937: 292. See also Coquery-Vidrovitch 1976: 396n.

40. Marseille 1984: 66; Coquery-Vidrovitch 1976: 399–400.

41. Ageron 1984: 236, 238.

42. On this, see Sauvy 1984: vol. 2, p. 131; Gignoux 1933: 118; Brelet 1923: 151.

43. Sauvy 1984: vol. 2, p. 151.

44. Lasserre 1933: 29.

45. Whetham 1974: 36–49; Self 1986: 405–19.

46. Lowe 1942: 92.

47. Lowe 1942: 82–83, 341.

48. Carr and Taplin 1962: 341; Boyce 1987: 124–25; Snyder 1971: 142.

49. The McKenna duties applied to motor cars, cycles, watches, clocks, musical instruments, film, and other luxury items.

50. The Dyestuffs act had several components. Part I, which was to be in effect for five years, created the Key Industry Duties (33.3 percent ad valorem), affecting more than 6,000 articles, mainly chemicals and scientific materials. The duties represented

a minute fraction of British imports. Part II established a procedure for the extension of the duties of part I to products that were victims of dumping, for example, fabric gloves (1922). Part II was to be in effect for three years.

51. These were the duties imposed under part II of the 1921 Act—fabric gloves, illuminating glassware, aluminum and enamelled hollow-ware, and gas mantles.

52. Commercial motor cars were added in 1925, and rubber tires in 1927.

53. Lace, gloves, cutlery, and gas mantles (1925), packing and wrapping paper (1926), items of pottery (1927), and buttons and enamelled hollow-ware (1928).

54. That is, lace, gloves, cutlery, and gas mantles.

55. *The Times*, 18 December 1924; cited by Lowe 1942: 78.

56. Abel 1945: 25, 27.

57. Carr and Taplin 1962: 469; Boyce 1987: 124.

58. Tolliday 1984: 54.

59. Turner 1984: 48.

60. Political and Economic Planning 1957: 26.

61. Hutchinson 1965: 77.

62. Political and Economic Planning 1944: 21.

63. For this paragraph and the next, see Hutchinson 1965: 75, 77, 137.

64. The woolens manufacturers were threatened with a cut in the initial level of protection granted to them under the Abnormal Importations Act of November 1931, an emergency measure to deter anticipatory importing, which IDAC was afterward mandated to adjust: Hutchinson 1965: 35.

65. Hutchinson 1965: 26. The same reasoning underlies the report of the (Milner) Tariff Advisory Committee constituted in 1923 by the Baldwin government: see Roberts 1984: 99.

66. Hutchinson 1965: 157.

67. On this confused moment of British party politics, see Williamson 1992.

68. Kaiser 1980: chap. 4.

69. Cited in Rowland, 1987: 94–95.

70. Tasca 1939: 133–35; Kaiser 1980: 291.

71. MacDonald 1972.

72. "Germany's Trade Offensive," *Economist*, 5 November 1938, 262–67; "Collective Security for Trade," *Economist*, 20 May 1939, 420–21; "The Fight for Rumania's Trade," *Economist*, 3 June 1939, 537–38; Kaiser 1980: 291–93.

73. Kottman 1968: 15n; Kreider 1943: 240.

74. Schatz 1970: 95.

75. Cited in Rowland 1987: 291.

76. On the role of economic interests, consult MacDonald 1972: 106, 115, 127; Kennedy 1981: 295–98.

77. Cited in Holland 1981: 294–98.

78. Tasca 1939: 94–95, 122, 152; Kottman 1968: 125–26; Rooth 1984.

79. Drummond 1972: 136–37.

80. Eichengreen 1982: 28.

81. Tolliday 1987: 294.

82. Roberts 1984.

83. On this, see Self 1986: 477; Tolliday 1987: 201–3, 276; Lucas 1937: 155; Allen 1970: 143.

84. Cited in Tolliday 1987: 201.

85. This paragraph draws from Williamson 1984: 116; Roberts 1984: 102; and Tolliday 1987: 205, 209, 296.

86. See Bamberg 1984: 259, 274; Roberts 1984: 96; Lucas 1937: 234–35, 239, 248–49.

87. Kirby 1977: chaps. 7–9; Allen 1970: chap. 3.

88. Departmental Committee on the Position of the Textile Trades after the War, Report, Cd. 9070, 1918, p. 113; cited in Grove 1962: 40–41.

89. The Machinery of Government Committee Report, 1918; cited in Political and Economic Planning 1950: 113.

90. Roberts 1984: 104.

91. Lucas 1937: 139; Bamberg 1984: 288; Cole 1948: 345.

92. Cited in Self 1986: 484.

93. Capie 1983: 93.

94. Rogow 1955: 85.

95. This paragraph draws from Bensel 1984: 128–47; Fite 1954: 211; Johnson 1978: 272–73; Allen 1954: 351; Myers 1929: 247, 249; and Sundquist 1973: 189.

96. Johnson 1978: 271–72.

97. This conflict is developed in several places. See, for instance, Fite 1954; Gardner 1964: 41–44; Adams 1976: 80–93; and Steward 1975: chap. 2.

98. U.S. Congress, House Committee on Ways and Means 1934, 1937, 1940. U.S. Congress, Senate Committee on Finance 1934, 1937, 1940.

99. Liechty 1972: 51; Humphrey 1955: 163; Vear 1956.

100. Brandes 1962: chaps. 8–10; Hawley 1974: 123; Arnold 1982.

101. Rothbard 1972: 120.

102. Schattschneider 1935.

103. Schattschneider 1935: 13, 86–98.

104. Schattschneider 1935: 128.

105. It is true that the public notice of the hearings invited witnesses to justify their request for protection in terms of higher costs of production at home than abroad. To entrust this task to interested parties, as the Republican Congress did, may have seemed naive, but to take this wishful directive literally, as the yardstick against which the quality of the evidence offered at the hearings ought to be assessed, is to miss the point. All the clerks and public officials working around the clock for a decade would not have sufficed to accomplish such a task. The claim to scientific validity in the writing of the tariff was meant for ideological consumption, especially to deflect progressive criticism that tariff begat trust; it was not intended to be rigorously implemented.

106. Taussig 1931: 489–500.

107. Macmahon February 1930; August 1930.

108. Based on dutiable schedules, and weighted with reference to imports in 1928: Macmahon August 1930: 923n.

109. Schattschneider's exclusive focus on what was said in the hearings led him to overlook the partisan nature of the farm-factory dispute: Schattschneider 1935: 137.

110. Theodore Lowi was first to expose the technical inadequacy of logrolling in high-quorum politics. See his famous review article, published in 1964.

111. Ferguson 1984.

112. Their lot resembled that of their Swedish counterparts, who, once it became clear that social democracy was going to last, agreed to the 1938 Saltsjobaden agreement, in which they gave up the fight in exchange for labor peace in labor markets,

recognition of private control in capital markets, and free trade. This comparison is well worked out in Gourevitch 1986: chap. 4.

113. They had no voice. For an in-depth study of this type of choice, see Hirschman 1970.

114. Hody 1986: 138, 158.

115. This paragraph draws from Hody 1986: 162–71.

116. Parrini 1969: 245–46; Wilson 1971: 73–82.

117. This paragraph draws from Dulles 1926: 31; Parrini 1969: 194–95, 200, 205–6; Wilson 1971: 106–19; and Adams 1976: 29–31.

118. Parrini 1969: 76–78.

119. Adams 1976: chap. 3.

120. Mikesell 1952: 65; Tasca 1938: chap. 12; Beckett 1941: chap. 6.

121. Devaluation had two simultaneous effects: it increased effective protection by pricing out foreign goods, and decreased nominal protection by reducing the ratio of specific duties relative to price—which is what the percentages given in this paragraph measure. An ad valorem duty would not be so affected, but most U.S. duties were specific.

122. Steward 1975: chaps. 7 and 8; Rowland 1987: 303.

123. Heston 1987: 439; Bauge 1987.

124. Whittlesey 1937: 65.

125. Diebold 1941: 19, 37.

126. Gordon 1941: 396.

127. Diebold 1941: 18.

128. Ibid.

129. Gordon 1941: 397.

130. Allen 1957: 126.

131. Kreider 1940: 318.

132. Kreider 1940: 332.

133. Kottman 1968: 222.

134. Ibid., 324.

135. This paragraph draws from Rowland 1987: 302.

136. Rowland 1987: 311. See also Megaw 1975.

137. Morgenthau Diary, 11 October 1938; cited in Kottman 1968: 257.

Chapter Eleven

1. Note the similarity with the small-country syndrome identified by Peter Katzenstein (1985), who argues that trade exposure led these countries to set up a formal or informal corporatist decisionmaking process that encompasses both economic and social domestic policies.

2. Even though the theory of hegemonic stability has come under serious attack, its relevance to the postwar era remains unchallenged. Its main proponents include Kindleberger (1975), Krasner (1976), and Lake (1988).

3. The postwar relationship between trade and security is also emphasized by Amacher, Tollison, and Willett (1979), Stein (1984), Aggarwal (1985), Pollard (1985: 2), Nelson (1989), and Gowa (1989).

4. *Congressional Quarterly* 1945: 304, 308; Watson 1956: 681.

5. Representative Noah M. Mason of Illinois apropos ITO, *Congressional Record*,

appendix, 10 March 1947, A963. Wall Street as a whole opposed the creation of the IMF, which they saw as an intrusion by the Treasury Department into international finance.

6. Wilkinson 1960: 41.

7. Grassmuck 1951: 134–41; Butler 1963: 651–52.

8. Westerfield 1955: 101.

9. Speech to the Senate, 22 April 1946; cited in Gardner 1956: 250. On Vandenberg's role in the passage of aid to Greece and Turkey, see Hartmann 1971, 64.

10. Leddy and Norwood 1963: 126–28.

11. Hartmann 1971: 183. Focusing on what he calls key motions and amendments, Richard A. Watson (1956: 679) describes the 1945–1951 period as one of continuation of the partisan battle.

12. The word "bipartisan" should not be taken to mean that there was no opposition to the administration's policy, but that there was no fundamental disagreement between the two party leaderships.

13. Gowa 1985: 189.

14. Humphrey 1955: 371–72.

15. For the traditional interpretation, see Price 1955; Jones 1955. For the revisionist view, see Kolko and Kolko 1972; Eakins 1969; and Ferguson and Rogers 1986: 49.

16. Kolko and Kolko 1972: 360.

17. Eakins 1969: 167.

18. Not taken into account was testimony given by administration officials, experts, or scholars. Also excluded was testimony given on behalf of public interest organizations (women, veterans, churches, parents, consumers, etc.) and industrywide, umbrella-type organizations (NAM, AFL-CIO, CNTP, etc.) on the grounds that organization leaders in pressure politics have little control over their rank and file: Bauer, Pool, and Dexter 1963: 332–40. Testimony on behalf of single firms was also dismissed as too parochial.

19. The deepest cuts in protection came in the late 1940s and early 1950s.

20. "Statement of Senator Hugh Butler [Republican, Nebraska], for Release to Sunday Morning Papers, 9 February 1947," U.S. Congress, House Committee on Ways and Means 1947: 745.

21. Schriftgiesser 1960: 160.

22. *Congressional Quarterly Almanac* 1953: 210–17. Bauer, Pool, and Dexter 1963: 10–39, 375–78.

23. Among its officers were executives from the Burroughs Corporation, Bell & Howell, Gillette, General Mills, Chase National Bank, and Macy's (*Congressional Quarterly Almanac* 1954: 271–72).

24. In addition to representatives from a few major oil corporations, others who testified represented Pepsi Cola, Caterpillar, Eastman Kodak, Bell & Howell, Bullock's, Bank of America, Solomon Brothers, McCormick, Ace Fasteners, and Rockwell Engineering (U.S. Congress, House Committee on Ways and Means 1955).

25. Bauer, Pool, and Dexter 1963: 383–87.

26. Wexler 1983: chap. 3; Wala 1986.

27. Arkes 1973: 265, 271. *Congressional Quarterly Almanac* 1949: 262, 336–37.

28. Arkes 1973: 273.

29. Mikesell 1952: 176–79.

30. Diebold 1952; Gardner 1956: 373–76.

31. Destler 1986: 22.

32. For examples of such quid pro quo, see Aggarwal 1985: chap. 4; *Congressional Quarterly Almanac* 1962: 289–90; Baldwin 1985: 143; Twiggs 1987: 81–82.

33. Leddy and Norwood 1963: 169–73.

34. Magee, Brock, and Young 1989: 262; Hufbauer, Berliner, and Elliott 1986: 3–5.

35. The only cross-sectoral study I have encountered for the period is that of Dougan of the 1954 nominal tariffs. Although Dougan's study is remarkable because it controls for the price elasticity of domestic demand, the results provide only weak support for the rent-seeking hypothesis Dougan champions. No support is found for the hypothesis that concentration increases influence. Not unsurprisingly, Dougan found a correlation between labor intensity and the tariff, as well as between unionization and the tariff. Less intuitively obvious is the negative correlation he found between industry size (measured by the value of shipments) and the tariff (Dougan 1984: 200).

36. Ehrmann 1957: chap. 2.

37. Jeanneney 1980.

38. Kuisel 1981: 169–72, 178–79.

39. Donnedieu de Vabres 1956: 235.

40. This paragraph draws from Lynch 1984.

41. Cited in Lynch 1984: 239–40. On Clémentel, see chap. 10.

42. Kuisel 1981: 201.

43. Even as early as 1946: see Kuisel 1981: 232.

44. See Cohen 1969: 101.

45. Gerbet 1956.

46. These percentages were calculated on the vote of confidence that took place on 12 December 1951, one day before the formal adoption of the bill; 240 deputies voted "no-confidence": see *Le Monde*, 13 December 1951.

47. This paragraph and the next draw from Carol L. Balassa's remarkable dissertation (1979: 162, 168, 178–79, 242–43, 264, 283).

48. See Mérigot 1943; Ehrmann 1957: chap. 2; Kuisel 1981: chap. 5. For a dissenting view, see Vinen 1991.

49. Ehrmann 1957: 113, 303, 397.

50. This, although Washington wanted to fight gigantism: see Hoffman 1951: 92. See also Cohen 1969: 90, 113; Sheahan 1963: 172.

51. Kuisel 1981; Ehrmann 1957: 290.

52. See Wickham 1963: 341.

53. Ehrmann 1954: 456.

54. Ehrmann 1957: 373.

55. Cohen 1969: 142; Sheahan 1963: 124; Naville et al. 1971: 75; Kuisel 1981: 261.

56. This paragraph draws from Mytelka 1982: 135–37.

57. Sheahan 1963: 135–36.

58. Mytelka 1982: 137.

59. Garanger 1960: 241.

60. Sheahan 1963: 94.

61. Jeanneney 1976: 561.

62. On ideological polarization under the Fourth Republic, see Sartori 1976.

63. Thomson 1975: 145.

64. Arnaud-Ameller 1970: 107–8.

65. Dobson 1986: 8–9; Harris 1972: 212.

66. Rogow 1955: 81.

67. For instance, Longstreth 1979.

68. Schmitter 1981.

69. To put it in game-theoretic terminology, the TUC and the FBI were engaged in an iterated Prisoner's Dilemma game.

70. For a similar argument, see S. A. Walkland's contribution to Gamble and Walkland 1984: 112.

71. Federation of British Industry 1944: 20; Milward 1979: 120.

72. Grove 1962: 61.

73. Rogow 1955: 49, 52, 61.

74. Federation of British Industry 1944: 12.

75. Federation of British Industry 1946.

76. Bain's presidential address, 14 April 1948; cited in Rogow 1955: 91–90.

77. Blank 1973: 79.

78. Blank 1973: 64, 124.

79. Hall 1986: 74.

80. Lord Dukeston, former trade union leader, address to the 1947 party conference; cited by Beer 1982: 209.

81. Morgan 1984: 111; Ovenden 1978: 25.

82. Blank 1973: 99–102.

83. "Neddy" refers to the National Economic Development Council (NEDC) and the National Economic Development Office (NEDO). The sectoral economic development councils (EDCs) created in 1963 were dubbed "Little Neddies." This paragraph and the next draw from Harris 1972: 240; Shanks 1977: 21–22; and Blank 1973: 178, 183.

84. Streat 1959: 4–5.

85. Lowi 1964.

86. The interpretation presented here draws from Beer 1965: 339.

87. Ovenden 1978: 17.

88. Rose 1967: chap. 6.

89. This paragraph draws from Lieber 1970.

90. Guillen 1989.

91. Balassa 1979: 131–33.

92. Claude 1961: 85–86; Balassa 1979: 226.

93. Grove 1962: 246–48.

94. McCrone 1969: 92, 117.

95. Harris 1972: 217–19.

96. Knight 1974: 102.

97. Grove 1962: 255; Harris 1972: 219–20.

98. Louis 1976: 15.

99. U.S. Tariff Commission 1967: 251, 256.

Chapter Twelve

1. The phrase was coined by Philippe Labarde, "Le libéral-interventionnisme," in Le Monde, L'Année Economique et Sociale: 1976: 144. See also Weber 1986: 252–55.

2. Hayward 1986.

3. Berger 1981: 304
4. Green 1984.
5. Dacier 1985: 105.
6. Portelli 1988: 27.
7. Berger 1981; Keeler 1985: 279.
8. Portelli 1988: 25–26.
9. Lavau, Grunberg, and Mayer 1983; see also Bernstein 1978.
10. Ibid. See the introduction and the contributions by Nonna Mayer and Gérard Grunberg and Etienne Schweisguth.
11. Mayer and Schweisguth 1985: 264. Equivalent figures were 8 percent for industrialists and large merchants, but 75 percent for workers, and 57 percent for service personnel.
12. Pineau 1981.
13. Le Gall 1988: 21.
14. Friedberg and Desjeux 1973: 14.
15. Suleiman 1974: 346.
16. Friedberg and Desjeux 1973: 29.
17. *Le Monde, L'Année Economique et Sociale: 1975*: 138.
18. PUK, Rhône-Poulenc, Elf-Erap, Creusot-Loire, CGE, Thomson, BSN, Saint-Gobain-Pont-à-Mousson: *Le Monde, L'Année économique et Sociale: 1975*: 90.
19. Morvan 1972: 272–74.
20. This paragraph draws from *Le Monde* 25 September 1979; Padioleau 1981: 83; Hough 1979: 205; and Deguen 1977: 145.
21. Green 1982: 30.
22. Cited in Hayward 1988.
23. Ibid.
24. This point is developed in Friedberg and Desjeux 1973, 1972: 567–85; Desjeux and Friedberg 1973; Friedberg 1974; Crozier and Friedberg 1977: 155–66; Lautman and Thoenig 1966.
25. For the wool industry trade association, see Friedberg and Desjeux 1973: 56.
26. Hayward 1974: 268.
27. Friedberg and Desjeux 1973: 48; Mytelka 1982: 142–45.
28. On this, consult the work of Friedberg and other researchers affiliated with the *Centre de sociologie des organisations*, note 24.
29. Weber 1986: 257
30. Underhill 1988: 504.
31. Aujac 1986: 13–35.
32. Barreau 1990: 59.
33. Cohen, Halimi, and Zysman 1984: 29.
34. Underhill 1988: 504.
35. Barreau 1990: 85.
36. Schlenker 1987; Schmidt 1988.
37. See articles by Eric le Boucher, *Le Monde*, 8 February 1989, and 15 November 1990.
38. Olson 1982: 75.
39. Pierre-Brossolette and Delanglade 1990.
40. Berger 1985: 231, 235.

41. In chap. 8 we saw that the movement toward the creation of business peak associations in the United States at the turn of the century was essentially motivated by the need to find a workable alternative to the partisan "football." The first French business peak association was created in 1919 at the prodding of the Commerce Ministry (see chap. 9).

42. Bauchard 1964: 45, 98–101. Weber 1986: 150. Another manifestation of this cleavage was the 1968 Grenelle accords. Afraid of a small business backlash following corporatist negotiations with the unions in 1968, the fourteen largest industrial groups of the CNPF, without reneging on their affiliation to that organization, gathered into a separate association—the *Association des grandes entreprises faisant appel à l'épargne* (AGREF).

43. Goldey 1985: 247.

44. Berger 1987: 196.

45. Bauer 1988: 60.

46. For instance, Pierre Bérégovoy opted for a case-by-case renationalization (*Le Figaro*, 16 September 1987), whereas Lionel Jospin defended wholesale renationalization (*Libération*, 23 October 1987).

47. *Economist*, 3 February 1990: 72

48. See articles by Eric le Boucher, *Le Monde*, 8 February 1989, and 15 November 1990.

49. *Le Monde*, 15 November 1990.

50. Messerlin 1982: 1012.

51. Nogués, Olechowski, and Winters 1986: table 3.

52. Messerlin 1982.

53. Stewart 1978: 40, 241.

54. Holmes 1982: 21.

55. Boston 1985.

56. King 1985: 17.

57. Kavanagh 1987: 299.

58. Gamble 1974: 78–81.

59. Grant 1980: 134.

60. Ibid.

61. *Financial Times*, 25 July 1979; cited in Grant 1980: 153.

62. Shepherd 1987: 169.

63. Grant 1980: 160.

64. Shanks 1977: 32.

65. Leruez 1975: 142, 145.

66. Ibid., 152.

67. CBI, "The National Economic Development Council and Office in History and Functions," duplicated, 1966: 4. Cited in Leruez 1975: 146.

68. Ganz 1977: 25–36.

69. Hayward 1975: 142.

70. Young and Lowe 1974: 32, 36.

71. Wilks 1981: 408.

72. Panitch 1979.

73. Leruez 1975: 152, 214–15.

74. Holmes 1982: 52, 79–80.

75. See details in Shanks 1977: 60.
76. Grant and Marsh 1977: 156; Ganz 1977: 40.
77. Shanks 1977: 77.
78. Young 1978; Wilks 1981.
79. Wilks 1981: 412.
80. Confederation of British Industry, 1976: 55. Cited in Wilks 1981: 407.
81. Wilks 1981: 410.
82. On this, see Sharp and Shepherd 1980: 122; Skuse 1983: 90–94; Young 1978.
83. Vincent Cable (1983: 222–25) reports that the government offered import quotas to consumer electronics, knitting, textiles, and footwear.
84. Grant 1987: 134.
85. Shepherd 1987: 169, 174.
86. Grant 1987: 93.
87. Holmes 1985: 154–61.
88. Grant and Sargent 1987: 137.
89. Report of the Commission of Inquiry into Industrial and Commercial Representations (Devlin report) 1972: 11.
90. Ibid.
91. Pinto-Duchinsky 1981: 234.
92. Grant 1980: 133, 154.
93. Holmes 1985: 154–61.
94. Walkland 1984: 134.
95. Report of a Labour study group, published by the Labour Party, London, 1973. See also Young and Lowe 1974: 209.
96. Cable 1983: 13.
97. Nairn 1972: 67.
98. That the two parties switched their position on the EEC to and fro should not be construed as evidence that the EEC was not a partisan issue. The inconsistency is only apparent. It derives from the fact that the two-party dynamic turns a center-extremes cleavage into a Left-Right cleavage, depending on relatively small shifts in the political center of gravity. In 1974, the center of gravity had moved to the left, thus strengthening the position of the extreme Left in the Labour party and that of the Center-Right in the Conservative party. Labour's party line thus was that of the extreme Left—nationalism—whereas the Conservatives' party line was pro-EEC. By 1983, the center of gravity had moved to the right, now privileging the preferences respectively of Labour Center-Left (pro-EEC) and Tory extreme Right (nationalist). The same logic rarely applies in multiparty systems, because of the possibility in such systems of a coalition of the centers, which makes it more difficult for extremes to see their views prevail.
99. Moravcsik 1991.
100. Oulton 1976: 81.
101. Cable and Rebelo 1980.
102. Ferguson and Rogers 1986.
103. See Figs. 11.2 and 11.3.
104. My thanks to Aaron Wildavsky for being the first to point this out to me.
105. The quote is from Cohen 1974: 129, 130.
106. Cited in Destler 1980: 170.

107. Metzger 1964: 87–92.

108. Lindeen 1970: 109.

109. Aggarwal 1985: chap. 4; *Congressional Quarterly Almanac* 1962: 289–90.

110. Baldwin 1985: 143.

111. Twiggs 1987: 81–82.

112. Finger, Hall, and Nelson 1982; Finger 1986.

113. The policy was functional. As an editorialist of the *Daily News Record* wrote about the 1962 MTN agreement, "the cotton textile pact is to be cited as an ideal example of how the U.S. can liberalize its trade policies while still protecting specialized industries from market disruption." *Daily News Record*, 13 December 1961; cited in Aggarwal 1985: 79.

114. Nelson ("High Track") 1989: 107.

115. On antiprotectionist activity, consult Destler and Odell 1987; and Milner 1988.

116. Mikesell 1952: 199.

117. Pastor 1980: 277.

118. Kenen 1960: 83; Baldwin 1966: 200–215.

119. Holliday 1975.

120. Rice 1963: 45; O'Leary 1967: chap. 4.

121. Destler 1980: 68.

122. Cohen 1977: chap. 4.

123. See testimony by William N. Walker, representing the U.S. Council of the International Chamber of Commerce: U.S. Congress, House Committee on Ways and Means 1979: 113. The bill can be found in U.S. Congress, Senate Committee on Government Operations 1979: 127–35. See also *National Journal*, 5 May 1979, 740.

124. U.S. Congress, Senate Committee of Governmental Affairs 1984; Senate Committee of Finance, Subcommittee on International Trade 1984.

125. Merciai 1981: 46.

126. Comparative data for 1980 show that the U.S. resorted to VERs seven times while the eight other largest trading countries in the world resorted to only one VER. In contrast, these other countries resorted to unilateral quotas much more so than the United States. These numbers do not include the voluntary export restraint arrangements negotiated under the auspices of the Multifiber Agreement. See Anjara et al. 1982: table 56, p. 118.

127. *Economist*, 18 February 1989, 52.

128. Milner and Yoffie 1989.

129. Hughes 1979: 23.

130. Hufbauer and Rosen 1986: 34; Richardson 1983: 395.

131. Among them, David Bonior of Michigan, Tim Wirth of Colorado, Richard Gephardt of Missouri, and Stan Lundine and John LaFalce, both of New York.

132. U.S. Congress, House Committee on Banking, Finance, and Urban Affairs, Subcommittee on Economic Stabilization 1983–1984.

133. See LaFalce's interventions, especially U.S. Congress, House Committee on Banking, Finance, and Urban Affairs, Subcommittee on Economic Stabilization, part 5, 26 October 1983, 415; part 3, 18 August 1983, 619; part 2, 14 July 1983, 191.

134. Oral presentations given by Sheldon Friedman and Owen Bieber, respectively

research director and president of the UAW (U.S. Congress, House Committee on Banking, Finance, and Urban Affairs, Subcommittee on Economic Stabilization, part 3, 3 August 1983, 288; part 4, 20 September 1983, 381.

135. Clark 1980; Ray 1981; Marvel and Ray 1983; Godek 1985.

136. Marvel and Ray (1983) found a positive relation. Cheh (1974), Fiekele (1976), Baldwin (1985: tables 4.2 and 4.8), and especially Lavergne (1983: table 7.3), at best found mixed results.

137. Marvel and Ray (1983: table 1) and Godek (1985) found a relation. Lavergne (1983: table 7.2) found none.

138. For 1965, Marvel and Ray (1983: table 1) found a positive significant relation between the consumer goods ratio and the nominal tariff, whereas Lavergne (1983: table 7.2) found a insignificant negative relation with the effective tariff.

139. Lavergne 1983: table 7.5.

140. Ibid., 165.

141. Finger 1986: 274.

142. Ray 1981; Clark 1980; Godek 1985.

143. Ray 1981.

144. Godek 1985.

145. Ray 1981; Marvel and Ray 1983.

146. Marvel and Ray 1983.

147. Shugart and Tollison 1985; Takacs 1981.

148. Hansen 1990.

149. Goldstein 1986.

150. Hansen 1990; Finger, Hall, and Nelson 1982.

151. Finger, Hall, and Nelson 1982: 462.

152. For the 1974 Trade Act, see Baldwin 1976. For the 1985 Textile Bill, see Tosini and Tower 1987. For the 1982 domestic content bill, see Coughlin 1985.

153. The French Méline tariff of 1892 is a historical example of this very move from executive to pressure politics by means of the creation of an oversized logrolling coalition: chap. 8.

Chapter Thirteen

1. That the French and American presidents proceed directly from a national constituency is no guarantee against rent seeking.

2. More generally, Harvard institutionalists view society as the source of instability or inefficiency, and institutions as the source of stability or efficiency. They argue that a weakening of state institutions alternatively lead to revolutions (Huntington 1968, Skocpol 1979), inefficient industrial policies (Katzenstein 1976, Zysman 1977), protection (Krasner 1976, 1978), and cycling voting equilibria (Shepsle and Weingast 1981).

3. See chap. 1, note 2.

4. Stigler 1971: 11.

5. Tocqueville 1945: vol. 1, pp. 243–44; for a debunking of that myth, see Waltz 1967.

6. Complementarity does not entail identity. Kenneth Waltz is a case in point. In *Foreign Policy and Democratic Politics* (1967), Waltz endeavors to show that decentralization is as effective, if not more so, as centralization in the making of foreign

policy. In *Theory of International Politics* (1979) he argues that domestic factors play a secondary role.

7. Nuclear weaponry was revolutionary in that its use promised negative externalities for everyone, including the privileged few, thereby stabilizing international relations in a world in which democracies were still a rare occurrence.

8. Doyle 1986.

Appendix One

1. I am more than grateful to Jim Fearon and Craig Koerner for helping me write this appendix. Mistakes and ambiguities probably are my largest contribution.

2. The assumption of oligopolistic competition does not entail a loss in generality—it is simply a more acurate description of reality than perfect competition. The same equation 5 can be derived, assuming perfect competition and increasing marginal production cost:

$$\pi = P(R)Q - C(Q,G)Q - L(R,G)$$

or a combination of oligopolistic competition and constant production cost:

$$\pi = P(Q,R)Q - C(G)Q - L(R,G)$$

The combination of perfect competition with constant production cost, however, yields no definite equilibrium.

Bibliography

Abel, Deryck. *A History of British Tariffs, 1923–1942*. London: Heath Cranton Ltd, 1945.

Abrahams, Paul P. "The Foreign Expansion of American Finance and its Relationship to the Foreign Economic Policies of the United States, 1907–1921." Ph.D. diss., University of Wisconsin, 1967.

Adams, Frederick C. *The Export-Import Bank and American Foreign Policy, 1934–1939*. Columbia: University of Missouri Press, 1976.

Ageron, Charles-Robert. "La perception de la puissance française en 1938–1939: le mythe impérial." In *La puissance en Europe, 1938–1940*, ed. René Girault and Robert Frank. Paris: Publications de la Sorbonne, 1984, 227–44.

Aggarwal, Vinod K. *Liberal Protectionism: The International Politics of Organized Textile Trade*. Berkeley and Los Angeles: University of California Press, 1985.

Alchian, Armen A., and Harold Demsetz, "Production, Information Costs, and Economic Organization." *American Economic Review* 62, no. 5 (1972): 777–95.

Allain, J-C. "La convention européenne de Bruxelles du 5 mars 1902 sur les sucres." *Relations Internationales* 15 (1978): 255–83.

Allen, G. C. *British Industries and Their Organization*. 5th ed. (London: Longman, 1970).

Allen, William R. "Issues in Congressional Tariff Debates, 1890–1930." *Southern Economic Journal* 20 (April 1954): 346–55.

———. "Cordell Hull and the Defense of the Trade Agreements Program, 1934–1940." In *Isolation and Security*, ed. Alexander de Conde. Durham, N.C.: Duke University Press, 1957, 107–32.

Amacher, Ryan C. Robert D. Tollison, and Thomas D. Willett. "The Divergence between Theory and Practice." In *Tariffs, Quotas and Trade: The Politics of Protectionism*, ed. Walter Adams et al. San Francisco: California Institute for Contemporary Studies, 1979, 35–66.

Amery, Julian. *The Life of Joseph*. Vol. 6. London: Macmillan, 1932.

Angelini, Pierre. *La politique du contingentement des importations*. Paris: Presses Universitaires de France, 1932.

Anjara, Shailendra J. et al. *Developments in International Trade Policy*, Occasional Paper No. 16. Washington, D.C.: International Monetary Fund, 1982.

Arkes, Hadley. *Bureaucracy, the Marshall Plan and the National Interest*. Princeton: Princeton University Press, 1973.

Armitage, S.M.H. *The Politics of Decontrol of Industry: Britain and the United States*. London: London School of Economics and Political Science, 1969.

Arnaud-Ameller, Paule, *La France à l'épreuve de la concurrence internationale, 1951–1966*. Paris: Colin, 1970.

Arnauné, Auguste. *Le commerce extérieur et les tariffs de douane*. Paris: Alcan, 1911.

Arnold, Peri E. "Ambivalent Leviathan: Herbert Hoover and the Positive State." In *Public Values and Private Power in American Politics*, ed. G. David Greenstone. Chicago: The University of Chicago Press, 1982, 109–36.

Ashley, P. *Modern Tariff History: Germany, U.S., France*. London: John Murray, 1920.

Ashley, William J. *The Tariff Problem*. London: King & Son, 1903.

Augé-Laribé, Michel. *La politique agricole de la France, 1880–1940*. Paris: Presses Universitaires de France, 1950.

Augier, Charles, and Angel Marvaud. *La politique douanière de la France*. Paris: F. Alcan, 1911.

Aujac, Henri. "An Introduction to French Industrial Policy." In *French Industrial Policy*, ed. W. J. Adams and Christian Stoffaës. Washington, D.C.: The Brookings Institution, 1986, 13–35.

Baack, Bennett D., and Edward J. Ray. "The Political Economy of Tariff Policy: A Case Study of the United States." *Explorations in Economic History* (20 January 1983): 73–93.

Baker, Richard C. *The Tariff Under Roosevelt and Taft*. Hastings: Nebraska Democrat Printing, 1941.

Balassa, Carol L. "Organized Business in France and the European Common Market: Interest Group Attitudes and Behavior." Ph.D. diss., Johns Hopkins University, 1979.

Baldwin, David A. *Foreign Aid and American Foreign Policy: A Documentary Analysis*. New York: Praeger, 1966.

Baldwin, Robert E. "The Political Economy of Postwar U.S. Trade Policy." *The Bulletin* 4. New York: New York University Center for the Study of Financial Institutions, 1976.

———. *The Political Economy of U.S. Import Policy*. Cambridge: MIT Press, 1985.

Bamberg, J. H. "The Government, the Banks and the Lancashire Cotton Industry, 1918–39." Ph.D. diss., Cambridge University, 1984.

Barral, Pierre. *Les agrariens français de Méline à Pisani*. Paris: Colin, 1968.

———. "Les groupes de pression et le tarif douanier français de 1812." *Revue d'histoire économique et sociale* 52, no. 3 (1974): 421–26.

Barreau, Jocelyne, ed. *L'Etat entrepreneur: Nationalisations, gestion du secteur public concurrentiel, construction européenne (1982–1993)*. Paris: L'Harmattan, 1990.

Bauchard, Philippe. *Bilan de la V République: L'économie au service du pouvoir*. Paris: Calmann-Lévy, 1964.

Bauer, Michel. "The Politics of State-Directed Privatisation: The Case of France, 1986–88." *West European Politics* 11, no. 4 (October 1988): 49–60.

Bauer, Raymond A., Ithiel de Sola Pool, and Lewis A. Dexter. *American Business and Public Policy*. Chicago: Aldine-Atherton, 1972 [1963].

Bauge, Kenneth L. *Voluntary Export Restriction as a Foreign Commercial Policy with Special Reference to Japanese Cotton Textiles, 1930–1962*. New York: Garland, 1987.

Beale, Howard K. "The Tariff and Reconstruction," *American Political Science Review* 35, no. 2 (January 1930): 276–94.

Beard, Charles, and Mary R. Beard. *The Rise of American Civilization*. New York: Macmillan, 1927.

Becker, Gary. "A Theory of Competition among Pressure Groups for Political Influence." *Quarterly Journal Of Economics* 98 (August 1983): 371–400.

Becker, William H. *The Dynamics of Business-Government Relations: Industry and Exports 1893–1921*. Chicago: University of Chicago Press, 1982.

Beckett, Grace L. *The Reciprocal Trade Agreements Program*. New York: Columbia University Press, 1941.

Beer, Samuel H. *Britain Against Itself.* New York: Norton, 1982.

———. *Modern British Politics: Parties and Pressure Groups in the Collectivist Age.* Rev. ed. New York: Norton, 1982.

Bensel, Richard F., *Sectionalism and American Political Development, 1880–1890.* Madison: University of Wisconsin Press, 1984.

Berger, Suzanne. "Lame Ducks and National Champions: Industrial Policy in the Fifth Republic." In *The Impact of the Fifth Republic on France,* ed. W. Andrews and Stanley Hoffmann. Albany: State University of New York Press, 1981, 160–78.

———. "The Socialists and the *Patronat*: The Dilemmas of Co-existence in a Mixed Economy." In *Economic Policy and Policy-Making under the Mitterand Presidency,* ed. Machin and Wright. New York: St. Martin's Press, 1985, 225–43.

———. "French Business: From Transition to Transition." In *The Mitterand Experiment. Continuity and Change in Modern France,* ed. George Ross, Stanley Hoffmann, and Sylvia Malzacher. Oxford: Oxford University Press, 1987, 187–98.

Bernstein, M. *Regulating Business by Independent Commission.* Princeton: Princeton University Press, 1955.

Bernstein, Serge. "Les conceptions du Parti Radical en matière de politique extérieure." *Relations internationales,* no. 13 (Spring 1978): 71–89.

Bézard-Falgas, Pierre. *Les syndicats patronaux de l'industrie métallurgique en France.* Paris: Editions de la vie universitaire, 1922.

Bhagwati, Jagdish N. "The Generalized Theory of Distortions and Welfare." In *Trade, Balance of Payments and Growth: Papers in International Economics in Honour of Charles P. Kindleberger,* ed. Jagdish N. Bhagwati et al. Amsterdam: North Holland, 1972, 69–90.

Bidwell, Percy W. *Tariff Policy of the United States.* New York: Council on Foreign Relations, 1933.

Blank, Stephen. *Industry and Government in Britain. The Federation of British Industries in Politics, 1945–65.* Lexington, Mass.: Lexington Books, 1973.

Blewett, Neal. "Free Fooders, Balfourites, Whole Hoggers, Factionalism within the Unionist Party, 1906–10." *Historical Journal* 11, no. 1 (1968): 95–124.

———. *The Peers, the Parties and the People: The British General Elections of 1910.* Toronto: University of Toronto Press, 1972.

Bobrie, François. "Finances publiques et conquête coloniale: le coût budgétaire de l'expansion française entre 1850 et 1913." *Annales Economies Sociétés Civilisations* 31, no. 6 (1976): 1225–44.

Borrelly-Bitsch, Marie-Thérèse. "Les répercussions du tarif douanier français de 1910 sur les relations franco-belges." *Relations Internationales* 15 (1978): 285–99.

Boston, Jonathan. "Corporatist Incomes Policies, the Free-Rider Problem and the British Labour Government's Social Contract." In *Organized Interests and the State,* ed. A. Cawson. Beverly Hills: Sage, 1985, 65–84.

Bouvier, Jean. "The Banking Mechanisms in France in the Late 19th Century." In *Essays in French Economic History,* ed. Rondo Cameron. Homewood, Ill.: Irwin, 1970, 341–69.

Boyce, Robert W. O. *British Capitalism at the Crossroads, 1919–1932.* Cambridge: Cambridge University Press, 1987.

Brady, David. "A Reevaluation of Realignments in American Politics: Evidence from the House of Representatives." *American Political Science Review* 79, no. 1 (1985): 28–49.

Brandes, Joseph. *Herbert Hoover and Economic Diplomacy: Department of Commerce Policy, 1921–1928.* Pittsburgh: University of Pittsburgh Press, 1962.

Brelet, M. *La crise de la métallurgie: la politique économique et sociale du Comité des forges.* Paris: Sagot & Cie, 1923.

Brown, Benjamin H. *The Tariff Reform Movement in Great Britain 1881–1885.* New York: Columbia University Press, 1943.

Brown, Harry J. "The National Association of Wool Manufacturers, 1864–1897." Ph.D. diss. Cornell University, 1949.

Brown, Kenneth D. "The Trade Union Tariff Reform Association, 1904–1913." *Journal of British Studies* 9, no. 2 (May 1970): 141–53.

Buck, Solon J. *The Agrarian Crusade: A Chronicle of the Farmer in Politics.* New Haven, Conn.: Yale University Press, 1920.

Burnham, Walter D. "The System of 1896: An Analysis." In *Evolution of American Electoral Systems,* ed. P. Kleppner et al. Westport, Conn.: Greenwood Press, 1981, 147–202.

Butler, David, and Anne Sloman. *British Political Facts, 1900–1975,* 4th ed. New York: St. Martin's Press, 1975.

Butler, Harold T. "Partisan Positions on Isolationism vs. Internationalism, 1918–1933." Ph.D. diss., Syracuse University, 1963.

Butler, Hugh. "Statement of Senator Hugh Butler (Republican, Nebraska), for Release to Sunday Morning Papers, February 9, 1947." *Reciprocal Trade Agreements Program Hearings,* U.S. Congress, House Committee on Ways and Means, 80th. Congress, 1st session, 1947.

Cable, Vincent, and Ivonia Rebelo. *Britain's Pattern of Specialization in Manufactured Goods with Developing Countries and Trade Protection.* World Bank, staff working paper no. 425, 1980

Cable, Vincent. *Protectionism and Industrial Decline.* London: Hodder and Stoughton, 1983.

Capie, Forrest. *Depression and Protectionism: Britain between the Wars.* London: Allen & Unwin, 1983.

Carr, J. C., and W. Taplin. *History of the British Steel Industry.* Cambridge, Mass.: Harvard University Press, 1962.

Cassing, James, Timothy J. McKeown, and Jack Ochs. "The Political Economy of the Tariff Cycle." *American Political Science Review* 80, no. 3 (September 1986); 843–62.

Central Statistical Office. *Annual Abstract of Statistics.* London: HMS Stationery Office, various years.

Chandler, Alfred D. "The Structure of American Industry in the Twentieth Century: A Historical Overview." *Business History Review* 43, no. 3 (Autumn 1959): 255–98.

———. *The Visible Hand: The Managerial Revolution in American Business.* Cambridge, Mass.: Belknap Press, 1977.

Cheh, John H. "United States Trade Policy and Short-Run Domestic Adjustment Costs." *Journal of International Economics* 4, no. 4 (1974): 323–40.

Clapham, Sir John. *Economic History of Modern Britain.* Vol. 3. Cambridge: Cambridge University Press, 1963.

Clark, Don P. "The Protection of Unskilled Labor in the United States Manufacturing Industries: Further Evidence." *Journal of Political Economy* 88, no. 6 (December 1980): 1249–54.

Clarke, P. F. *Lancashire and the New Liberalism*. Cambridge: Cambridge University Press, 1971.

―――. "The End of Laissez Faire and the Politics of Cotton." *Historical Journal* 15, no. 3 (1972): 513–32.

Claude, Henry. *Gaullisme et grand capital*. Paris: Editions Sociales, 1961.

Cleary, M. C. *Peasants, Politicians and Producers. The Organization of Agriculture in France since 1918*. Cambridge: Cambridge University Press, 1989.

Cline, Peter. "Winding Down the War Economy: British Plans for Peacetime Recovery, 1916–19." In *War and the State: The Transformation of British Government, 1914–1919*, ed. Kathleen Burk. London: Allen & Unwin, 1982, 157–81.

Coats, A. W. "Political Economy and the Tariff Reform Campaign of 1903." *Journal of Law and Economics* 11 (April 1968): 181–229.

Coben, Stanley. "Northeastern Business and Radical Reconstruction: A Re-examination." *Mississippi Valley Historical Review* 46, no. 1 (June 1959): 67–90.

Coetzee, Frans. "Pressure Groups, Tory Businessmen and the Aura of Political Corruption Before the First World War." *Historical Journal* 29, no. 4 (1986): 833–52.

Cohen, Benjamin J. "The Revolution in Atlantic Economic Relations: A Bargain Comes Unstuck." In *The United States and Western Europe: Political, Economic and Strategic Perspectives*, ed. Wolfram F. Hanrieder. Cambridge, Mass.: Winthrop, 1974, 106–33.

Cohen, Stephen D. *The Making of United States International Economic Policy: Principles, Problems and Proposals for Reform*. New York: Praeger, 1977.

Cohen, Stephen S. *Modern Capitalist Planning: The French Experience*. Cambridge, Mass.: Harvard University Press, 1969.

Cohen, Stephen S. Serge Halimi, and John Zysman. *Institutions, Politics, and Industrial Policy in France*. BRIE Working Paper, University of California, Berkeley, January 1984.

Cole, G.D.G. *A History of the Labour Party from 1914*. London: Routledge and Kegan Paul, 1948.

Coleman, D. C. ed. *Revisions in Mercantilism*. London: Methuen, 1969.

Commission des Communautés européennes. *Premier rapport sur les aides d'état dans la Communauté européenne*. Luxembourg: Office des publications officielles des Communautés européennes, 1989.

Commission des Communautés européennes. *Second rapport sur les aides d'état dans les secteurs des produits manufacturés et certains autres secteurs dans la Communauté européenne*. Luxembourg: Office des publications officielles des Communautés européennes, 1990.

Commission du tariff général des douanes. *Procès-verbaux des séances*. Paris: Librairie des publications législatives, 1878–1879.

Comparison of the Customs Law of 1883 with the New Law of 1890. Washington, D.C.: U.S. Government Printing Office, 1890.

Confederation of British Industry. *The Road to Recovery*. London: CBI, 1976.

Conseil supérieur du commerce, de l'industries et des colonies. *Enquête sur le régime douanier. Questionnaire. Analyse sommaire des réponses*. Paris: Imprimerie Nationale, 1889–1890.

Conybeare, John A. C. "Voting for Protection: An Electoral Model of Tariff Policy." *International Organization* 45, no. 1 (Winter 1991): 57–82.

Coquery-Vidrovitch, Catherine. "L'Afrique coloniale française et la crise de 1930: crise structurelle et genèse du sous-dévelopment." *Revue française d'histoire d'outre-mer* 63 (1976): 386–424.

Corden, W. M., and G. Fels. *Public Assistance to Industry*. London: Macmillan, 1976.

Corey, Lewis. *The House of Morgan*. New York: G. Howard Watt, 1930.

Coughlin, Cletus C. "Domestic Content Legislation: House Voting and the Economic Theory of Regulation." *Economic Inquiry* 23, no. 3 (July 1985): 437–48.

Crouzet, François. "Recherches sur la production d'armements en France (1815–1913)." *Revue historique* 251, no. 509 (Winter 1974): 45–84.

———. "Remarques sur l'industrie des armements en France (du milieu du XIXe siècle à 1914). *Revue historique* 251, no. 510 (Spring 1974): 409–22.

———. "Essor, déclin et renaissance de l'industrie française des locomotives, 1838–1914." *Revue d'histoire économique et sociale* 55, nos. 1–2 (1977): 189–92.

Crozier, Michel, and Erhard Friedberg. *L'acteur et le système*. Paris: Seuil, 1977.

Crozier, Michel, Samuel P. Hungtington, and Joji Watanuki. *The Crisis of Democracy; Report on the Governability of Democracies to the Trilateral Commission*. New York: New York University Press, 1975.

Dacier, Jean-Louis, et al. *Les dossiers noirs de l'industrie française*. Paris: Fayard, 1985.

Deguen, Daniel. "Les moyens de la politique industrielle." In *Politique industrielle et stratégies d'entreprises*. Paris: Masson, 1977.

Desjeux, Dominique, and Erhard Friedberg. "Le Ministère de l'industrie et son environnement." Paris: Hachette, 1973, microfiche.

Destler, I. M. *American Trade Politics*. Washington, D.C. and New York: Institute for International Economics and Twentieth Century Fund, 1986.

———. *Making Foreign Economic Policy*. Washington, D.C.: The Brookings Institution, 1980.

Destler, I. M., and John S. Odell. "Anti-Protection: Changing Forces in United States Trade Politics." *Policy Analyses in International Economics*, no. 21. Washington, D.C.: Institute for International Economics, September 1987.

Detzer, David W. "The Politics of the Payne-Aldrich Tariff of 1909." Ph.D. diss., University of Connecticut, 1970.

———. "Business Reformers, and Tariff Revision: The Payne-Aldrich Tariff of 1909." *The Historian* 35 (February 1973): 196–204.

Dewey, Davis R. *Financial History of the United States*. New York: Longmen, Green & Co., 1903.

Diebold, William. *New Directions in Our Trade Policy*. New Jersey: Council on Foreign Relations, 1941.

———. *The End of the ITO*. Essays in International Finance, no. 16. Princeton: October 1952.

Dobson, Alan P. *U.S. Wartime Aid to Britain*. New York: St. Martin's Press, 1986.

Donnedieu de Vabres, Jacques. "The Formation of Economic and Financial Policy." *International Social Science Bulletin* 8, no. 2 (1956): 228–39.

Dougan, William R. "Tariffs and the Economic Theory of Regulation." In *Research in Law and Economics* 6. JAI Press, 1984, 187–210.

Dougan, William R., and M. C. Munger. "The Rationality of Ideology." *Journal of Law and Economics* 32 (April 1989): 119–42.

Downs, Anthony. *An Economic Theory of Democracy*. New York: Harper and Row, 1957.

Doyle, Michael. "Liberalism and World Politics." *American Political Science Review* 80, no. 4 (1986): 1151–69.

Drummond, Ian M. *British Economic Policy and the Empire, 1919–1939*. London: Allen & Unwin, 1972.

Dulles, John F. "Our Foreign Loan Policy." *Foreign Affairs* 5, no. 1 (October 1926): 33–48.

Dunham, Arthur L. *The Anglo-French Treaty of Commerce of 1860 and the Progress of the Industrial Revolution in France*. Ann Arbor: University of Michigan Publications, 1930.

Eakins, David W. "Business Planners and America's Postwar Expansion." In *Corporations and the Cold War*, ed. David Horowitz. New York: Monthly Review Press, 1969, 143–71.

Ecole Nationale d'Administration. "Les interventions financières de l'Etat en faveur des investissements industriels privés." Rapport de séminaire, 1973.

Edelman, Murray. "Symbols and Political Quiescence." *American Political Science Review* 54, no. 3 (September 1960): 695–704.

Ehrmann, Henry. "The French Trade Associations and the Ratification of the Schuman Plan." *World Politics* 6, no. 4 (July 1954): 453–81.

———. *Organized Business in France*. Princeton: Princeton University Press, 1957.

Eichengreen, Barry J. "The Eternal Fiscal Question: Free Trade and Protection in Britain, 1860–1929." Harvard Institute of Economic Research, discussion paper no. 949, December 1982.

Elwitt, Sanford. *The Making of the Third Republic: Class and Politics in France, 1868–1884*. Baton Rouge: Louisiana State University Press, 1975.

Esping-Andersen, Gøsta. *Politics Against Markets: The Social Democratic Road to Power*. Princeton: Princeton University Press, 1985.

Farnie, D. A. *The English Cotton Industry and the World Market, 1815–1896*. Oxford: Clarendon Press, 1979.

Federation of British Industry. *Organization of British Industry. Report of the FBI. Organization of Industry Committee*. London: FBI, October 1944.

———. *Trade Organization: Relationship with Government. Report of the Trade Organization Committee*. London: FBI, 9 October 1946.

Ferguson, Thomas. "From Normalcy to New Deal: Industrial Structure, Party Competition, and American Public Policy in the Great Depression." *International Organization* 38, no. 1 (Winter 1984): 41–94.

———. "Party Realignment and American Industrial Structure: The Investment Theory of Political Parties in Historical Perspective." In *Research in Political Economy*, vol. 6, ed. Paul Zarembka. (Greenwich, Conn.: JAI Press, 1983, 1–82.

Ferguson, Thomas, and Joel Rogers. *Right Turn: The Decline of the Democrats and the Future of American Politics*. New York: Hill and Wang, 1986.

Fiekele, Norman S. "The Tariff Structure for Manufacturing Industries in the United States: A Test of Some Traditional Explanations." *Columbia Journal of World Business* (Winter 1976): 98–104.

Finger, J. M. "Ideas Count, Words Inform." In *Issues in World Trade Policy; GATT at the Crossroads*, ed. R. H. Snape. New York: St. Martin's Press, 1986, 257–80.

Finger, J. M., H. Keith Hall, and Douglas R. Nelson. "The Political Economy of Administered Protection." *American Economic Review* 72, no. 3 (June 1982): 452–66.

Fiorina, Morris P. *Representatives, Roll-Calls, and Constituencies.* Lexington, Mass.: Lexington Books, 1974.

Fitch, Edwin M. "The Lumber Industry and the Tariff." Ph.D. diss., University of Wisconsin, 1933.

Fite, Gilbert C. *George N. Peek and the Fight for Farm Parity.* Norman: University of Oklahoma Press, 1954.

Fohlen, Claude. *L'industrie textile au temps du Second empire.* Paris: Plon, 1956.

François-Poncet, André. *La vie et l'oeuvre de Robert Pinot.* Paris: Colin, 1927.

Fraser, Peter. "The Unionist Debacle of 1911 and Balfour's Retirement." *Journal of Modern History* 35, no. 4 (December 1963): 354–65.

Friedberg, Erhard. "Administration et entreprises." In *Où va l'administration française?* ed. Michel Crozier et al. Paris: Les Éditions d'Organisation, 1974, 101–40.

Friedberg, Erhard, and Dominique Desjeux. "Les Systèmes d'intervention de l'Etat en matière industrielle." Paris: Hachette, 1973, microfiche.

———. "Fonctions de l'Etat et role des grands corps: le cas du corps des Mines." *Annuaire international de la fonction publique* (Fall 1972): 567–85.

Fuchs, Carl J. *The Trade Policy of Great Britain and Her Colonies since 1860.* London: Macmillan, 1905.

Galambos, Louis. *Competition and Cooperation: The Emergence of a Modern Trade Association.* Baltimore: Johns Hopkins University Press, 1967.

Gallarotti, Giulio M. "Toward a Business-Cycle Model of Tariffs." *International Organization* 39, no. 1 (Winter 1985): 155–88.

Gamble, A. M., and S. A. Walkland. *The British Party System and Economic Policy, 1945–1983: Studies in Adversary Politics.* Oxford: Clarendon Press, 1984.

Gamble, Andrew. *The Conservative Nation.* London: Routledge and Kegan Paul, 1974.

Ganz, Gabriele. *Government and Industry: The Provision of Financial Assistance to Industry.* Abingdon: Professional Books, 1977.

Garanger, André A. *Petite histoire d'une grande industrie.* Neuilly-sur-Seine: Société d'édition pour la mécanique et la machine-outil, 1960.

Gardner, Lloyd C. *Economic Aspects of New Deal Diplomacy.* Madison: University of Wisconsin Press, 1964.

Gardner, Richard N. *Sterling-Dollar Diplomacy; Anglo-American Collaboration in the Reconstruction of Multilateral Trade.* Oxford: Clarendon Press, 1956.

Gaston, Jack W. T. "Policy Making and Free-Trade Diplomacy: Britain's Commercial Relations with Western Europe." Ph.D. diss., University of Saskatchewan, 1975.

Gavin McCrone. *Regional Policy in Britain.* London: Allen & Unwin, 1969.

George, Alexander L., and Timothy J. McKeown. "Case Studies and Theories of Organizational Decision Making." *Advances in Information Processing in Organizations* 2 (1985): 21–58.

Gerbet, Pierre. "La Genèse du Plan Schuman; Des origines à la déclaration du 9 mai 1950." *Revue française de science politique* 6, no. 3 (July–August 1956): 525–53.

Gignoux, Claude J. *L'Après-guerre et la politique commerciale,* 2d ed. Paris: Colin, 1933.

Gille, Bertrand. "Esquisse d'une histoire du syndicalisme patronal dans l'industrie sidérurgique française." *Revue d'histoire de la sidérurgie* 5, no. 3 (July–September 1964): 209–49.

———. *La sidérurgie française au XIXe siècle.* Geneva: Droz, 1968.

Gillet, Marcel. *Les charbonnages du Nord de la France au 19ème siècle.* Paris: Mouton, 1973.

Gilpin, Robert. *The Political Economy of International Relations.* Princeton: Princeton University Press, 1987.

Girault, Arthur. *The Colonial Tariff Policy of France.* Oxford: Clarendon Press, 1916.

Godek, Paul E. "Industry Structure and Redistribution Through Trade Restrictions." *Journal of Law and Economics* 28, no. 3 (October 1985): 687–703.

Godfrey, John F. *Capitalism at War: Industrial Policy and Bureaucracy in France.* Leamington Spa: Berg, 1987.

Goldey, David. "Comment." In *Economic Policy and Policy-Making Under the Mitterand Presidency 1981–84,* ed. Howard Machin and Vincent Wright. New York: St. Martin's Press, 1985, 244–54.

Goldstein, Judith. "The Political Economy of Trade: Institutions of Protection." *American Political Science Review* 80, no. 1 (March 1986): 161–84.

———. "Ideas, Institutions, and American Trade Policy." *International Organization* 42, no. 1 (Winter 1988): 179–218.

Goldstein, Judith, and Barry R. Weingast. "The Origins of American Trade Policy: Rules, Coalitions and International Politics." SSRC Conference on Congress and Foreign Policy, April 21–22, 1991.

Gollin, Alfred M. *Balfour's Burden: Arthur Balfour and Imperial Preference.* London: A. Blond, 1965.

Golob, Eugene O. *The Méline Tariff: French Agriculture and Nationalist Economic Policy.* New York: Columbia University Press, 1944.

Gordon, Margaret S. *Barriers to World Trade: A Study of Recent Commercial Policy.* New York: Macmillan, 1941.

Goujet, Robert. *Protectionnisme en France depuis la guerre dans les faits et la doctrine.* Paris: La vie universitaire, 1922.

Gourevitch, Peter A. *Politics in Hard Times.* Ithaca, N.Y.: Cornell University Press, 1986.

Gowa, Joanne. "Subsidizing American Corporate Expansion Abroad: Pitfalls in the Analysis of Public and Private Power." *World Politics* 37, no. 2 (Jan. 1985): 181–203.

———. "Bipolarity, Multipolarity, and Free Trade." *American Political Science Review* 83, no. 4 (December 1989): 1245–56.

Gramsci, Antonio. *Prison Notebooks.* New York: International Publishers, 1971.

Grant, Wyn. "Business Interests and the British Conservative Party." *Government and Opposition* 15, no. 2 (Spring 1980): 143–61.

Grant, Wyn, and David Marsh. *The Confederation of British Industry.* London: Hodder and Stoughton, 1977.

Grant, Wyn, and Stephen Wilks. "British Industrial Policy: Structural Change, Policy Inertia." *Journal of Public Policy* 3, no. 1 (1983).

Grant, Wyn, with J. Sargent. *Business and Politics in Britain.* London: Macmillan, 1987.

Grassmuck, George L. *Sectional Biases in Congress on Foreign Policy.* Baltimore: Johns Hopkins University Press, 1952.

Green, Diana. "Government and Industry in France: A Contractual Approach." *Public Money* (September 1982): 27–31.

———. "Industrial Policy and Policy-Making, 1974–82." In *Continuity and Change in France,* ed. Vincent Wright. London: Allen & Unwin, 1984, 139–58.

Grove, J. W. *Government and Industry in Britain* London: Longmans, 1962.

Guillen, Pierre. "La politique douanière de la France dans les années vingt." *Relations Internationales* 16 (Winter 1978): 315–31.

Guillen, Pierre. "L'échec des tentatives d'entente économique avec l'Italie (1922–1929)." *Relations Internationales* 13 (Spring 1978): 51–69.

———. "L'avenir de l'Union française dans la négociation des traités de Rome." *Relations Internationales* 57 (Spring 1989): 103–12.

Habermas, Jürgen. *Legitimation Crisis*. Boston: Beacon Press, 1975 [1973].

Haggard, Stephan. "The Institutional Foundations of Hegemony: Explaining the Reciprocal Trade Agreements Act of 1934." *International Organization* 42, no. 1 (Winter 1988): 91–120.

Haight, Frank A. *French Import Quotas: A New Instrument of Commercial Policy*. London: P. S. King, 1935.

———. *A History of French Commercial Policies*. New York: Macmillan, 1941.

Hall, Peter. *Governing the Economy*. New York: Oxford University Press, 1986.

Hansen, John Mark. "Taxation and the Political Economy of the Tariff." *International Organization* 44, no. 4 (Autumn 1990): 527–53.

———. *Gaining Access: Congress and the Farm Lobby, 1919–1981*. Chicago: University of Chicago Press, 1991.

Hansen, Wendy L. "The International Trade Commission and the Politics of Protectionism." *American Political Science Review* 84, no. 1 (March 1990): 21–46.

Hara, Terushi. "Les investissements ferroviaires français en Algérie au XXe siècle." *Revue d'histoire économique et sociale* 54 (1976): 185–211.

Hardach, Gerd. *The First World War, 1914–1918*. Berkeley: University of California Press, 1977.

Harris, Nigel. *Competition and the Corporate Society: British Conservatives, the State and Industry, 1945–64*. London: Methuen, 1972.

Hartmann, Susan M. *Truman and the 80th Congress*. Columbia: University of Missouri Press, 1971.

Hawley, Ellis W. "Herbert Hoover, the Commerce Secretariat, and the Vision of an 'Associate State,' 1921–1928." *Journal of American History* 61 (June 1974): 120.

Hayward, Jack. "Steel." In *Big Business and the State*, ed. R. Vernon. Cambridge, Mass.: Harvard University Press, 1974.

———. "Employers' Associations and the State in France and Britain." In *Industrial Policies in Western Europe*, ed. J. Warnecke and Ezra N. Suleiman. New York: Praeger, 1975, 118–47.

———. *The State and the Market Economy: Industrial Patriotism and Economic Intervention in France*. Brighton, Eng.: Harvester Press, 1986.

Hechter, Kenneth. *Insurgency: Personalities and Politics of the Taft Era*. New York: Columbia University Press, 1940.

Hennebicque, Alain. "Albert Thomas." In *The French Home Front 1914–1918*. Providence, R.I.: Borg, 1992.

Heston, Thomas J. *Sweet Subsidy*. New York: Garland, 1987.

Hirschman, Albert O. *Exit, Voice and Loyalty: Responses to Decline in Firms, Organizations, and States*. Cambridge, Mass.: Harvard University Press, 1970.

Hody, Cynthia A. "From Protectionism to Liberalism: Institutional Change and the Politics of American Trade Policy." Ph.D. diss., University of California, Los Angeles, 1986.

Hoffher, René, ed. *La politique commerciale de la France*. Paris: 1939.

Hoffman, Arthur S. *The European Recovery Program in France: A Case Study in Concentration in Human Society*. Paris: Imprimerie Dippe, 1951.

Holland, R. F. "The Federation of British Industries and the International Economy, 1929–39." *Economic History Review* 34, no. 2 (May 1981): 287–300.

Holliday, George D. "History of the Export-Import Bank of the United States." In *U.S. Financing of East-West Trade: The Political Economy of Government Credits and the National Interest,* ed. Paul Marer. Bloomington, Ind.: International Development Research Center, 1975, 343–48.

Holmes, Martin. *Political Pressure and Economic Policy: British Government 1970–1974.* London: Butterworth Scientific, 1982.

————. *The First Thatcher Government 1979–1983.* London: Harvester Press, 1985.

Holt, Byron W. *Home and Foreign Price of American-made Goods.* New York Tariff Reform Club pamphlet reprinted in *Congressional Record* 40, part 8, (7 June 1906): 8024–33.

Hough, J. R. "Government Intervention in the Economy of France." In *Government Intervention in the Developed Economy,* ed. Peter Maunder. London: Croom Helm, 1979.

Houston, David F. *Eight Years with Wilson's Cabinet.* Garden City: Doubleday, Page and Co., 1926.

Hufbauer, Gary C., Diane T. Berliner, and Kimberly A. Elliott. *Trade Protection in the United States: 31 Case Studies.* Washington, D.C.: Institute for International Economics, 1986.

Hufbauer, Gary C., and Howard Rosen. *Trade Policy for Troubled Industries.* Washington, D.C.: Institute for International Economics, 1986.

Hughes, Kent H. *Trade, Taxes, and Transnationals: International Economic Decision Making in Congress.* New York: Praeger, 1979.

Humphrey, Don D. *American Imports.* New York: Twentieth Century Fund, 1955.

Huntington, Samuel P. *Political Order in Changing Societies.* New Haven, Conn.: Yale University Press, 1968.

Hutchinson, Sir Herbert. *Tariff-Making and Industrial Reconstruction.* London: Harrap, 1965.

Ilersic, A. R. *Parliament of Commerce: The Story of the Association of British Chambers of Commerce.* London: Association of British Chambers of Commerce, 1960.

Ingham, John N. "Robber Barons and the Old Elites." *Mid-America* 52, no. 3 (July 1970): 198–99.

Institut National de la Statistique et des Etudes Economiques (INSEE). *Annuaire statistique de la France.* Paris: Imprimerie Nationale, various years.

Irwin, Douglas A. "Free Trade and Protection in Nineteenth Century Britain and France Revisited." University of Chicago School of Business, unpub. manuscript. Chicago, 1992.

Jeanneney, Jean-Noël. *François de Wendel en république: l'argent et le pouvoir, 1914–1940.* Paris: Seuil, 1976.

————. "Hommes d'affaires au piquet." *Revue historique* 533 (January–March 1980): 81–100.

Jeans, Stephen S. "The British Iron and Steel Industries: Their Conditions and Outlook." In *British Industries,* ed. W. J. Ashley. London: Longmans, Green and Co., 1903, 1–37.

Johnson, Donald B. *National Party Platforms,* rev. ed. Urbana: University of Illinois Press, 1978.

Jones, Joseph M. *The Fifteen Weeks: An Inside Account of the Genesis of the Marshall Plan*. New York: Viking Press, 1955.

Kaiser, David E. *Economic Diplomacy and the Origins of the Second World War*. Princeton: Princeton University Press, 1980.

Katzenstein, Peter. "International Relations and Domestic Structures: Foreign Economic Policies of Advanced Industrial States." *International Organization* 30, no. 1 (Winter 1976): 1–45.

———. *Small States in World Markets: Industrial Policy in Europe*. Ithaca, N.Y.: Cornell University Press, 1985.

———. "Conclusion: Domestic Structures and Strategies of Foreign Economic Policy." In *Between Power and Plenty: Foreign Economic Policies of Advanced Industrial States*, ed. P. Katzenstein. Wisconsin: The University of Wisconsin Press, 1977, 295–336.

Kavanagh, Dennis. *Thatcherism and British Politics. The End of Consensus?* Oxford: Oxford University Press, 1987.

Keeler, John T. S. "Corporatist Decentralization and Commercial Modernization in France: the Royer Law's Impact on Shopkeepers, Supermarkets and the State." In *Socialism, the State and Public Policy in France*, ed. Philip G. Cerny and Martin A. Schain. New York: Methuen, 1985.

Kenen, Peter B. *Giant among Nations: Problems in United States Foreign Economic Policy*. New York: Harcourt, Brace, 1960.

Kenkel, Joseph F. *Tariff Commission Movement: The Search for a Non-Partisan Solution of the Tariff Question*. Ph.D. diss., University of Maryland, 1962.

Kennedy, Paul. *The Realities behind Diplomacy*. London: Fontana, 1981.

Keohane, Robert. *After Hegemony*. Princeton: Princeton University Press, 1984.

Kiewiet, D. Roderick, and Matthew D. McCubbins. *The Logic of Delegation: Congressional Parties and the Appropriations Process*. Chicago: University of Chicago Press, 1991.

Kindleberger, Charles. "Group Behavior and International Trade." *Journal of Political Economy* 59 (February–December 1951): 30–46.

———. "The Rise of Free Trade in Western Europe, 1820–1875." *Journal of Economic History* 35, no. 1 (1975): 20–55.

King, Anthony. "Thatcher's First Term." In *Britain and the Polls 1983. A Study of the General Election*, ed. Austin Ranney. American Enterprise Institute, 1985, 1–38.

Kirby, M. W. *The British Coalmining Industry, 1870–1946: A Political and Economic History*. Hamden, Conn.: Archon Books, 1977.

Kirchheimer, Otto. "The Transformation of the Western European Party Systems." In *Political Parties and Political Development*, ed. La Palombara and Weiner. Princeton: Princeton University Press, 1966, 177–200.

Knight, A. *Private Enterprise and Public Intervention: The Courtaulds Experience*. London: Allen and Unwin, 1974.

Kolboom, Ingo. *La revanche des patrons: le patronat français face au Front Populaire*. Paris: Flammarion, 1986.

Kolko, Gabriel. *The Triumph of Conservatism*. Chicago: Quadrangle, 1963.

———. *The Roots of American Foreign Policy*. Boston: Beacon Press, 1969.

Kolko, Gabriel, and Joyce Kolko. *The Limits of Power: The World and United States Foreign Policy, 1945–1954*. New York: Harper and Row, 1972.

Kottman, Richard N. *Reciprocity and the North Atlantic Triangle*. Ithaca, N.Y.: Cornell University Press, 1968.

Krasner, Stephen D. "State Power and the Structure of International Trade." *World Politics* 28 (April 1976): 317–47.

———. "United States Commercial and Monetary Policy: Unravelling the Paradox of External Strength and Internal Weakness." In *Between Power and Plenty*, ed. P. Katzenstein. Madison: University of Wisconsin Press, 1977, 51–88.

———. *Defending the National Interest*. Princeton: Princeton University Press, 1978.

———. "Approaches to the State: Alternative Conceptions and Historical Dynamics." *Comparative Politics* 16, no. 2 (January 1984): 223–46.

Kreider, Carl J. "International Affairs: Domestic Processes in the Trade Agreements Program." *American Political Science Review* 34, no. 2 (April 1940): 317–32.

———. *The Anglo-American Trade Agreement: A Study of British and American Commercial Policies, 1934–1939*. Princeton: Princeton University Press, 1943.

Krueger, Anne O. "The Political Economy of the Rent-Seeking Society." *American Economic Review* 64 (1974): 291–303.

Kuisel, Richard F. *Capitalism and the State in Modern France: Renovation and Economic Management in the Twentieth Century*. Cambridge: Cambridge University Press, 1981.

Kurth, James. "The Political Consequences of the Product Cycle: Industrial History and Political Outcomes." *International Organization* 33, no. 1 (Winter 1979): 1–34.

Laffey, John F. "The Roots of French Imperialism: The Case of Lyon." *French Historical Studies* 6, no. 1 (Spring 1969): 78–93.

Lake, David A. *Power, Protection, and Free Trade: International Sources of U.S. Commercial Strategy, 1887–1939*. Ithaca, N.Y.: Cornell University Press, 1988.

Lasserre, Marc. *Les nouvelles orientations de la politique commerciale française*. Paris: Presses Universitaires de France, 1933.

Laughlin, James L., and Willis Parker. *Reciprocity*. New York: Baker and Taylor, 1903.

Lauren, Paul G. *Institutional Responses to Twentieth-Century Diplomacy in France and Germany*. Stanford, Calif.: Hoover Institute, 1976.

Lautman, Jacques, and Jean-Claude Thoenig. "La planification, agent de changement dans quelques administrations publiques françaises." In *Tendances et volontés de la société française*. Paris: SEDEIS, 1966, 229–47.

Lavau, Georges, Gérard Grunberg, and Nonna Mayer, eds. *L'univers politique des classes moyennes*. Paris: Presses de la Fondation nationale des sciences politiques, 1983.

Lavergne, Réal P. *The Political Economy of U.S. Tariffs*. Toronto: Academic Press, 1983.

Leach, Duave M. "The Tariff and the Western Farmer: 1860–1890." Ph.D. diss., University of Oklahoma, 1965.

Lebovics, Herman. *The Alliance of Iron and Wheat in the Third French Republic, 1860–1914*. Baton Rouge: Louisiana State University Press, 1988.

Leddy, John M., and John W. Norwood. "The Escape Clause." In *Studies in United States Commercial Policy*, ed. Wiliam B. Kelly. Chapel Hill: University of North Carolina Press, 1963, 124–73.

Lefranc, Georges. *Les organisations patronales en France; du passé au présent*. Paris: Payot, 1976.

Le Gall, Gérard. "Printemps 1988: retour à une gauche majoritaire." *Revue politique et parlementaire* 90, no. 936 (July–August 1988): 14–24.

Lehmbruch, Gerhard. "Liberal Corporatism and Party government." In *Trend Toward Corporatist Intermediation*, ed. P. C. Schmitter and G. Lehmbruch. London: Sage, 1979, 147–84.

———. "Interest Groups, Government, and the Politics of Protectionism." *Aussenwirtschaft* 41, nos. 2–3 (1986): 273–302.

Leruez, Jacques. *Economic Planning and Politics in Britain*. Oxford: Martin Robertson, 1975.

Levasseur, E. *Histoire du commerce de la France. Deuxième partie: de 1789 à nos jours.* Paris: Arthur Rousseau, 1912.

Lewis, Cleona. *America's Stake in International Investments*. Washington, D.C.: Brookings Institution, 1938.

Lhomme, Jean. *La grande bourgeoisie au pouvoir, 1830–1880*. Paris: Presses Universitaires de France, 1960.

Lieber, Robert J. *British Politics and European Unity*. Berkeley: University of California Press, 1970.

Liechty, Elden E. "Economic and Political Forces Shaping the Smoot-Hawley Tariff Act of 1930." Ph.D. diss., University of Utah, 1972.

Lindeen, James W. "Interest-group Attitudes Toward Reciprocal Legislation." *Public Opinion Quarterly* 34, no. 1 (Spring 1970): 108–12.

Link, Arthur S. *Wilson; The New Freedom*. Vol. 2. Princeton: Princeton University Press, 1956.

Lipset, Seymour M., and Stein Rokkan. "Cleavage Structures, Party Systems and Voter Alignments: An Introduction." In *Party Systems and Voter Alignments*, ed. Lipset and Rokkan. New York: Free Press, 1967, 1–64.

Lohmann, Susanne, and Sharyn O'Halloran. "Delegation and Accommodation in U.S. Trade Policy." Stanford University, October 21, 1991, unpub. manuscript.

Longstreth, Frank. "The City, Industry and the State." In *State and Economy in Contemporary Capitalism*, ed. Colin Crouch. New York: St. Martin's Press, 1979, 157–90.

Louis, Pierre. "Aide publique et dévelopement économique régional." *Economie et statistique* 80 (July–August 1976): 13–24.

Lowe, Marvin E. *The British Tariff Movement*. Washington, D.C.: American Council on Public Affairs, 1942.

Lowi, Theodore. "American Business, Public Policy, Case-Studies, and Political Theory." *World Politics* 16, no. 4 (July 1964): 677–715.

Lubenow, W. C. *Parliamentary Politics and the Home Rule Crisis: The British House of Commons in 1886*. Oxford: Clarendon Press, 1988.

Lucas, Arthur F. *Industrial Reorganization and the Control of Competition: The British Experiment*. London: Longmans, Green and Co., 1937.

Luebbert, Gregory M. *Comparative Democracy: Policymaking and Governing Coalitions in Europe and Israel*. New York: Columbia University Press, 1986.

———. *Liberalism, Fascism, or Social Democracy: Social Classes and the Political Origins of Regimes in Interwar Europe*. Oxford: Oxford University Press, 1991.

Lynch, Frances M. B. "Resolving the Paradox of the Monnet Plan: National and International Planning in French Reconstruction." *Economic History Review* 37, no. 2 (May 1984): 229–43.

MacDonald, A. C. "Economic Appeasement and the German Moderates, 1937–1939. An Introductory Essay." *Past and Present* 56 (August 1972): 105–35.

Macmahon, Arthur W. "American Government and Politics." *American Political Science Review* 24, no. 1 (February 1930): 50–56.

———. "American Government and Politics." *American Political Science Review* 24, no. 2 (August 1930): 920–26.

Maddison, Angus. *Phases of Capitalist Development.* Oxford: Oxford University Press, 1982.

Magee, Stephen P., William A. Brock, and Leslie Young. *Black Hole Tariffs and Endogenous Policy Theory.* Cambridge: Cambridge University Press, 1989.

Maier, Charles S. *Recasting Bourgeois Europe: Stabilization in France, Germany, and Italy in the Decade after World War I.* Princeton: Princeton University Press, 1975.

March, James G., and Johan P. Olsen. *Rediscovering Institutions. The Organizational Basis of Politics.* New York: Free Press, 1989.

Margairaz, Michel. "Les propositions de politique économique, financière et monétaire de la S.F.I.O. de 1934 à 1936: la reflation." Mémoire de Maîtrise, Université de Paris 8, 1972. Paris: Publications de l'A.U.D.I.R. and Hachette, 1973, also on microfiche.

Marks, Stephen V., and John McArthur. "Empirical Analyses of the Determinants of Protection: A Survey and Some New Results." In *International Trade Policies,* ed. John S. Odell and Thomas D. Willett. Ann Arbor: University of Michigan Press, 1990, 105–39.

Marrison, A. J. "British Businessmen and the Scientific Tariff: A Study of Joseph Chamberlain's Tariff Commission, 1903–1921." Ph.D. diss., University of Hull, 1980.

———. "Businessmen, Industries, and Tariff Reform in Great Britain, 1903–1930." *Business History* 25, no. 2 (July 1983): 148–78.

Marseille, Jacques. *Empire colonial et capitalisme français: histoire d'un divorce.* Paris: Albin Michel, 1984.

Marvel, Howard P., and Edward J. Ray. "The Kennedy Round: Evidence on the Regulation of International Trade in the United States." *American Economic Review* 73, no. 1 (March 1983): 190–97.

Maunder, Peter. *Government Intervention in the Developed Economy.* London: Croom Helm, 1979.

Mayer, Nonna, and Etienne Schweisguth. "Classe, position sociale et vote." In *Explication du vote: un bilan des études électorales en France,* ed. Daniel Gaxie. Paris: Presses de la Fondation nationale des sciences politiques, 1985, 263–90.

Mayer, Nonna, and Pascal Perrineau, eds. *Le Front National à découvert.* Paris: Presses de la Fondation Nationale des Sciences Politiques, 1991.

Mayer, Robert S. *The Influence of Frank A. Vanderlip and the National City Bank on American Commerce and Foreign Policy, 1910–1920.* New York: Garland, 1987.

Mayer, Wolfgang. "Endogenous Tariff Formation." *American Economic Review* 74 (1984): 970–85.

McCormack, R. "Prelude to Progressivism, 1890–1910." *New York History* 59 (1978): 253–76.

McCrone, Gavin. *Regional Policy in Britain.* London: Allen & Unwin, 1969.

McCubbins, Matthew, Roger Noll, and Barry Weingast. "Administrative Procedures as an Instrument of Political Control." *Journal of Law, Economics, and Organization* 3 (1987): 243–77.

McPherson, C. P. "Tariff Structures and Political Exchange." Ph.D. diss., University of Chicago, 1972.

Megaw, M. Ruth. "Australia and the Anglo-American Trade Agreement, 1938." *Journal of Imperial and Commonwealth History* 3 (1975): 192–211.

Merciai, Patrizio. "Safeguard Measures in GATT." *Journal of World Trade Law* 75, no. 1 (1972): 41–46.

Mérigot, Jean Guy. *Essai sur les comités d'organisation professionnelle.* Paris: Librairie générale de droit et de jurisprudence, 1943.

Messerlin, Patrick A. "Les déterminants de la demande de protection: le cas français." *Revue économique* 33, no. 6 (November 1982): 1001–23.

———. "Bureaucracies and the Political Economy of Protection." World Bank Staff Report, no. 568. Washington, D.C.: The World Bank, 1983.

Metzger, Stanley D. *Trade Agreements and the Kennedy Round: An Analysis of the Economic, Legal, and Political Aspects of the Trade Expansion Act of 1962 and the Prospects for the Kennedy Round of Tariff Negotiations.* Fairfax, Va.: Coiner, 1964.

Meynier, Gilbert. *L'Algérie révélée: la guerre de 1914–1918 et le premier quart du XXe siècle.* Geneva: Droz, 1981.

Middlemas, Keith. *Politics in Industrial Society: The Experience of the British System since 1911.* London: André Deutsch, 1979.

Mikesell, Raymond F. *United States Economic Policy and International Relations.* New York: McGraw-Hill, 1952.

Miller, Clarence L. *The States of the Old Northwest and the Tariff.* Emporia, Kans.: Emporia Gazette Press, 1929.

Milner, Helen. "Trading Places: Industries for Free Trade." *World Politics* 40 (April 1988): 350–76.

Milward, Alan S. *War, Economy and Society, 1939–1945.* Berkeley: Univeristy of California Press, 1979.

Mitchell, B. R. *European Historical Statistics. 1750–1975.* New York: Facts on File, 1980.

Moore, Barrington. *Social Origins of Dictatorship and Democracy: Lord and Peasant in the Making of the Modern World.* Boston: Beacon Press, 1966.

Moravcsik, Andrew. "Negotiating the Single European Act: National Interests and Conventional Statecraft in the European Community." *International Organization* 45, no. 1 (Winter 1991): 19–56.

Morgan, Kenneth O. *Labour in Power, 1945–1951.* Oxford: Clarendon Press, 1984.

Morvan, Yves. *La concentration de l'industrie en France.* Paris: Colin, 1972.

Mueller, Dennis C. *Public Choice II.* Cambridge: Cambridge University Press, 1989.

Murray, Bruce K. *The People's Budget 1909/10: Lloyd George and Liberal Politics.* Oxford: Clarendon Press, 1980.

Myers, William S. "The Republican Party and the Tariff." *Annals of the American Academy of Political and Social Science.* Vol. CXLI. 1929.

Mytelka, Lynn. "The French Textile Industry: Crisis and Adjustment." In *The Emerging International Economic Order: Dynamics, Constraints and Possibilities,* ed. H. K. Jacobson and D. Sidjanski. Beverly Hills, Calif.: Sage, 1982, 129–66.

Nairn, Tom. "The Left against Europe." *New Left Review* 75 (1972), special issue.

National Planning Association. "The Foreign Aid Program and the United States Economy." In *Foreign Aid Program: Compilation of Studies and Surveys*. U.S. Senate, 85th. Congress, 1st session, Doc. no. 52, March 1957.

Naudin, Jean. *Les accords commerciaux de la France depuis la guerre*. Paris: Recueil Sirey, 1928.

Naville, Pierre. et al. *L'Etat entrepreneur: le cas de la Régie Renault*. Paris: Anthropos, 1971.

Nelson, Douglas. "On the High Track to Protection: The U.S. Automobile Industry, 1979–1981." In *Pacific Dynamics*, ed. Stephen Haggard and Chung-in Moon. Boulder, Colo.: Westview Press, 1989, 97–128.

————. "The Domestic Political Preconditions of U.S. Trade Policy: Liberal Structure and Protectionist Dynamics." *Journal of Public Policy* 9, no. 1 (January–March 1989): 83–109.

Nichols, Jeannette P. "Silver Diplomacy." *Political Science Quarterly* 48, no. 4 (1933).

Niskanen, W. A., Jr. *Bureaucracy and Representative Government*. Chicago: Aldine-Atherton, 1971.

Nogués, Julio J., Andrzej Olechowski, and L. Alan Winters. "The Extent of Nontariff Barriers to Industrial Countries' Imports." *World Bank Economic Review* 1, no. 1 (1986): 181–99.

Noll, Roger. "The Political Foundations of Regulatory Policy." *Journal of Institutional and Theoretical Economics* 139 (1983): 377–404. See also, chap. 2, note 26.

North, Douglass C. *Institutions, Institutional Change, and Economic Performance*. Cambridge, Mass.: Harvard University Press, 1991.

Nye, John Vincent. "The Myth of Free-Trade Britain and Fortress France: Tariffs and Trade in the Nineteenth Century." *Journal of Economic History* 51 (March 1991): 23–46.

O'Halloran, Sharyn. "Congress, Parties, and the Tariff, 1878–1934." Paper presented at the Midwest Political Science Association meeting, Chicago, April 1991.

O'Leary, Michael K. *The Politics of American Foreign Aid*. New York: Atherton Press, 1967.

Ogburn, W., and W. Jaffé. *The Economic Development of Post-War France*. New York: Colombia University Press, 1929.

Olson, Mancur, Jr. *The Logic of Collective Action*. Cambridge, Mass.: Harvard University Press, 1965.

————. *The Rise and Decline of Nations*. New Haven, Conn.: Yale University Press, 1982.

Organization for Economic Cooperation and Development. *Industrial Support Policies in OECD Countries, 1986–1989*. Paris: OECD, 1992.

Oulton, Nicholas. "Effective Protection of British Industry." In *Public Assistance to Industry*, ed. W. M. Corden and G. Fels. London: Macmillan, 1976, 46–90.

Ovenden, Keith. *The Politics of Steel*. London: Macmillan, 1978.

Padioleau, Jean G. *Quand la France s'enferre*. Paris: Presses Universitaires de France, 1981.

Panitch, Leo. "The Development of Corporatism in Liberal Democracies." In *Trend Toward Corporatist Intermediation*, ed. P. C. Schmitter and G. Lehmbruch. London: Sage, 1979, 119–46.

Parrini, Carl P. *Heir to Empire: United States Economic Diplomacy, 1916–1923.* Pittsburgh: University of Pittsburgh Press, 1969.

Parsons, J. G. *Protection's Favors to Foreigners.* Reprinted in U.S. Congress, Senate, *Senate Documents,* 61st Congress, 1st session, vol. 54, 1910, 9–59.

Pastor, Robert A. *Congress and the Politics of U.S. Foreign Economic Policy.* Berkeley and Los Angeles: University of California Press, 1980.

Pelling, Henry. *Social Geography of British Elections 1885–1910.* London: Macmillan, 1967.

Peltzman, Sam. "Towards a More General Theory of Regulation." *Journal of Law and Economics* 9 (August 1976): 211–40.

Perry, O. H. "Proposed Tariff Legislation Since 1883." *Quarterly Journal of Economics* 2 (October 1887): 69–78.

Pierre-Brossolette, Sylvie, and Sabine Delanglade. "Les nouveaux réseaux de la gauche." *L'Express.* 5 January 1990): 56–62.

Pincus, Jonathan J. *Pressure Group and Politics in Antebellum Tariffs.* New York: Columbia University Press, 1977.

Pineau, Pierre. "Les artisans-commerçants et la nouvelle structure politique." *Eglise aujourd'hui en monde rural* 433 (December 1981): 585–97.

Pinot, Robert. "La métallurgie et la révision du tarif douanier." *Revue politique et parlementaire* 60, no. 179 (May 1909): 238–63.

———. "La métallurgie, la construction mécanique et la révision du tarif douanier." *Revue politique et parlementaire* 60, no. 180 (June 1909): 490–516.

———. *Le Comité des Forges de France au service de la nation.* Paris: Colin, 1919.

Pinto-Duschinsky, Michael. *British Political Finance, 1830–1980.* Washington, D.C.: American Enterprise Institute, 1981.

Pitkin, Hanna F. *The Concept of Representation.* Berkeley: University of California Press, 1967.

Pitkin, Thomas M. "Western Republicans and the Tariff in 1860." *Mississippi Valley Historical Review* 27, no. 3 (December 1940): 401–20.

Platt, D.C.M. *Finance, Trade, and Politics in British Foreign Policy 1815–1914.* Oxford: Clarendon Press, 1968.

Plowden, Willian. *The Motor Car and Politics, 1896–1970.* London: Bodley Head, 1971.

Poidevin, Raymond. *Les relations économiques et financières entre la France et l'Allemagne de 1898 à 1914.* Paris: Colin, 1969.

———. "Fabricants d'armes et relations internationales au début du XXe siècle." *Relations internationales* 1 (1971): 39–56.

———. "Protectionnisme et relations internationales: l'exemple du tariff douanier français de 1910." *Relations internationales* 15 (1978): 47–62.

Political and Economic Planning. "British Trade Associations." *Planning* 10, no. 221 (12 May 1944): 1–23.

———. "Government and Industry." *Planning* 17, no. 318 (18 September 1950): 41–59.

———. *Industrial Trade Associations: Activities and Organization.* London: Allen & Unwin, 1957.

Pollard, Robert A. *Economic Security and the Origins of the Cold War, 1945–1950.* New York: Columbia University Press, 1985.

Pontusson, Jonas. *The Limits of Social Democracy: Investment Politics in Sweden*. Ithaca, N.Y.: Cornell University Press, 1992.

Portelli, Hugues. "La résistible ascension du libéral-conservatisme." *Revue politique et parlementaire* 90, no. 935 (May–June 1988): 23–28.

Posner, R. "Theories of Economic Regulation." *Bell Journal of Economics* 5 (1974): 335–58.

Price, Harry B. *The Marshall Plan and its Meaning*. Ithaca, N.Y.: Cornell University Press, 1955.

Priouret, Roger. *Origines du patronat français*. Paris: Grasset, 1963.

Przeworski, Adam. *Democracy and Market*. Cambridge: Cambridge University Press, 1991.

Ramsden, John. *The Age of Balfour and Baldwin, 1902–1940*. London: Longmans, 1978.

Ratcliffe, Barrie M. "The Tariff Reform in France, 1831–1836." *Journal of European Economic History* 7, no. 1 (Spring 1978): 61–138.

Ray, Edward J. "Determinants of Tariff and Nontariff Trade Restrictions in the U.S." *Journal of Political Economy* 89, no. 1 (1981): 105–21.

Rempel, Richard A. *Unionists Divided. Arthur Balfour, Joseph Chamberlain and the Unionist Free Traders*. Hamden, Conn.: Archon Books, 1972.

Report of the Commission of Inquiry into Industrial and Commercial Representations. (Devlin Report), London, Association of British Chambers of Commerce; Confederation of British Industry, 1972.

Report of the Tariff Commission, 7 vols. London: King & Son, 1904–1907.

Rice, Andrew E. "Building a Constituency for the Foreign Aid Program: The Record of the Eisenhower Years." Ph.D. diss., Syracuse University, 1963.

Richardson, J. David. "Worker Adjustment to U.S. International Trade: Programs and Prospects." In *Trade Policy in the 1980s*, ed. William Cline. Washington, D.C.: Institute for International Economics, 1983.

Riker, William H., and Steven J. Brams. "The Paradox of Vote Trading." *American Political Science Review* 67 (1973): 1235–47.

Riker, William H. "Implications from the Disequilibrium of Majority Rule for the Study of Institutions." *American Political Science Review* 74, no. 2 (June 1980): 432–46.

Rist, M. "Une expérience française de libération des échanges au dix-neuvième siècle: le traité de 1860." *Revue d'économie politique* (November–December 1956): 908–61.

Roberts, Richard. "The Administrative Origins of Industrial Diplomacy: An Aspect of Government Industry Relations, 1929–1935." In *Businessmen and Politics*, ed. John Turner. London: Heinemann, 1984, 93–104.

Roberts, Stephen H. *History of French Colonial Policy, 1870–1925*. London: King & Son, 1929.

Rogow, Arnold A. *The Labour Government and British Industry, 1945–1951*. Oxford: Blackwell, 1955.

Rogowski, Ronald. "Trade and the Variety of Democratic Institutions." *International Organization* 41, no. 2 (Spring 1987): 203–24.

———. *Commerce and Coalitions*. Princeton: Princeton University Press, 1989.

Rohrlich, Paul E. "Economic Culture and Foreign Policy." *International Organization* 41, no. 1 (Winter 1987): 61–92.

Rooth, T.J.T. "Limits of Leverage: The Anglo-Danish Trade Agreement of 1933." *Economic History Review* 2d ser., no. 37 (May 1984): 211–28.

Rose, Richard. *Influencing Voters.* New York: St. Martin's Press, 1967.

Rosenstock-Franck. "Facteurs politiques." In *La politique commerciale de la France*, ed. René Hoffherr. Paris: 1939.

Rothbard, Murray N. "War Collectivism in World War I." In *A New History of Leviathan*, ed. Ronald Radosh and Murray N. Rothbard. New York: Dutton & Co., 1972, 66–110.

Rowland, Benjamin M. *Commercial Conflict and Foreign Policy: A Study in Anglo-American Relations, 1932–1938.* New York: Garland Publishing, 1987.

Rowley, Charles K., and Robert D. Tollison. "Rent-Seeking and Trade Protection." *Aussenwirtschaft* 41, nos. 2–3 (1986): 303–28.

Royal Commission. *Depression of Trade and Industry.* London: Eyre and Spottiswoode, 1886.

Royal Institute of International Affairs. *The Colonial Problem.* London: Oxford University Press, 1937.

Ruggie, John G. "International Regimes, Transactions, and Change: Embedded Liberalism in the Postwar Economic Order." *International Organization* 36 (Spring 1982): 379–415.

Rust, Michael J. "Business and Politics in the Third Republic: The Comité des Forges and the French Steel Industry, 1896–1914." Ph.D. diss., Princeton University, 1973.

Sartori, Giovanni. *Parties and Party Systems: A Framework for Analysis.* Cambridge: Cambridge University Press, 1976.

Saul, S. B. "The Motor Industry in Britain to 1914." *Business History* 5 (1962–63): 22–44.

Sauvy, Alfred. *Histoire économique de la France entre les deux guerres (1918–1931): de l'armistice à la dévaluation de la livre.* 3 vols. Paris: Economica, 1984.

Scally, R. J. *The Origins of the Lloyd George Coalition.* Princeton: Princeton University Press, 1975.

Schattschneider, E. E. *Politics, Pressures and the Tariff: A Study of Free Enterprise in Pressure Politics, as Shown in the 1929–1930 Revision of the Tariff.* New York: Prentice-Hall, 1935.

———. *The Semisovereign People: A Realist's View of Democracy in America.* New York: Holt, Rinehart, and Winston, 1960.

Schatz, Arthur W. "The Anglo-American Trade Agreement and Cordell Hull's Search for Peace 1936–1938." *Mississippi Valley Historical Review* 57 (June 1970): 85–103.

Schlenker, L. H. "Local Industrial Strategies. A Key to French Economic Planning in the Eighties?" *Comparative Politics* 19, no. 3 (April 1987): 267–81.

Schmidt, Vivien A. "Industrial Management under the Socialists in France. Decentralized *Dirigism* at the National and Local Levels." *Comparative Politics* 21, no. 1 (October 1988): 53–74.

Schmieder, Eric. "La Chambre de 1885–1889 et les affaires du Tonkin." *Revue française d'histoire d'outre-mer* 53, nos. 192–93 (Summer and Fall 1966): 153–214.

Schmitter, Philippe C. "Interest Intermediation and Regimes Governability: Contemporary Western Europe and North America." In *Organizing Interests in Western Europe*, ed. Suzanne Berger. Cambridge: Cambridge University Press, 1981, 287–330.

Schriftgiesser, Karl. *Business Comes of Age: The Story of the Committee for Economic Development and Its Impact upon the Economic Policies of the United States, 1942–1960*. New York: Harper, 1960.

Self, Robert C. *Tories and Tariffs: The Conservative Party and the Politics of Tariff Reform, 1922–1932*. New York: Garland Publishing, 1986.

Sémars, Fernand. *Relations économiques des colonies avec la métropole*. Nancy: Imprimerie L. Kreis, 1905.

Semmel, Bernard. *Imperialism and Social Reform*. London: Unwin, 1960.

Shanks, Michael. *Planning and Politics*. London: Allen & Unwin, 1977.

Sharp, M., and Geoffrey Shepherd. *Managing Change in British Industry*. Geneva: International Labor Organization, late 1980s.

Sheahan, James. *Promotion and Control of Industry in Postwar France*. Cambridge, Mass.: Harvard University Press, 1963.

Shepherd, Geoffrey. "United Kingdom: A Resistance to Change." In *Managing Industrial Change in Westyern Europe*, ed. François Duchêne and Geoffrey Shepherd. London: Frances Pinter, 1987, 145–77.

Shepsle, Kenneth A., and Barry R. Weingast. "Structure Induced Equilibrium and Legislative Choice." *Public Choice* 37 (1981): 503–19.

Shugart, William F., and Robert D. Tollison. "The Cyclical Character of Regulatory Activity." *Public Choice* 45, no. 3 (1985): 303–11.

Silberman, Bernard S. *The Rationalization of State Bureaucracy: A Comparative Strategic Choice Analysis of France, Japan, The United States and Great Britain*. Chicago: University of Chicago Press, 1993.

Sklar, Martin J. "Woodrow Wilson and the Political Economy of United States Liberalism." *Studies on the Left* 1 (1959–60): 17–47.

Skocpol, Theda. *States and Social Revolutions*. Cambridge: Cambridge University Press, 1979.

———. "Bringing the State Back In: Strategies of Analysis in Current Research." In *Bringing the State Back In*, ed. Peter E. Evans, Dietrich Rueschemeyer, and Theda Skocpol. Cambridge: Cambridge University Press, 1985, 3–43.

Skowronek, Stephen. *Building a New American State*. Cambridge: Cambridge University Press, 1982.

Skuse, Allen. *Government Intervention and Industrial Policy*, 3d ed. London: Heinemann, 1983.

Smith, Michael S. "Free Trade Versus Protection in the Early Third Republic: Economic Interests, Tariff Policy, and the Making of the Republican Synthesis." *French Historical Studies* 10, no. 2 (Fall 1977): 293–314.

Smith, Michael S. *Tariff Reform in France, 1860–1900*. Ithaca, N.Y.: Cornell University Press, 1980.

Snyder, Jack. *Myths of Empire: Domestic Politics and International Ambition*. Ithaca, N.Y.: Cornell University Press, 1991.

Snyder, Rixford K. *The Tariff Problem in Great Britain, 1918–1923*. New York: AMS Press, 1971.

Soulier, Auguste. *L'instabilité ministérielle sous la Troisième République, 1871–1938*. Paris: Recueil Sirey, 1939.

Stanwood, Edward. *American Tariff Controversies in the Nineteenth Century*. Boston: Houghton Mifflin, 1903.

Steigerwalt, Albert K. *The National Association of Manufacturers, 1895–1914: A Study in Leadership.* Ann Arbor: University of Michigan Graduate School of Business Administration, 1964.

Stein, Arthur A. "The Hegemon's Dilemma: Great Britain, the United States, and the International Economic Order." *International Organization* 38, no. 1 (Spring 1984): 355–86.

―――. *Why Nations Cooperate.* Ithaca, N.Y.: Cornell University Press, 1991.

Stephenson, Nathaniel W. *Nelson W. Aldrich: A Leader in American Politics.* New York: Charles Scribner's Sons, 1930.

Stern, Clarence A. *Golden Republicanism: The Crusade for Hard Money.* Ann Arbor, Mich.: 1964.

Steward, Dick. *Trade and Hemisphere.* Columbia: University of Missouri Press, 1975.

Stewart, M. *Politics and Economic Policy in the UK since 1964: The Jekyll and Hyde Years.* Oxford: Pergamon, 1978.

Stigler, George J. "The Theory of Economic Regulation." *The Bell Journal of Economics and Management Science* 2, no. 1 (Spring 1971): 3–21.

Stolper, Wolfgang F., and Paul A. Samuelson. "Protection and Real Wages." *Review of Economic Studies* 9–10 (1941–43), 58–73.

Stopford, John M. "The Origins of British-Based Multinational Manufacturing Enterprises." *Business History Review* 48, no. 3 (Autumn 1974): 303–35.

Streat, Sir Raymond. "Government Consultation with Industry." *Public Administration* 37 (Spring 1959): 1–8.

Suleiman, Ezra. *Politics, Power and Bureaucracy.* Princeton: Princeton University Press, 1974.

Summers, Festus P. *William L. Wilson and Tariff Reform; a Biography.* New Brunswick, N.J.: Rutgers University Press, 1953.

Sundquist, James L. *Dynamics of the Party System.* Washington, D.C.: The Brookings Institution, 1973.

Sykes, Alan. *Tariff Reform in British Politics, 1903–1913.* Oxford: Clarendon Press, 1979.

Takacs, Wendy E. "Pressures for Protectionism: An Empirical Analysis." *Economic Inquiry* 19 (October 1981): 687–93.

Tarbell, Ida. *The Tariff in Our Times.* New York: Macmillan, 1911.

Tasca, Henry J. *The Reciprocal Trade Policy of the United States: A Study in Trade Philosophy.* Philadelphia: University of Pennsylvania Press, 1938.

―――. *World Trading Systems.* Paris: International Institute of Intellectual Cooperation, 1939.

Taussig, Frank W. *The Silver Situation in the United States.* Baltimore, Md.: Guggenheim, Weil, 1893.

―――. *Some Aspects of the Tariff Question: An Examination of the Development of American Industries Under Protection,* 3d ed. New York: Greenwood Press, 1969 [1915].

―――. *Tariff History of the United States.* New York: G. P. Putnam, 1931.

Tawney, R. H. "The Abolition of Economic Controls, 1918–1921." *Economic History Review* 13, nos. 1–2 (1943): 1–30.

Tedesco, Paul H. "Patriotism, Protection, and Prosperity: James Moore Swank, the American Iron and Steel Association, and the Tariff, 1873–1913." Ph.D. diss., Boston University, 1970.

Terrill, T. E. *The Tariff, Politics, and American Foreign Policy 1874–1901*. Westport, Conn.: Greenwood Press, 1973.

Thobie, Jacques. "Finance et politique: le refus en France de l'emprunt ottoman de 1910." *Revue historique* 239 (Spring 1968): 327–50.

Thomas, J. A. *The House of Commons, 1832–1901*. Cardiff: University of Wales Press Board, 1939.

Thomson, Virginia, and Richard Adloff. "French Economic Policy in Tropical Africa." In *Colonialism in Africa, 1870–1960*, Vol. 4, *The Economics of Colonialism*, ed. Peter Duignan and Lewis H. Gann. Cambridge: Cambridge University Press, 1975, 127–64.

Tinbergen, Jan. *Economic Policy: Principles and Designs*, 4th ed. Amsterdam: North-Holland, 1967.

Tocqueville, Alexis de. *Democracy in America*, trans. Phillips Bradley. New York: Random House, 1945.

Tolliday, Steven. "Tariffs and Steel, 1916–34: The Politics of Industrial Decline." In *Businessmen and Politics*, ed. John Turner. London: Heinemann, 1984, 50–75.

———. *Business, Banking, and Politics: The Case of British Steel, 1918–39*. Cambridge, Mass.: Harvard University Press, 1987.

Tosini, Suzanne, and Edward Tower. "The Textile Bill of 1985: The Determinants of Congressional Voting Patterns." *Public Choice* 54 (1987): 19–25.

Trachtenberg, Marc. " 'A New Economic Order': Etienne Clémentel and French Economic Diplomacy during the First World War." *French Historical Studies* 10, no. 2 (Fall 1977): 315–41.

Tsebelis, George. *Nested Games: Rational Choice in Comparative Politics*. Berkeley and Los Angeles: University of California Press, 1990.

Turner, John. "The Politics of 'Organized Business' in the First World War." In *Businessmen and Politics*, ed. John Turner. London: Heinemann, 1984: 33–49.

Twiggs, Joan E. *The Tokyo Round of Multilateral Trade Negotiations: A Case Study in Building Domestic Support for Diplomacy*. Lanham, Md.: University Press of America, 1987.

U.S. Bureau of the Census. *Historical Statistics of the United States: Colonial Times to 1970*. Washington, D.C.: U.S. Government Printing Office, 1976.

———. *Statistical Abstract of the United States*. Washington, D.C.: U.S. Government Printing Office, various years.

U.S. Congress, House Committee on Banking, Finance and Urban Affairs, Subcommittee on Economic Stabilization. *Industrial Policy Hearings*. 98th Congress, parts 1–6 (1983–84).

U.S. Congress, House Committee on Ways and Means. *Tariff Hearings*. Washington, D.C.: U.S. Government Printing Office, 1893.

———. *Revision of the Tariff*. 51st Congress, 1st session, 1889–90 Washington, D.C.: U.S. Government Printing Office, 1890.

———. *Reciprocal Trade Agreements: Hearings*. (1934).

———. *Federal Government International Trade Functions Reorganization. Hearings*, (6 September 1979.

———. *Extending Reciprocal Foreign Trade Agreement Act: Hearings* (1937).

———. *Extension of Reciprocal Trade Agreements Act: Hearings* (1940).

———. *Trade Agreements Extension. Hearings*, 84th. Congress, 1st session (1955).

U.S. Congress, Joint Economic Committee. *Industrial Policy, Economic Growth and the Competitiveness of Industry. Hearings.* 98th Congress, 1st session, parts 1–2 (1983).

U.S. Congress, Senate Committee of Governmental Affairs. *Trade Reorganization Act of 1983. Hearings.* 96th Congress, 2d session (1984).

U.S. Congress, Senate Committee on Finance. *Reciprocal Trade Agreements: Hearings* (1934).

———. *Extending Reciprocal Trade Agreement Act: Hearings* (1937).

———. *Extension of Reciprocal Trade Agreements Act: Hearings* (1940).

U.S. Congress, Senate Committee on Finance, Subcommittee on International Trade. *Trade Reorganization Plans. Hearings.* 96th Congress, 2d session (1984).

U.S. Congress, Senate Committee on Government Operations. *Proposed Foreign Trade Reorganization. Hearings* (10 September 1979).

U.S. Tariff Commission. *Handbook of Commercial Treaties.* Washington, D.C.: U.S. Government Printing Office, 1922.

———. *Operation of the Trade Agreements Program. 19th Report.* Washington, D.C.: U.S. Government Printing Office, 1967.

———. *Reciprocity and Commercial Treaties.* Washington, D.C.: U.S. Government Printing Office, 1918.

———. *Report of the Tariff Commission.* 2 vols. Washington, D.C.: U.S. Government Printing Office, 1882.

Underhill, Geoffrey R. D. "Neo-Corporatist Theory and the Politics of Industrial Policy." *European Journal of Political Research* 16 (1988): 489–511.

Vear, Charles W. "Organized Labor and the Tariff." Ph.D. diss., Fletcher School of Law and Diplomacy, Tufts University, 1956.

Verdier, Daniel. "Between Party and Faction: The Politics Behind the Repeal of the Corn Laws." Paper presented at the American Political Science Association meeting, Atlanta, 1989.

Villey, Etienne. *L'organisation professionnelle des employeurs dans l'industrie française.* Paris: Alcan, 1913.

Vinen, Richard. *The Politics of French Business, 1936–1945.* Cambridge: Cambridge University Press, 1991.

Viner, Jacob. *Dumping: A Problem in International Trade.* Chicago: University of Chicago Press, 1923.

Wala, Michael. "Selling the Marshall Plan to Aid European Recovery." *Diplomatic History* 10, no. 3 (Summer 1986): 221–66.

Waltz, Kenneth N. *Foreign Policy and Democratic Politics.* Boston: Little, Brown, 1967.

———. *Theory of International Politics.* New York: Random House, 1979.

Watson, Richard A. "The Tariff Revolution: A Study of Shifting Party Attitudes." *Journal of Politics* 18, no. 4 (November 1956): 678–701.

Weber, Henri. *Le parti des patrons.* Paris: Seuil, 1986.

Wehler, Hans-Ulrich. *The German Empire, 1871–1918.* New York: Berg, 1985.

Weill, Georges. *La France sous la monarchie constitutionnelle.* Paris: Alcan, 1912.

Weingast, Barry R. "The Congressional-Bureaucratic System: A Principal-Agent Perspective (with Applications to the SEC)." *Public Choice* 44 (1984): 147–91.

Westerfield, H. Bradford. *Foreign Policy and Party Politics: Pearl Harbor to Korea.* New Haven, Conn.: Yale University Press, 1955.

Wexler, Imanuel. *The Marshall Plan Revisited: The European Recovery Program in Economic Perspective.* Westport, Conn.: Greenwood Press, 1983.

Whetham, Edith H. "The Agricultural Act, 1920 and its Repeal—the 'Great Betrayal.'" *Agricultural History Review* 22, no. 1 (1974): 36–49.

Whittlesey, C. R. "Import Quotas in the United States." *Quarterly Journal of Economics* 52, no. 1 (November 1937): 37–65.

Wickham, S. "French Planning: Retrospect and Prospect." *Review of Economics and Statistics* 45, no. 4 (Nov. 1963): 335–47.

Wiebe, Robert H. *Businessmen and Reform: A Study of the Progressive Movement.* Cambridge, Mass.: Harvard University Press, 1962.

Wilkins, Mira. *The Maturing of Multinational Enterprise: American Business Abroad from 1914 to 1970.* Cambridge, Mass.: Harvard University Press, 1974.

Wilks, Stephen. "Planning Agreements: The Making of a Paper Tiger." *Public Administration* 59 (Winter 1981): 399–419.

Williamson, Oliver E. *The Economic Institutions of Capitalism.* New York: Free Press, 1987.

Williamson, Philip. "Financiers, the Gold Standard and British Politics, 1925–1931." In *Businessmen and Politics,* ed. John Turner. London: Heinemann, 1984, 105–29.

———. *National Crisis and National Government.* Cambridge: Cambridge University Press, 1992.

Wills, Henry T. *Scientific Tariff Making: A History of the Movement to Create a Tariff Commission.* New York: Blanchard Press, 1913.

Wilson, Joan H. *American Business and Foreign Policy, 1920–1933.* Lexington: University Press of Kentucky, 1971.

Wright, Gordon. *Rural Revolution in France.* Stanford, Calif.: Stanford University Press, 1964.

Wright, Philip G. *Tariff-Making by Commission: A Study of One Attempt at an Improved Method for Making Tariffs.* Washington, D.C.: The Rawleigh Tariff Bureau, 1930.

Yandle, Bruce, and Elizabeth Young. "Regulating the Function, Not the Industry." *Public Choice* 51 (1986): 59–70.

Yandle, Bruce. "Bootleggers and Baptists in the Market for Regulation." In *The Political Economy of Government Regulation,* ed. Jason F. Shogren. Boston: Kluwer Academic Publishers, 1989, 29–53.

Yarbrough, Beth V., and Robert M. Yarbrough. "Cooperation in the Liberalization of International Trade: After Hegemony, What?" *International Organization* 41, no. 1 (Winter 1987): 1–26.

Young, Edward. *Special Report on the Customs-Tariff Legislation of the United States.* Washington, D.C.: U.S. Government Printing Office, 1874.

Young, Stephen, and A. V. Lowe. *Intervention in the Mixed Economy: The Evolution of British Industrial Policy, 1964–72.* London: Croom Helm, 1974.

Young, Stephen. "Industrial Policy in Britain, 1972–1977." In *Planning in Europe,* ed. Jack Hayward and Olga A. Narkiewicz. London: Croom Helm, 1978.

Zebel, Sydney H. "Fair Trade: An English Reaction to the Breakdown of the Cobden Treaty System." *Journal of Modern History* 12, no. 1 (March–December 1940): 161–85.

Zysman, John. *Political Strategies for Industrial Order: State, Market and Industry in France.* Berkeley: University of California Press, 1977.

———. *Governments, Markets, and Growth: Financial Systems and the Politics of Industrial Change.* Ithaca, N.Y.: Cornell University Press, 1983.